D0040696

ASTORIA

ASTORIA

JOHN JACOB ASTOR
AND THOMAS JEFFERSON'S
LOST PACIFIC EMPIRE

A STORY OF WEALTH,
AMBITION, AND SURVIVAL

PETER STARK

ecco

An Imprint of HarperCollins*Publishers*

HarperCollins books may be purchased for educational, business, or sales promotional use. For information please e-mail the Special Markets Department at SPsales@harpercollins.com.

FIRST EDITION

Designed by Suet Yee Chong
Maps designed by Kevin McCann, Cartographics, LLC
Title page photograph by Nejron Photo/Shutterstock, Inc.

Library of Congress Cataloging-in-Publication
Data has been applied for.

ISBN 978-0-06-221829-2

14 15 16 17 18   OV/RRD   10 9 8 7 6 5 4 3 2 1

To Murray and Rosa, and to Rags

[T]his is the land of *liberty* and *equality,* where a man sees and feels that he is a man merely, and that he can no longer exist, [except if] he can himself procure the means of support.

—Robert Stuart, *journal postscript for October 13, 1812,*
while starving in today's Wyoming,
shortly before discovering the South Pass

CONTENTS

PART THREE

PACIFIC EMPIRE AND WAR

LIST OF MAPS

CAST OF CHARACTERS

SEAGOING PARTY

Captain of the *Tonquin*

CAPTAIN JONATHAN THORN—age thirty-one. U.S. naval hero whom Astor hired to captain the *Tonquin* on the voyage around Cape Horn to the West Coast and then to China.

Partners Aboard the *Tonquin*

ALEXANDER MCKAY—age forty at the time he joined. Highly respected for his experience as explorer, trader, and friend of the Indians in many years' service in Canada with the North West Company, he was a shareholding partner and trader with Astor's enterprise, sailing aboard the *Tonquin*.

DUNCAN MCDOUGALL—age unknown. Scottish fur trader from Canada and former North West Company employee appointed by Astor to be second in command for his "emporium" on the West Coast and to lead it whenever Wilson Price Hunt was absent.

DAVID STUART—age forty-five. One of the oldest members of the Astor enterprise, the Scottish emigrant had lived some years in Canada, probably in the fur trade, before going out aboard the *Tonquin* as shareholding partner and fur trader.

ROBERT STUART—age twenty-five. The younger Stuart, also Scottish-born, worked briefly as a clerk for the North West Company in Canada before joining Astor's company with his uncle David, and also held a small number of shares.

Notable Clerks Aboard the *Tonquin*

GABRIEL FRANCHÈRE—age twenty-four. A French Canadian born in Montreal to a merchant family, Franchère sailed aboard the *Tonquin* as a clerk and kept his own journal account of the expedition.

ALEXANDER ROSS—age twenty-seven. Scottish-born, Ross worked as a schoolteacher in Canada before seeking his fortune by joining Astor's Pacific enterprise as a clerk, sailing aboard the *Tonquin* but staying at Astoria when she sailed on. He also kept his own journal.

JAMES LEWIS—clerk from New York who sailed aboard the *Tonquin*.

THOMAS MCKAY—son of Alexander McKay (above) who stayed at Astoria when the *Tonquin* sailed onward.

The Seagoing Party also included seven additional clerks, about fifteen French-Canadian voyageurs, and about five craftsmen such as blacksmiths and carpenters.

Crew of the *Tonquin*

In addition, the *Tonquin* carried officers and crew, totaling about twenty-three people, and, after stopping at Hawaii, Hawaiians numbering about twenty-four individuals.

THE OVERLAND PARTY

Leader

WILSON PRICE HUNT—age twenty-seven. The young New Jersey–born businessman, who had worked as a fur trade supplier in St. Louis, was appointed by Astor to lead the Overland Party across the continent and head Astor's West Coast operations.

Partners

DONALD MACKENZIE—age twenty-six. Scottish fur trader from Canada and former employee of the North West Company (NWC) who possessed considerable wilderness experience and great physical energy. Unhappy with the NWC, he joined Astor's enterprise, initially helping Hunt to co-lead the Overland Party.

RAMSAY CROOKS—age twenty-three. Scottish-born Canadian fur trader who had worked in the American fur trade along the Missouri River, befriending Hunt in St. Louis and eventually joining the Overland Party as partner in Astor's West Coast enterprise.

ROBERT McCLELLAN—age forty. Born in Pennsylvania to parents of Scottish descent, McClellan had fought in Ohio Valley Indian wars and eventually worked as a fur trader along the Missouri, for a time in a partnership with Ramsay Crooks. Joined Hunt's Overland Party as a partner at St. Louis, given two and a half shares, compared to most partners' five shares.

JOSEPH MILLER—age thirty, approximately. Member of a respected family in Baltimore, Miller had quit the military to come west as a fur trader, and joined the Overland Party in St. Louis, also holding two and a half shares.

Clerk with Overland Party

JOHN REED—An Irishman, Reed joined the Overland Party at Montreal or Mackinac Island and served as clerk as Hunt's party made its way west.

Other Notable Members of Overland Party

JOHN DAY—forty-year-old Virginian who joined the Overland Party as a hunter.

MARIE DORION—Iowa Indian woman with two toddlers and married to Pierre Dorion, interpreter for Hunt's Overland Party.

PIERRE DORION—half-Sioux interpreter for Hunt's Overland Party and son of Old Dorion, interpreter for Lewis and Clark.

In addition, the Overland Party included nearly forty French-Canadian voyageurs, several other American hunters, and several trappers met on the Missouri.

Notable Clerks Aboard the *Beaver*

ROSS COX—age nineteen. The Dublin-born Cox emigrated to New York and joined Astor's enterprise as clerk with the hope of making his fortune. He kept a journal of his experiences.

ALFRED SETON—A young New Yorker of good family that was down on its luck, Seton dropped out of Columbia to join Astor's enterprise as clerk. He also kept a journal of his own.

JOHN CLARKE—age twenty-nine. From Montreal, and a former employee of the North West Company, Clarke may have been related to Astor through his mother. He sailed to the West Coast aboard the *Beaver,* and may have soon been made a shareholding partner.

Captain and Crew of the *Beaver*

CAPTAIN CORNELIUS SOWLE—age forty-two. A native of Rhode Island, Sowle had sailed on Pacific and Far East trading voyages for a number of years previous to joining Astor.

The *Beaver* also carried other Astor clerks, craftsmen, voyageurs, and Hawaiians, in addition to the captain and his crew.

Nearly two centuries ago, the story that follows was well-known to Americans. In the Epilogue to the following account, I touch on some of the reasons why it has now been largely forgotten. It has been told before by various authors, a number of them participants in these events in the early 1800s who kept journals or logbooks at the time or later wrote memoirs. Among these participant-writers are Gabriel Franchère, John Bradbury, H. M. Brackenridge, Alexander Ross, Ross Cox, Alfred Seton, Duncan McDougall, and Robert Stuart.

The best-known account from the early 1800s was published in 1836, after a retired John Jacob Astor commissioned Washington Irving, then one of America's most famous authors, to write an account of these events two decades past. Irving's book, *Astoria, or Anecdotes of an Enterprise Beyond the Rocky Mountains* (1836), became a bestseller of its day and was soon published in editions abroad.

Global

Russia

Europe

London

China

Canton

Africa

Chinese Goods for London and New York

Australia

N
W E
S

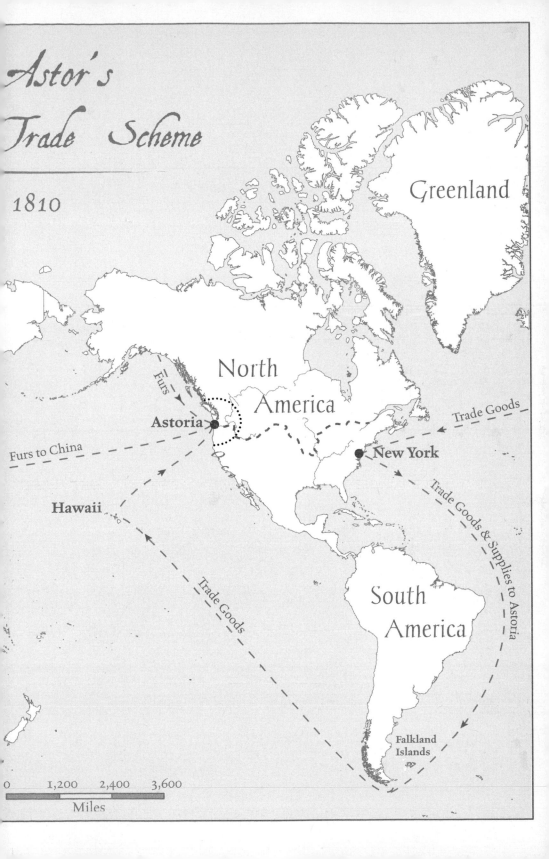

Astor's Trade Scheme

1810

Greenland

North America

Furs

Astoria

Furs to China

Hawaii

Trade Goods

New York

Trade Goods

Trade Goods & Supplies to Astoria

South America

Falkland Islands

| 0 | 1,200 | 2,400 | 3,600 |

Miles

VIEW OF THE FALKLAND ISLANDS.
Boat and five passengers pulling after Ship Tonquin.

ON AUGUST 13, 1813, GALE WINDS BLEW UP AS JOHN JACOB Astor's ship the *Lark* sailed in the open Pacific. At the time, the ship lay about two hundred miles off the coast of Maui, bound for Astor's settlement on the Northwest Coast of America. Huge seas overtook the *Lark,* and Astor's trusted Captain Samuel Northrup fought to keep her steady. For a moment the Captain took a break belowdecks, leaving her in the hands of less experienced officers. Suddenly she swung sideways to the onrush of wind and water and was "knocked down" by an enormous wave. She slowly heaved herself upright, decks lashed by spray, rigging screaming in the wind.

"[W]e were in great Confusion and disorder," reported Captain Northrup.

The ship was short of experienced officers and crew, due in part to the recent outbreak of war between Britain and the United States on the East Coast. Another wave hit, knocking her almost entirely over, keel out of the water. This was now beyond an emergency. The yardarms, masts, and rigging dragged underwater like fishing nets, pulling the ship over, straining every fitting and line in the screaming winds, threatening to overturn the *Lark* completely. As the inexperienced crew clung to the rails and rigging of the wildly heeled ship in this tumult of wind and spray, the fate of John Jacob Astor's West Coast empire literally hung in the balance.

Captain Northrup had to decide in a matter of a few moments whether to issue one of sailing's most desperate commands—to order the masts knocked out of their fittings and rigging cut down to try to right the *Lark*.

ASTOR'S SETTLEMENT, "ASTORIA," was the first American colony on the West Coast of North America, much in the way that Jamestown and Plymouth were the first British colonies on its East Coast. For John Jacob Astor, the West Coast colony would serve as the epicenter of a global commercial empire that leveraged nearly all the wealth of western North America into one vast trade network that passed through his own hands. For Thomas Jefferson, who had enthusiastically encouraged Astor to start the colony, it would provide the beginnings of a separate country on the West Coast—a sister democracy to the United States that looked out to the Pacific. Both men grasped far ahead of most of their contemporaries that the Pacific would one day take on the central importance in world affairs and trade that the Atlantic held in their day.

As it was, however, the West Coast lay nearly as remote as a separate planet. Jefferson had added a huge swath of territory to the United States just a few years before, with the Louisiana Purchase. But even this addition extended U.S. territories only as far as the

Rockies. No nation had a solid claim to that enormous region of land, much of it unexplored despite the recent expedition by Lewis and Clark, between the crest of the Rockies and the Pacific shore. The Spanish, coming up from Mexico, had planted missions on the coast as far north as San Francisco Bay. Russian fur traders, coming across the Bering Sea in recent decades, had established a few fur outposts in Alaska, and contemplated adding a post down near San Francisco Bay. But in between those two points lay a vast coastal no-man's-land nearly two thousand miles long that was essentially up for grabs. It was as if the East Coast of the United States from Florida to Maine were there for the taking.

It was Astor's vision to capture its wealth. It was Jefferson's vision to make it a democracy.

IF CAPTAIN NORTHRUP CHOSE TO DISMAST HER, the ship's hull would probably right itself and her crew and cargo survive. But the crew would be rendered helpless aboard a drifting, mastless hulk— thereby ending the rescue mission that was aimed at saving Mr. Astor's West Coast empire. If Captain Northrup chose not to cut away the masts and rigging, in these long suspended moments tipped on her beam ends in the raging storm, the ship still might right herself and sail on unharmed. Or she might not. She might capsize completely, slowly disappear beneath the tumbling seas, and then quietly sink to the depths of the Pacific Ocean along with Astor's and Jefferson's grandest plans.

As the *Lark* began to capsize, turning her bottom up toward the raging wind and monstrous seas, dragging her rigging and yardarms in the heaving ocean like a giant net, Captain Northrup issued the fateful command: *Dismast her.*

PART ONE

THE LAUNCH

ENTRANCE OF THE COLUMBIA RIVER.

Ship Tonquin, crossing the bar, 25th March, 1811.

CHAPTER ONE

*[Y]our name will be handed down with that of Columbus &
Raleigh, as the father of the establishment and the founder of such
an empire.* —THOMAS JEFFERSON TO JOHN JACOB ASTOR

AFTER AN EARLY DINNER, JOHN JACOB ASTOR LIKED TO
play a game of solitaire in the outdoor portico—or in winter, in
front of the fire in one of the sitting rooms—of his brick row house on
New York City's Lower Broadway. He smoked his pipe, sipped from a
glass of beer, and slowly turned over the cards from the rows dealt on
the table, reordering them to try to make the hands. In his native Germany, where the game originated and was known as "Patience," it was
said that when your luck ran well in the card game, the time was right
to make life's important decisions. When it ran poorly at Patience, you
should avoid them.

Astor definitely believed in runs of luck. He also believed in meticulous planning, bold vision, huge risk, and relentless focus on his bottom line. As the game's name implied, he was willing to wait many
years for his risk, vision, and planning to reach fruition. He treated
money—and men—as something to be invested for the long term, and
he knew that along the way there were sure to be some heavy losses,
whether measured in dollars or in human lives.

The game of Patience, likewise, demanded astute calculation of
risk, constant rearrangement of cards into proper order, and suffering of losses in pursuit of a grander vision. One might say that John

Jacob Astor turned over his first card when he left a difficult home and a narrow future in the small German town of Walldorf, one of seven "forest villages" near Heidelberg, to follow his three older brothers' footsteps out into a far wider world. The eldest Astor brother, George, had already emigrated to London and joined a musical instrument maker. Another worked on a prince's estate elsewhere in Germany. A third brother, Henry, had sailed to America during the Revolutionary War. Following the family trade, he had become a butcher, selling meat from a wheelbarrow in the streets of New York, then a small port city. The youngest brother, John Jacob, had remained behind as a Walldorf schoolboy.

Home was a deeply unhappy place for John Jacob. He was five years old when his mother died giving birth to a daughter. His father was a Huguenot, descended from the French Protestants who, under persecution from the French Crown, had fled to other countries such as Germany in the late 1600s. Known as a friendly and upright butcher who enjoyed the cheer of local taverns, the senior Astor promptly remarried after his first wife's death and fathered several more children with his second wife. According to Walldorf stories told years later by those who knew the family, his stepmother "loved not . . . John Jacob." Nor would his father pay, or perhaps couldn't afford, to apprentice John Jacob to a clockmaker or master carpenter or other "higher" profession. Rather, he wanted his remaining and youngest son to help run his Walldorf butcher shop.

The teenage Astor started planning his escape from Walldorf long before he made the break.

"I'm not afraid of John Jacob; he'll get through the world," the village schoolteacher, Valentine Jeune, also descended from French Huguenots, was said to have remarked. "He has a clear head and everything right behind the ears."

In 1779, after laboring as a butcher's assistant to his father for two years, John Jacob left Walldorf at age sixteen, as the old stories put it, "with a bundle over his shoulder . . . to walk to the Rhine." Working his way downriver as deckhand on a lumber boat, he then spent a few years in England with his older brother, George, in the musical instrument business. There he formulated a plan: work to earn his passage across the Atlantic, learn English well enough to get along, and wait for the War of Independence to end in the American British colonies. Already, at this young age, John Jacob displayed the talent and discipline to look to the future—and to plan for it to his utmost advantage—that would serve him well in later life.

Straw-blond, stocky, exuding energy and alertness, the young Astor was endlessly inquisitive. At age twenty-one, in March 1784, the butcher's son from Walldorf climbed down from his passenger ship onto the frozen surface of Chesapeake Bay. The winter had been an especially severe one in North America. While the ship attempted to make landfall, the Chesapeake had frozen and locked the ship in ice for three months. Along with his fellow passengers, Astor walked to shore toting a sack of seven finely crafted flutes and a few other imported goods—his initial capital to start life in, as the Germans called it, the New Land.

Making his way to New York City, Astor quickly turned down his older brother Henry's offer for a job in his Manhattan meat stall, having heard of more promising ways to make money in America. While on his Atlantic passage, he'd met aboard the ship a friendly fellow German passenger who traded furs. From him John Jacob learned that substantial profits could be made by starting with just a few trinkets to trade for individual pelts, especially if the trader developed good London contacts.

Years later, Astor liked to tell the story of his days as a struggling immigrant in the mid-1780s when he was a young man and the United States only a few years old. One day he walked through Lower Broadway in Manhattan where big, new houses were under construction for the prosperous merchants in the fast-growing city, then with a population of twenty-three thousand, and reaching no farther north than Cortlandt Street, but soon to triple in size.

"I'll build . . . a grander house than any of these," he pledged to himself, "and in this very street."

When Astor arrived in Manhattan and made his pledge, the United States was still very much an inchoate nation a mere six years old. Its thirteen colonies had united and declared themselves separate from Great Britain and had recently fought and won a War of Independence against the mother country, but many of the basic workings of its government were still being settled. When Astor walked Lower Broadway envying the solid houses, the U.S. Constitution hadn't been adopted, nor had the Bill of Rights. The United States didn't have its own workable form of money. Taxation remained in a state of confusion. George Washington still hadn't been chosen president, Alexander Hamilton and James Madison worked on what would become the Federalist Papers, and a youngish and recently widowed Thomas Jefferson held the post of U.S. diplomat in Paris.

The economy likewise was only a tiny fraction of what it would one day become. Slaves worked large plantations in the southeastern states that grew tobacco and cotton, while small-scale farming, fishing, and the beginnings of manufacturing supported the economies of northeastern states. But almost all this economic activity and population clustered on the eastern seaboard within a few hundred miles of the Atlantic Ocean. European settlement had barely crossed the Appalachian Mountains. In interior North America lay an expanse of wilderness, inhabited by Indian tribes, that extended an almost unimaginable distance, much of it unknown and unexplored by Europeans.

But the unformed nature of the young United States also opened up tremendous possibility, economic and otherwise. Upon his arrival in New York, young Astor found a ready market for his fine European musical instruments in a fledgling city hungry for culture. Taking his German shipmate's advice, he also hung about the New York docks to seek out travelers who had picked up a few individual furs—beaver, bear, fox, whatever—from frontier settlers or Indians in the interior wilds. Within a year or so, he'd accumulated enough furs to make a voyage back to London, where he learned the incredible markups that fashion-conscious patrons would pay for elegant, scarce luxury goods.

Astor showed a precocious grasp of international markets, understanding that America lacked refined manufactories while Europe lacked large expanses of wilderness. Selling the fruits of one to the hungry markets of the other yielded steep profits. Thus the immigrant John Jacob Astor set himself up in the mid-1780s in the small city of Manhattan as the purveyor of an unlikely combination of goods—fine musical instruments and wild-animal pelts. While Astor's chosen markets might have seemed haphazard, in reality he had identified two powerful economic veins in the young North American economy.

"Jacob Astor [has] just imported an elegant assortment of Piano Fortes," read one 1788 ad in the New York *Packet;* "he also buys and sells for Cash all kinds of furs."

Astor's competitive nature blossomed early, a trait his own siblings may have inadvertently fostered by displaying both an affectionate and yet also dismissive quality in their dealings with their younger brother. When he first arrived in New York, he worked for a time selling bread and cakes from a basket in the streets. "Jacob was nothing but a baker's boy," his older sister would later remark. Later, needing to raise capital to expand his trading of furs and instruments, John Jacob approached his older brother Henry, who virtually controlled retail selling prices in the Manhattan meat stalls by reaching outside the city to buy cheaper meat and using aggressive selling tactics. John Jacob asked his flush older sibling for a loan of two hundred dollars.

"I will give you $100 if you will agree never to ask me to loan you any money," Henry replied.

It's easy to imagine John Jacob pledging to out-succeed Henry, as well as outbuild the prosperous merchants with their big houses on Lower Broadway.

Only a year and a half after arriving in America, John Jacob married his landlady's daughter, Sarah Todd, whose widowed mother ran a boardinghouse at 81 Queen Street. Deeply religious, Sarah Todd displayed a shrewdness for business matters in her own right (Astor called her the best judge of furs he ever knew), and brought to their marriage a dowry of three hundred dollars, which he badly needed for capital, as well as talents that complemented his own. Related to one of New York's oldest Dutch families, the Brevoorts, Sarah urged the awkward young immigrant with the thick German accent to befriend the city's prominent traders who hung out at merchants' coffeehouses like the Tontine at Wall and Water streets, a kind of precursor to the New York Stock Exchange when the city was a small but growing Atlantic port.

Mutually ambitious, both lovers of good music and fond of family life, the couple took two upstairs rooms in Mrs. Todd's boardinghouse—a room in front for their music-and-fur shop and one in back to sleep. Children soon arrived in this warm and busy household. Sarah's family had lived in Manhattan for decades and had witnessed the little settlement's creeping growth northward from the tip of the island. Perhaps it was Sarah who suggested that she and John Jacob invest surplus fur profits in purchasing building lots and bare land farther north up Manhattan Island, beyond the leading edge of the town. Eventually they bought a parcel of largely rural land known—as it still is today—as Greenwich Village, and another property called Eden Farm, which would one day be the site of Times Square and much of Midtown.

JOHN JACOB AND SARAH ASTOR both viscerally understood that, in those early days, the great riches of interior North America were in furs. Furs and land. Where the Spanish conquistadores captured troves of gold and silver far to the south, the early French and British in the cold forests of the north instead had discovered a wealth of mammals growing luxurious coats—beaver, lynx, mink, fox—that fetched staggeringly high prices among Europe's status-conscious aristocrats. Men killed each other staking claims to fur territory. It was the raison d'être for the great trading companies of the Canadian north, such as the Hudson's Bay Company and the North West Company.

By the time Astor arrived in North America in the late 1700s, French traders, intermixing with Native Americans, had been gathering furs from the continent's interior wilds, largely centering on the Great Lakes, for two centuries. Still farther to the north, British merchants had organized the Hudson's Bay Company, acquiring a royal British monopoly to furs from lands draining into Hudson Bay. The French and British fur traders, guided by Indians, had discovered canoe routes not only through the Great Lakes and Hudson Bay regions, but deep into the continent's northern and western interior as far as Lake Athabasca, another five hundred miles beyond Hudson Bay. But a great deal of the North American interior, especially to the west, remained unexplored by Europeans.

As Astor delved into the business of buying and selling furs in the 1780s and 1790s, his own travels took him farther from the docks of America's Atlantic seaports and deeper into the interior. With Sarah's blessing, the stocky, energetic, young family man John Jacob left their lively household full of young children and boarded sailing sloops on long journeys up the Hudson River to visit the Indian tribes of upstate New York. He walked the forest paths with a backpack of trinkets, or drove a wagon that bogged down on the muddy tracks. He slept in front of the big kitchen fireplaces in settlers' wilderness homes. He learned how to barter with Indians, who had been trading goods between tribes for untold centuries and were highly astute bargainers. The conscientious young trader picked up enough of their languages and techniques to close his deals in Seneca, Mohawk, or Oneida.

"Many times," reminisced an old resident of Schenectady, New York, "I have seen John Jacob Astor with his coat off, unpacking in a vacant yard near my residence a lot of furs he had bought dog-cheap off the Indians. . . ."

Soon Astor's fur-buying trips took him to Montreal—then the continent's center of the fur trade, and the portal to the great interior wildernesses where the Canadian companies captured their furs. In Montreal, Astor was wined and dined by the partners of Canada's North West Company, the more southerly counterpart to the Hudson's Bay Company, at their luxurious Beaver House. One summer in the mid-1790s the company's Scottish fur traders invited their valued New York customer, who bought pelts in volume, to accompany them as their guest in a huge voyageur canoe all the way to the key North West Company post at Grand Portage, on the western shore of Lake Superior. This served as the jumping-off point to the waterways of the western interior. Astor thus became one of the few white men in the late 1700s, except for the traders themselves, to travel so deeply into North America's wild heart.

This journey and his contact with these traders was pivotal in Astor's life—and the continent's destiny. Here, at the edge of the great western wilderness, he heard stories directly from the mouths of the *coureurs de bois*—the French-Canadian "runners of the forest"—and from knowledgeable Indian chiefs of the continent's vastness and its incredible abundance of furs farther to the west. He gained an understanding of its unmapped western geography—the run of its rivers, the lay of its mountains, and, so very far away, the glimmering Pacific Ocean, which marked the continent's edge. Only one white man, Alexander Mackenzie, a Scottish trader with the North West Company, and his little party had paddled the northern forests and portaged the mountain spines to see it, arriving at the Pacific in the summer of 1793. At just about the same time, the first British and American trading vessels had begun to explore the fur-trading potential of the continent's Northwest Coast.

Astor never forgot the vision of continental geography that he glimpsed from the wild western shore of Lake Superior and the stories of the traders who frequented it. He married this vision with the stories he'd begun to hear about the first British and American fur-trading ships landing on the Northwest Coast. These first ships had landed just a few years earlier, starting in 1788, bartered with Coastal Indians for sea otter and other pelts, and taken them across the Pacific to sell in Chinese ports for unheard-of sums. Astor's genius turned in part on his ability to look far beyond the obvious horizons of time and place and meld fragments of information on geography, politics, and trade potential into a much greater vision. He quickly came to the realization that, one day, a wealthy trading empire would exist on the West Coast of North America. The Pacific Rim would emerge as a new world stage—a much larger version of what the North Atlantic was during his own era, a vast, globally important region ringed by powerful countries and fueled by a busy transoceanic trade.

The question was, whose West Coast empire would it be?

Alexander Mackenzie posed exactly that same question to his British readership in his account of his Canadian overland journey to the Pacific. Writing in his *Travels,* published in 1801, Mackenzie highlighted the enormous stakes that would go to whichever nation first established settlements on the Pacific Coast and the Columbia River and connected these via an inland water route to the East Coast and the Atlantic. That nation, Mackenzie wrote, would possess "the entire command of the fur trade of North America . . . from latitude 48, North to the pole . . . the fishing of both seas, and the markets of the four quarters of the globe."

THE MOMENT FOR ASTOR TO ACT on his vision arrived in early 1808. It had been twenty-three years since the immigrant baker's boy had hawked his cakes on Lower Broadway and enviously eyed the big brick houses. Now a wealthy fur merchant, he lived comfortably in one of them, a double row house at 223 Broadway, just a few steps up the street from St. Paul's Church. He also worked the profitable tea trade from China with several of his own ships and was a substantial Manhattan landowner. One day that winter of 1808, Astor, still a relatively young man in his mid-forties, sat at his writing desk, dipped his pen, and began a letter of introduction to be dispatched to the Federal City in Washington.

Five years earlier, in 1803, President Jefferson had acquired the Louisiana Purchase from Napoleon at bargain prices, and, with Congress's eventual approval, added to U.S. territory nearly a million square miles up to the Rockies' spine. Enormous as it was, the Louisiana Purchase still stopped far short of the Pacific Coast. The Northwest remained a mostly unknown and largely unclaimed (by Western powers) region of North America, a piece of real estate roughly the size of Western Europe available by squatters' rights.

President Jefferson dispatched Lewis and Clark on their 1804–1806 expedition to discover a river route through the new lands and push beyond the Louisiana Purchase border, over the Rockies, and down the mountains' far slope to the Pacific. He had read Alexander Mackenzie's 1801 warnings to his British countrymen about the urgent necessity of controlling the Columbia's mouth and Pacific Coast. With Britain distracted by the Napoleonic Wars, President Jefferson felt compelled to get there first—before his long-hated British, with their "bastard liberty," and who, as he contemptuously put it, "would not lose the sale of a bale of fur for the freedom of the whole world."

On his triumphant return to Washington, D.C., Meriwether Lewis strongly urged President Jefferson, as Mackenzie had urged the British, to create a seaport on the Pacific Rim as an outlet to China for furs from the western sector of North America, despite the lack of an easy water route through the Rockies. But President Jefferson felt that the U.S. government by itself had neither the will nor the funds to extend itself far west enough to settle the far edges of the continent. However much he wished to see it, he thought a Pacific Rim seaport was best left to private enterprise.

Astor's timing was perfect. Not long after Lewis reported in to Jefferson about the need for a port on the Pacific, a letter posted from

New York and dated "27 Feb 1808" in a flowing, deeply forward-slanted hand, arrived at the president's house in Washington.

> *Sir,*
>
> *It was my intention to have presented myself before you & to have stated to you my wish of engaging in an extensive trade with the Indians . . . [that] may in time embrace the greater part of the fur trade on this continent the most of which passes now through Canada. . . .*

President Jefferson vetted Astor through his New York contacts. He learned that Astor was "a man of large property & fair character, and well acquainted with the fur & peltry business."

The president replied enthusiastically to Mr. Astor:

> *The field is immense, & would occupy a vast amount of capital. . . .*
>
> *You may be assured that in order to get the whole of this business passed into the hands of our own citizens . . . every reasonable patronage & facility in the power of the Executive will be afforded.*

Thus introduced to each other via letter, President Jefferson and John Jacob Astor then arranged a meeting at the president's house in Washington, D.C., in the spring or early summer of 1808.

TWO YEARS LATER, on a warm summer Sunday in 1810, a strange craft came winging from the north down the Hudson River, bearing the first recruits of the great undertaking. Hundreds of spectators—out of the city's ninety-six thousand people—crowded to the docks that were clustered at the southern tip of Manhattan Island. The huge birch bark canoe, nearly forty feet long, surged through the water far faster than any Yankee rowboat. This was a vessel of the North, the racehorse of the fur trade, propelled by nine French-Canadian voyageurs who had paddled from the great fur-trading center of Montreal. The canoe jumped forward as they planted each stroke of their blades. Feathers and ribbons fixed to their hats streamed jauntily behind them on the breeze. The lyrics to their French boat songs, chanted in unison to the rhythm of their paddles, punctuated by the lilting solos of the steersman, echoed across the water and rolled along the Hudson's wooded shores. The Sunday strollers had never seen anything like it.

Dans mon chemin j'ai rencontré
*Trois cabalières bien montées**

The canoe glided alongside the lower Manhattan docks, now so packed with spectators—sailors, strolling couples, vagrants, wharf rats, curious young men, mothers and children, stout businessmen— that the voyageurs could barely find a spot to land. They hopped out. With graceful Gallic manners and dipping flourishes of their feathery hats, they cordially greeted the crowd. They were short men— few over five feet six, the better to fold their legs into cargo-jammed canoes. They wore gaudy sashes tied around their waists, from which hung beaded tobacco pouches, easily accessible for their regular pipe breaks while paddling for long days through wilderness lakes and rivers. Deerskin moccasins and leather leggings covered their spindly legs. Their upper bodies, however—arms, shoulders, and torsos— bulged with outsized strength.

Two of the voyageurs now reached down, one at the bow and one at the stern of the canoe that was thinly sheathed with birch bark, its seams stitched with spruce roots and caulked with spruce gum. The two men seized it by the thwarts, plucked it out of the water, and easily slung the giant, dripping hull on their shoulders.

---

*   Coming along met on my way
    Three cavaliers in fine array

The crowd gasped with astonishment at their strength.

Astor now stepped forward from the crowd. In his mid-forties, he was prosperously stout and dressed simply but emanated a lively energy, intensified by his long shocks of straw-colored hair and bright, curious eyes. In his thick German accent, he greeted this exotic feather-bunted flock. Reaching into his pocket, he approached the two voyageurs hefting the big, featherweight craft.

"[D]elighted with the vivacity and dexterity of the two men," a witness reported, "he gave them an eagle to drink his health."

The ten-dollar coin, a half ounce of solid gold, represented a small fortune. John Jacob had come a long way from his start as a baker's boy. He turned to a group of gentleman acquaintances.

"Six Americans," he told them, "couldn't do what these two brawny fellows just did."

Proud Yankee wharf rats jeered. His prosperous New York acquaintances took issue. But the voyageurs' leader, the Scottish fur trader McKay, spoke up to challenge the crowd: They would race any boat in New York Harbor over a three-mile course at ten-to-one odds.

No one stepped forward.

Satisfied that he had hired the best in the business, taking pride in their skill and strength as a harbinger for the success of his bold, continent-changing undertaking, Astor directed his French-Canadian voyageurs across New York Harbor to his Brooklyn staging area. Here more of his recruits would assemble to board his ship, *Tonquin,* bound in a month for the Pacific Coast, to lay the first foundations of the great empire.

No exact record exists of that meeting between President Jefferson and John Jacob Astor two years earlier at the president's house. Jefferson was so passionately engaged in the possibilities of the western continent that he was known to crawl around on hands and knees in the president's office studying maps spread out on the floor. It's clear that Astor and Jefferson fueled each other with their mutual enthusiasm and vision of the West Coast's limitless possibilities. Jefferson was a philosophical idealist (but practical statesman) possessed of a continent-wide vision and deeply committed to the concept of nations living free from royal rule. Astor was an extremely focused and yet far-seeing businessman whose deepest loyalties, besides to his family and closest acquaintances, were to his business empire: extending it as far as possible, preferably in the form of a monopoly, while maximizing his bottom line. For these two energized individuals meeting in Washington, the Pacific Coast hovered over the western horizon like a giant blank slate—a tabula rasa for statecraft on a hemispherical scale and trade on a global one.

"A powerful company is at length forming for taking up the Indian commerce on a large scale," Jefferson wrote to Meriwether Lewis after his meeting with Astor. Lewis was governor of the Louisiana Territory and based in St. Louis at the time. "It will be under the direction of a most excellent man, a Mr. Astor, merch't of New, long engaged in the business, & perfectly master of it."

After their meeting, Astor had framed his global commercial vision into an overarching strategy and meticulous business plan that dovetailed with Jefferson's geopolitical thinking. As soon as possible, in 1809, Astor would dispatch his first ship, the *Enterprise,* to test the profitability of his transglobal trading scheme with a quick stop at the Northwest Coast. The following year, in 1810, he would send two advance parties—one around Cape Horn by sea on the *Tonquin* and one across America by land. The Overland Party would begin to lay out a vast network of fur posts reaching up the Missouri River, over the Rockies, and to the Pacific Ocean, and open a "line of communication" across the continent along which both messages and furs could travel.

The two advance parties, Seagoing and Overland, would meet at the mouth of the Columbia River. Here, overlooking the Pacific, they would construct the first American colony on the West Coast. This great trading "emporium" would gather furs from the western half of the North American continent. It would form the apex of an

elegant and fantastically profitable triangle trade between three continents that employed a fleet of Astor's ships continuously circling the
globe. From manufactories in London and New York the ships would
carry inexpensive trade goods valued by the Indians—knives, blankets, pots, beads—around Cape Horn to the Northwest Coast. Here,
along two thousand miles of the forested, indented Pacific coastline,
Astor's agents would exchange the trade goods with Coastal Indians
for valuable furs such as sea otter. They would also load the ships with
furs funneled to the emporium from Astor's interior network of trading posts, which covered tens of thousands of square miles, as well as
gather furs from Russian posts on the Alaskan coast.

The Astor ships would transport the heavy fur packets—sea
otter, beaver, lynx, bear—across the Pacific. His captains would sell
them at a tremendous markup in Canton, where a powerful demand
existed from wealthy Chinese. Then, in China, Astor's ships would
load porcelain, silk, tea, and yellow nankeen cloth and sail these car-
gos around the other half of the globe (or return via the same route,
depending on conditions) to the markets of London and New York,
completing the circumnavigation and reaping another astronomical
profit from fashionable and eager European and American consumers
of Chinese luxury goods.

The scale of the plan was staggering. As of this date, 1810, the
entire tradable wealth of largely unexplored western North America
lay in its furs. There was no gold. There were no commercial fisheries.
There was no wheat grown or timber harvested. Astor, this still-young
and very ambitious immigrant, had conceived a plan that funneled the
entire tradable wealth of the westernmost sector of the North American continent north of Mexico through his own hands. It was, as the
early accounts described it, "the largest commercial enterprise the
world has ever known."

Barely twenty-five years had elapsed since the Revolutionary War
ended. To most spectators milling about the lower Manhattan docks
that summer day in 1810 gawking at the voyageurs' canoe, the North

American continent didn't extend much farther west than the Ohio Valley—the far edge of European settlement. That a West Coast of the continent even existed remained the haziest of notions to them, and that the vast Pacific Ocean reached far beyond it to China lay almost beyond imagination. The idea of colonizing the West Coast—to start a commercial empire or a kind of sister country on the Pacific, as Thomas Jefferson hoped, one that looked west toward China instead of east toward Europe—would make as much sense to most of the New York spectators, had they known about the great plan, as colonizing the stars or building a city on the moon.

As the voyageurs' big canoe sliced across New York Harbor, headed toward the Brooklyn staging grounds, with its echoing French boat songs and surging prow wave, Astor was pleased with the great scheme that he had set in motion. On this happy, bright Sunday in August 1810, however, neither John Jacob Astor nor Thomas Jefferson, nor anyone who had signed on as a participant, possessed the least inkling of the toll the "grand venture" would exact. It would be a toll in lives, in fortunes, in sanity, and in the ultimate configuration of America.

It was an easy walk of six blocks or so from John Jacob Astor's fur shop at 71 Liberty Street—on today's Zuccotti Park—to his home at 223 Broadway. Turning up Broadway, he passed three-story brick houses in the Federal style, then the pillared façade of St. Paul's Church. Astor surely turned his plans over in his head as he made that daily walk. Returning home to his early dinner, and his peaceful game of checkers or solitaire, did he think about the choices he'd made, and the risks he took, and, especially, the leaders he had recruited so carefully for his grand enterprise? As if turning over more face cards in his game of Patience, feeling the reach of his skill and the run of his luck, Astor, in the months ahead, would discover much about his chosen leaders as they staggered under extreme stress—in the roaring

Pacific, in the unmapped canyons of the West, and, perhaps most profoundly, in their own minds.

There was Wilson Price Hunt, the young businessman from Trenton, New Jersey. An acquaintance of Astor's, and an American, and thus trusted by Astor to be wholly loyal to the cause, Hunt would serve as Mr. Astor's stand-in to head the West Coast colony and emporium, overseeing the entire Pacific Rim trade empire. Leaving from Astor's offices in Manhattan in early summer of 1810, Hunt traveled to Montreal in company with two Scottish fur traders to recruit those first voyageurs who had canoed so dramatically down the Hudson River. From there he was to lead the Overland Party to the Columbia River. Known almost universally to friends as a kind, thoughtful, and consensus-seeking person with good business sense and a fascination with the West, he had most recently lived in St. Louis selling supplies to the first fur trappers heading up the Missouri into the new U.S. Louisiana Territory. Though Hunt had no experience in the wilderness, Astor had faith that this quick-learning newcomer, who would have the help and company of more experienced fur traders during the journey, could lead a large party across one of the largest, least known, and most rugged wildernesses in the world.

For second in command of the West Coast emporium, Astor chose Duncan McDougall. McDougall was to travel to the West Coast aboard the *Tonquin* as a member of the Seagoing Party. Also a Scottish-born fur trader from Montreal, and thus a British subject, McDougall was short, proud, energetic, and quick to take command—as well as take offense. Astor would have preferred that McDougall and the several other Scottish fur traders he recruited be American citizens, especially in light of rising tensions between the United States and Britain over territorial issues, but Astor wanted to hire the best fur traders in North America. The best in the business, by far, were the Scottish traders and French-Canadian voyageurs in the Canadian trade. Many of these traders were employees of the Montreal-based North West Company, whose sprawling operations stretched over thousands of square miles of wilderness from the Great Lakes nearly to the Rockies, while the Hudson's Bay Company operated farther to the north.

Astor knew many of the North West Company traders from his fur-buying trips to Montreal and dinners and dances there. He identified several willing to throw in their lot with his bold new enterprise, either because they were unhappy with their roles in the North West Company or enticed by the mind-boggling prospects of Astor's expedition. He made them a tempting offer. Christening his new entity the Pacific Fur Company and incorporating it in early 1810, he divvied it up into one hundred shares and extended capital up to $400,000. That was just to start—more funding could be made available if needed. If they signed on with him, Astor would give each of these Scottish-born fur traders five of those hundred shares and would name them a "partner" or "shareholder." Should Astor's vast plan succeed, they all knew, their shares would be worth a fortune.

Four signed on, filling the roster of Astor partners with a tangle of Scottish clans: in addition to Duncan McDougall, there were Donald Mackenzie, Alexander McKay, and David Stuart, who would split his shares with his young nephew, Robert. Three other partners, two of them also of Scottish descent, would join en route.

The third of Astor's chosen leaders was an American patriot and U.S. naval hero, Captain Jonathan Thorn. Astor referred to Thorn as his "gunpowder fellow." A thirty-one-year-old lieutenant taking a leave of absence from the U.S. Navy, Thorn would captain the *Tonquin* and command a crew of twenty-three. Sailing around Cape Horn, captain and crew would carry aboard the *Tonquin* as passengers the first wave of Scottish fur traders and French-Canadian voyageurs to start the emporium on the Northwest Coast. Thorn had made a name in 1804 by sailing directly into enemy fire off Tripoli in the Mediterranean during a fierce battle against North Africa's Barbary pirates, who had attacked American shipping there. While the youngish Captain Thorn had never commanded a civilian ship before, his utter fearlessness in battle and his unquestioned American patriotism—as well as his strict adherence to orders—appealed to Mr. Astor. Astor had confidently assured his Scottish partners that if there was fighting at sea to be done to establish the West Coast empire, Captain Thorn would "blow all out of the water."

According to Astor's plan, his chosen leaders would recruit other participants en route. Many would play prominent roles: fur trader Ramsay Crooks, Virginia hunter John Day, and an incredibly tough Native American woman leading her two toddlers. Known by her Europeanized name, Marie Dorion, she would stumble out of the wintry wilderness many months later with an incredible story to tell.

By August 1810, when that first canoe of recruited voyageurs landed at the lower Manhattan docks, John Jacob Astor had been laying his plans for more than two years. He had allowed for every possible problem. He had backup plans for his backup plans. He had worked diplomatic channels from Washington all the way to St. Petersburg, Russia. He had received the enthusiastic endorsement of Jefferson and his pledge of "every reasonable patronage & facility in the power of the Executive." He had proposed partnerships with his potential rival, the North West Company. His emissaries were convincing Russia with its Alaskan fur posts to use his ships to carry Russian furs to China, hoping to lock up a world monopoly on fur, or something close to it. He had interviewed recruits, chosen leaders, and instructed his agents to recruit still more voyageurs and hunters, Hawaiian swimmers, and Indian interpreters. He was prepared to put tremendous capital behind this epic undertaking, one of the greatest business ventures the world has known: a global trading empire, a colony—perhaps even a country—of his own.

In all his meticulous planning and preparation, however, Astor had not allowed for one major factor. Mountain climbers talk about "exposure," meaning one's level of physical risk in a particular situation—on a very narrow ledge on a cliff face, for instance—when a small mistake can result in major consequences. In 1810, when John Jacob Astor launched his great endeavor, this far, wild edge of the North American continent—with its brutal North Pacific storms, hostile natives, extreme remoteness, difficulty of communication, vulnerability to foreign empires, dense rain forests, and surf-battered coasts—was as exposed as any habitable place on earth.

Nor was it possible to predict the powerful distorting effect that this degree of exposure would have on the personalities and leadership abilities of the men Astor had chosen to head his West Coast empire. Under extreme stress, each leader succumbed to his own best and worst traits.

For anyone who stood to gain from it, however, Astor's vision was too mesmerizing not to embrace. His great trading scheme harmoniously and profoundly joined the dreams of two powerful and far-seeing men. Astor would dominate the world fur market, the Pacific Rim trade, and reap fantastic profits, as would his fur-trader partners. Through John Jacob Astor's powerful global trade network and West Coast colony, President Jefferson and his successors would establish a democratic outpost on the dim, distant Pacific Coast. Jefferson's vision embraced the entirety of North America and accorded Astor's enterprise a powerful role in shaping the continent's political destiny.

"I view [your undertaking]," Jefferson would write to Astor, "as the germ of a great, free and independent empire on that side of our continent, and that liberty and self-government spreading from that side as well as this side, will ensure their complete establishment over the whole."

THE BICKERING ABOARD THE *TONQUIN* STARTED THAT first night out of New York Harbor, on September 8, 1810. Captain Thorn, following his naval discipline, ordered all lights out at 8:00 P.M. His salt-hardened crew diligently obeyed. But the four clannish, woodsy, Scottish fur traders on board as passengers hadn't finished their socializing on deck, chatting and smoking their pipes as if sitting around a campfire. Nor had the dozen sinewy, French-Canadian voyageurs. Nor the eight literate young men from Canada who had signed on as clerks with Mr. Astor, some of them scribbling away in their journals.

The argumentative Scottish fur traders flatly refused Captain Thorn's order for bedtime. Mr. Astor had made them *partners* in the great scheme, they retorted. They held a financial interest. That meant, as shareholders, they *owned* part of the *Tonquin*. How could Captain Thorn tell them what to do aboard their own ship? they demanded.

Another question arose: Who would sleep where? The 300-ton *Tonquin,* ninety-six feet long, square-rigged with three masts, a newly built and fast-sailing ship, was crammed full of the crew of twenty-three plus the twenty-six passengers plus mounds of supplies for the emporium's warehouses-to-be. Captain Thorn had assigned to the Spartan quarters before the mast the passengers known as "mechanics"—the blacksmith, carpenter, and cooper for the West Coast emporium—as well as several clerks-in-training. Here they would share quarters with the *Tonquin*'s common sailors and help out with sailors' duties. The Scottish partners and clerks took this as an insult. They confronted Captain Thorn and asked him to move their mechanics and clerks-in-training aft to the more luxurious main cabin with the other clerks.

"He was a strict disciplinarian," wrote one of the clerks, Gabriel Franchère, who kept a journal, "of a quick and passionate temper, accustomed to exact obedience, considering nothing but duty, and giving himself no trouble about the murmurs of his crew, taking counsel of nobody, and following Mr. Astor's instructions to the letter. Such was the man who had been selected to command our ship."

Astor had anticipated that the mossy, comradely, forest-grown hierarchy among the passengers aboard the *Tonquin* might collide headlong with Captain Thorn's iron chain of naval command. He had written out detailed instructions to his chosen leaders before the voyage began. To Thorn, Astor had written that the captain needed to pay careful attention to the health of all aboard, and foster harmony and good humor aboard the ship.

"To prevent any misunderstandings," Astor wrote to Captain Thorn, "will require your particular good management."

But "good management" was a phrase open to interpretation. The captain refused to budge to the partners' request. The mechanics would stay where he had assigned them—in the forecastle with the common sailors—and work as he ordered.

McDougall, the small, proud Scottish partner, was incensed. It was McKay, however, who served as their de facto spokesman. At forty years old, the former North West Company employee was deeply respected in fur-trading circles for having crossed the continent to the Pacific with Alexander Mackenzie in 1793. Known for his expertise in scouting wilderness trails and working harmoniously with Indians, he was described by clerk Franchère as both "bold and enterprising," while also "whimsical and eccentric."

Perhaps incited by the short, feisty McDougall, McKay now

stepped forward from the Canadian contingent to address Captain Thorn.

"We will defend ourselves rather than suffer such treatment."

Captain Thorn, just then turning to leave, suddenly spun around on his heel to face McKay.

"I will blow out the brains of the first man who dares disobey my orders aboard my own ship."

"In the midst of this scene," wrote another clerk, Alexander Ross, "Mr. David Stuart, a good old soul, stept up, and by his gentle and timely interference put an end to the threatening altercation.

"This was the first specimen we had of the captain's disposition," Ross continued, "and it laid the foundation of a rankling hatred between the partners and himself."

And so went the great venture's first hours at sea.

Despite the tension, the *Tonquin*'s passage was relatively uneventful until she had sailed from New York Harbor well down into the Southern Hemisphere. As the horizon of the East Coast dropped from sight and they sailed out into the Atlantic, Franchère sensed just how deeply into the wilds he was headed. It would be nine thousand miles and three and a half months to Cape Horn, and that would mark only the halfway point to the Northwest Coast. He admitted that, as a sensitive person, he would have abandoned the venture right then if it were possible.

"One must have experienced it one's self," he wrote, "to be able to conceive of the melancholy which takes possession of the soul of a man of sensibility, at the instant that he leaves his country and the civilized world, to go to inhabit with strangers in the wild and unknown lands."

By September 14, only a week out of New York Harbor, the first flying fish, indicating warmer tropical waters, zipped through the ship's rigging and fell to the *Tonquin*'s deck. Ten days later the crew and passengers caught two dolphins and cooked them, a delicious break from the monotony of hard bread, salt beef, and salt pork. On October 5, sailing southeast across the Atlantic toward Africa to take advantage of the trade winds, they spotted the hazy, rocky headlands of the Cape Verde Islands, off Africa's coast.

Some of the younger passengers asked Captain Thorn to land at the islands so they could claim they had touched Africa. Captain Thorn refused what he thought a frivolous request, despite the chance to refill the *Tonquin*'s emptying water barrels. They sailed onward toward the equator. A few days off Cape Verde, a large ship fell in at a distance behind the *Tonquin*—a brig carrying twenty cannon but no identifying flag. As the big, threatening mystery ship shadowed them, Captain Thorn, glassing the vessel from afar, believed she might be a British warship preparing to board the *Tonquin*.

It was a growing problem and festering point of irritation for the young, proud U.S. republic, having fought free of its British colonial bonds barely twenty-five years earlier. British warships cruising in the Atlantic recently had boarded American commercial vessels to search for British subjects aboard as crew or passengers—of which there were often many, as in the case of the *Tonquin*. The British ships dragooned these errant subjects of the Crown into the ongoing war against Napoleon, where Britain needed all available men. The young U.S. government deeply resented this British "stop-and-search" inter-ference in American shipping, a resentment that would only grow. Cap-tain Thorn had steered clear of the Cape Verde Islands in part to avoid British vessels that might be lurking there.

Now came the game of cat-and-mouse, and Captain Thorn played it to his strengths. Known as a fast and well-constructed ship, Astor's *Tonquin* was only three years old, and her hull was sheathed in copper, which kept it free of boring worms and clinging weed growth, and gave her extra speed compared to a simple wooden hull. She carried ten guns, plus gunports that made it look as if she carried twenty, plus two fake guns in her bow. She also carried on this voyage a great number of available hands in the form of crew plus passengers, to load and fire the guns in rapid succession if it came to a fight. This gave Captain

Thorn an advantage, as the other ship appeared to carry a small crew to man its guns.

First trying to outrace the big brig, Captain Thorn ordered all sails set. The wind blew fair as he coaxed from the *Tonquin* maximum speed. All day the stranger easily stayed with the *Tonquin*. As dusk fell, she broke away and vanished into the quick tropical night. It appeared they'd finally shaken the ominous vessel. When dawn broke, however, they spotted the twenty-gun stranger still trailing them, even closer, seeming to want the *Tonquin* to identify herself without it doing likewise. Captain Thorn showed no American colors, knowing this could provoke a boarding, with many of his passengers then hauled off to fight Napoleon.

The foaming prow of the big mystery brig now closed to a mere cable's length, or about two hundred yards, from the wake swashing off the *Tonquin*'s stern. This sudden nearness of the ship, Franchère reported, put Captain Thorn in a state of "some alarm."

But this was also precisely why Astor had hired naval hero Thorn. Astor's "gunpowder fellow" now came into his element—bristling confrontations between armed ships in the lawless reaches of the open sea. Realizing the *Tonquin* couldn't outsail the brig, Thorn, as daylight brightened, ordered all crew and passengers on deck and had the ship's drum "beat to quarters"—the rhythm that signaled to prepare the gun decks—and make as if all crew and the many passengers were loading all cannon. The mystery ship could hear the beat of the drum and see the scurry of activity toward the guns.

Captain Thorn's ruse worked. The sudden threat of the *Tonquin*'s twenty-plus cannon (or so it looked), manned by a large and energetic crew and a determined captain, apparently daunted the brig.

"[A]bout ten A.M. the stranger again changed her course," reported Franchère, "and we soon lost sight of her entirely."

As the southern journey progressed, Captain Thorn grew fed up with the "lubberly" whims of his unseamanlike passengers and became ever more rigid in his command. It was as if he were trying to discipline the entire sprawling Canadian wilderness in a sailing ship just one hundred feet long. He forbade the Scottish partners from gathering on the starboard side of the quarterdeck, the ceremonial area near the wheel where commanders of warships customarily stood. He banned the scribbling clerks from the quarterdeck altogether. He was shocked with the casual manner in which the Scottish partners, such as the wilderness veteran McKay or the genial David Stuart, supposedly dignified managers of Mr. Astor's venture, would sit on deck passing a pipe as equals with common voyageurs, telling stories. When he found his amiable first mate, Mr. Fox of Boston, joining this shaggy Scottish-Canadian social circle, Thorn confined him belowdecks for three days.

Thorn wrote long letters back to his boss, Mr. Astor, to be sent on any passing ship they met or port where they should happen to call, complaining how the partners impeded Astor's great mission to the Pacific Coast. He railed against the partners' "effeminacy," their delicacy of habits, their need for entertainment and luxury, as if they expected "Fly-market on the forecastle, Covent-garden on the poop, and a cool spring from Canada on the main top."

And they whined about the food—this despite the hams and puddings he had them served in the luxury of the cabin.

"When thwarted in their cravings for delicacies, they would exclaim it was d-d hard they could not live as they pleased on their own ship, freighted with their own merchandise. And these are the fine fellows who made such a boast that they could 'eat dogs.'"

It wasn't just the partners who drove Captain Thorn wild. He complained in his letters to Astor that the scribbling clerks, far from being educated, had received their learning in barrooms and around billiard tables and had never ventured deeper into the woods than Montreal, except one, a schoolteacher, who was "as foolish a pedant as ever lived." The assorted artisans or mechanics his ship carried as passengers were as worthless as anyone "that ever broke sea biscuit." The voyageurs themselves—these wilderness hippies of their era—were a

slovenly lot, with their singing and dancing at all hours, their bragga-
docio, their dirty leather leggings, their overcoats cut from blankets.
Like some angry father with teenage sons sleeping until noon after last
night's carouse, Captain Thorn periodically stormed into the forward
cabin to roust the voyageurs from their "lubber nests" and make them
bathe and get exercise on deck.

This cultural clash aboard the *Tonquin* had its origins in the earliest European settlement of North America. The ship in many ways was
a microcosm of the continent itself at that moment in 1810—national
boundaries still undefined, and different peoples, even Northern European ones, largely unblended in what would eventually become known
as the melting pot.

The earliest French colonists in North America were aristocratic
adventurers and entrepreneurs who established a settlement in
today's Nova Scotia shortly before Sir Walter Raleigh's British colonists founded Jamestown in Virginia in 1607. Where these English
colonists at Jamestown, and later, Plymouth, painstakingly chopped
the forest acre by acre and planted seed by seed, the French soon discovered that their wealth was not in agriculture, but in the rich harvests of furs—especially beaver—from the millions of square miles
of the continent's vast interior. These fetched high prices in Europe,
where the aristocracy increasingly valued furs and beaver felt hats as
high-fashion items. Europe's own wild, fur-bearing animals had been
largely depleted by about 1600.

The French in America held two tremendous advantages over the
English for reaping that wealth in pelts, one geographic and one cultural. While the English had the Appalachians to cross to travel westward from their Atlantic settlements, no similar geographic barrier
stood between the French settlements and the continent's interior. An
easy water route—the St. Lawrence River, the Great Lakes, and chains
of rivers and lakes beyond—led directly from the French settlements
to North America's heart. Culturally, the French held an advantage in
the fur trade because they, unlike the English, had few qualms about

intermarrying with Native Americans and acculturating to an Indian way of life. They learned to hunt deer and moose like the natives, fish, live in the woods, trap the abundant beaver, paddle hundreds of miles by birch bark canoe or, in winter, make their way by snowshoe and toboggan.

The early French also enjoyed a lighthearted streak and cheerful resilience about their travails in the North American wilds that the English decidedly lacked. While the Pilgrims grimly read their Bibles through the long dark nights, the first winters for the French in the New World wilderness centered around an eating and drinking society they named L'Ordre de Bon Temps—"The Order of the Good Times"—whose mission was to provide nightly feasts of wild game and generous quantities of wine accompanied by song and even comedy theater.

The cultural mix of the French fur trade changed fundamentally after 1763—a change that was reflected in the cultural mix aboard the *Tonquin*—when Britain won Canada from France in the Seven Years' War. From then on, Scottish Highlanders, immigrating from Britain, took over management of what had been the French-Canadian fur trade. With their main headquarters at Montreal, these Highland Scots eventually ran long strings of wilderness trading posts out of a great baronial hall on the shores of Lake Superior known as Fort William. Indians brought furs to the posts to trade for manufactured goods. Scots or French Canadians usually managed the posts and employed the French-Canadian voyageurs, as well as Indian guides and interpreters, to transport the ninety-pound packets of beaver and other furs. They loaded several tons of these packets into the big birch-bark freight canoes, carrying the furs from the wilderness posts back through the interior waterways of North America and into the warehouses in Montreal. From there they were shipped to the East Coast, or across the Atlantic to Europe.

The fur trade embodied the economic differences between these groups that coexisted on the North American continent. The trade in

Canada came under regulation by the British Crown, the great swaths of territory held by Hudson's Bay Company and the North West Company granted by royal charter as monopolies. In the United States and its territories, despite the efforts of merchants to acquire government-backed monopolies, the trade was unregulated by charter and fell to individual operators. These American traders competed fiercely and with a free-for-all and cutthroat—at times literally—attitude in their dealings with one another and with Native Americans who supplied the furs. Certain aspects of the economic systems of North America remained works in progress.

At least three distinct cultures were jammed together on the *Tonquin,* cheek-by-jowl, for five or six months: the chummy Scottish fur traders who had run Canadian wilderness posts and managed the Canadian trade, the good-time French-Canadian voyageurs who paddled their canoes, and the iron-fisted Yankee naval hero and his crew of American sailors. The Scotsmen and voyageurs had worked side by side for several decades in the fur trade and understood each other's quirks. Not so the Yankee and the Scots. Tensions still ran deep between Americans and British from the Revolutionary War and its aftermath. Captain Thorn, an unyielding disciplinarian and ardent patriot, clearly hated the Scotsmen. And the Scotsmen, like a clannish yet argumentative family that sticks together against all outsiders, gladly—and en masse—returned the favor.

By MID-NOVEMBER, they'd crossed the equator and sailed well down into the Southern Hemisphere. The ship now had altered course, once again taking advantage of the winds, and steered southwest toward the tip of South America and Cape Horn, advancing from tropical calms toward the powerful winds of the southerly latitudes known as the Roaring Forties and the Furious Fifties. On the night of November 11, the wind suddenly shifted and a tremendous storm struck. While they had paddled their canoes through plenty of storms on

Canada's lakes and rivers, it was the first time many of the voyageurs and clerks had ridden out a tempest on a ship on the open sea—"with nothing," as Franchère put it, "but the frail machine which bore me between the abyss of waters and the immensity of sky."

It was a frightening experience. The gale shrieked through the rigging, and rain and wind lashed the sea into a ghostly fury. Flashes of lightning and blasts of thunder surrounded the tossing ship, so that the tumult of the sea, wrote Franchère, "appeared all a-fire."

"[The] terrible tempest," he wrote, "seemed to have sworn our destruction."

Toppling seas washed over the deck's wooden planking, which, over the past weeks, had shrunk in the hot tropical sun. Seawater poured through the resulting gaps and drenched the men in the hammocks below.

The gale subsided. Crew and passengers scrambled about below-decks and worked together to plug a leak that had sprung in the ship's hull, as well as to repair a jib boom that the wind had ripped. The wind shifted again, to the southwest. Now came a difficult judgment call for the commanding officer. On a square-rigger, fully bringing in the sails was a big job—the crew had to scramble aloft on ratlines, or rope ladders, then gather up and lash the canvas sails in tight bundles to the horizontal spars of the yardarms. On a large square-rigger, bringing in all the sails could take several hours, so if a gale threatened, the timing of an order to "shorten sail" was of utmost importance.

The order went out from the quarterdeck for the crew to furl the top and topgallant sails, but, whether for lack of anticipation or underestimating its force, the *Tonquin* still carried too much sail when struck by the full force of the second gale. A particularly powerful gust typically appears like a dark shape ruffling across the sea's surface. When it slams into a square-rigger, the whole ship strains, the deck tilting as she heels over, the hull surging forward through the swells, the rigging running taut like the strings of a giant musical

instrument, the scream of wind through the lines suddenly jumping to a shriek. If a ship has too much sail, with a sudden *BOOM*
the sails will start to "blow out," the fabric splitting apart under the
enormous pressure of the gust like an overfilled balloon, the canvas
exploding into ragged shreds. Then *BOOM,* another, and another, the
shreds flapping madly from the yardarms like kite tails while the ship
careens over the sea.

The *Tonquin,* Ross reported, lost many sails in this storm. As the
ship tossed through the heavy seas, six cannon tore loose from their
moorings and rolled about on the deck "like thunder." For seventeen
straight hours, the ship "scudded" or was shoved from behind by the
gale, making a distance downwind of 220 miles, or close to fourteen
miles per hour, madly sailing on the verge of control.

At 8:00 A.M. on November 14, a rogue wave curled ten feet above
the stern of the *Tonquin* and toppled downward. Voyageurs, clerks,
crew, Scottish partners, Captain Thorn—whatever their animosities
toward each other—all grabbed for rigging and rails as the giant wave
smashed onto the *Tonquin's* deck around the mainmast and broke into
a tumult of white water.

"[B]y that means," reported Ross, "[we] saved ourselves."

The concussive force of the wave threw the sailor manning the
wheel clear across the quarterdeck, slamming him into rigging or rail,
breaking two of his ribs, and sending him to his berth for a week.

After forty hours of battering the ship, the gale eased. The ship's
carpenter went to work repairing leaks in the *Tonquin's* otherwise solid
and copper-sheathed hull while the sailmaker stitched his canvas.

With the pause in the gales, Captain Thorn reassessed the ship's
supplies of freshwater and realized they were running dangerously
low. On November 20, he reduced the water ration further to a pint and
a half per day. Ten days later, on December 2, he cut it yet again—to
a pint per day. This, the passengers complained, was a hardship when
the diet consisted of so much salted meat. Thirsty men bargained with
one another, saying they would give a gallon of brandy for a pint of

water. Finally, on December 5, an officer in the masthead spotted one of the Falkland Islands.

"[I]t is only those who have been three or four months at sea," wrote Franchère, "who know how to appreciate the pleasure which one then feels even at the sight of such barren and bristling rocks as form the Falkland Isles."

Only whaling ships visited the treeless and surf-battered isles far out in the South Atlantic, inhabited by great numbers of seals, penguins, and seabirds. To the relief of everyone, Captain Thorn ordered the *Tonquin* to put in at the barren and unpeopled islands for freshwater.

The trouble at the Falklands started when several of the *Tonquin*'s passengers, who were amusing themselves by casually exploring onshore, discovered two graves. While the carved lettering on the old wooden headboards was barely legible, they discerned that one was the grave of a young sailor who died in a fall from a Falklands rock in 1794, and the other a victim of smallpox in 1803. The little group of touring *Tonquin* passengers decided to ask the ship's carpenter for two fresh boards so they could recarve the lettering.

"This pious attention to two dead men," wrote Franchère, who was one of the carvers, "nearly proved fatal to a greater number of the living."

It took several days for the ship's cooper to repair the water casks, and the sailors to fill them at a spring a few hundred yards inland, then row them out to the *Tonquin,* anchored just offshore in the sheltered bay. To pass the time, the clerks and voyageurs had been exploring ashore and the Scottish partners had been hunting the island's abundant waterfowl with their shotguns. On this particular day, as the sailors finished filling the casks and rowing them to the ship, and the clerks carved the new headboards, Captain Thorn came ashore, carrying his own fowling piece, with the idea to do a little hunting. Stepping from the rowboat, he spotted a gray goose standing on nearby rocks. He raised his shotgun and fired. The goose fluttered. The captain quickly reloaded and fired again. The goose fluttered again. Captain Thorn hurried over to the presumably wounded goose before it fluttered away and escaped.

As he approached, he saw that the goose's leg was tied to a rock. This had been the work of one of the clerks, Farnham, who wanted to have some "sport" with it.

"[W]hen he discovered his mistake," wrote Ross, " . . . we all burst out laughing."

Captain Thorn was not amused. He spun around and immediately returned to his boat and ordered it to take him back to the *Tonquin*.

A stray sailor ashore had already put Captain Thorn in a foul mood about lack of discipline on land. Nor was it exactly clear when the *Tonquin* was due to weigh anchor after refilling the water casks. The Scottish partners understood that it wouldn't be until the following day. As the captain stalked off angrily to the *Tonquin* after being tricked, the passengers went on with their carving, and two of the Scottish partners hiked over a sand spit to hunt birds.

"While we were thus eagerly employed, little did we suspect what was going on in another quarter," reported Ross, "for, about two o'clock in the afternoon, one of our party called out, 'The ship's off!'— when all of us, running to the top of a little eminence, beheld, to our infinite surprise and dismay, the *Tonquin,* under full sail, steering out of the bay."

WHILE THE *TONQUIN* WORKED ITS SQUABBLING WAY toward Cape Horn that late fall of 1810, Wilson Price Hunt and his Overland Party stopped their travels for the winter about four hundred miles up the Missouri River from St. Louis. Already they'd fallen behind Astor's schedule. Explored by Lewis and Clark only six years earlier, the Missouri was the only known route across the vast terra incognita of this part of the North American continent. It made sense to follow that known route and stay at the Lewis and Clark wintering camp at the Mandan villages, in what is today North Dakota. But Hunt's accommodating and loyal nature, compounded by his inexperience, slowed the Overland Party from the start. He'd fallen a thousand miles short of the Lewis and Clark winter camp. The consequences of this and other delays would build like a gathering storm.

Hunt had insisted on stopping at various points along the way to recruit more personnel, though Donald Mackenzie, the Scottish partner traveling with Hunt, had warned him about the folly of this. Astor, valuing Mackenzie's decade's worth of wilderness experience with the North West Company, and thinking he would make a good counterbalance to Hunt, initially appointed Mackenzie and Hunt as co-leaders of the Overland Party, or had at least given this arrangement his tacit approval. Together they'd left Manhattan for Montreal in the early summer of 1810 to gather recruits for the Seagoing Party, passing around Astor's "gilded prospectus," as Ross, one of the recruited clerks, put it.

Hunt and Mackenzie had sent the Scottish clerks and French-Canadian voyageurs to New York to board the *Tonquin*. But when it came time at Montreal to hire for their own Overland Party, Hunt balked. Mr. Astor had instructed them to include as many Americans as possible for the West Coast settlement; Hunt didn't want to go against his wishes, by hiring the British subjects available in Montreal.

Mackenzie objected—forcefully. Not only did the "Northwesters" possess far more experience in the fur trade than the Americans, but it would be tough to hire competent woodsmen of any stripe once the Overland Party traveled beyond Montreal. He told Hunt that the good men at interior settlements or posts would already be engaged in work, and only good-for-nothing rabble would be available to hire.

The big Scotsman presented an intimidating figure for young Hunt to challenge. Powerfully built, he was an expert marksman and woodsman who had received a "liberal" education as a youth in Scotland, but, as the embodiment of a man of action, he hated to sit still to write or keep a journal, except for the briefest of directional notes scrawled in charcoal on beaver skins.

"To travel a day's journey on snowshoes was his delight," wrote Ross, who knew Mackenzie well. "When not asleep, he was always on foot, strolling backwards and forwards, full of plans and projects; so peculiar was his pedestrian habit, that he went by the name of 'Perpetual Motion.'"

Mackenzie's presence on the Overland Party was a major reason Astor felt comfortable allowing Hunt, a neophyte in the woods, to co-lead it. But now the first difference in philosophy arose between the two, and the argument grew fierce before they could reach a compromise. Finally, they agreed to hire twelve voyageurs at Montreal to paddle them up the Great Lakes to Mackinac Island. The remainder they'd hire en route when they passed through two major fur trading centers in the continent's interior—Mackinac Island and St. Louis.

Before heading into the wilderness, the voyageurs accompanying Hunt and Mackenzie underwent their ritual leave-taking from their vil-

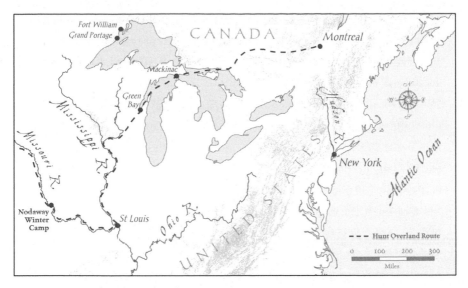

HUNT OVERLAND PARTY, JULY–NOVEMBER 1810

lage near Montreal—farewells with family and friends, carousals with drink and women, a confession at the Chapel of St. Anne, the patroness of voyageurs. Their big freight canoe, called a Montreal canoe or a *canot du maître,* was close to forty feet long and about six feet wide, able to carry about four tons. Once the voyageurs were ready, and with Hunt and Mackenzie aboard, they paddled their canoe briskly from Montreal on the regular route up a network of rivers toward the head of the Great Lakes, about five hundred miles away.

A voyageur canoe, for several centuries, was by far the fastest mode of transportation into the wild heart of the North American continent. Propelled by the powerful arms of the voyageurs, commanded by the steersman, and paddling in exact unison at forty to sixty strokes per minute, these canoes surged through the water at four to six miles per hour, a remarkable speed. Paddling twelve to fifteen hours per day, with short breaks while afloat for a pipe of tobacco (they measured distances in terms of "pipes") or a stop ashore for a mug of tea, they could cover fifty to ninety miles per day, unless they faced strong headwinds or waves that forced them to the shelter of shore, a state called *degradé.* During that single day each voyageur would make more than thirty thousand paddle strokes. On the upper Great Lakes, the canoes traversed hundreds of miles of empty, forested shorelines and vast stretches of clear water without ports or settlements or sails, except for the scattered Indian encampment. They camped along shore wherever convenient, kindling a fire and wrapping themselves in blankets or furs beneath the shelter of their overturned canoes. During portages, each voyageur hauled two 90-pound packets of pelts on his back—a staggering 180 pounds, one packet suspended from a tumpline around his forehead, the other resting atop it on his back—a half mile at a time between designated rest stops, then returned for additional loads. Some of the portages went on for ten miles, and a notorious one lasted for forty.

A Great Lakes traveler in the early 1800s timed the voyageurs with whom he rode during a shore break. They landed their canoe, climbed out, unloaded its cargo, kindled a fire, melted spruce pitch, repaired a tear in the overturned birch-bark hull, reloaded the canoe, cooked breakfast, shaved, washed, climbed back in the canoe, and paddled off, in fifty-seven minutes.

"I can liken them to nothing but their own ponies," he wrote. "They are short, thick set, and active, and never tire."

Wrote another: "[T]hey haven't lost an iota of French gaiety, which differs so strikingly from the glacial sang-froid of Americans."

Unlike the sprawling egalitarianism of the American trade, a strict sense of hierarchy prevailed in the Canadian fur trade. On its lowest rung stood the *mangeurs de lard,* or "pork-eaters," so named because, subsisting on preserved or salted pork, they were mostly a waterborne porter service where newcomers started. They simply paddled the big freight canoes the hundreds of miles from Montreal to the main interior posts such as Mackinac Island on Lake Huron, or Fort William on Lake Superior. There they dropped off a load of trade goods and supplies brought from Montreal, picked up several tons of the ninety-pound packets of pelts, and paddled back to Montreal.

In contrast to the pork-eater, the higher-ståtus *hivernant,* or "win-terer," lived off wild game while managing the remote wilderness fur posts of the interior throughout the winter, where he traded goods directly with the Indian hunters and trappers for furs. At the top of the hierarchy stood the *bourgeois*—or "proprietor" or "partner"—who actually owned part of the enterprise. Originally held by French Cana-dians, these proprietor roles were largely taken over by Scottish fur traders after Britain won Canada from France in 1763. For the ambi-tious Scots fur trader, usually a young immigrant from the Highlands, the system offered a vast hierarchy to climb to success and wealth, from apprentice, to clerk, to partner. For many of the French-Canadian voyageurs, however, the paddling life remained an end in itself:

"I could carry, paddle, walk and sing with any man I ever saw," claimed one seventy-year-plus voyageur, as quoted by historian Grace Lee Nute, writing in the early 1900s. "I have been twenty-four years a canoe man, and forty-one years in service; no portage was ever too long for me. Fifty songs could I sing. I have saved the lives of ten voyageurs. Have had twelve wives and six running dogs. I spent all my money in pleasure. Were I young again, I should spend my life the same way over. There is no life so happy as a voyageur's life!"

On July 22, 1810, about three weeks after leaving Montreal, Hunt and Mackenzie's birch-bark freight canoe surged into the cove and toward the crescent of beach at Michilmackinac Island. Known as "Mackinac" for short (and pronounced "Mackinaw"), the strategically placed island sits where lakes Huron, Michigan, and Superior con-verge. It thus served as a major waterway crossroads for the interior fur trade. Atop a bluff over the cove and its crescent beach stood an impos-ing fort. Strung out along the beachfront directly beneath its ramparts and cannon tumbled an array of shacks and cabins from which fiddle music drifted out over the chill, crystalline northern waters.

The steersman directed the canoe toward the beach, paddling at top speed, voyageurs singing at the top of their lungs, their finest feathers and sashes flying to impress spectators ashore. The canoe glided into the shallows of the gravelly beach and out of it stepped Wilson Price Hunt, determined to hire *Americans* for Mr. Astor's West Coast empire. He walked into a scene such as he'd never witnessed before.

"Every nook and corner in the whole island swarmed, at all hours of the day and night, with motley groups of uproarious tipplers and whisky-hunters," wrote one contemptuous Scots-Canadian observer. "[It] resembled a great bedlam, the frantic inmates running to and fro in wild forgetfulness."

"That Canadians in general drink, sometimes to excess, must be admitted," he continued, "but to see drunkenness and debauchery, with all their concomitant vices, carried on systematically, it is necessary to see Mackinaw. . . . [I]n the morning [the Americans] were found drinking, at noon drunk, in the evening dead drunk. . . ."

Mackenzie had warned Hunt. It was going to be tough to hire competent voyageurs or woodsmen once they'd reached the interior, and, in any case, the Americans they did find would make far inferior hires to Canadians.

Established as an outpost nearly a century and a half earlier, in the 1670s, by Jesuit missionaries, Mackinac for a century had served as a major collection point of the Canadian fur trade in the upper Great Lakes. But in the late 1700s, the Canadians or "Northwesters" extended their reach still deeper into North America's interior across what is today Minnesota, Manitoba, and Saskatchewan. By this point, in 1810, their sophisticated system of canoe relays and fur posts threaded for one thousand miles through rivers and lake chains all the way from the western shore of Lake Superior to the foot of the Rocky Mountains.

As it pushed deeper into the continent's wild interior, the North West Company shifted its regional headquarters from Mackinac Island another three hundred miles westward to Superior's western shore. Here it established a post at Grand Portage—so named because the voyageurs and fur traders portaged nine miles over Lake Superior's western bluffs to gain access to the river systems of the continent's western interior. At Grand Portage, they transferred their trade goods from the huge Montreal canoes to smaller *canot du nord,* about twenty-five feet long and capable of carrying about three thousand pounds plus paddlers. With one of these smaller canoes, the *hivernant* and his voyageurs made their way to his remote wilderness post.

While Grand Portage opened the trade to the northern and western wilderness, the old fur post at Mackinac Island remained the hub of the fur trade to the south—what we'd now call the upper Midwest. After long, lonely fall and winter months tending their traplines, these "southwestern" woodsmen, many of them Americans, paddled into Mackinac with pelts to sell, eager for company and with a yen to cut loose—drinking, dancing, singing, whoring, fighting, buying knick-knacks and finery from the beach's shacks and stalls. These Americans were generally independent or freelance contractors compared to the northwestern company men, who considered themselves vastly superior professionals and looked down on this undisciplined southwestern mob that caroused at Mackinac Island, although many voyageurs were present at Mackinac, too.

"Perhaps Satan never reigned with less control in any place than he has here," wrote one missionary's wife in 1803 of the Mackinac Island beach scene.

The American woodsmen didn't even bother with the offer from the earnest, young Mr. Hunt. A whispering campaign rippled among the Mackinac rum shacks that Astor's was a losing enterprise headed on a death trip into hostile Indian realms and starvation deserts. Even if the rumors weren't true, to sign the contract Hunt offered on John Jacob Astor's behalf was a tremendous commitment, even by the standards of today; it would mean handing five years of one's life to a start-up venture bound for the unknown.

Desperate to hire, Hunt and Mackenzie upped their offer—the recruits, if they wished, could sign for only three years instead of committing to a full five. Finally, on the last day of July 1810, the first Mackinac recruit signed—a French-Canadian voyageur, François Landry.

This was a victory of sorts for Hunt and Mackenzie and their Overland Party. Landry might convince some of his fellow French-Canadian voyageurs at Mackinac to join the great Astor enterprise, serving, as one early Astorian chronicler put it, as the "stool-pigeon" to lure in more recruits.

But the voyageurs were cleverer than that. John Jacob Astor had money and Wilson Price Hunt was authorized to spend it and the voyageurs knew it. The voyageurs now stepped forward, in twos and threes, willing to sign on with the stipulation that they receive partial wages in advance.

Hunt agreed.

There were a few other matters, the voyageurs added.

Several claimed they'd already committed to other fur outfits. They needed money to buy out their contracts. Another said that he couldn't depart Mackinac Island before he paid off his debts. And still another, the voyageur Joseph Perrault, asked Mr. Hunt to pony up the $11.25 fine levied against him for a recent barroom brawl on Mackinac, plus another $8.50 to pay for the repair of the table he'd smashed.

Hunt paid. These voyageurs signed. But Hunt and Mackenzie still needed more.

For all his inexperience in the wilderness, Wilson Price Hunt had a knack for reading people's character. He and Mackenzie now struck on another lure. In addition to their free-spending habits and free-living lifestyle when off duty, voyageurs had a well-deserved reputation, especially when ashore, for favoring flamboyant clothing. To this, Hunt and Mackenzie made their appeal.

The well-dressed voyageur boasted a look that was something between a soft-footed Indian hunter below the waist and a swash-buckling French pirate above it. This unusual sartorial configuration reflected the voyageurs' origins in the melding of seventeenth-century French immigrants in eastern North America with the native Indian peoples already living there who were familiar with travel through its lakes, rivers, and forests, and the dress and equipment best suited to it.

The voyageurs wore soft Indian moccasins on their feet and deerskin leggings up over their knees that were held up by a garter-like string tied to a belt around the waist. In warm seasons they typically wore a breechcloth, in the Indian style, leaving thighs bare. This waist-down garb gave them exceptional maneuverability for sitting or squatting for hours in a cramped, luggage-crammed canoe, climbing in and out over the high gunwales, and hauling two nincty-pound packets of pelts at a time during a portage. The footwear and leggings also offered a certain resistance to wading in cold water or snow, essential in these northern climes.

Above the waist, the voyageurs wore a loose-fitting and colorful plaid shirt, perhaps a blue or red, and over it, depending on the weather, a long, hooded, capelike coat called a *capote*. In cold winds they cinched this closed with a waist sash—the gaudier the better, often red. From the striking sash dangled a beaded pouch that contained their fire-making materials and tobacco for their "inevitable pipe." Topping off this rainbow-hued, multicultural ensemble, the well-dressed voyageur sported either a colorful headscarf or a red wool hat, on which the French-Canadian voyageurs loved to display badges of their status.

"Je suis un homme du nord!"

The true "Man of the North" wore a brightly colored feather in his cap to distinguish himself from the rabble, fixing it in place before landing at a fur post. As it happened, Hunt and Mackenzie possessed an abundant supply of large, colorful feathers, including flouncy ostrich plumes, among the trade goods they'd purchased at Montreal. Desperate for recruits at Mackinac, they struck on the clever idea of offering an ostentatious feather to every voyageur who signed on. Soon the short, arcing beach at Mackinac Island fluttered with the feathers of newly recruited French-Canadian voyageurs who had joined John Jacob Astor's great Pacific Coast enterprise.

But ostrich feathers, to Hunt's dismay, worked no magic with the hard-drinking, no-frills American woodsmen. He and Mackenzie still needed more recruits for the West Coast empire. Leaving Mackinac Island in mid-August, the Overland Party paddled southwest toward their next destination, St. Louis. En route, they had to cross a geographic barrier that is almost unrecognized today but that determined the route of much pre-industrial travel (and even cultural patterns) in North America. This subtle rise of land known to geographers as the Mid-Continental Divide separates the watershed of the Great Lakes, running east to the Atlantic via the St. Lawrence, from the watershed of the Ohio-Mississippi-Missouri river system, which drains the center of the continent south into the Gulf of Mexico. In the fifteen thousand or more years since arriving in North America from Asia, Native Americans had discovered the most efficient places to portage canoes across this divide, laying out their waterway equivalent of the Interstate Highway System, and along which, centuries later, they guided the first Jesuit missionaries and voyageurs.

Following one of these ancient Indian travel corridors, the Overland Party now paddled down Lake Michigan to Green Bay, up the Fox River, and portaged over a short stretch of marshy ground that marks the Mid-Continental Divide in central Wisconsin. Then they relaunched their birch-bark vessels on the smooth, steady current of the Wisconsin River's tea-colored waters. A day or two later, the current swept them out onto the languorous, blue Mississippi River, half a mile wide, dotted with wooded islands and shouldered by tall, forested bluffs. Now they rode the current down the great central drainage system of North America. About three weeks after leaving Mackinac Island, they pulled into the French village and fur post at St. Louis, where the Missouri, flowing from the Rockies and western plains, joins the Mississippi.

Wilson Price Hunt struck a recruiting wall at St. Louis, too. For six weeks Hunt lingered in the village where he'd lived a few years before, a collection of old French homes surrounded by verandas and new, brick-built American shops, in addition to log cabins and crude shacks. As the hazy heat of late summer advanced to the clear cool of mid-autumn, Hunt, surrounded by old friends in a familiar place, may not have felt the urgency to leave. Men to hire were in short supply due in part to other fur companies hiring, companies headed up the Missouri, which was busier since the Lewis and Clark expedition had explored its length just six years before. The huge new U.S. territory, the Louisiana Purchase, was now opening for fur commerce. Meriwether Lewis had died the previous year and William Clark was serving as U.S. Indian Agent in St. Louis. He and Hunt probably consulted on the most plausible route to the Pacific.

There was also a certain anxiety in the air about the journey west. Another fur outfit, under the leadership of Andrew Henry, had set off up the Missouri a year and a half earlier to establish a remote post at Three Forks, the river's headwater streams near the Rocky Mountains. Reports had come downriver of attacks by Blackfeet. In the streets of St. Louis the worry grew: Had something terrible happened to them?

Hunt and Mackenzie knew they had to get a start, at the least, before winter set in. On October 21, the Overland Party turned their boats up the Missouri. By mid-November they'd made about four hundred miles. This was still nearly a thousand miles short of Astor's hope for a winter camp at the Mandan villages where Lewis and Clark had wintered. The temperature plummeted. Arctic winds blew unimpeded down the barren plains. Fine needles of frazil ice congealed on the gently swirling Missouri, clumped together, and drifted downstream in slushy rafts. The Overland Party pitched its winter camp on November 16, 1810, at the mouth of the Nodaway River, in what today is northeastern Missouri. Two days later the clumpy rafts of frazil ice locked together in the arctic cold and the Missouri River froze shut for the winter.

CHAPTER FOUR

S EVEN THOUSAND MILES TO THE SOUTH OF THE ICEBOUND
Missouri, summer was arriving in the Falklands. This made the islands no less barren and the prospect of being stranded on them no less forbidding.

The alarm instantly spread among the passengers amusing themselves ashore—the *Tonquin* was sailing out of the bay! Two or three of the headboard-carving clerks scrambled over the top of the sand spit, firing guns, to signal to the Scottish partners hunting birds on the far side of it, McDougall and Stuart, to return immediately. Other clerks made for the rowboat beached in the bay. A half hour had passed by the time they all gathered at the ship's boat. By then, the *Tonquin,* making good speed on a good wind under Captain Thorn's command, had already sailed three miles out to sea.

All nine of the partners and clerks stranded on the island piled into the boat—twenty feet in length, built for half that number—and took to the oars. Backs bent in unison with each grunting stroke, they rowed hard after the *Tonquin,* expecting that the ship would "heave to" into the wind at any moment and wait for them to catch up. It did not. The *Tonquin* proceeded to sail onward, displaying full billowing canvas to the tops of the masts, into the open South Atlantic.

They strained harder at the oars, fighting a tidal current. The ship was fast outpacing them. As they left the sheltered bay and pulled into the open ocean, the full force of wind and waves and spray swept over the little rowboat, drenching them in cold seawater. The *Tonquin* now had sailed ahead by more than two leagues—or six miles. Ever larger swells broke over the rowboat's gunwales, dumping in seawater that sloshed around their feet. Taking turns with a bailing bucket, the passengers furiously scooped water from the bilge and tossed it overboard. The Falklands lie only six hundred miles from Antarctica. The water remains frigid even at the height of the Antarctic summer. If the rowboat swamped, the clerks and Scottish traders, even those who knew how to swim, would have no chance of survival.

They momentarily paused at the oars. A brief, urgent discussion broke out: Should they chase onward into the tumultuous open sea after the *Tonquin,* or turn back to the immediate safety of the shore, where eventual death by exposure, starvation, or simply years of barehanded isolation might await them?

As they debated, the man who was bailing lost his grip on the bucket. It danced away on the heaving swells. Those at the oars heaved hard to swivel the rowboat to catch the errant bucket. One of the oars snapped. Now they were bobbing on the open swells, without a bailing bucket, and missing one oar, with the *Tonquin* still sailing away from them.

They hesitated once more. Should they return to the barren island or chase after the *Tonquin*? A decision was made: They would reach the ship—or die trying.

"The weather now grew more violent," reported Ross, "the wind increased. . . ."

It was then, Ross wrote, as they despaired of reaching her, that they noticed the *Tonquin* begin to swing on the wind. Soon she had shifted course entirely. She bore down toward the oared vessel. After considerable maneuvering in the rough seas, the two vessels finally managed to pull alongside each other. The abandoned passengers climbed aboard from the tossing boat to the safety of the big ship.

Franchère, who was in the boat, wrote that there was never any doubt of Captain Thorn's clear intention to abandon them "upon those barren rocks of the Falkland isles, where we must inevitably have perished."

The timely intervention of young Robert Stuart had saved them. Robert was the nephew of Scottish partner David Stuart, the kinder and older trader who had mediated the power struggle the first night at sea out of New York Harbor. David Stuart, the uncle, was among the passengers in the struggling oared boat. When it had become clear on board the *Tonquin* that Captain Thorn had no intention of turning her around to save the boat and its passengers, the younger Stuart strode up to the captain on the quarterdeck. Whipping out two loaded pistols, he commanded Captain Thorn to alter course immediately.

Do it, young Stuart demanded, or "you are a dead man this instant."

ON FEBRUARY 11, 1811, two months after leaving the Falklands and rounding Cape Horn, the *Tonquin's* crew spotted from fifty miles away the snowcapped cone of Mauna Loa volcano rising two and a half miles above the blue Pacific swells. The volcano marked the largest isle of the group that Captain Cook had named the Sandwich Islands when he had "discovered" them for Britain three decades earlier. The seafaring natives who lived there for centuries called them Owyhee and we know them today as Hawaii. All hands and passengers scrambled on deck as the *Tonquin,* spanking along on the lusciously warm trade winds, sailed toward the Big Island at a brisk eight or nine knots.

"The coast of the island," wrote Franchère, "viewed from the sea, offers the most picturesque *coup d'oeil* and the loveliest prospect; from the beach to the mountains the land rises amphitheatrically, all along which is a border of lower country covered with cocoa-trees and bananas, through the thick foliage whereof you perceive the huts of the islanders. . . ."

The intoxicating view captured all eyes as the ship neared the emerald isle. A teenage Canadian boy accompanying the voyageurs, Guillaume Perrault, was watching the island's approach from a perch high aloft in the foremast when he suddenly lost his grip and plummeted out of the rigging toward the deck far below. Just before hitting the wooden planking, his falling body struck upon the taught triangle of guyline shrouds that supported the mast. He bounced "like a ball" off the webbing, as Franchère put it, and flew out into the sea a good twenty feet beyond the ship's rail. The boy didn't know how to swim. In the best of circumstances, it would take a square-rigged ship like the *Tonquin* a considerable distance to slow or reverse course to rescue him.

"We perceived his fall," wrote Franchère, "and threw over to him chairs, barrels, benches, hen-coops, in a word everything we could lay hands on. . . ."

The floating furniture was intended to mark the boy's location in the big swells. It would presumably also give him something to which to cling—if he could somehow make his way to one of the items.

It was an irony that the accident occurred amid fair winds and subtropical islands, rather than the much-feared and often violent waters off Cape Horn. The *Tonquin* had rounded the Horn uneventfully several weeks earlier in decent weather, making the transition from Atlantic to Pacific on Christmas Day of 1810. The truly bad weather had prevailed during this latest leg of the voyage not around Cape Horn, but between Captain Thorn and his passengers. Captain Thorn's attempt to abandon them on the Falklands, wrote Ross, dwarfed into insignificance all the "former feuds and squabbles."

He described the thick tension that wrapped the deck of the *Tonquin* en route to Hawaii.

"Sullen and silent, both parties passed and repassed each other in their promenades on deck without uttering a word," wrote Ross, "but their looks bespoke the hatred that burnt within. The partners on the quarter-deck made it now a point to speak nothing but the Scotch dialect; while the Canadians on the forecastle spoke French—neither of which did the captain understand; and as both groups frequently passed hours together, cracking their jokes and chanting their outlandish songs, the commander seemed much annoyed on these occasions, pacing the deck in great agitation."

Captain Thorn, for his part, believed that both he and Mr. Astor would have been far better off if he'd succeeded in abandoning the passengers on the Falklands. He attributed his decision to turn back not to Robert Stuart's hair-trigger pistols pointed at him but to a sudden shift in the wind.

"Had the wind not hauled ahead soon after leaving the harbor's mouth," he wrote to Mr. Astor, "I should positively have left them; and, indeed, I cannot but think it an unfortunate circumstance for you that it so happened . . . as they seem to have no idea of the value of property, nor any apparent regard for your interest, although interwoven with their own."

When the *Tonquin* had rounded Cape Horn she had sailed 9,165 miles from New York Harbor, according to her officers' calculations. Another roughly 7,200 miles brought them to the Hawaiian Islands, for a total distance of more than 15,000 miles and five months simply to reach Hawaii, trapped with one's enemies in a cargo-jammed space one hundred feet long, surrounded by nothing but one another and the infinite wilderness of the sea.

Nothing in our daily world remotely compares to this extreme confinement, except perhaps space travel or a winter in Antarctica. Imagine an airline flight of five months with one brief stop, no movies, porridge for breakfast, salt pork for dinner, and a bottle and a half of fresh water per day. The cultural clashes between factions—American sailors, Scottish fur traders, French-Canadian voyageurs, and naval heroes—exacerbated the pressures of extreme confinement, a phenomenon noted by modern psychological studies of crews that winter in Antarctica stations.

"Crews with clique structures," according to a summary of these studies, "report significantly more depression, anxiety, anger, fatigue and confusion than crews with core-periphery structures."

The *Tonquin*'s example offers abundant lessons in leadership, especially in the hazards of overlapping spheres of authority. During the long Pacific leg of the passage, two of the Scottish partners, McKay and McDougall, passed their time by designing the fort and living quarters they would build as the central node of Astor's empire on the West Coast. Arguments and power struggles soon erupted between the two of them over the exact details of fort layout. Like Captain Thorn, each believed he best represented John Jacob Astor's interests. Astor had, in fact, vested each of these individuals with his own authority in a specific sphere—Captain Thorn in matters having to do with the *Tonquin,* McKay in his expertise dealing with Indians at wilderness posts, McDougall as second in command in Hunt's absence at the West Coast emporium. But these clear spheres frequently overlapped. Among the partners aboard the *Tonquin,* McDougall proved the most forceful and managed to come out on top. Short, proud, and quick to take control, he settled the architectural argument with McKay by pulling out his letter from Mr. Astor and pointing to the language putting him in charge of the emporium when Hunt was not around.

"[A]nd within fifteen minutes," Captain Thorn reported to Astor, "they would be caressing each other like children."

While at first glance of the map, Hawaii appears to lie far out in the Pacific, due to prevailing winds it offered a convenient resupply stop for sailing ships en route between Cape Horn and the Northwest Coast. Astor had instructed Captain Thorn and the Scottish partners to hire Hawaiians before proceeding to the West Coast. The islanders possessed skills that would be indispensable in founding a colony, such as growing lush gardens and raising pigs. They were also exceptional swimmers and boatmen. Many North Atlantic sailors and Canadian voyageurs never learned to swim, having grown up around waters so cold that the skill was difficult to learn and often regarded as largely pointless should they fall overboard in the open ocean, where chances of rescue were slim.

So it was with young Perrault. As the *Tonquin* flew on a stiff breeze along the Hawaiian coast and he dropped from the foremast into the sea, the thrashing boy disappeared in the ship's wake while passengers and crew threw benches and barrels overboard. Captain Thorn called out the "heave to" order. The helmsman instantly spun the wheel to steer the *Tonquin* into the wind, backing the sails to slow the ship. Officers and crew jumped at one of the small boats lashed in davits on deck, jerked out their clasp knives, sliced the lines that secured it, and lowered the boat over the side.

Fifteen minutes had elapsed by the time they reached Perrault, reported Franchère. His waterlogged body rose and sunk with the swells. His head lolled beneath the surface. But his greasy and tar-stained coveralls had managed to keep his legs and torso afloat. They hauled his lifeless body into the boat and rowed him back to the *Tonquin,* where they went to work trying to revive him by rolling him in blankets and rubbing him with salt. Soon he came to consciousness.

"[I]n a few hours he was able to run upon the deck," wrote Franchère.

Not all crew and passengers doused overboard from the *Tonquin* would be so lucky as young Guillaume.

The Hawaiians warmly welcomed the *Tonquin*'s passengers and crew—too warmly, thought Captain Thorn. The ship anchored on the west side of the Big Island of Hawaii at Kealakekua Bay. Dozens of native canoes paddled out from the bay's two large villages bearing mounds of breadfruit, bananas, watermelons, coconuts, yams, cabbages, and poultry—a spectacular culinary vacation from porridge and salt pork. The tattooed paddlers gladly traded their fresh vegetables and meat for glass beads, rings of iron, sewing needles, cotton cloth, and other glass and metal manufactures.

A contingent of passengers and crew from the *Tonquin* returned the visit, rowing from the ship to the village under the palms. Nineteen young women and one man danced for them in welcome, swaying rhythmically in unison as they sang. Their performance enchanted the passengers and sailors after the months of confinement in the dark,

claustrophobic quarters of the *Tonquin* under the unyielding hand
of Captain Thorn. The young women, as Franchère described them,
each wore a "becoming" garland of flowers. The dumbfounded young
visitors from the Bible-toting lands of New England and Scotland and
Montreal had never seen anything like it.

"For other traits, they are very lascivious," he reported, "and far
from observing a modest reserve, especially toward strangers."

An old man led the visitors down the beach to a shelf of coral rock.
He pointed out the very spot where Captain Cook had fallen, on February 14, 1779—which Franchère realized was exactly thirty-two years
before, to the day. The old man filled in the details of Cook's famous
demise. Initially the Hawaiians had welcomed Cook; and Cook in turn
had treated them with respect. After several misunderstandings,
however, the Hawaiians had stolen a rowboat. Captain Cook and his
marines rowed ashore and marched under the palms to the Hawaiian king's house to take him hostage until the islanders returned the
ship's boat.

Hawaiian chiefs and warriors clustered around their sacred leader
to protect him. Captain Cook, "not accustomed to have his intentions
frustrated," recorded one crew member who was an eyewitness, " . . .
had but little command over himself in his anger." A crowd of two or
three thousand Hawaiians pressed in. The enraged Cook beat them
back with the butt of his shotgun. His Lieutenant Phillips warned
Cook that he was in mortal danger and should leave immediately.
Cook fired once, wounding a Hawaiian, then again, killing one. Followed by the crowd of angry Hawaiians, he retreated to the nearby
beach with his marines while other marines in his oared boats just
offshore opened fire.

Cook strode into the surf and, facing the ocean, raised his hands
to order the marines in boats to cease firing at the Hawaiians and pick
him up. James Cook, like so many of the sailors of the era, had never
learned to swim well, either; if he knew how, he may have waded out
from shore into deeper water and events could have transpired very

differently. As Cook stood in the shallows facing seaward, one of the Hawaiian chiefs, "more daring than the rest," stepped forward with dagger in hand and stabbed Cook between the shoulders. Instantly, another warrior clubbed him over the head. Cook collapsed into the shallow surf. They pounced on him, holding him underwater for several minutes. Then they dragged him up and beat his head against the nearby coral rocks to ensure that he was dead.

Thrown into chaos by the sudden fall of their vaunted leader, and some of them also falling under knife stabs and club blows, Cook's men scrambled for the boats and retreated to the ships anchored in the bay, unable to retrieve their commander's body. They then opened fire with cannon loaded with jagged iron shrapnel aimed at the hundreds of Hawaiians gathered on the beach.

Three decades later, the *Tonquin*'s partners and clerks strolled about the beach, enthralled by the old Hawaiian's story and their own presence on the very spot where one of the greatest British heroes of the age had forever fallen. Captain Thorn would have been well served to learn from Captain Cook's temperamental treatment of the native peoples, but the captain had apparently remained aboard ship. Accompanied by their knowledgeable local guide, the *Tonquin* contingent ashore was, in effect, one of Hawaii's first tourist groups. Like most tourists, they now wanted souvenirs. Pulling out pocketknives, they pried chunks of wood from the coconut trees that still bore the bullet and shrapnel scars of Captain Cook's last stand and chipped off pieces of the coral rock where Hawaiian warriors bashed his head.

Finally, the enchanting day ashore drew to a close and they headed for the rowboat. The Scottish partners and young clerks had an incentive to return to the *Tonquin*—the possibility of great wealth as founders and shareholders of Mr. Astor's West Coast empire. The *Tonquin*'s sailors, however, faced only the prospect of Captain Thorn's harsh discipline at sea for many months to come. Several deserted right there on the paradisal beach at Kealakekua Bay.

When, with the shore party back on board, Captain Thorn heard that several of his sailors were missing, he flew into a rage.

"Storming and stamping on deck," Ross wrote, "the captain called up all hands; he swore, he threatened, and abused the whole ship's company. . . ."

The captain demanded that the Hawaiian islanders bring back the deserters, which they eventually did. He had one deserter confined belowdecks. Another was tied up and flogged. A third, reported Ross, was put in irons. Captain Thorn didn't bother to round up the deserting boatswain Anderson, however, because he felt Anderson was worthless as a sailor anyway.

With the *Tonquin* now undermanned, Ross momentarily felt sorry for the captain, while also pointing out in his account of the incident that Captain Thorn had brought on all his woes himself. Thorn was steeped in a rigid system of order, discipline, and deprivation designed for the sole purpose of combat at sea. Through the long reach of Astor's empire, this ethic had collided head-on at the beach of Kealakekua Bay with the charming allures of what appeared, for an outsider at least, to be a far more permissive, harmonious, and easygoing culture. Captain Thorn's situation was a bit like that of a besieged summer camp director trying to corral his high-spirited lads from escaping during the night to the girls' camp across the lake.

"[W]ith all his faults he had some good qualities," Ross wrote, "and in his present trying situation we all forgot our wrongs, and cheerfully exerted ourselves to help him out of his difficulties."

But the difficulties in Hawaii didn't end at Kealakekua Bay, nor did Captain Thorn's frustrations. Before sailing the 2,600 miles to America's West Coast, the *Tonquin* needed more personnel to staff the emporium as well as a stock of live Hawaiian pigs, both to consume en route and to raise at the new colony. Royal Hawaiian decree, however, banned the villagers from selling their own pigs to passing ships, as this was a trading right reserved for the king. Two days after the shore visit to Captain Cook's last stand, the *Tonquin* sailed about twenty miles up the west coast of the Big Island and put in at Tohehigh Bay, residence of the island's governor, for permission to buy pigs. To the surprise of all aboard, the governor of the Big Island turned out to be a Scotsman and former sailor named John Young, who twenty years earlier had served as boatswain aboard a New England ship, the *Eleanora,* one of the first trading vessels to call at the Northwest Coast after Cook's voyage.

Young had been taken captive during an altercation between the ship's captain and the Hawaiians and left behind by the *Eleanora.* Kamekameha, the head of the Big Island at the time and a far-sighted leader, had taken in the boatswain, given him land, and used him as a trusted advisor on military matters and Western technology. Kamekameha eventually united the other islands and established his royal seat at the more fertile island of Oahu, with its good harbor at what is now the city of Honolulu. He promoted Young to be governor of the Big Island, where he had ruled.

Captain Thorn, the Scottish partners McDougall and McKay, and some of the clerks, such as Ross, were rowed ashore at Tohehigh Bay on the Big Island to meet Governor Young, then about sixty years old, shrewd, and in good health, to ask about buying pigs.

"He received us kindly," wrote Ross, "and with every mark of attention peculiar to an Indian chief; showed us his wife, his daughter, his household, and vassals. . . . [F]rom his long residence among the natives, he has imbibed so much of their habits and peculiarities, that he is now more Indian than white man."

But to buy pigs, Governor Young told them, they had to sail to Oahu and call on King Kamekameha himself, who kept a monopoly on the sale of pigs to foreign ships as a means of generating profits for the royal treasury.

The *Tonquin* sailed from the Big Island to Oahu and anchored in Waikiki Bay. Over several days, the Scottish partners exchanged formal visits with King Kamekameha to negotiate the sale of pigs. Arriving at the *Tonquin* in a huge double canoe paddled by sixteen chiefs and accompanied by three enormous wives in traditional garb, the Hawaiian king wore a mix of Western dress that included a blue coat with velvet collar, a beaver top hat, and a long sword given to him by his "brother," King George III of England. The *Tonquin's* passengers and crew, no doubt laboring under the popular image that savages and cannibals inhabited the islands of the Pacific, were impressed by the sophistication of the Hawaiians' traditional culture. They noted the finely crafted outrigger canoes and seafaring skills, the hundreds of woven-walled, thatched-roofed houses of the town, the personal cleanliness and industriousness of the Hawaiian people, and their careful respect of taboos, religious customs, and rules laid down by their king.

None of it impressed Captain Thorn. Chafing to be under way, he wrote to Mr. Astor from Waikiki, "It would be difficult to imagine the frantic gambols that are daily played off here. To enumerate the thousand instances of ignorance, filth, &c . . . would require Volumes."

Not to be outdone in the displays of power and refinement, the Scottish partners rose to the same level of formality as the Hawaiians. Dressing up in their kilts, they paid a visit to King Kamekameha and called themselves "The Great Eris of the Northwest," using the Hawaiian word for king. They pledged to Kamekameha to establish permanent and very profitable trade relations with his islands once they'd founded their West Coast colony.

Finally the negotiations with King Kamekameha concluded. Dozens of canoes were dispatched from shore, heaped with more fruit, vegetables, and a hundred squealing pigs to stock the *Tonquin*. The Scottish partners wanted to hire thirty or forty Hawaiians to work at the West Coast emporium, impressed with their extraordinary ability to handle canoes, swim like seals, and hold their breath underwater for up to four minutes while diving deep for a pulley the ship had lost overboard. This was all encouraged by King Kamekameha. He urged his subjects to travel to foreign lands and learn new skills to bring back and further Hawaii. But Captain Thorn said no—the *Tonquin* couldn't carry that many extra men and supplies. Eventually, he and the partners reached a compromise: twelve Hawaiians to serve as sailors and twelve to work the West Coast emporium for a total of twenty-four carried as additional passengers aboard the ship.

As the ship prepared to sail, it appeared that the *Tonquin* would achieve a tranquil leave-taking from Hawaii, unlike the stormy departures from New York Harbor and the Falkland Islands.

"[F]rom the good conduct of the sailors since our arrival, we began to think matters would go smoothly for the future," wrote Ross, "but these hopes were of short duration. . . ."

One of the sailors, Edward Aymes, from New York, missed the longboat that was leaving the Waikiki beach for the *Tonquin*. He quickly hired Hawaiians to take him out to the ship, but an enraged Captain Thorn jumped into the boat when it pulled alongside the *Tonquin* where Aymes was ready to climb aboard, seized stalks of sugarcane in the boat destined to feed the pigs, and beat Aymes senseless with them. Then he ordered Aymes thrown overboard.

A native canoe nearby rescued Aymes and took him to shore. He returned a few hours later and, from a canoe alongside the ship, called up to Captain Thorn, apologizing and asking to be taken aboard. Captain Thorn threatened to kill Aymes if he set foot on the *Tonquin*. Aymes asked for his clothes and sailors papers. Thorn didn't reply. The sympathetic first mate, Mr. Fox, surreptitiously threw down the articles into the canoe for Aymes.

And so sailor Aymes was left on Hawaii. As his canoe pushed off from the *Tonquin,* he shouted up to Captain Thorn that he knew his rights as an American citizen. If they ever met on American soil, he said, Captain Thorn would find himself in deep trouble.

W HEN THE *TONQUIN* ARRIVED OFF THE NORTHWEST Coast and mouth of the Columbia River on March 22, 1811, it had left all tropical antics far in its wake. Here wind squalls from the northwest swept across the charcoal sea. Huge swells tossed the ship. Roaring white breakers smashed against the shoreline of this far edge of the North American continent, stretching away endlessly north and south in a misty gray-green band of impenetrable forest and rocky headlands, backed by ranges of snowy mountains. Here was the fabled destination—the epicenter of the great empire-to-be! If they hadn't understood just how wild and remote and storm-battered the Northwest Coast was when they left the bustle of New York and the scented islands of Hawaii, they did now. From this spot, sending and receiving any communication to their familiar world would take roughly one year.

But whatever safety and shelter was offered by this wild coast was blocked by a four-mile-long sandbar across the Columbia's mouth. Still today one of the world's most dangerous navigational hazards, here the power of the largest river of the western continent, discharging an average of 265,000 cubic feet of water per second, collides head-on with the power of the world's largest ocean. The Pacific tides and swells entering the river's mouth fight against the outgoing river's discharge. This battle throws up ferociously steep mounds of water, up to twelve feet high, known as standing waves. They can literally stand a boat up on end. At the same time, incoming swells from the North Pacific, generated by powerful storms thousands of miles out at sea and thirty feet and more in height, tower over the shallows of the bar. Crashing down in a tumult of foam and spray further churned by the winds and tidal currents, these waves create what seems to be a giant cauldron where the earth's hydraulic forces converge.

Somewhere in this chaos of wind and wave and powerful tides the Seagoing Party had to find the gap in the shallow sandbar. It was only through this single channel that the main current of the Columbia River exited the continent, and they could enter.

"The wind was blowing in heavy squalls, and the sea ran very high," wrote Franchère, about their arrival off the Columbia's mouth, adding that they could plainly see the breakers crashing from three miles off.

Captain Thorn gave orders to prepare the whaleboat. Mr. Fox, he ordered, would act as captain. For his crew, Mr. Fox would take the French-Canadian brothers Lapensée, in addition to Joseph Nadeau, and John Martin. Their mission was to row into the wild confusion of wind and wave and current and "sound" the bottom—measure the water's depth to locate the deeper channel across the shallow bar.

Fox was taken aback. Three of the four men assigned to pull the oars of the whaleboat into one of the most treacherous spots in the world's oceans were French Canadians who had never before been to sea—Nadeau was a barber from Montreal and the two brothers had worked as porters at Lachine Rapids, just above Montreal. John Martin, an experienced but aging Yankee seaman, didn't have the power of youth at the oars.

Couldn't Captain Thorn assign a more experienced crew to man the oars? asked Fox.

No, replied Thorn. He needed all experienced sailors aboard the *Tonquin* to handle her in these conditions.

"Mr. Fox," wrote Alexander Ross, who witnessed this scene unfolding on the deck of the *Tonquin*, "then represented the impossibility of performing the business in such weather, and on such a rough sea, even with the best seamen."

"[T]he waves [are] too high for any boat to live in," Fox pleaded to Captain Thorn.

The captain had already turned away. He now spun around to face Fox.

"Mr. Fox, if you are afraid of water, you should have remained in Boston."

Fox didn't reply. He simply turned to the crew and issued the fateful order: *Lower the boat.*

A mere twenty ships had, by this time, crossed the Columbia bar. The Columbia River itself had been discovered by Europeans only eighteen years earlier. For European sailing ships, almost all the other coastlines of the world were on the way to somewhere. The Northwest Coast was not and remained obscure, unknown, and impossibly remote for centuries after most other coastlines of the world had been charted.

Spaniards first had sailed northward from their colonies in Mexico as far as today's Oregon in the 1600s. But the cool, wet, rugged Northwest Coast inhabited by Indian tribes living in wooden longhouses and traveling in large cedar canoes didn't compel them like the benign climates and monumental, gold-encrusted civilizations of the Aztecs and Incas far to the south. For a century and a half, the Northwest Coast, in geopolitical terms at least, remained a vast no-man's-land while Europe's seafaring powers, such as Spain, France, and Britain, assembled their colonial empires elsewhere on the globe.*

In the second half of the 1700s, a flurry of interest from several

---

* Franchère tells of meeting an old blind man living among Indians along the lower Columbia who claimed to be the son of a Spanish sailor long since shipwrecked at the mouth of the Columbia with three other survivors. The four Spaniards married native women but eventually struck southward in an attempt to rejoin their countrymen, presumably in California. Franchère, *Narrative of a Voyage to the Northwest Coast of America,* pp. 112–13.

European powers converged on the Northwest Coast. After pushing their empire across Siberia to the Far East, the Russians, with the Bering Expedition in 1741, sailed across the North Pacific to the Aleutian Islands and Alaskan coast, and quietly began to develop a fur trade with natives there. With Russia poking around Alaska's Pacific Coast, Spain felt threatened and swung her attention northward from Mexico. Starting in 1769, Franciscan Father Junípero Serra planted a string of missions up the Pacific Coast as far north as today's San Francisco Bay. Beyond this point, however, the coastline grew colder, wetter, more forested, and less attractive for settlement.

As Father Serra built his missions for Christianity in California, and small Russian ships traded for furs up in the Aleutians, Captain Cook explored the South Pacific for Britain and for science. On his Third Voyage in 1776, however, British authorities assigned Cook a secret mission in the North Pacific that also had much to do with commerce—locate the Pacific end of the legendary Northwest Passage. The Passage had been a coveted geographical object sought since Columbus—a water route across North America that offered European merchants a shortcut to the trading wealth of the Orient.

Hoping to find the Northwest Passage—and to collect the resulting 20,000-pound prize from the British government—Cook captained two ships, the *Resolution* and *Discovery,* which made landfall at present-day Oregon, then coasted northward all the way to the Arctic Ocean probing for the Passage or the mouth of the long-rumored Great River of the West. Legends abounded about this river, passed along from Indian tribes deep in the interior. The European explorers fervently hoped that the rumors referred to an actual waterway that linked the Great Lakes with the Pacific Ocean. Almost the entire stretch of this coast was terra incognita—outside the arctic realms, this was the last major section of the earth's continental coastline that hadn't yet been charted. The expedition, however, didn't work out as planned. Cook didn't locate the Pacific mouth of the great cross-continental waterway on his first attempt. It was while resupplying

and repairing in Hawaii for another foray that he was killed by islanders in the surf at Kealakekua Bay. But Cook's surviving officers and
crew nevertheless made a discovery that would determine the future
of the Pacific Rim.

While seeking the mysterious waterway amid the deep inlets of
the Northwest Coast on their initial visit, Cook's men had traded trinkets with Indian tribes for furs. To the amazement of Cook's officers
and crew, when they reached China after his death they discovered
that the spectacularly lustrous sea otter furs purchased for one dollar's
worth of trinkets from Northwest Coastal Indians sold for the equivalent of a hundred dollars cash in Macao and Canton.

"The rage with which our seamen were possessed to return to [the
Northwest Coast]," reported one of Cook's officers, "and, by another
cargo of skins, to make their fortunes, at one time, was not far short of
mutiny."

Although its huge and wealthy empire had existed for millennia,
China was then an inward-looking country hardly known to the West.
The Son of Heaven, as China's emperor was called, ruled over an elaborate and entrenched bureaucracy of mandarins who, besides carrying
out his bidding, celebrated their refined tastes in literature, cuisine,
and dress. This official class happened to covet robes trimmed with
luxurious furs. They had caressed the lustrous pelt of the sea otter
furs brought by the Russian *promyshlenniki* from Alaska that made
it across the Middle Kingdom's restrictive borders. There may have
even been official decrees that mandarins trim parts of their robes
with sea otter fur.

Among the Cook expedition's British sailors hoping to make a fortune in sea otters was a lone New Englander, John Ledyard. With the
Cook voyage, he had become the first native-born American citizen to
set foot on North America's Pacific Coast. A romantic and footloose
son and grandson of sea captains who had died young, Ledyard had
dropped out of Dartmouth College and a career in the ministry, built
a dugout canoe, and paddled down the Connecticut River and out into

the wide world, eventually signing on with Cook and his *Resolution* and *Discovery*.

After the Third Voyage's end in 1780, the thirty-year-old Ledyard returned to New England. In a four-month flurry of writing, Ledyard knocked out a memoir about his travels with Cook in which he reported the sea otter discoveries, as did other memoirists of the voyage. Promoting with his memoir the idea of setting up a beaver skin and otter fur trade, Ledyard assembled a consortium of Philadelphia and Boston merchants to finance ships to the Northwest Coast and launch the first American—or European—fur trade with China. As the plan neared fruition, however, the partners intrigued against each other. Ledyard's great scheme collapsed. He would, however, play a significant if largely unsung role in planting the first American colony on the West Coast.

The ever-restless Ledyard didn't quit after the Boston fiasco, sailing for Europe in 1784 and assembling a consortium of Brittany merchants. When this also fell apart, he traveled to Paris and called on the newly appointed American minister to France, forty-two-year-old Thomas Jefferson. The two hit it off instantly. They shared a passion for exploration, geography, native tribes, and Indian vocabularies. Both of their fathers had been adventurous men who had died young. Ledyard, having visited both Asia and the Northwest Coast, expounded to Minister Jefferson on his innovative theory that native tribes had traveled from Asia across the narrow Bering Strait to populate the Americas. Jefferson was fascinated. They often dined together at Jefferson's Paris house in Jefferson's fine gilt chairs, in front of a crackling fire, amid a wide-ranging welter of conversation with other footloose young Americans who were living in the Paris of the Enlightenment. Jefferson also lent the ever-broke Ledyard sums equivalent today to a thousand dollars simply to survive.

"My friend, my brother, my Father," Ledyard wrote to Jefferson, "I know not by what title to address you. . . ."

Jefferson's own father had been a Virginia planter and pioneering surveyor who, when Thomas was a young boy, had joined an exploratory surveying expedition deep into Virginia's western wilderness. Due in part to this legacy of exploration and mapmaking, Jefferson grasped the geography of North America on a far more continental scale than most of his contemporaries. Starting as a young man, he looked west to the wilderness that lay beyond the Appalachians. As governor of Virginia from 1779 to 1781, he commissioned military expeditions far beyond Virginia's settlements into the wilderness lands that lay over the Appalachians, including a proposal to erect a fort—its design meticulously sketched by his own hand—where the Ohio River meets the Mississippi some seven hundred miles west of Virginia's coast.

Ledyard's stories opened Jefferson's eyes to the wealth in furs and geographical possibilities of the Northwest Coast. At their "petite soupers" in front of his Parisian fireplace in 1785 he enthusiastically embraced Ledyard's scheme for an American sea voyage to the Northwest Coast to trade for furs and sell them on the rich Chinese market. Jefferson was also suspicious of a French scientific expedition similar to Cook's that was just then sailing for the Pacific under Lapérouse; he believed it, too, had hidden commercial designs on the West Coast.

After a third attempt to assemble a consortium of merchants came to nothing, a frustrated Ledyard, brainstorming with Jefferson, hatched a plan to set off alone to the Northwest Coast. Like the ancient native peoples in his migration theory, Ledyard planned to cross Siberia by foot and coach, hop the Bering Strait by small Russian fur boat to Alaska, then, as explorer rather than trader, *walk* across North America to his home in Connecticut.

"[M]y tour round the world by Land," Ledyard described it to Jefferson.

And off John Ledyard went—twenty years before the Lewis and Clark expedition—having planted in the future president's mind a glimpse of the potential economic and political significance of the Northwest Coast and Pacific Rim.

As the lone romantic adventurer struck off into the Russian winter (later to be arrested by Russian authorities), expeditions from several nations simultaneously prepared to sail for the Northwest Coast in the mid-1780s with the exclusive commercial purpose of trading at high profit for sea otter and other valuable furs. John Meares, a former Royal Navy officer, sailed for the Northwest Coast in 1786 to trade and got trapped in ice far in the north, in Alaska's Prince William Sound, losing twenty-three of his crew to scurvy. Russian traders built a permanent fur post in Alaska in 1784. Boston merchants under Charles Bulfinch raised funds for two American ships, the *Columbia Rediviva* and the *Lady Washington*. Commanded by Captain Robert Gray and Captain John Kendrick, these sailed out of Boston Harbor in 1787 to round Cape Horn and head for the West Coast.

It's a measure of the scale and remoteness of the Northwest trade that it took three years for Captain Gray to complete his trading mission. (Kendrick didn't return with him.) After acquiring sea otter furs in late 1788 and early 1789, he sailed across the Pacific to Canton, traded the *Columbia*'s cargo of pelts and loaded up with Chinese tea, and sailed across the Indian Ocean, around Africa's Cape of Good Hope then up the South and North Atlantic, finally returning home to Boston Harbor in August 1790. He was welcomed by a parade celebrating his feat for captaining the first American ship to circumnavigate the globe. Captain Gray, however, wasted little time celebrating. Seeing vast opportunities in the Pacific, a mere six weeks after arriving in Boston, he and the *Columbia* again sailed for the Northwest Coast.

Trading practices had changed just in the four years since his first visit. Enough merchant ships, both American and British, had touched at the Northwest Coast in the rush for fur that the natives trading with the "Boston men," as they knew whites, charged far higher prices in nails, knives, and other goods than during his first voyage. Gray wasn't inclined to negotiate. He and other sea captains began to take furs by force. The Indians retaliated, and the violence escalated in the Coastal Indian villages of today's Vancouver Island.

"I was sent," wrote John Boit, one of Gray's officers, in his journal entry for March 27, 1792, "with three boats all well man'd and arm'd, to destroy the village of Opitsatah. . . . [I] am grieved to think Capt. Gray shou'd let his passions go so far. . . . This fine village [of two hundred houses and massive ceremonial wood carvings], the work of Ages, was in a short time totally destroy'd."

Investigating the coast southward for new trading opportunities, Captain Gray guided his ship across a treacherous bar ripped by currents and pounded by heavy surf. He found himself in the mouth of a large and powerful river that discharged into the Pacific. On May 12, 1792, Captain Gray, during his second visit to the Northwest Coast, thus became the official Euro-American discoverer of the long-rumored Great River of the West. Sailing thirteen miles up it, he named it after his ship—the *Columbia*. He realized from its volume that it was a very large river but he had no idea how far into the North American continent it might reach.

Five months later a rival explorer, British naval officer George Vancouver, on a four-year mission to chart the entire Northwest Coast, arrived at the river's mouth. Sending small boats one hundred miles up it, Vancouver officially claimed the river and its enormous unexplored interior basin for Britain, setting up a potential conflict of claims to a chunk of territory whose size no one knew and to a river whose source was unknown.*

---

* Two of the nations in the burgeoning Northwest Coast fur trade, Spain and Britain, both attempted to colonize the region, quite coincidentally, in early 1789. Landing first at Nootka Sound by two months, the Spaniards seized several of the British vessels that soon arrived, placing the first emissary of King George III and his crew under arrest and holding them in Mexico. This seemingly minor incident brought to the brink of war the two greatest empires in the world at the time. Realizing the gravity of the situation, they quickly convened diplomatic negotiations to avoid violence. In October 1790, both nations signed the Nootka Sound Convention, by which the Spanish would pay reparations for the seized ships and trade goods, and both agreed to what amounted to a free-trade agreement for the Pacific Coast of the Americas. Each facing crises at home due to the French Revolution, by 1795 both nations had abandoned Nootka Sound as a settlement.

By the time Astor's ship, the *Tonquin,* arrived at the Columbia bar in 1811, American and British merchant ships, using Hawaii as a port of call, had been sailing to the Northwest Coast for more than twenty years, since Captain Gray's first arrival. Thus John Jacob Astor didn't originate the idea of trading goods for furs on the Northwest Coast and selling them across the Pacific in China. What Astor did was to conceive it on a scale far larger, more global, more intricate, more elegant, and more profitable than anyone had before. His innovation was to link the interior North American fur trade over the Rockies with the Pacific coastal fur trade and link that to the Russian Alaskan fur trade, and link that to China, to London, to Paris, to New York. Astor's thinking revolved on entire continents and oceans.

Astor, along with Thomas Jefferson, understood the global implications of the Pacific Rim and its role in a future world far more clearly than his contemporaries—that one day it would serve a role equal to or greater than the Atlantic's, and finally knit the globe into one great trading empire. Those passengers arriving at the mouth of the Columbia aboard the *Tonquin* under Captain Thorn's command in late March 1811 would be the first emissaries to make that global empire a reality.

ONE WONDERS WHY CAPTAIN THORN simply didn't wait for the weather to settle a bit before sending Mr. Fox in a small boat into the tumult of wave and squall and current to look for a channel through the Columbia Bar. Trying to fathom the captain's exact reasoning is as imprecise an exercise as trying to sound the Columbia Bar. Captain Thorn had been undermined and humiliated by the Scottish partners, clerks, and voyageurs throughout the six-month voyage from New York Harbor. He trusted no one aboard his ship. In his eyes, even his first mate, Mr. Fox, had grown far too friendly with the Scottish partners. In Hawaii, Captain Thorn had heard rumors from passing ship captains that diplomatic tensions were rising between the United

States and Britain. He prepared himself should the partners who were British citizens attempt mutiny aboard his ship. Deeply isolated— from his passengers, his own officers and crew—and surrounded by the infinite and uncaring Pacific, Thorn's mind took its own turns. No one, including Thorn himself, could say exactly what those were. Irving and Ross claim that it was simply malice on Thorn's part. It's conceivable, however, that in his regimented adherence to mission, configured with his anger and humiliation and paranoia, he believed he was doing his commander in chief, Mr. Astor, a favor by dispatching the whaleboat over the bar in this tumultuous weather, carrying a load of bad apples, and thus weeding out these, the most expendable of the men.

In the shrieking northwest squalls, the Scottish partners could see that this mission amounted to near suicide for the men assigned to the boat. McKay and McDougall approached Captain Thorn on deck and asked that he wait for a break in the weather.

"But he was deaf to entreaties," reported Ross, "stamped, and swore that a combination was formed to frustrate all his designs. The partners' interference, therefore, only riveted him the more in his determination, and Mr. Fox was peremptorily ordered to proceed."

Fox was now visibly upset. He had personal ghosts that haunted the Columbia Bar. He turned to the Scottish partners, Ross wrote, with tears in his eyes.

"'My uncle was drowned here not many years ago, and now I am going to lay my bones with his.'"

Fox then shook hands with the partners and others standing near him on deck, and climbed down into the boat. One of the partners handed him a pair of bedsheets, which could serve as a sail.

"Farewell, my friends!" Fox called out. "We will perhaps meet again in the next world."

The small boat then pushed off from the side of the tossing *Tonquin,* and all hands aboard lined the rail in silence to watch her row into the chaos.

———◆◉◆———

WHERE JOHN JACOB ASTOR LED WITH BROAD VISION AND careful planning, and Wilson Price Hunt led with care and consensus, Captain Jonathan Thorn led with force. And in the face of danger, he insisted on raw, head-on bravery. Yet in the power of the Pacific Coast his approach may have met its match.

It was 1:30 P.M. on March, 22, 1811, when Mr. Fox pushed off from the tossing *Tonquin* with three voyageurs and an aging sailor manning the oars of the small whaleboat. His shipmates watched the whaleboat pull out into the heaving seas from the *Tonquin* where she sailed on the open ocean a few miles off the Columbia Bar. Looking north and south, they could see the gray-green coastline of the continent's western edge—the strip of sand, the rocky headlands, the band of forest, the coastline thinning and dimming for miles in each direction, slowly disappearing amid the fine sea mist tossed up by the crashing Pacific surf, without seeing a single trace of a human presence. Mr. Fox's mission was to locate the channel across the bar for the *Tonquin* to follow and lay the first foundations of empire on this most remote of coasts.

Alexander Ross watched from the rail with the others. The seas were so rough that by the time the whaleboat moved one hundred yards from the ship, he wrote, the onlookers at the rail frequently lost sight of it among the whitecapping swells. Mr. Fox's whaleboat soon became "utterly unmanageable." It turned sideways to the "foaming surges," spun around, then was flung up to a wave crest, before disappearing again into a deep trough.

"At last she hoisted the flag," wrote Ross. "[T]he meaning could not be mistaken; we knew it was a signal of distress. At this instant all the people crowded round the captain, and implored him to try and save the boat; but in an angry tone he ordered about ship, and we saw the ill-fated boat no more."

Ross believed Captain Thorn was taking his revenge on his first mate for befriending the Scottish traders and French-Canadian voyageurs during the six-month voyage. Or Captain Thorn may have thought he was doing Mr. Astor a favor by getting rid of them. There may have been other explanations for Thorn's seemingly cruel behavior.

Captain Thorn had trained in a military and naval tradition in which lives were sacrificed in the name of a mission for the good of country. He remained an officer in the U.S. Navy, on leave with permission to pursue Astor's hugely ambitious enterprise in the Pacific. He burned with an unrelenting determination and patriotism to carry out his mission per his orders from Astor—in this case, to cross the Columbia Bar as expediently as possible and land the first American colony on the West Coast. But Astor's great expedition served at least as much a commercial as a nationalistic purpose. Captain Thorn appears not to have reflected on this: What cost in human lives was a commercial mission worth? Or if he did reflect on this weighty issue, he kept it to himself. He may have felt unsure of himself in this, his first command, but sealed it off with his outward toughness. The more perceptive passengers might have sometimes caught a hint of a softer Thorn. Franchère reported that when those aboard the *Tonquin* realized that Fox's whaleboat was lost, Captain Thorn looked as distressed as anyone. Was this for the loss of human life, or the setback it represented to his mission?

The ship spent the next day searching for the missing boat, followed by "an anxious night" tacking back and forth a distance off the

Columbia's mouth in powerful winds and heavy seas. Captain Thorn, who surely had been forewarned about the extreme hazards of the Columbia Bar, was giving it a good deal of berth and respect. Should he run aground on the bar with the *Tonquin* amid the surging tidal currents and pounding breakers, the loss of lives and property would be far greater than what was lost with the whaleboat.

By noon two days after they'd arrived, March 24, the wind had dropped. Now Mr. Mumford, the second mate aboard the *Tonquin,* made another attempt at finding the channel across the bar. Joining him in the longboat were two Scottish partners, Alexander McKay and David Stuart, as well as clerk Alexander Ross, and several others at the oars. The longboat, wrote Ross, was "well manned and armed" and hoped to cross the bar and make a landing on the "wild and gloomy" shore.

They were approaching the bar but still two miles from shore when those in the longboat suddenly found themselves pulled into the ripping maelstrom of current and surf and wind and shallows for which the Columbia Bar was already infamous. Ross, at the oars, described "the terrific chain of breakers . . . rolling one after another in rapid succession" while a "fearful suction" pulled the longboat toward the bar. Before they had time to respond fully, the current had dragged the longboat into the bar's breakers, the crashing tons of water spinning them this way and that.

"[A]t this instant, Mr. Mumford, who was at the helm called out, 'Let us turn back, and pull for your lives; pull hard, or you are all dead men.'"

For twelve minutes, Ross wrote, the longboat hung in the balance, the men pulling with all their strength, but neither winning nor losing the battle against the current sucking them farther into the bar's breaking surf. Finally, "the boat obeyed the oars," he wrote. They managed to row themselves out of the imminent danger and to the relative safety of the heaving but open sea.

The next morning, March 25, 1811, Mumford and crew again

attempted to find the channel, now probing southward along the bar. Although the wind was calm, and the sea not choppy, the big smooth-backed swells rolling in off the Pacific still crashed over the bar in heavy breakers, almost trapping them again. They returned to the *Tonquin* without locating the channel. Captain Thorn, reported Ross, appeared dissatisfied with his officers—as well as himself. He surely felt the weight of the enterprise resting heavily on his shoulders. For four days the Seagoing Party had been stuck outside the mouth of the Columbia. How could they launch Mr. Astor's great Pacific trade empire if Captain Thorn and his ship couldn't even cross the Columbia Bar?

Captain Thorn now summoned one of Astor's men, Job Aiken, a Scotsman and ship's rigger, who was a strong sailor. He ordered Aiken to take the pinnace, the ship's launch used to ferry passengers and supplies back and forth to shore, and sound the bar slightly farther north, with a crew made up of sailmaker John Coles, armorer Stephen Weeks, and two Hawaiians. Aiken and his crew were to measure the depth of the water by dropping a sounding line with a lead weight attached. If they found water deeper than three and a half fathoms—three and a half times the distance of a man's outstretched arms, or about twenty feet—they were to raise a flag to signal the *Tonquin* to follow this channel across the bar.

It was already late in the day, 3:00 P.M., when Aitken and his crew rowed away from the *Tonquin*. A slight sea breeze had sprung up over the swells, a favorable and gentle wind to ride across the bar toward shore. Soon the hands aboard the *Tonquin* spotted the flag hoisted in Aitken's boat—they had found the channel across the bar. Captain Thorn ordered the *Tonquin*'s anchor raised. The ship now slowly sailed toward the bar, moving at three knots on the gentle breeze, toward the calmer gap in the heavy breakers that indicated where the deeper water of the channel lay. The task demanded Captain Thorn's utmost concentration—looking seaward to gauge the wind, looking up to determine the set of the sails, looking ahead to keep a steady course toward the gap in the breakers.

At the same time, Aiken's pinnace, after sounding for the channel, rowed her way back out toward the ship coming in. As the pinnace neared the ship, Aiken veered a bit off to the ship's starboard to let the ship pass, expecting the *Tonquin* to pause or throw a rope so Aiken and party could rejoin the ship. But no one aboard ship made a move to help, reported Ross. As the pinnace began to fall to the rear, McKay finally spoke up.

"Who is going to throw a rope to the boat?"

No one replied. No sailor left his post to help.

Aiken's boat had now dropped behind the *Tonquin,* which was still gliding in toward the bar, aiming at the channel through the breakers, threading this needle of calm in the chaos of surf and current. The men in the pinnace began to row to catch up to the ship sailing landward but the powerful current of the outgoing tide worked against them.

"The boat, the boat!" shouted the partners at the rail on the *Tonquin.* They turned to Captain Thorn "entreating" him to pick up the pinnace and its crew.

"I can give them no assistance," he replied coolly, according to Ross.

"Back a sail, throw a rope overboard," shouted the partners. Second Mate Mumford said it would not take a minute.

"No," replied Captain Thorn. "I will not endanger the ship."

As the pinnace disappeared off the ship's stern in the swells, the *Tonquin* sailed in toward the bar and the chaos of breakers, "the sight of which," reported Ross, "was appalling." She steered accurately into the channel through which the Columbia's current exited the continent. Then the water suddenly grew shallower. She struck bottom on a second sandbar. The breakers tossed her up and slammed her down onto the hard sand bottom. Breakers ten feet high crashed over her stern. Everyone aboard who was able leapt up to grab the rigging before being tossed or washed overboard. She slammed seven or eight times with a keel-jarring shock. Then she broke free into deeper water on the inside of the bar. The wind now had died. The sails flapped. As darkness fell, the *Tonquin,* now without wind or headway of her own in

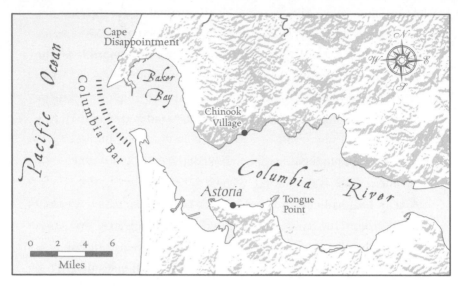

MOUTH OF COLUMBIA RIVER AND COLUMBIA BAR

order to steer her, but still surrounded by breakers, was being washed toward the foot of the high rocky headland that lay just inside the bar, called Cape Disappointment.

"We are all lost," someone shouted, wrote Ross. "The ship is among the rocks."

Captain Thorn ordered two anchors dropped to hold the ship in place. They were, in effect, caught inside the line of scrimmage between two opposing continental forces. Pushed by the Pacific surf in the darkness, pulled by the flow of the outgoing tide and current coming out of the Columbia, the ship slowly began to drag her two anchors over the bottom toward the rocky base of Cape Disappointment, which would surely smash her to pieces even if the sandbar had not.

The pinnace, meanwhile, was caught outside the bar. The breakers had worsened. Now that the ocean's tide had turned, it flowed outward, drawing water out of the Columbia's mouth. This outward flow pushed against the incoming waves—in effect shoving the rolling, breaking inbound waves upward into steep, high peaks. Aitken ordered the boat to drift with the outgoing tidal current, farther out to sea, trying to keep her steady in the turbulence. But one of the steep, toppling waves slammed into the pinnace amidships and knocked her over, spilling the crew.

The surf instantly washed away Aiken and sailmaker John Coles. Stephen Weeks, the armorer, grabbed hold of an oar and used it for flotation while managing to stay near the overturned pinnace. The two Hawaiians immediately stripped off their clothes in the surging breakers and set to work righting the pinnace. After they managed to flip it right side up, the boat remained full of water. Swimming beside it, they emptied the pinnace by jerking the boat rapidly back and forth, end to end, so the water inside her slopped out over the gunwales. It was an extraordinary display of boat handling in rough seas.

One of the many ironies of the Astoria story is that the expert swimmers brought from Hawaii—and they were indeed expert swimmers, ocean canoeists and longboard surfers—had never before touched a cold ocean. The water temperature at Waikiki Beach in Hawaii is about 80 degrees Fahrenheit, the temperature of a swimming pool. The water temperature at the mouth of the Columbia in March, when the *Tonquin* arrived, averages about 45 degrees, the temperature of an ice bath. At this temperature, someone who is immersed and lightly clothed loses body heat at an astonishing rate. In the first one to two minutes, as the water's cold hits sensors buried deep in the skin, the victim will hyperventilate and the heart rate will jump—the gasping, yelping "shock" of hitting cold water—before elevated heart rate and breathing level off. For the expert Hawaiian swimmers, this moment must have come as a painful surprise.

After about ten minutes, the body's core temperature begins a steady decline of roughly one-tenth of a degree per minute, although humans with thicker skin fold and more subcutaneous fat will show a slower cooling rate. After about fifty minutes of immersion, when the body's core temperature reaches about 93 degrees, the average victim has lost a good part of his or her ability to manipulate extremities—fingers, arms, and legs. (The hands of "cold-water immersion" survivors have been found totally "locked" on to frozen ropes to which they clung during their ordeal; the ropes had to be cut to free them.) After roughly two hours in the water, when the body's core temperature falls to 86 degrees, the subject typically loses consciousness. At this point the victim usually drowns. After four hours in water this cold the victim is almost surely dead.

Yankee sailors and Hawaiian swimmers both possessed their own advantages in these extreme circumstances. While not expert swimmers, and often not swimmers at all, the Yankee sailors knew the shock of cold water, and from all their cold-ocean seafaring, also knew of that state of drowsiness and lassitude that foretells the slip into hypothermia. What the Hawaiians had going for them, besides their extraordinary swimming ability and centuries-old tradition of small boats on the open sea, was their stockier body types and subcutaneous fat. Modern research shows that Asiatic peoples tend to have a thicker layer of under-the-skin fat, especially in the upper body, than do Caucasians. This would serve them as an insulating layer, but when the warning symptoms of hypothermia commenced, unlike the Yankee sailor, they probably wouldn't recognize them or know the warning signs of hypothermia and how to fight it.*

Despite the water's incredible chill as they swam beside the small boat, the Hawaiians managed to slosh water from the pinnace until it was buoyant enough to hold one of them. As darkness descended on the Pacific, one of the Hawaiians climbed over the gunwales into the swamped boat and resumed bailing by rapidly scooping water with his hands and splashing it over the side. The currents of the outgoing

---

*   The thicker subcutaneous fat layer of females also gives an insulating advantage in cold-water immersion. In terms of body type, a tall, thin male, such as a skinny Yankee sailor, is at a disadvantage.

tide now carried them out to sea, away from the immediate danger of the breakers on the bar. Soon the pinnace was afloat, bobbing on the waves. The other Hawaiian climbed in, too.

They noticed Weeks nearby, clinging to his oar. They maneuvered the pinnace near to him. Weeks was now so tired and cold he could barely hold himself to his oar. The two Hawaiians tried to pull him into the pinnace, but their hands, with fingers stiffened by the extreme cold water, didn't possess the strength to grip him. Finally, the two Hawaiians leaned over the gunwales, seized Weeks's clothing in their teeth, and by wrenching upward with their heads, pulled him aboard the pinnace.

Now the true ordeal began. The three were wet, very cold, nearly naked, and at sea in a small boat along a dangerous coast smashed by heavy breakers, in the dark of the night. One of the Hawaiians, exhausted and deeply chilled, eventually lay down in the bottom of the boat, having seemingly given up hope. The other also seemed to fall into a stupor, refusing to move. Weeks, despite the difficulty of holding himself upright in his condition, struggled to the oars and began to row, trying to keep the boat far enough offshore to avoid the breakers. He understood that he had to row not only to stay out of the surf, but to keep working his muscles to generate body heat and avoid being overcome by a hypothermic stupor

Around midnight, the Hawaiian lying in the bottom of the boat died. The other Hawaiian lay on top of him and stayed there, unmoving and silent.

Weeks kept on rowing, for all purposes alone.

Just across the bar, the *Tonquin* also struggled as night fell over the Pacific. Her two anchors dragged over the bottom as the tide flowed out and the wind died, leaving her without sail power, slowly but irrevocably pulling her toward the rocks and surf of the headland of Cape Disappointment. The crew worked desperately to keep the ship from running aground and breaking up in the violent surf. But as the night deepened, reported Ross, the tide began to turn. First was a slack tide—that period between an outgoing tide and an incoming one. Then the tide began to flow inward, the tidal currents now pushing into the Columbia's broad mouth instead of exiting it. Around midnight, with a rising wind that helped power the ship, these tidal currents carried the *Tonquin* into the safety of the cove just inside Cape Disappointment, known as Baker's Bay. With their ship safely anchored, the exhausted sailors took to their berths for a rest.

The following morning, March 26, a party rowed across the placid bay to the shore. It consisted of Captain Thorn, McKay, Ross, and several others. They planned to climb to the summit of Cape Disappointment, which looked like a smaller version of Gibraltar, topped by a few wind-gnarled evergreen trees, and scout the coast for survivors or signs of the two missing boats.

"We had not proceeded fifty yards," reported Ross, "when we saw Steven Weeks, the armourer, standing under the shelter of a rock, shivering and half-dead with cold."

They couldn't get him to talk, or perhaps he wasn't able, to tell what happened to his boat mates in the pinnace. The party brought him back to the *Tonquin,* warmed him, and gave him food and clothes. (Franchère, also a witness to the rescue, reported Weeks was stark naked when found.) When Weeks finally began to talk, he could barely be understood, he "appeared so overpowered with grief and vexation."

"You did it purposely," he finally exclaimed in anger to the assembled group.

Weeks calmed down a bit after those aboard the *Tonquin* recounted how the ship had slammed over and over on the bar and had struggled, too, through the night, in danger of being smashed on the rocks of the cape.

Weeks then told his story. After the Hawaiian had died in the bottom of the pinnace about midnight, and the other Hawaiian lay down atop him, Weeks continued to row. When the incoming tide began to flow toward shore, the pinnace was pulled toward the breakers, and he rowed all the harder to stay at sea to avoid them. When dawn broke, he was only a quarter mile from the breakers, and perhaps a half mile offshore from Cape Disappointment itself.

"I paused for a moment, 'What is to be done?' I said to myself; 'death itself is preferable to this protracted struggle.'"

Weeks turned the prow of the boat to the shore and decided he'd reach land, or die trying.

As he rowed into the breakers, they swept up the boat from the stern and pushed it forward toward shore, as if surfing. As the sun was just rising, he found himself and the boat "thrown up high and dry on the beach."

With "benumbed limbs," Weeks dragged himself from the boat. He also managed to drag out the Hawaiian who was still barely alive and haul him to the edge of the forest, where "covering him with leaves I left him to die."

As he gathered leaves, Weeks happened to spot a beaten path at the forest's edge. He followed it around the base of Cape Disappointment to the bay on its inside, where he ran into the *Tonquin* and the party led ashore by Captain Thorn.

The Hawaiian whom Weeks buried in the leaves still lived. Discovered the next day, feet bleeding, legs swollen, nearly dead, he was warmed by a giant bonfire on the beach and carried back to the *Tonquin*. The Hawaiian in the bottom of the boat, however, had perished. The other twenty-three Hawaiians aboard the *Tonquin* came ashore the following day and held an elaborate burial ceremony on the sandy beach, placing sea biscuit and pork under his arms and tobacco under his genitals for the journey to the next world. The Hawaiians prayed and chanted in unison over him, which gave the *Tonquin* diarists to understand that these Pacific islanders possessed a greater spiritual sophistication than they had guessed.

Neither of the two other members of the pinnace, the mariner Job Aitken and sailmaker Coles, was ever seen again. Nor was any sign of the genial Mr. Fox and his boat ever found, nor his crew of voyageurs, which included the popular brothers Lapensée and Joseph Nadeau, all of respectable Canadian families, and the old sailor John Martin. In the three attempts sent by Captain Thorn, eight of the approximately sixty of Mr. Astor's men aboard the *Tonquin* had died simply trying to land the expedition at the Columbia's mouth.

It was not a good beginning for John Jacob Astor's Pacific empire.

PART TWO

THE JOURNEY

M R. ASTOR, MEANWHILE, WROTE TO WILSON PRICE Hunt of the Overland Party about possible rivals.

John Jacob Astor usually dealt with rival enterprises in one of three ways. First he tried to buy them out. If that didn't work, he tried to form a partnership with them. If he failed to join them, he tried, through relentless competition, to crush them.

He had scrupulously planned for two years how to deal with possible rivals for his West Coast empire. He had tried several times, over months of negotiations, to forge a West Coast partnership with the firm most likely to challenge him—the North West Company, that consortium of Scottish fur traders based in Montreal with outposts stretching from Lake Superior all the way to the Rockies.

Astor knew the Scottish partners well from previous trips to Montreal, where, over the years, he'd purchased many thousands of dollars' worth of their furs. They in turn had wined and dined him at their Beaver Club and at dinner parties in their homes. On one occasion in 1808, Astor's daughter Magdalen accompanied him to one of these parties, and the after-dinner dancing had lasted until midnight, with a French cotillion, then all the rage in New York, performed in her honor. Beyond their sociability, Astor knew them as expert, efficient, and far-flung fur traders. One of their men, Alexander Mackenzie—no relation to Donald Mackenzie of the Overland Party—had reached the Pacific Coast twelve years before Lewis and Clark by traveling through

Canada and crossing the Rockies, all far to the north of the Missouri route. They in turn knew Astor as an innovative businessman and a take-no-prisoners competitor with money to burn.

The negotiations went down to a final round. It was a complicated deal that Astor offered the North West Company, made more complicated by certain trade embargoes the United States had recently imposed on Canada. In essence, Astor would buy into the existing North West Company fur operations in the upper Midwest, and they'd buy into his start-up fur operations on the Pacific Coast. The proposal was, by any standards, a gargantuan deal. It embraced much of the tradable wealth of the western half of the continent and converted it into global trading capital. Whether measured by market share, percentage of gross domestic product, or geographical scope, Astor's commercial scheme, unregulated by government bodies, existed on a scale that would probably dwarf even the largest mergers of our era. He was striving for a near-global monopoly on fur.

For months, Astor waited impatiently in New York as the North West Company partners debated his proposal, one group in Montreal, another at a meeting in July 1810 at the great baronial hall of Fort William on Lake Superior, the major post and staging area that the NWC had built some distance up the shoreline from Grand Portage. A strict decorum prevailed at these North West Company annual July gatherings. The Scottish partners sat at the long polished table before the huge fireplace, while clerks and those of lesser rank occupied wooden tables further back in the Great Hall. A maitre d' from Montreal oversaw the serving staff, which presented a feast with china and white linen tablecloths. From this elegant hall and simple Council House in the wilderness of Lake Superior, surrounded by all the gunsmithing shops and warehouses and kitchens and other supporting outbuildings of the fort, the Scottish partners of the North West Company controlled the trade in thousands upon thousands of square miles of northern forest.

In considering Astor's proposal, the partners had huge issues to resolve, and there was much at stake. Not only could the future of the company turn on these deliberations, but the future political configuration of North America itself and the role of the Pacific Ocean in global trade. The debate raged onward, over hours, over days, in formal meetings in the spare Council House. How to split the profits with Astor? How long would it take even to turn a profit? And who took the losses?

Between meetings, the former Highlanders adjourned to the Great Hall next door and feasted on wilderness delicacies such as fatty beaver tail and spit-roasted venison, braised moose heart and smoked whitefish, as well as the roast beef, veal, and legs of mutton provided by the fort's own farm. They drank French wines, port, Madeira, and brandy, imported by freight canoe from Montreal, along with savory Double Gloucester cheeses as they considered how much of their best fur territory to concede in order to join this endeavor. Would it be worth the risk of giving up half ownership of what they knew to be profitable in the Great Lakes region? It was necessary also to decide whose Pacific "empire" it would be, and whether they could establish a better Pacific fur trade without Astor. But to answer this question, they had to decide who had the better claim to the West Coast. Did the Americans have any rightful claim whatsoever to any lands west of the crest of the Rocky Mountains at the western boundary of the Louisiana Purchase?

The questions were difficult, in many cases unanswerable, and in all cases the outcome remained extremely uncertain. Their sense of doubt—perhaps a legacy from their wind-blasted Scottish Highlands backgrounds—finally prevailed over Astor's vision, optimism, and drive.

As the wintering partners at Fort William debated the proposal, the North West Company partners who remained in Montreal decided to vote no, their answer arriving first via express messenger at Astor's offices in New York. Consensus between the two groups was complicated by long lags in communication with the partners at Fort William. Not having received news of the Montreal partners' decision, wintering partners voted in favor of accepting Astor's offer, with caveats—he could give them a third of his Pacific enterprise and they would work with him, but they also wanted to guard their own interests on the Pacific side of the Rockies.

Having heard only "no," Astor now had to reconfigure his plans for the enterprise, rearranging the players he had assembled—who led, and who followed, and who might be loyal to whom. He thought carefully about how to make adjustments, restlessly working over the problem from his offices on Liberty Street. He may have mulled over this great business problem, this continental destiny, when, for exercise and amusement, he rode his horse along country paths of upper Manhattan Island looking at properties to buy, or in the evenings, when he and Sarah attended the opera.

He and Sarah were increasingly well-known New Yorkers. Music lovers who maintained a comparatively modest way of life, they nevertheless had begun to nurture more refined tastes, in the arts, in the company they kept, even in their pride in the Parisian silver tea set they liked to bring out for guests. A driven, focused businessman from the start, John Jacob Astor also was driven by the need to be someone important, to be recognized, to prevail, as he'd pledged when a young man selling bread and cakes. He had chosen a far larger destiny than the life of a butcher's son in Walldorf. Of all the places in the world, North America compelled him toward it, where the sheer scale and vast wilds of the continent offered an enormous blank slate for someone of his ambition. With his grand plan now launched, he had moved decisively toward putting much of the western half of the continent within his personal domination and profit. He could eventually prevail at a level far beyond the burghers he once envied with their big brick houses on Broadway—indeed, at a level that was global in scope.

Within this grand vision, the issues Astor had to contend with day by day were nonetheless practical ones: With the merger off, would the North West Company now make a run at the rich Pacific Rim sea otter trade, too? What about the interior Northwest trade, and the Missouri

River trade? Could he trust his own men who had formerly worked for the North West Company to stay loyal to him if a fierce rivalry unfolded on the West Coast and across the Pacific? Would his empire and fleet end up staring down the cannon barrels of the world's most powerful fighting force—the British Royal Navy?

Astor wrote to Hunt, who was at the time in St. Louis trying to gather more recruits to take to the Nodaway winter camp. He told Hunt that as any partnership with the North West Company was no longer possible, he had demoted Donald Mackenzie and promoted Hunt to sole leader of the Overland Party. International tensions continued to rise with Great Britain over the boarding of ships in the Atlantic and other territorial issues, and without the North West Company merger, Astor wanted to ensure that the leadership of his Overland Party and West Coast empire stayed with the loyal Mr. Hunt of Trenton, New Jersey, rather than with a British subject, former North West Company employee, and Highlander like Donald Mackenzie—no matter how expert the latter was in the wilds.

Once its Montreal partners had voted down the proposed partnership with Astor, the Montreal headquarters of the North West Company did, in fact, begin to make its own countermoves. Its Scottish fur trading partners weren't about to give over the entire western continent to John Jacob Astor. Their own trader Alexander Mackenzie, after being the first European to reach the Pacific Coast overland from Canada, had written that whichever country first established settlements at the Columbia River would control a vast empire. As far as they were concerned, the Columbia River basin was *British,* not U.S., territory. They claimed it on the strength of the earlier coastal explorations of Captain Cook, George Vancouver, and Alexander Mackenzie himself, thus laying their own claim to a chunk of the Pacific Rim the size of France—and possibly far larger.

"No establishment of the [United] States on that river or on the coast of the Pacific should therefore be sanctioned," the Montreal partners had earlier warned authorities in London.

The "wintering" partners at Fort William dispatched their "maybe" after meeting on the Astor proposal. But, instead of east to London, they dispatched it and instructions accompanying it westward by express canoe out on the chain of rivers and lakes that led into the wilderness beyond Lake Superior. The message was addressed to David Thompson, already a legend for the thousands of square miles of unknown terrain in interior North America he'd explored and mapped for the North West Company. The Indians knew him as "Koo-koo-Sint"—"Star-Looker"—in reference to the many celestial observations he'd made with navigational instruments. With an aptitude for mathematics, refined mapmaking abilities, and expert skills for surviving in the wilds, David Thompson was a professional where Hunt was a beginner.

While the wintering partners at Fort William had voted to consider joining forces with Astor in some way, they also very much wanted to protect their own interests on the West Coast. The message from the North West Company wintering partners at Fort William ordered Thompson to proceed directly to the mouth of the Columbia.

The game for Astor had shifted. It no longer resembled solitaire, arranging and rearranging the cards, but rather another game he played frequently on his outdoor portico—checkers. He now had a tenacious opponent working the board across from him with thousands of square miles of North American terrain and the Pacific Rim empire at stake, as well as fortunes—and lives—that would be made or lost based on the fitness of his strategy.

CHAPTER EIGHT

B Y LATE MAY 1811, HUNT'S OVERLAND PARTY, FOLLOW-
ing the Lewis and Clark route across the wilderness of the western continent, had ascended well up the Missouri from their Nodaway
winter camp, where they'd been stuck since the previous November.
On the morning of May 26, the party pulled over to the riverbank for
breakfast, as they routinely did after an early start. As they sat on the
bank, eating, smoking, and resting from their early morning exertions,
they were surprised to spot three white men in two canoes riding
swiftly downstream on the Missouri's spring current.

They fired a rifle to signal to the distant boats, which paddled
across the current to the shore. One of canoeists was well into middle
age and wore a bandana wrapped around his head. Underneath the
bandana, he bore a massive scar. He had been scalped.

He had this message for Wilson Price Hunt and his Overland Party:
Avoid the Blackfeet at all costs.

This was not the first story they had heard about the Blackfeet.
Experienced travelers heading into troubled regions have a rule of
thumb: From afar, the physical danger often sounds worse than it is up
close, as distance tends to darken rumors. This was not the case, however, for Wilson Price Hunt and his Overland Party. As they ascended
the Missouri en route to the Pacific Coast, the rumors they heard
about the Indian tribes that lay ahead, especially the Blackfeet, grew
ever more frightening.

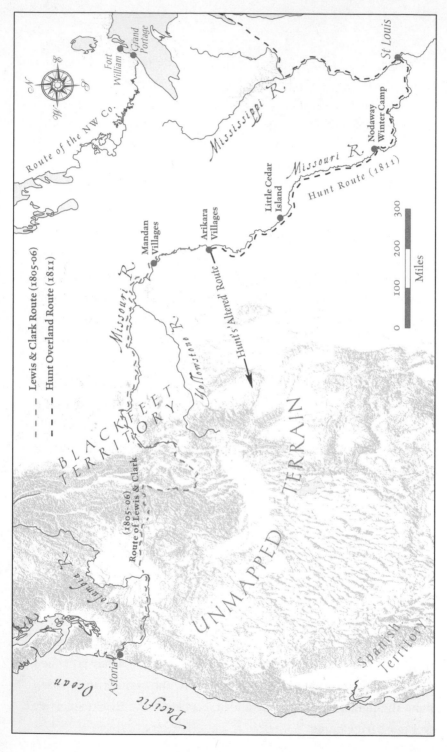

HUNT OVERLAND PARTY, APRIL–JULY 1811

Route of the NW Co.

Fort William

Grand Portage

Mississippi R.

St Louis

Nodaway Winter Camp

Missouri R.

Hunt Route (1811)

Little Cedar Island

Arikara Villages

Mandan Villages

Missouri R.

Yellowstone R.

Hunt's Altered Route

B L A C K F E E T   T E R R I T O R Y

Route of Lewis & Clark (1805–06)

Columbia R.

Astoria

U N M A P P E D   T E R R A I N

Pacific Ocean

Spanish Territory

N

- - - Lewis & Clark Route (1805–06)
- - - Hunt Overland Route (1811)

Miles

0   100   200   300

Get more men. So Hunt had been warned by traders like Ramsay Crooks. Crooks, who had joined the expedition back at Mackinac Island, had undergone his own hair-raising encounter the previous year while heading up the Missouri and trying to establish a trade among the Plains Indian tribes. Six hundred mounted Sioux warriors had suddenly appeared on the riverbank and ordered Crooks's river captains, whose boats were laden with trade goods, to pull over and trade with them. Crooks and company had done as ordered and started to trade, but as soon as the Sioux went back to their villages, they had fled downstream salvaging the goods that they could.

Though he took Crooks's advice, Hunt had found men in short supply. Throughout the winter, while his Overland Party remained at Nodaway winter camp, Hunt had shuttled from winter camp about four hundred miles downriver to St. Louis trying to boost the party from its original thirty-some members to a full sixty. Besides recruiting, Hunt had to contend with several American hunters who, claiming mistreatment, had quit at the winter camp, and at the same time keep his eye on Mr. Astor's schedule, which called for him to reach the Pacific Ocean and to establish his line of communication and supply of furs from the interior regions to the coast.

"Mr. Hunt, in his eagerness to press forward," reported Ross, "was perfectly worn out with anxiety."

Hunt had finally left St. Louis in early March 1811, bound for his Nodaway camp, and traveling in a ten-oared riverboat that carried his latest batch of recruits. Besides voyageurs at the oars, the boat carried rifle-toting American woodsmen to serve as the Overland Party's hunters, an Indian interpreter with his wife and their two small boys, and two eccentric British botanists. The latter had been urged into the unexplored West by Thomas Jefferson and his scientific friends back at Philadelphia's American Philosophical Society. Botany, in the late eighteenth and early nineteenth centuries, had become an exalted science since it was a way of investigating the many newly explored regions of the earth. Wealthy Europeans maintained gardens of exotic and foreign plant species the way the wealthy collect art today. Astor had promised Jefferson to share any scientific information that his expeditions gathered, and, as a result, Hunt was eager to have the two botanists along.

The botanists, for their part, welcomed the opportunity to collect undocumented plant species in the American interior, but they might not have been entirely aware of what lay ahead. As foreigners and scientists—a different tribe of sorts—they may have felt themselves partly immunized from any grudges between Plains Indians and American woodsmen. The young and plant-obsessed Thomas Nuttall, for instance, was known to use his musket barrel as a spade to dig up the rootballs of plants, hopelessly clogging the weapon's muzzle with mud and rendering it useless in times of danger.

A short ways upriver from St. Louis, Hunt's riverboat with the new recruits had stroked past a hamlet, La Charette, where an old man stood on the riverbank. Some of the party recognized him. It was eighty-four-year-old Daniel Boone, who had retired here from the too-crowded Kentucky wilderness that he'd originally opened to settlement; he still trapped for beaver pelts farther up the Missouri. Here in the flesh stood what would become a central irony in the exploration of the West—those trailblazers who marked the path for "civilization" to follow still felt an emotional tug to keep it wild and pure, knowing that this wildness, like the native peoples and animals, was diminishing with every passing year. Pulling a few miles farther upstream, Hunt's riverboat had encountered another American woodsman who, although only in his later thirties, was already something of a legend, too—John Colter.

The botanist John Bradbury, less single-mindedly obsessive about plants than Nuttall, but energetically curious nevertheless, had heard that Colter, in his wilderness wanderings, had discovered the massive fossil of a forty-foot-long fish. Colter had served with Lewis and Clark five years earlier on their journey to the Pacific and then stayed in the Upper Missouri region for several years to trap, before finally returning the previous spring to St. Louis. Summoned from his nearby cabin to the riverbank, Colter told the awaiting botanist that he didn't know anything about a huge fish fossil. But Colter nevertheless held Bradbury spellbound with other stories from the unexplored Rocky Mountains, which Bradbury wrote down. One of these served as further warning to Hunt's Overland Party of what lay ahead and has since become infamous in the annals of Western exploration.

Colter and his trapping partner, a man named John Potts, were paddling their canoe one day along a small tributary of the Jefferson's Fork of the Upper Missouri when, without warning, they encountered a group of some five or six hundred mounted Blackfeet warriors emerging from cottonwood groves on both sides of the river. Colter steered the canoe ashore. As the canoe touched the shore, one of the Indians plucked out a rifle that lay in the canoe. Stepping out, Colter pulled away the rifle from the Indian. Despite Colter's warnings to stay put, Potts made a start to escape in the canoe. Potts had barely pushed off from the bank when a warrior unleashed an arrow.

"Colter, I am wounded!" Potts shouted.

Leveling his rifle from the canoe, Potts fired at one of the many warriors on the riverbank. The Indian fell over, dead. There was the sudden twang of bows and a whooshing of air. Potts, sitting in the canoe, was instantly pierced by dozens of arrows. His body appeared, as Colter phrased it to Bradbury, who recorded it with a botanist's precision, as though "he was made a riddle of."*

After having Colter seized by his warriors, the Blackfeet chief asked Colter if he was a fast runner.

Colter, guessing what was about to happen, told the chief that he was a very bad runner.

---

* The word *riddle*, among its other meanings, once described a board with pins projecting out of it that was used to straighten bent pieces of wire, as defined in the *Oxford English Dictionary*. Colter no doubt was comparing Potts's arrow-pierced body to this pin-studded board.

The chief had him stripped naked and led Colter out onto a broad and open plain nearby. The several hundred warriors, armed with spears, eagerly waited three or four hundred yards back.

"The chief," recorded Bradbury, "now . . . released him, bidding him *to save himself if he could.*"

At that moment, the warriors emitted a piercing scream, and the race was on.

Colter was, in fact, a very fast runner. He sprinted off barefoot across the plain, heading toward the Jefferson Fork of the Missouri, six miles away, the Blackfeet equivalent of a ten-kilometer footrace. Prickly pear cactus buried themselves in the soles of his feet as he ran three miles without looking back. The whoops grew fainter and blood began to pour from his mouth and nostrils, as happens with racehorses and athletes when extreme exertion causes lung tissue to hemorrhage. Finally, Colter dared to spin around for a look. He'd far outrun all the warriors except one, in pursuit only a hundred yards back and closing.

Sprinting onward, Colter heard the footsteps and heavy panting draw closer, and expected at any moment to feel a flung spear pierce his back. He abruptly stopped, whirled about, and spread out his arms, displaying a chest splattered with the blood spilling from his nose. The exhausted Blackfeet warrior, suddenly surprised, raised his spear to throw, tripped, fell, and broke the spear. Colter grabbed the blade end and rammed it through the warrior's body, pinning him to the ground like a skewered fish.

Colter raced onward and, finally reaching the Jefferson Fork, plunged in and hid himself under a logjam. Like a beaver in his lodge, he held his body underwater and his head in the airspace between logs. The Blackfeet, shrieking "like so many devils," scrambled over the log-jam without detecting him, although he feared they might light it on fire. At nightfall, Colter slipped out, stealthily swam downstream, and took to shore. It was a seven-day trek, totally naked, back to an isolated fur post on the Yellowstone River that had been recently founded by St. Louis fur trader Manuel Lisa. Colter, a rugged American hunter, noted Bradbury, survived his trek by eating a root known to the Indians; the botanist, who'd been commissioned by the Linnaean Society of Liverpool to gather American plant specimens, carefully identified the plant by its Latin name, *Psoralea esculenta* (known today as prairie turnip).

Colter pointed to Meriwether Lewis as being at least partly responsible for the Blackfeet's vehemence toward whites. On the return trip from the Pacific, Lewis and a small party had taken a scouting foray in what is today northern Montana. Several young Blackfeet tried to steal the Lewis party's rifles and horses. In the altercation, one of Lewis's men stabbed to death one of the Blackfeet, and Lewis shot and probably fatally wounded another. In his anger about the cheeky raid, Lewis had left a Jefferson peace medal around the neck of the dead man, to show to all who had killed him.

Before the main bands of Blackfeet could exact retribution, Lewis and his scouting party fled day and night on horseback to the Missouri. Here he rejoined another contingent of his men who were in canoes and together they paddled at high speed down the Missouri and out of Blackfeet territory. The Blackfeet, one of the fiercest of the Plains warrior tribes, with a strict code of vengeance for the death of their own, hadn't forgotten five years later. Lewis had been lucky, but whatever American who followed would pay the price.

Colter strode along the bank for several miles as Hunt's boat laboriously made its way upstream toward the winter camp at Nodaway. He seemed to miss the excitement of the wilderness, reported botanist Bradbury, and appeared tempted to join the Overland Party, even though he'd only returned from the Rocky Mountains the previous spring, had since married, and had started a homestead of his own. Colter warned the party to take all possible precautions when traversing Blackfeet territory, even suggesting they might find a different, safer route than the Lewis and Clark route. The one he proposed left the Missouri River and skirted south below the extremely dangerous Blackfeet territory.

Finally Colter turned away from the riverbank and back toward his cabin where his bride, Sallie, waited. Hunt, with his boatload of additional recruits, continued upriver for the Nodaway camp, pondering Colter's idea of a new, untested, and possibly safer route to the Pacific.

By mid-April 1811, after wintering at the Nodaway camp, the full Overland Party readied themselves for the big push up the Missouri and over the Rockies to the Pacific. They now numbered around sixty people—about forty French-Canadian voyageurs, several American woodsmen, the two British botanists, the interpreter and his family, a ledger-keeping clerk by the name of John Reed, and five shareholding partners including Hunt and Donald Mackenzie, along with Hunt's friend from their St. Louis days, twenty-four-year-old Ramsay Crooks. Crooks, like Hunt, was known to be steady, even-tempered, and considered—even gentle. Opposite in temperament to this pair was a fourth partner in the Overland Party, Robert McClellan. The small, wiry, intense McClellan, with piercing, deep-set, dark eyes, was of Scottish heritage but born in frontier Pennsylvania. Considerably older than most of the Overland Party, at just over forty, he had fought in the Ohio Valley Indian wars in the late 1700s. Like a land-based version of Captain Thorn, he was known both for his acts of bravery under fire and for his hair-trigger personality.

Joseph Miller was the fifth shareholding Astor partner traveling with the Overland Party. Born in Baltimore to a respectable family, having benefited from a good education, the adventurous Miller, in a dispute over leave time, had quit an officer's position in the army to come west as a fur trapper and trader. The previous spring he had ascended the Missouri with Crooks and McClellan to establish a trade with the Indians but had run into problems with a band of six hundred Teton Sioux. McClellan, the former Pennsylvanian Indian fighter, was convinced that rival businessman Manuel Lisa, a New Orleans native, had incited the Sioux to stop the competing trading party. Now based in St. Louis and known as an aggressive businessman, Lisa had established a few trading posts partway up the Missouri. McClellan swore that if he ever encountered Lisa in the wilds beyond the reach of law, he would shoot him on sight.

Hunt had encountered the greatest difficulty in hiring an Indian interpreter for his Overland Party, tangling in St. Louis with Manuel Lisa over who would get Pierre Dorion. Dorion's father, Old Dorion, had served as a Sioux interpreter on the Lewis and Clark expedition. His son, Pierre Jr., part Sioux, part French, had interpreted for Lisa on a trading foray up the Missouri. Lisa claimed that Dorion still owed him for a large liquor bill from that journey. Dorion disputed the bill as wildly inflated.

Manuel Lisa still badly wanted Dorion to serve as his interpreter, as he was sending a trading expedition up the Missouri the same spring that Hunt set out upriver with the Astor Overland Party. Lisa's party was destined for the post he had established at the Mandan villages, some sixteen hundred miles upstream. He also hoped his expedition would discover what had happened to a missing party of trappers sent by his concern, the Missouri Fur Company, almost two years earlier to establish a post at the Missouri headwaters at Three Forks.

In St. Louis, Lisa tried to detain Dorion over his disputed liquor debt, sending authorities to keep him from joining Hunt's party. But Dorion, somehow forewarned, slipped out of St. Louis at night and joined Hunt's riverboat en route. Still another complicating factor intervened when Dorion insisted that his wife and their two young boys accompany the Overland Party. His wife, a member of the Iowa tribe and known by her Anglicized name of Marie Dorion, apparently resisted the idea. Dorion beat her, and she escaped into the woods along the river with her two boys. Hunt dispatched a search party. After a night in the woods, she returned to the riverbank and rejoined her husband and the Overland Party.

Did Marie Dorion grasp the magnitude of what the Overland Party was about to attempt perhaps more clearly than anyone else on the Astor expedition? Five-year-old Jean Baptiste walking at her side and tiny two-year-old Paul riding on her back contrasted with the vastness of the wilderness and the sprawling ambition of Astor's enterprise. Marie Dorion may have spoken—and probably did, at some point—directly with Sacagawea herself, wife of interpreter Toussaint Charbonneau of the Lewis and Clark expedition as well as a member of the Shoshone tribe from what today is Idaho. Apparently, Sacagawea was in St. Louis as Hunt's riverboat departed up the Missouri in March, with its additional recruits and the Dorion family, bound for winter camp. It's likely Marie Dorion and Sacagawea knew each other: two Indian women in the small settlement of St. Louis, both wives of interpreters in the burgeoning Missouri fur trade.

What would Sacagawea have told Marie Dorion?

It will be very long, and very difficult to reach the ocean. . . . You and your children will suffer. . . .

By then, five years after her journey with Lewis and Clark, Sacagawea had adopted European dress and manners. She may have understood that whites, with their powerful guns and endless numbers and relentless urge for furs and farmland and profit, had just begun their long reach toward the western ocean. She may have understood that these first expeditions heading westward represented the beginning of the end for her people's ancient, seminomadic way of life.

One imagines her saying to Marie Dorion, *Don't go. . . .*

Or . . . *Yes, join them, because they will come to our homelands whether we join them or not. . . . Or . . . Go. You will see amazing things. . . .*

Organizing into four riverboats laden with approximately twenty tons of goods and equipped with oars, sails, and towropes, the Overland Party embarked from Nodaway winter camp on April 21, 1811, with sails set in a favorable upriver wind. They hoped to reach the Pacific—as Astor expected—in late summer or autumn.

It rained nearly every day at first. The river flowed high with the spring rains, and the swift current shoved against the prows of the riverboats working slowly upstream. Sitting in rows on benches, the voyageurs pulled the oars in tandem strokes. These experienced steersmen hugged the boats to the inside of the bends where the current ran slack, instead of fighting the full swirling force of midstream. In swift sections they stood and shoved their way upriver with long "setting poles," or stepped out of the boats onto the riverbank and dragged them upstream, hauling together on 200-foot-long towropes called *cordelles.*

The American hunters, among them John Day, a lanky, good-natured, forty-year-old Virginian, ranged the grassy banks or forested bottomlands stalking deer, bear, and other game to feed the sixty-person party. The botanists, Bradbury and Nuttall, walked ashore whenever they could to study and dig plant specimens. Here on the plains, Indian villages lay at great distances from one another and they encountered few other humans. At night the expedition moored along the grass-and-mud riverbanks or on islands, pitching tents in which partners and botanists and the clerk usually slept, while voyageurs rolled themselves in bison robes or blankets under the stars. Bradbury noted that at night the skies glowed a distant orange from fires set by war parties covering their tracks across the prairie grasses.

Each day they pushed onward up the Missouri. The spring current undercut the soft, muddy banks, and uprooted cottonwood trees that tumbled into the river. Still attached to the banks by their rootballs, these downed trees, known to the voyageurs as *embarrass,* or "impediment," projected from shore like arms reaching into the river and straining out drifting wood from the flow. These partial dams of driftwood sticking out from the banks had the effect of speeding up the river's current around their projecting ends. The voyageurs worked hard with oars and poles and towlines to round these obstacles or crossed the river to avoid them.

Although they would have preferred paddles and their lightweight birch-bark canoes to the heavy wooden riverboats and oars, the voyageurs kept up their good cheer and their paddling songs. Bradbury, with a knowledge of Latin and French, translated one of their favorite songs into English, its lighthearted verses about life on the farm back in Quebec contrasting with the enormity and uncertainty of the wilderness that lay ahead:

> *Behind our house there is a pond,*
> *Fal lal de ra,*
> *There came three ducks to swim thereon. . . .*

One can hear, in the cadence of these lines, the quick, swirling stroke of the oars in the water, the brief, dripping pause after the stroke, followed by the next hard pull and the sudden forward surge of the riverboat, repeated thousands and thousands of times each day.

They had pulled themselves upstream for two months by that day in late May when, over breakfast, they saw two canoes with three white men coming down the river. The man wearing the bandana over his scalped pate, they learned, was a sixty-six-year-old Kentuckian and former Indian fighter named Edward Robinson. He belonged to the missing party Manuel Lisa sought. Two years earlier, in the spring of 1809, Robinson and the other two Kentuckians in the canoes with him, Jacob Reznor and John Hoback, had ascended the Missouri with a large trapping party sent by Lisa and the Missouri Fur Company to establish a fur post at Three Forks. Rich in beaver and other fur-bearing animals, Three Forks lay near the Missouri headwaters. It also happened to lie in the heart of Blackfeet territory. Robinson and company described how the Blackfeet relentlessly attacked the trapping parties whenever they emerged from the small, fortified post at Three Forks, even to try to negotiate. In various ambushes, they killed an estimated twenty to thirty trappers.

"The [Blackfeet] Indians were so intensely hostile," as early fur-trade historian Hiram Chittenden described the Three Forks incident, "that there seemed to be no possibility of an interview except at the rifle's mouth."

After several months of relentless ambush, the white trappers abandoned the Three Forks outpost and fled in two different directions. One group headed down the Missouri toward St. Louis with the beaver pelts they'd gathered. Another group, led by Andrew Henry, and including the Kentuckians Robinson, Reznor, and Hoback, scrambled southwest over the nearby crest of the Rockies hoping to escape the Blackfeet and continue trapping. There, in the winter of 1810–11, along a small river, they built makeshift cabins and wintered. They believed this river was a headwater stream of the Columbia River, flowing to the Pacific Ocean.

After suffering a hard winter, the little party abandoned their mountain hideout and scattered farther, some heading south hoping to reach Spanish territory in Mexico, while Robinson, Reznor, and Hoback headed east, through unknown mountain ranges and broad valleys, back toward the Missouri River. After traversing a huge stretch of unmapped terrain that skirted south of Blackfeet territory, they finally struck the Missouri. They had been paddling downstream on the swift spring snowmelt bound for their Kentucky farms, when, on that morning, May 26, 1811, they ran into Wilson Price Hunt and his party breakfasting on the riverbank.

Even after all the harrowing experiences they'd undergone—or perhaps because of them—the sight of Hunt's large Overland Party was too tempting to the three Kentucky trappers, as were the possible riches they might accrue under Astor's transcontinental scheme. They abandoned their plans to head back to their family farms and signed with Hunt's and Astor's enterprise. Immediately after signing, they transferred their baggage to the riverboats and let their empty canoes drift away downstream.

Despite their eagerness to join, the three Kentuckians, echoing John Colter, strongly advised Hunt to avoid the Blackfeet. The Blackfeet were implacable and still furious that Meriwether Lewis had killed one of their young men. Hunt and his Overland Party, the Kentuckians claimed, could easily bypass Blackfeet territory. They simply had to continue up the Missouri a few days farther from where they were now, to the Arikara villages. They would have to purchase horses from the friendly Arikara, then leave the Missouri River, and the Lewis and Clark route more generally, traveling overland, due west, across the Rockies, to that unnamed headwater stream of the Columbia where Robinson, Reznor, and Hoback had recently abandoned their winter camp. Once at the stream, the big group simply had to build canoes and the forty voyageurs could paddle the entire Overland Party and its tons of trade goods and trapping equipment downstream to the Pacific—setting up posts along the way—and rendezvous with the *Tonquin* at the Columbia's mouth. Not only would the route provide safety from the Blackfeet, they claimed; if they followed certain mountain passes through the Rockies, their way would also prove far easier than the Lewis and Clark route, which included a long and difficult mountain crossing.

Hunt deliberated. He had never been placed in anything like this situation. The incredible ferocity of the Blackfeet on one hand and, on the other, a great unknown chunk of territory? To choose the latter, he'd have to leave behind the Missouri and his big cargo boats equipped with lethal swivel guns, and travel for many vulnerable weeks on foot and horseback through uncharted lands. More difficult still, he'd have to disregard Mr. Astor's instructions. The party now numbered at least sixty and possibly could withstand a fierce Blackfeet attack, but the French-Canadian voyageurs, infused more with the spirit of brotherly love than mortal combat, didn't relish the idea of fighting and surely preferred what amounted to a very long portage. And the Kentucky and Virginia hunters, though happy to fight, didn't much like the odds.

The massive scar under the bandana on Robinson's hairless pate seems to have made a deep impression on Hunt, as if a symbol, in puckered flesh, of what lay farther up the Missouri. Old photographs of scalping victims—survivors were more common than is thought— call to mind circus clowns in the utterly bald, peeled-bare top of the victim's head, with frizzed tufts of hair protruding on the sides and a narrow fringe of locks running above the forehead.

Hunt surely also heard how it had been done. To scalp, the perpetrator typically turned his victim—alive or dead—facedown on the earth. With a knife—a stone knife in the pre-European days, and metal thereafter—he scored around the top of the head, cutting through the scalp to the underlying bone of the skull. Seizing a forelock of hair in his hand and placing one knee in the victim's back, the perpetrator then gave a sharp upward jerk and ripped the large flap of scalp with its hair intact clean off the victim's skull. Victims who were still alive at this point later reported that the tearing sounded like "distant thunder." The blood loss, of course, was considerable, but stanching factors, such as cold or the raggedness of the tear, could constrict the blood vessels quickly and slow the loss. Edward Robinson, scalped some years earlier fighting in Ohio Valley Indian wars, had been among the lucky survivors.

Whatever it meant for survivors, for Native American tribes the act of scalping held special meaning beyond simple vengeance. This close personal contact with the enemy and the removal of part of his person allowed the victor to absorb the victim's power. Once removed, the fleshy underside of the scalp was scraped clean and stretched over a wooden hoop. This was then mounted on a tall shaft and displayed aloft as a ceremonial trophy. Though some suggest that Europeans first introduced scalping to Native Americans, other evidence indicates the practice existed long before white men arrived in Sioux or Blackfeet territory. Archaeologists digging near this same section of the Missouri discovered a massacre site from tribe-against-tribe warfare that dates to the 1300s. It contains nearly five hundred human skeletons. According to archaeological interpretation, most of the skulls display the stone-knife scores of scalping.

The warrior tribes of the Plains had good reasons to display their ferocity to outsiders who infringed on their territory—whether the outsiders were other tribes, or, later, Europeans like Hunt and his companions. The Blackfeet and other Plains tribes sat atop of—and claimed as their own—one of the largest reservoirs of easily accessible protein the world has ever known: the vast herds of bison placidly grazing on prairie grasses. The Plains tribes, and especially the Blackfeet, jealously guarded these resources—a living storehouse of some 15 billion pounds of meat, as well as the hides to make their tipis and thick winter robes—by instilling in would-be thieves the fear of a terrible death.* Fear was a way to enforce the national boundary of a scattered nomadic tribe.

After listening to the case for leaving the Missouri and detouring south of Blackfeet territory, and hearing a similar opinion from two other wide-ranging trappers who had recently joined the Overland Party, Benjamin Jones and Alexander Carson, Hunt wrestled with this new alternative. He bore a deep sense of responsibility both to Astor and to the party under his own leadership. Were their interests the same in this case? What would Mr. Astor have him do?

Hunt had been the sole leader of the Overland expedition since his stay in St. Louis. It was there, while visiting the settlement from Nodaway winter camp to recruit more men, that Hunt had received a letter from Astor in New York. Unnerved by political tensions between the Americans and the British, and unable to come to an agreement with rival trapping companies, Astor decided he'd rather an American citizen take sole charge of the Overland Party, relegating the Scot Donald Mackenzie to an equal status with the other partners. Wilson Price Hunt, in effect, had riding on his shoulders alone the welfare of the sixty-person Overland Party and much of the fate of John Jacob Astor's West Coast empire.

They camped together on the night of May 26, on a beautiful stretch of the Missouri, amid gentle grassy hills, abundant feeder streams, and stretches of willow-fringed bottomlands. The next day the Overland Party resumed its upstream push, now accompanied by the three Ken-

---

* This estimate is based on a North American Plains bison population before the arrival of Europeans of about 30 million animals, with an average carcass weight (the slaughtered animal without hide, head, or innards) of about five hundred pounds.

tuckian trappers. The wind blew fair that day from the southeast and the weather held warm and sunny. The party hoisted the boats' sails and made good mileage, reported Bradbury, despite the protests of the voyageurs, who, accustomed to controlling a canoe's every movement with their paddles, grew panicky whenever the riverboats heeled in the brisk breeze.

"*O mon Dieu! Abattez le voile!*" Oh my God! Stop the sail!

Meanwhile, the eccentric young Nuttall leapt for the shore at every opportunity in his head-down pursuit of new plants, to the ignorance of all else, including personal safety.

The voyageurs had taken to calling him *le fou*.

Ou est le fou? Where is the fool?

Il est après ramasser des racines. He is gathering roots.

The four boats made good progress upriver under sail that day and camped that night, May 27, 1811, on Little Cedar Island. They were now an estimated 1,075 miles up the Missouri River from St. Louis. The island was a botanical wonderland—a grove of cedar trees grew in its center surrounded by gardenlike beds of vines and flowers. Voyageurs and woodsmen chopped new boat masts from the cedars to replace damaged ones, while Bradbury and Nuttall scrambled about collecting plants. Hunt, however, was distracted by his own problems. He had to decide, and soon, whether to turn away from the Missouri.

"[T]he best possible route . . . became a subject of anxious enquiry," wrote Bradbury of that night camping on Little Cedar Island.

Hunt closely questioned the three Kentuckians about their proposal. He consulted with the two other trappers who had traveled the Upper Missouri, Carson and Jones. Mr. Astor had instructed him to try, whenever possible, to reach consensus among the partners. Hunt polled them, as he would throughout the journey, on their opinions about which way to go.

One pictures Hunt's party camped on the grassy bank of the narrow island—islands in the river granted a certain safety from Indian attack—with a large fire of long driftwood logs throwing yellow sparks up toward the diamond-bright prairie stars. The sixty men, one woman, and two children press in toward the fire's warmth and comfort. Perhaps Hunt moves between the fire and his tent, interviewing and deliberating. What lay out there, in the vast prairie night, in the whole western continent, beyond this tiny glowing circle of warmth and humanity? Which mountains would let them pass, which rivers, which tribes that roamed unseen in the continental darkness? On Little Cedar Island, Wilson Price Hunt, for the first time, tasted the unknown. Though its flavor might intoxicate an eager, lone young man like John Colter, Hunt, responsible for a large group of people and the expectations of great men, probably found it neither exhilarating nor romantic. On the one hand there were the Blackfeet warriors that surely awaited him on the known route up the Missouri. On the other lay the route that left the Missouri and struck overland, skirting south of the Blackfeet, where his party might wander lost over snowy mountain ranges and through the starvation deserts.

What might have come as a startling revelation about striking out into the unknown is that though the questions confronting one are often mundane—this route or that, this river drainage or another—the implications are profound, and sometimes fatal.

By morning, Hunt had decided.

It's not surprising that in the choice between a near-certain, violent confrontation with the Blackfeet and venturing out into a great stretch of unexplored terrain, Hunt, avoiding conflict, finally chose the latter. One could call it a bold choice in the true spirit of exploration, or cowardice, a retreat into fear for the safety of his party, and for himself. Whatever an expedition member's perspective, Hunt had made the fateful decision: The Overland Party would leave the Missouri and veer to the south of the planned route, avoiding the Blackfeet, and trek, on foot and horseback, into the great swath of uncharted terrain.

The decision made, Hunt sat down to write Mr. Astor of his change in plans.

M EN SHOUTED, CURSED, AND SANG PARTING WORDS above the heaving of horses and creaking of packsaddles as the long procession of the Overland Party left the Arikara villages, mounted the Missouri riverbank, and strode onto the great, grassy plains. Wilson Price Hunt had made his decision after that restless night on Little Cedar Island: The Overland Party would avoid the Blackfeet territory, leave the Missouri and the known Lewis and Clark route, and strike across a great stretch of unknown terrain, guided by the three trappers, in search of the headwaters of the Columbia.

With the decision made, Hunt had to worry about whether they would find enough horses for the journey. Did the three trappers know where they were going? What other tribes might they encounter besides the Blackfeet? How long would it take to reach the Rocky Mountains and then the Pacific?

But what Hunt didn't seem to feel was any sense of urgency. With his lack of wilderness experience, Hunt had never seen winter in the mountains and how difficult travel there could be.

After his restless night on Little Cedar Island and his decision to leave the Lewis and Clark route and head into the unknown territory, his party worked their way another two weeks upstream on the Missouri by riverboat until they reached the riverbank opposite the Arikara villages on the morning of June 12, 1811. Though this was to be their jumping-off point across the prairie, Hunt lingered there for nearly five weeks.

Just as Hunt's party arrived opposite the Arikara villages, Manuel Lisa's party landed nearby. Lisa's big riverboat, its voyageurs pulling for all they were worth in the thousand-some miles since St. Louis, had a week earlier caught up with the Hunt party. It had rained during the night and soaked both parties' bedding. While their blankets and bison robes dried in the sun, an Arikara chief called from the villages across the river to both parties. The chief's powerful Indian oratorical voice, the syllables of speech accented evenly and clearly, carried easily across the half-mile-wide Missouri. He invited the whites to cross the river for a council.

The rival parties had previously agreed, using as intermediaries Bradbury and his friend in the Lisa party, Henry Brackenridge, to arrive at the Arikara villages at exactly the same moment. This way neither would have won a trade advantage by getting there first. But, even as the two parties prepared to cross the Missouri simultaneously to the villages, suspicions lingered.

"M'Clellan, in particular, carefully watched [Lisa's] motions," wrote Bradbury, "determined to shoot him if he attempted to cross the river before us. . . ."

The rival riverboats shoved off—oars dipping into the Missouri's surface, which swirled with spring snowmelt from the distant mountains. Brackenridge, an ambitious young St. Louis journalist and lawyer in Lisa's boat, described seeing Arikara women bobbing down the Missouri's pillows of current in circular boats as they crossed. The boats were made of a single bison hide stretched over a willow frame, known as "bullboats," and helped the women tote bundles of firewood for their hearths. Hunt's and Lisa's riverboats touched simultaneously on the opposite bank, where a crowd of Arikaras met them. The Arikara chief, known to French fur traders as Le Gauche—"Left-Handed"—escorted them through the village's two hundred or so conical earthen lodges to the council house. Inside they were seated ceremoniously on bison robes. The further progress of the Overland Party to the Pacific would pivot on this council between Le Gauche, Manuel Lisa, and Wilson Price Hunt. Could Hunt obtain from Le Gauche horses to carry the sixty people in his party and their tons of supplies for the long trek across the plains, over the Rockies, and to the Columbia headwaters?

Or would Manuel Lisa, the rival trader, somehow sabotage Hunt's efforts with the Arikara, undermining Astor's grand plans for the Rocky Mountain and Pacific fur empire?

Fights and threats had instantly erupted when the two parties first met each other on the Missouri riverbank a week before, when Lisa's boat had overtaken Hunt's group. As in St. Louis, Lisa had once again tried to hire the Indian interpreter, Pierre Dorion, away from Hunt by offering him whisky and reminding him of the large whisky debt Dorion still owed Lisa's Missouri Fur Company.

Dorion, enraged, had slugged Lisa on the riverbank.

"O meu Dieu! Ou est mon couteau!" Oh my God! Where is my big knife! Lisa had cried in indignation, recorded the botanist and eyewitness Bradbury.

While Lisa hurried off to get his weapon, Dorion had grabbed two pistols from Hunt, who didn't seem inclined to put an end to the frontier melee, perhaps seeing this brawl as a convenient way to rid himself and Mr. Astor of a rival. Both McClellan and Crooks also itched to take on Lisa personally, convinced that he'd incited the Sioux against them on their previous trade journey up the Missouri. As Lisa returned with his big *couteau* stuck in his belt, Brackenridge tried to stop the violence.

"I had several times to stand between him and the interpreter, who has a pistol in each hand," Brackenridge wrote.

The enraged Lisa, no doubt feeling his honor deeply impugned by the Indian interpreter's blow, then turned on Hunt, insulting him with an expression, as Bradbury delicately put it, "conveying an imputation upon himself."

Whatever it was, Lisa's insult set off the normally placid Wilson Price Hunt.

"[Hunt] told Lisa that the matter should be settled by themselves," wrote Bradbury, "and desired him to fetch his pistols."

Duels were still in vogue then among gentlemen and military officers, with the Burr-Hamilton duel fought only seven years before. Many duels never came to actual sword blows exchanged or bullets fired. Honor for both parties could more simply be satisfied on the "field of honor" by each appearing at the appointed hour ready to kill the other man, then employing various techniques for calling it off gracefully. Perhaps both Hunt and Lisa knew that the cooler heads of the botanist and journalist would eventually prevail.

"I followed Lisa to his boat, accompanied by Mr. Brackenridge," wrote Bradbury, "and we with difficulty prevented a meeting, which, in the present temper of the parties, would certainly have been a bloody one."

From that point forward, Bradbury and Brackenridge served as intermediaries between the Hunt and Lisa parties. (The other young British botanist, Nuttall, or *Le Fou,* apparently remained focused on finding new plants, oblivious to the threats of violence nearby.) In order to ease suspicions that anyone might angle for position with the Arikara, both parties had agreed to reach the villages at exactly the same moment, although it was anyone's guess what would happen next between them.

With both Lisa and Hunt sitting in the Arikara council lodge that morning of their arrival at the villages, an elderly chief, or priest, climbed to the lodge's rooftop and in that powerful voice summoned all other chiefs to the meeting. With a group of twenty or more assembled in the lodge, the priest lit the long-stemmed pipe. Le Gauche took up the pipe and offered puffs to the Great Spirit—puffs to the sky, to the earth, and to the cardinal directions—then carried it around the group and, in a gesture of respect, pressed it to each person's lips for several puffs.

Le Gauche opened with a short speech. His people were poor, he said, and he was glad to see the white traders; he would be happy to trade with them.

Manuel Lisa replied with a gift of tobacco and said that he would like to trade for bison skins and beaver pelts if the prices weren't too high. Lisa, reported Brackenridge, pointed to Hunt and his colleagues sitting on the bison robes and told Le Gauche and the assembled chiefs that Mr. Hunt was a friend of his.

"[Hunt and his party] were going on a long journey to the great Salt lake, to the west," Lisa told the chief, "and he hoped would meet with favourable treatment; and that any injury offered them, he would consider as done to himself. . . ."

For Hunt and his fellow partners, this came as a startling departure from Lisa's behavior the week before.

"This candid and frank declaration," reported Brackenridge, also sitting on a bison robe in the council house, "at once removed all suspicion from the minds of the others, who had become seriously apprehensive that Lisa . . . might betray them."

It was now Hunt's turn. Hunt also offered a gift of tobacco to Le Gauche, then spoke. His mission was not to trade with the Arikara, he told Le Gauche and the assembled chiefs, but to meet with his brothers far away at the great salt lake to the west. He would leave the river and travel overland from these villages toward the great body of water. He needed many horses for the journey and had plenty of goods to trade for the Arikara horses.

Hunt spoke in French to Dorion, who translated his speech into native language intelligible to the chiefs. Bradbury made a point of sitting next to Dorion to get as nuanced a sense of the exchange as possible without understanding the language. While waiting for translation, the scientist and his friend the journalist Brackenridge noted the details of Arikara lodge construction: the roof supported by four tall forked posts planted in the earth, joined by crossbeams, and the whole covered with woven osier branches topped by the thick layer of earth that offered insulation in the cold winters and hot summers and gave the lodge its conical shape. A raised altar in these lodges typically held two elaborately painted bison skulls; displayed above them were consecrated objects like shields and quivers of arrows. While the lodges themselves were snug, and the people bathed twice a day, the Arikara villages sat on a level plain along the riverbank backed by bluffs and suffered from poor drainage. Aswarm with children, and with thirty or forty dogs per family, the villages became, both Bradbury and Brackenridge complained, a stinking pool of unhygienic filth whenever it rained.

Le Gauche, sitting on his slightly raised dais in the council house, now responded to both Lisa's and Hunt's requests. He and his people were fond of white men, he said, and glad they'd come. He needed some time to fix the exact price of bison robes for Lisa; he was currently thinking about thirty loads of ball and powder per robe. For Hunt, however, Le Gauche had bad news:

"[H]e was certain they could not spare the number of horses that he understood [Hunt] wanted," reported Bradbury, "and that he did not think they ought to sell any horses."

Le Gauche didn't give a reason why, at least not one that Bradbury reported. Surely McClellan, the Astor partner also sitting on a bison robe in the council lodge, suspected that Manuel Lisa had somehow got word to the chief telling him not to help the Overland Party. A more likely reason, however, is that the Arikara were at war with the Sioux and Le Gauche may have felt the Arikara needed to keep their horses at hand.

Ten days earlier, the Sioux had blockaded Hunt's riverboats on their laborious ascent of the Missouri, charging down the bank with five or six hundred warriors to stop them at a narrows. Only after Hunt ordered all swivel guns, howitzers, rifles, and pistols loaded and aimed at the Sioux warriors, to show his willingness to fight, did the chiefs on the shore wave bison robes signaling their willingness to talk. They let Hunt and his party pass, contingent on Hunt's promise that he wouldn't sell arms to their upstream enemies, the Arikara.

After Le Gauche denied Hunt's request for horses, another Arikara chief, named Les Yeux Gris (Gray Eyes), spoke up.

Les Yeux Gris stated, contrary to Le Gauche, that indeed the Arikara could sell many horses to Hunt. The sold horses could easily be replaced, he said, by "stealing or smoking." Horse stealing was a highly honorable practice among Plains tribes and denoted besting one's enemies in the most humiliating way possible. Some tribes prided themselves on being absolute masters at it. "Smoking," on the other hand, as Crooks explained to Bradbury, referred to a custom among tribes friendly to one another. If one tribe lacked in some item—food, horses, whatever—that tribe could send emissaries to the other tribe, smoke together, and ask the other tribe to help provide the missing item. Someday, both tribes knew, the favor would be returned.

Les Yeux Gris's idea met the general approval of the gathered chiefs, including Le Gauche. At the right price—and Hunt seemed eager to pay well, including with arms and powder, despite his promises to the Sioux—they would sell horses to Hunt, replacing the horses by smoking or stealing.

The meeting broke up. Bradbury and colleagues were led off to another lodge for a feast of boiled sweet corn mixed with bison fat, which Bradbury found delicious.

But there were still delays. Horses had to be found and prices negotiated. Manuel Lisa himself offered to sell Hunt some of his own horses, kept at his post at the Mandan villages, another few hundred miles upriver. A small party from Hunt's group, including Ramsay Crooks, traveled from the Arikara villages to the Mandan villages to get Lisa's horses and bring them back.

While the Overland Party was delayed for logistical reasons, the elaborate Plains Indian hospitality have may have sapped the group's desire to be on its way. Bradbury, who frequently wandered the Arikara villages, described how on entering an earthen lodge, the master always shook his hand, set him down on a bearskin or bison hide, and prepared a pipe for him while the woman of the lodge prepared him food. This done, she took up her leather sewing bag containing bone awl and split-sinew thread to repair any of his torn clothing or footwear. Then, if night was near, the guest was offered both a place to sleep and someone to sleep with.

"No people on earth discharge the duties of hospitality with more cordial good-will than the Indians," he wrote.

His colleague Brackenridge noted that a guest's refusing the offer of "wife, sister, or maid servant, according to the estimation in which the guest is held . . . is considered as treating the host with contempt."

Brackenridge was also astounded at the volume of the kind of sexual barter system between the voyageurs and the Arikara women, in which the price for their services in blue beads and other trade goods was worked out in advance between the women—their husbands if the women were married—and the voyageurs. On seeing an Arikara chief in a thoughtful mood one day, Brackenridge asked the chief what was the matter. "'I was wondering,' said he, 'whether you white people have any women amongst you.' I assured him in the affirmative. 'Then,' said he, 'why is it that your people are so fond of our women, one might suppose they had never seen any before?'"

On July 18, 1811, Wilson Price Hunt's Overland Party finally left the Arikara villages, turned its back on the Missouri, and stepped out onto the plains. Most of them walked. The party had a total of eighty-two horses—still not enough to carry more than sixty people, plus the goods they needed to establish an interior trading network beyond the Rockies to the Pacific. The five Astor partners rode on horseback—Hunt, Mackenzie, Crooks, McClellan, and Miller, plus clerk John Reed. The other fifty-six men strode along on foot. Packed with weighty, swaying loads of trade goods for the Indians, along with the traps, food, ammunition, and other supplies unloaded from the riverboats, the remaining seventy-five or so horses carried what was probably between ten and fifteen tons' worth of expedition baggage.

Marie Dorion and her two young boys had a single horse at their disposal. Marie herself, to the wonder of the men, mostly walked. She had shown a reluctance about this epic journey since its very beginning. Now, nearly fifteen hundred miles up the Missouri, as the expedition struck out overland through unknown terrain toward the Rockies, Marie Dorion had something else to contend with. She was three months pregnant.

She could calculate that the infant would come in the moon of the shortest days, or December. She must have wondered whether she and her two young children would have food and shelter in the wintry month when the baby arrived. Would they have reached the settlement on the Pacific or would the Overland Party still be walking?

Marie Dorion may have talked more with Sacagawea since leaving St. Louis. According to Brackenridge, both Sacagawea and her husband, Toussaint Charbonneau, were also on Lisa's riverboat. Sacagawea was ill and wanted to return to her native people, while Charbonneau had hired on with Lisa. They had left their son, Jean Baptiste, the infant who'd traveled with Sacagawea on the Lewis and Clark journey, behind in St. Louis. He was now six years old, and William Clark, serving as the U.S. Indian agent in St. Louis, wanted a good education for the boy who had accompanied his expedition. Sacagawea and Marie Dorion, both heading up the Missouri River, were thus together at the Arikara villages for that week of June 12, 1811, while Lisa's party lingered before heading further upriver and Hunt negotiated with the Arikara for horses.

Sacagawea was only in her early twenties. According to written records, she'd be dead of typhus in a little more than a year at Lisa's fur post at the Mandan villages. (Some oral traditions say she lived many years longer.)

But Marie Dorion, pregnant, would go onward. So would her husband, Pierre, and their two boys. She would bring her own resilience to the journey, and in some ways her own vision would help determine the course of an empire on the Pacific.

The voyageurs had their own apprehensions as the party turned its back to the Missouri. They vastly preferred paddles and canoes—or even riverboats and oars—to foot and horseback. Manuel Lisa's men, during their stay together at the Arikara villages, had filled their heads with horror stories of what awaited them—horses stolen by the master-thief Crows, perishing of hunger and thirst in the starvation deserts, lost in the mountains, massacred at the hands of the ruthless Blackfeet. Lisa's men claimed that the three Kentuckian trappers, Robinson, Hoback, and Reznor, didn't know where they were heading—no white man did.

Summer was passing. The Rocky Mountains still lay a long way off. With or without enough horses, Hunt and his party knew they had to make a start, whatever their fears of what lay ahead and however comforting the Arikara hospitality they left behind.

"[T]he grass was knee-high," recorded Hunt, who now kept his own journal, as the great procession moved out onto the plains, "and the horses could graze contentedly."

They walked past huge herds of grazing bison and camped under brilliant summer stars. Despite their resolution to leave, no one seemed inclined to hurry, even Hunt. They'd trekked less than a week, and covered a mere sixty-seven miles, when they had to stop again. Several of the party had fallen ill, among them Ramsay Crooks. He was so weak, possibly with malarial fever, that he had to be placed on a travois and dragged behind his horse.[*]

By this time the restless Mackenzie, always pushing forward, but now deprived of a co-leadership role, may have simply thrown up his hands and let Hunt take all the delays he wished. If Astor didn't want Mackenzie as a leader of the party, then Hunt, Mackenzie might have felt, could hang himself with his tardiness and lack of wilderness experience.

Hunt, for his part, felt deeply committed to the unity of the group. But now one of the group had fallen badly ill. Was he to leave an ill member behind, and proceed ahead with his and Mr. Astor's schedule? In response to this tension between the cohesion of the group and the

---

[*]   Meriwether Lewis also suffered from malarial fever during his expedition, and at other times in his life. It was then referred to as the "ague."

success of his mission, Hunt chose to rest for two weeks at a camp near the friendly Cheyenne villages. The Cheyenne were an "honest and clean" people, as Hunt described them, and traded with Hunt for thirty-six more horses. Living in tipis of tanned bison hides, the Cheyenne moved frequently and hunted the great herds of bison on the plains, instead of residing in permanent earthen lodges and growing corn like the Arikara.

It wasn't until early August, when a cool breath of fall already blew on the high plains, that Hunt's party resumed its journey toward the Pacific. With the additional animals purchased from the Cheyenne, the voyageurs now each shared a horse, taking turns riding and walking. Crooks still rode in the travois. Astor partner Joseph Miller suffered extreme discomfort from the hard wooden Indian saddles.

Meanwhile, Hunt's riverboats, having been sold to Lisa, were whisking down the Missouri on a brisk current making close to nine miles per hour toward St. Louis. They carried botanist Bradbury, his friend Brackenridge, and Bradbury's enormous plant collection packed in seventeen trunks that he had purchased from the voyageurs, who no longer needed them on horseback. Once Bradbury and Brackenridge's riverboat pulled into the settlement of St. Louis, Charles Gratiot, a St. Louis trader originally from Switzerland, and, like John Jacob Astor, of Huguenot descent, wrote to his business correspondent Astor in New York. Gratiot ominously described to Astor the rumors he was hearing in St. Louis about Hunt's delays.

"It was to be apprehended [Hunt] would experience many difficulties before he could cross the mountains and would be exposed to winter on the roads before he could reach the place of his destination."

As Hunt's party continued its trek, the country began to rise, to break into ridges and draws, and grow drier, as if the thick untanned hide of the earth itself had dried and shrunk and cracked. They'd crossed what's now known as the 100th meridian, an imaginary dividing line between the moist, fertile Midwest and the high, arid West. The bison herds, avoiding the driest areas, grazed in the big, grassy

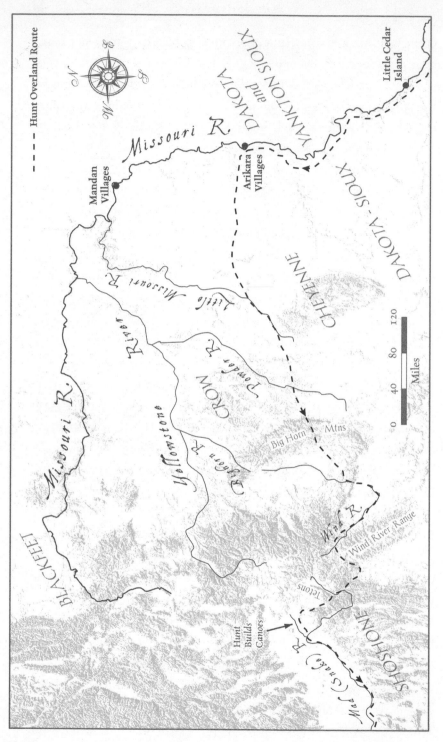

HUNT OVERLAND PARTY, JULY–OCTOBER 1811

- - - - Hunt Overland Route

Little Cedar
Island

DAKOTA AND
YANKTON SIOUX

DAKOTA-SIOUX

Missouri R.

Mandan
Villages

Arikara
Villages

CHEYENNE

Little Missouri R.

Missouri R.

River

Yellowstone R.

CROW

Powder R.

Big Horn R.

Big Horn Mtns

Miles

0   40   80   120

BLACKFEET

Wind R.

Wind River Range

Tetons

Hunt
Builds
Canoes

Mad (Snake) R.

SHOSHONE

basins, where at times they clustered and formed a vast sea of brown, woolly backs.

"They made a frightful noise," wrote Hunt of breeding bison crowding nearby. "The males tore up the earth with their hooves and horns."

The six hunters with the Overland Party rode off on horseback to supplement the expedition's food supplies. They went missing for a week, having lost their bearings in relation to the Hunt party, not sure if they were north or south, in front of or behind the main group, despite signal fires lighted by Hunt's party to guide them back. Finally rejoining the party while it was on the march, they brought with them the meat of eight bison.

The temperature swung wildly between night's cold and day's warmth on the high, dry plains at the end of summer. On August 20, the night turned cold enough to lay a skim of ice "as thick as a dollar" on standing water. A few days later the day turned so hot and dry that the party suffered from thirst crossing a patch of broken country. Horses' hooves and voyageur moccasins slowly trod over the baked, cracked earth. The sun blazed. Mackenzie's dog died of heat. From the dusty heights, they spotted in the distance the snow-patched peaks of the Bighorn Mountains, the first true range of the Rockies, and the first in a series of great north-south ridges running like enormous corrugations up and down the continent.

On August 30, a party of mounted Crow Indians—master riders and master horse thieves, able to traverse "the craggy heights as if they were galloping in a riding school," as Hunt put it—discovered the camp of the Overland Party and invited them to the nearby Crow encampment.

The Crow chief received the leaders in his tipi with the same gracious hospitality they'd experienced with the Arikara and Cheyenne. A similar code of hospitality traditionally extends to wayfarers among many nomadic societies across the world—among Inuit hunters in the Arctic, Bedouin dwellers in the desert, Tibetan nomads on the high

Asian plateaus. In these places the population is widely scattered over sweeping landscapes, the climate often fierce, and food a day-to-day uncertainty. One extends hospitality to wayfarers in need with the unspoken knowledge that one day it will be returned. Here on the high plains, if the strangers violated that hospitality, infringed on it, or killed someone, their hosts could transform into enemies relentlessly bent on revenge.

Hunt and his Overland Party spent a day with the Crow, trading for fresh and additional horses to replace tired animals. They now had 121 animals; most of the party could ride instead of walk. The party set out again on September 2, attempting to cross the Bighorns, but "precipices and bare mountain heights," as Hunt described them, blocked their way. They wandered uncertainly in the valleys, looking for a passage. The hospitable chief of the Crow, learning of the problem, sent an emissary to guide Hunt and his party to the easiest route across the Bighorns. Following the guide, they traveled through passes that Native Americans had discovered many centuries before—and game animals before them—climbing through piney forests up to verdant spring-fed valleys and heathery carpets of alpine tundra to nearly ten thousand feet. This, like most of the interior "wilderness" of the North and South American continents, was hardly a blank spot to the native peoples, although it surely was to white explorers. Archaeologists have discovered that as the glaciers of the Ice Age receded some eleven thousand years ago, Clovis hunters butchered giant mammoth near this same route Hunt followed over the Bighorns.

A band of mounted Crow crossed the Bighorns in tandem with Hunt, displaying "truly remarkable" horsemanship.

"There, among others," marveled Hunt, "was a child tied to a two-year-old colt. He held the reins in one hand and frequently used his whip. I asked about his age and was told that he had seen two winters. He did not yet talk!"

The Overland Party dropped from the crest of the Bighorns down into the first of the valleys, lying between the giant corrugations.

They were in what is today north-central Wyoming, near the Yellow-stone region. The three trappers—Robinson, Reznor, and Hoback—had some familiarity with this terrain, as they had vouched when they had first met Hunt's party on the Missouri. They guided the party on horseback upstream along the Wind River through a beautiful and treeless high valley. The tall patches of nostril-tingling sagebrush and thickets of ripe gooseberry bushes brushed the horses' flanks. With splashing, clunking hooves fording the Wind River's gravel bars, their horses negotiated the tumbled rocks scoured clean from the past spring's torrential mountain snowmelts. They saw no bison here. Wary of the fierce grizzly bear lurking in the berry patches, but unable to approach the more docile black bears near enough to kill them, they instead fished in the river for trout or grayling to supple-ment their dwindling supplies of dried bison meat.

They left the narrowing valley of the Wind River and, bearing west, followed an Indian trail that crested another of those great cor-rugations, known as the Wind River Range. It was while crossing this nine-thousand-foot-high pass on September 15, 1811, that one of the three trappers climbed a slope above the pass's notch and scanned the jumbled terrain unfolding below and to the west. There their land-mark stood, clearly visible even at sixty miles' distance—three jag-ged, snowcapped peaks rising in a cluster like shark's teeth, nearly a mile above the surrounding landscape. At the foot of those mountains, said Robinson, ran the headwater stream that would take the party to the Columbia River.

The Overland Party celebrated.

"[The three mountains] were hailed by the travellers," wrote Wash-ington Irving, in his account of Astor's enterprise, "with that joy with which a beacon on a seashore is hailed by the mariners after a long and dangerous voyage. . . ."

Wilson Price Hunt, weighted by his Yankee reserve and need for geographic grounding in this unmapped wilderness, called them the Pilot Knobs. The buoyant French-Canadian voyageurs called them as they saw them, the Trois Tetons—"the three breasts." It's the voya-geurs' name that has stuck for these grand mountains that tower above today's Jackson Hole, Wyoming.

Robinson, Reznor, and Hoback had been right. At the base of those mountains flowed a river westbound for the Pacific Ocean. Once they reached that headwater stream, it would be an easy paddle to the Columbia and the rendezvous with Astor's ship at the Pacific Coast. The start of the great Pacific empire now lay in sight.

It took another month of walking, until mid-October, before they actually stepped into canoes and embarked on the river journey to the Columbia and Pacific. First they had to restock their meat supplies and build canoes. They also had to ensure, as best they could, that they'd chosen the right river to descend to the Pacific. Here, in the Teton and Yellowstone region, they had entered a confusing and uplifted complex of mountains, valleys, and drainages that, in some ways, is an apex of the North American continent. Within a hundred or so miles of each other, several major rivers begin here and flow in different directions across western North America, like water poured on top of a rounded but fissured boulder that trickles down four different sides. For the next few weeks, they would work their way over that rounded, fissured boulder until they reached the river that flowed west.

When they had stood at the crest of the Wind River Range, spot-ting the Trois Tetons in the distance, the explorers had just crossed the Continental Divide, leaving behind the tributary rivers that flowed eastward to the Missouri. Just over the divide they spent a few days stalking and shooting bison in a high valley at the headwaters of what they called the "Spanish River." They met Shoshone Indians hunting bison with bows and arrows, who told them this river flowed far to the south, to settlements of the Spanish.* Hunt bought two thousand

---

* This was a remarkable—and accurate—piece of geographic knowledge that the Shoshone hunters gave to the Hunt Party. Hunt's "Spanish River" was in fact what we today know as the Green River, a main branch of the Colorado. It flows all

pounds of dried bison from these Shoshone hunters, supplementing another four thousand pounds the Overland Party had just hunted and dried themselves. The party traveled northwest from the Spanish River headwaters and soon crossed another low divide. Following a stream downward, they met a swift-flowing river that the three trappers recognized—the river that flowed past the base of the Tetons and would lead them to the Columbia. Due to its swift current, the American trappers called it, reported Hunt, the "Mad River."

The French-Canadian voyageurs clamored to paddle it. Hunt, however, had reservations about embarking on their canoe voyage right here. While the Mad River flowed swiftly through riffles and bends, no large rapids were readily visible. On the other hand, he didn't like the way the Mad River abruptly swung around the southern end of the Trois Tetons, heading west, toward the Pacific, but then disappeared from sight into an adjacent mountain range.

Despite his own reservations, he polled the group, attentive to both the harmony within the group and his orders from Mr. Astor.

He posed the question: Should they build canoes here and descend this swift unknown river that leads westward into a mountain range, or should they continue to trek on foot, much more slowly, toward the Columbia?

Almost everyone voted to paddle down the Mad River by canoe. Thus did the gentle-handed Hunt once again shape a consensus among a large, and culturally disparate group, so unlike the fierce and fractious leadership of Captain Thorn aboard the *Tonquin*. Hunt had shown himself a master at cannily appealing to others' desires. A few weeks earlier, a rogue trapper named Edward Rose, who had been living with the Crow Indians, had joined the Overland Party. On hearing rumors

the way from northwestern Wyoming and, after joining the Colorado and coursing through the Grand Canyon, enters the Gulf of California near what then were Spanish missions in Sonora, Mexico, and Baja California. The Shoshone hunters a thousand miles to the north knew this geography and knew of the far-off settlements, in 1811, even though many of them had never seen a white man.

that the "very unpleasant and insolent" Rose planned to incite members of the Hunt party to desert, steal the party's horses, and join the Crow, Hunt had ably defused the threat. He graciously offered Rose a half year's wages and traps to go off on his own, which Rose accepted as a good deal.

In spite of such efforts, there comes a juncture in the geography of the unknown where the power of the terrain itself can shred the delicate web of consensus.

Problems arose even before they started building canoes. First it was a matter of materials. Birch bark, as the French Canadians two centuries earlier had learned from Indians on the East Coast, made the perfect hull covering for a lightweight, maneuverable canoe. But the right kind of birches didn't grow in these western mountains. The voyageurs instead planned to hew canoes from hollowed-out tree trunks—an acceptable, while clumsier and heavier, alternative to the birch-bark canoe. But the party discovered that the spruce trees growing near the Mad River were gnarled with too many tough knots to carve with axes, while the softer cottonwoods along its banks were too small to hollow into durable one-piece canoe hulls.

As the voyageurs wrestled with the materials issue in these mountain valleys where altitude and cold stunted tree growth, Hunt sent a small scouting party led by John Reed, a game young Irish clerk, down along the riverbank on horseback to explore the Mad River where it disappeared into the mountain range. Three days later, Reed returned saying he'd followed the river into an impassable canyon, choked with too many rapids for canoes, too steep for horses to pass along the riverbank, and too rugged even to traverse on foot.

"So far as Mr. Reed could see," reported Hunt, "the river continued to flow through the heart of the mountains."

But Robinson, Hoback, and Reznor spoke up again. They knew of *another* headwater river, located just on the *other* side of the Trois Tetons, that also flowed to the Columbia. The year before, they had wintered on its banks in the makeshift cabins with Andrew Henry after fleeing the Blackfeet at Three Forks. The river was placid, the three trappers reported, the trees on its banks large and abundant. This, the group decided, would serve as a better spot to build their canoes and launch downstream toward the Pacific.

A Shoshone camping with them along the Mad River knew an easy pass over the Tetons frequently traveled by Indians. On October 5, after a two-day storm had plastered the rocky spires of the Tetons white with snow, the Overland Party crossed what is today called Teton Pass, just west of Jackson, Wyoming, and dropped into a high, wide, pleasant valley on its far side—"a beautiful plain," as Hunt described it (today's Teton Valley, Idaho). Snow melted in the still-warm October sun. Within a few short, easy days of traveling across the pretty valley, they had reached the abandoned huts that Andrew Henry and the fleeing trappers, among them the three Kentuckians, had built the year before. These sat on the bank of a gentle river one hundred yards wide that meandered through grassy meadows and willow bushes, interspersed with groves of big cottonwood trees turning yellow in autumn. They saw abundant signs of beaver. Looking back across the valley the way they'd come, they had a clear view of the Tetons' snowy and rocky peaks.

"[T]he mountain," reported Hunt, "we believed was our last."

Although the season was growing late—it was now early October—they'd arrived at the start of their final leg to the Pacific and the foundation of John Jacob Astor's empire. They weren't overly worried. Headed downstream by canoe and leaving the mountains, they could cover distance much more quickly than by foot and horse. They weren't entirely sure how far off the Pacific Ocean might be, or exactly where they would join the Columbia. They had neither the equipment—sextant and chronometer—nor the mathematical skills to take longitude, which would have definitively established their distance from the Pacific Coast. But they thought it couldn't be far off. They didn't realize that the mouth of the Columbia still lay hundreds and hundreds of miles away and nearly five thousand feet below them. Even a sextant, however, couldn't have told them of the horrors that lay between here and there.

On October 19, 1811, they left their horses in the high valley's rich, grassy meadows with two young Shoshone Indians, promising to return. The members of the Overland Party then stepped into the fifteen large and heavily loaded canoes they'd hewn from massive cottonwood trunks. It was a joyous moment, especially for the voyageurs, delighted to dismount horses and get on the water, trading the clunking of hooves over dry stones for the swish and drip of the paddle. Pushing off from the bank into the steady current of this unknown river, they now pushed beyond the absolute limits of the white man's knowledge of western North America.

The smooth river twisting through the high valley meadows resonated with their songs and with the cadence of their strokes.

> *Three bonnie ducks go swimming 'round,*
> *On, roll on my ball, on!*
> *The prince goes off a-hunting bound,*
> *On, roll on my ball, on!*

I T WAS GLORIOUS TO BE ON THE WATER, AT FIRST. THE LIT-tle river wound smoothly through a broad, high mountain valley dotted with grassy meadows and groves of old cottonwood trees. The voyageurs paddled rhythmically to chansons sung out by the fifteen steersmen who swung the big canoes agilely around the river's tight bends and along its willow banks, heading generally southwest. Autumn-yellow leaves fluttered down and settled on the gentle swirls of current. A few miles to their left, or eastward, rose the great barrier of the Tetons they had just crossed, the gray rock spires of its uppermost peaks veined with white from winter's first snowfall.

No European had paddled this river. No European knew where it ran. It was a guess, as if they had taken up a random piece in a vast geographic puzzle that measured a thousand or more miles across and now tried to click that piece into its proper place. Likely from Indian information and its westward flow, the partners, Hunt and Crooks, Mackenzie and McClellan, believed this small river eventually joined a branch of the Columbia and would lead them to the "great salt lake"— the Pacific Ocean.

Despite the gentle current and beautiful scenery, the weather was brisk that first day. Flocks of ducks and geese bobbed in the riverbank eddies, driven down from the north by the first wave of cold. The paddlers pointed out to one another encouraging signs of beaver in the form of gnawed trees and stick-built lodges. Periodic snow flurries swept across the little river in white veils, casting the flotilla in shades of gray, with the voyageurs in their *capotes,* or hooded cloaks, like a procession of singing monks gliding down the smooth water. They were happy. These "Men of the North" well knew this weather and this paddling. Winter was coming. But as they believed they had crossed the final range of the Rockies, the Pacific felt near.

They paddled the small river's twisting course nearly thirty miles that first day. The smaller river then joined a larger flow. This was the Mad River. It coursed in from their left, or east, after exiting the mountain range south of the Tetons that had so frustrated John Reed on his scouting foray a few weeks earlier. They found this encouraging, too.

"As we went on downstream," Hunt recorded, "the river became more beautiful and much larger. . . ."

The combined flow of the two rivers left the mountains, which began to recede in the distance behind them. Ahead lay a broad lava plain stubbled with sagebrush, where the riverbed widened to more than a thousand feet. Hunt noted that it could easily float a canoe of any size—good information to have when establishing Mr. Astor's network of fur posts in these unknown regions. The Mad River—or the Canoe River, as Hunt dubbed it, putting the best possible spin on its name as an artery to carry future fur commerce—danced along in a clear, beautiful green. The river cut through the broad lava plain, straightening and gaining speed, as if to whisk them, and future loads of Mr. Astor's furs, straight to the Pacific, thence across to China, to complete the great, golden triangle trade.

On the second day, they had paddled nearly forty miles when, late in the day, they heard rapids. Typically the lead canoe guided the way. Its bowman scouted the best route between the boulders and among the waves, through the holes and tongues of current, pulling the bow with his paddle this way and that to avoid the obstacles, while, in the stern, the steersman pried on his paddle like a rudder to swing the stern about to follow the bow. In one sense, the Overland Party stood at a disadvantage on the Mad River. Their cottonwood canoes were heavier and less maneuverable than the lightweight birch-bark canoes of the North. Moreover, each craft was freighted with many hundreds of pounds of dried meat, trade goods, and trapping equipment as well as four or five paddlers and passengers. This hefty weight settled the canoes deep in the water, allowing relatively little freeboard—the distance between the upper edge of the canoe and the river's surface. It was precisely for situations like this, however, that John Jacob Astor, through his proxies Hunt and Mackenzie, had hired the finest canoeists available—the Canadian voyageurs. Awkward canoes or not, this was their element.

Although the rapids that second day were relatively mild, waves poured over the gunwales of two of the heavily laden canoes. The added weight of the water settled them still deeper in the turbulent current. The two craft took in more water, then swamped, filling to the gunwales like an overflowing bathtub, losing all maneuverability and stability as they swept downstream.

"I sent my canoe and one other to the rescue," wrote Hunt in his journal.

The rescuers managed to pluck all the men from the water, but couldn't corral one of the two swamped canoes. It washed away downstream, carrying off its load of trade goods, food, and traps.

Food was important, merchandise crucial. The Overland Party needed all the trade goods possible to establish the sprawling network of fur posts planned for this western slope of the Rockies. Already they had laid the first foundations of this interior trade. Two weeks earlier, while still on the east side of the Tetons, Hunt had split off the first "string" or "leash" of trappers to work these headwater streams, which appeared rich in beaver and untrapped by whites.

An estimated 60–400 million beaver had lived in North American rivers and streams before the arrival of Europeans. The continent's largest rodent, weighing twenty-five to seventy pounds and able to stay underwater for up to fifteen minutes with one breath, makes its home along streams and rivers, ponds and lakes. It has an astonishing ability to create its own ideal habitat by building dams across streams to create ponds. Gnawing through branches and cutting down trees with powerful jaws and chisel-like teeth, it drags sticks and branches to the stream, plants them in mud, and interweaves other branches to dam the water's flow. In the pond backed up by its dam, the beaver builds its lodge, surrounded by water, by assembling a great mass of sticks and branches that protrudes a few feet above the pond's surface, sealing it with mud and hollowing out chambers in which to spend the winter and raise its young, protected from foxes and other predators. Beneath the pond's surface, it stores a supply of aspen or willow branches or other vegetation to eat during the winter.

Its lodge remained nearly impenetrable, but the beaver's system of marking its territory made it vulnerable to trappers. While its eyesight is poor, its sense of smell is acute. Small scent glands located near its genitals produce a powerful substance called castoreum, which they use to mark their territory, applying it to mud and stick piles that they constantly maintain and check for the scent of other beaver. Fur trappers exploited this habit by pounding a stake in the pond's water and attaching to it a chain about five feet long with a trap at the end. Having set the trap at pond's edge a few inches underwater, trappers would smear an unguent of beaver scent and spices on a stick and place it on the bank just above the trap, splashing it with water to erase any human scent. Smelling the scent from as far as two hundred yards away, the resident beaver would swim over to check it out. As the rodent climbed onto the bank, the trap would close around its leg. When it tried to swim away to escape, the heavy trap and chain would pull the beaver underwater, drowning it.

The trappers worked in pairs, or groups—the "leashes" that Hunt released from the main group. The first leash had split off on the other side of the Tetons. While the voyageurs hewed the cottonwood canoes, after crossing the Tetons, Hunt had split off another leash that included the three Kentucky hunters, Robinson, Hoback, and Reznor, plus another trapper, Martin Cass. As they made their preparations to leave the Overland Party, Joseph Miller, the Baltimore gentleman and military officer turned adventurer, announced to the amazement—even shock—of everyone that he would not be going to the Pacific Coast with Hunt's Overland Party after all. He would instead join the Kentucky trappers. Even though he stood to profit enormously from them, he "threw in" his two and a half shares of John Jacob Astor's enterprise and quit.

Hunt tried to convince him to continue to the Pacific. He promised Miller, an acquaintance from St. Louis whom he had urged to join the venture in the first place, passage on the first Astor ship back to New York. Miller, known to be stubborn, adamantly refused.

"[He] had been in a gloomy and irritable state of mind for some time past," wrote Irving, who surely heard this directly from one of the participants, "being troubled with a bodily malady that rendered travelling on horseback extremely irksome to him. . . ."

One wonders what malady plagued him. Saddle sores? Bad back? Hemorrhoids? Any of these would have been painful, especially on the wooden saddles they used, but Irving was too delicate to say. Here was one example of how some mundane but acutely persistent pain could make an extremely strenuous expedition unbearable. Miller also resented the fact that he had been given only half the stock as the other partners—two and a half shares to their five each. The Overland Party had traveled exactly twelve months and some two thousand miles since St. Louis, as far as Joseph Miller would go. Even Wilson Price Hunt's diplomatic skills couldn't smooth over this fracture as his party pushed deeper into the unknown.

On the third day, the banks of the Mad River steepened. The paddlers glimpsed exposed masses of black basalt, the lava rock that so long ago had bubbled up from within the earth and spread in a great flow, hardening into ledges and angular, hexagonal-like columns that undergirded the broad sagebrush plain. That day the river's breadth, formerly a thousand feet, narrowed, spilling into a tight channel, as if the hardening sheet of lava had split with a long crack. For about half a mile, the river squeezed to a mere sixty feet wide, then tumbled over a ledge of lava rock in a low waterfall. Accustomed to portages, able to haul two hundred pounds on their backs, the voyageurs cleared the canoes of passengers, hefted the packets of trade goods and gear, and carried them around on the riverbank. They then "lined" the empty canoes through the rapids with ropes, lowering the craft through the churning water while holding the ropes from shore.

They made only six miles that day. The next day, their fourth on the river, they made only six miles more, negotiating another two portages, capsizing a smaller canoe, and dumping more supplies, including dried bison meat, into the river. The first flickers of doubt arose. Just where did this river lead? No one knew. They met no natives along the bank who could tell them, and the river itself was not saying.

By the fifth day they were learning how to negotiate the Mad River and made good distance on fast water, seventy-five miles, portaging their baggage in a few patches of rougher water to lighten the canoes. Running generally southwest, the river bent through cottonwood and willow bottomlands in another shallow valley cut through the lava plains. Sagebrush and fescue grew on the riverbanks, amid scattered, ground-hugging lobes of prickly pear cactus. Flocks of ducks and geese quacked ahead of them, pausing on their autumn migration from the North, paddling along in great rafts down the river, occasionally taking flight with the rushed beating of wings and splashing of feet on water, only to glide down again, farther ahead of the canoes, with an attenuated *ploosh* followed by contented quacking as they settled in.

The Overland Party usually didn't bother to hunt them—too much time and ammunition for too little meat. They wanted big animals. The hunters spotted a few old bison tracks on the arid sagebrush plain above the river, but no bison.

More than anything, Hunt sought information, and late on the fifth day they saw their first humans on the river—a small band of Shoshone

Indians camped onshore. When Hunt tried to approach, the Indians fled. A short ways downstream, the flotilla met three more Shoshone crossing the river on a raft made of bundled reeds, naked except for a stole of hare skin draped over the shoulders. Hunt attempted to ask the Indians if they knew what lay ahead, but the Shoshone sheered away, avoiding him. After portaging around a thirty-foot-high waterfall and rapids and losing more trade goods to swamped canoes, they spotted another Shoshone camp. These ran, too. But one Shoshone mounted on horseback apparently felt more secure. Hunt managed to signal him with friendly signs back to the riverbank.

It was an unvarnished meeting of wildly disparate cultures. The Shoshone clearly had never seen a European before, much less a large party of them. The blue eyes of Northern Europeans set in hairy faces—like the eyes of a wolf—disconcerted Native Americans. It would not be a great leap for the Shoshone man to identify these strange creatures as animal spirits in human form. This spiritual power granted to him by the Shoshone, however, worked against Hunt and his Overland Party in this case.

"[H]is fear of us was so great," wrote Hunt, "that I could not get him to show me, by sign language, the route that I should take. His only concern was that I not take away his fish and meat and that I commend him to the care of the Great Spirit."

Perhaps the question simply didn't make sense to the Shoshone: Why would a fellow being of the Great Spirit need to know what route to follow? Why ask the Shoshone and not the Great Spirit? Or perhaps the trembling Shoshone simply didn't know a trail to the great salt lake to the west.

Unanswered, they carried on. The flotilla made seventy miles that day, their seventh, the river now swinging almost due west across the lava plains. The next day, the eighth, they made a good forty. The river broadened again, to half a mile, with lots of beaver lodges. It rained. Could wetter weather indicate the ocean lay near? At this brisk pace— averaging some fifty miles a day on the seventh day and eighth days—

in ten days more they could make five hundred miles. The Pacific couldn't lie many days away. The river might serve as a fine conduit for Mr. Astor's furs to the great emporium at the Columbia's mouth.

Even after splitting off two leashes of trappers, they remained a very large party of about fifty-six people in fourteen canoes, having lost one boat. Hunt still led the group. Ramsay Crooks rode in the second canoe, helping to navigate with the popular veteran steersman Antoine Clappine behind him at the stern paddle. McClellan, the Indian fighter of the hair-trigger temper, rode in one of the canoes, as did Mackenzie, the former Northwester of deep wilderness experience. Additionally there were John Day, the Virginia hunter; John Reed, the young Irish clerk; plus the Dorion family; and some forty voyageurs, for whom these long days on the river, paddling tens of thousands of strokes, was routine.

On the ninth day, October 28, 1811, however, the routine changed. The river channel tightened. On each bank, lava walls rose sharply in gray-black columns of basalt, clumps of minty sagebrush and tufts of tawny autumn grasses sprouting from cliff ledges. The current swiftened, the green water bunching up against the black walls and shoreline boulders. The lead canoe picked its way, bowman scanning for the best route, steersman prying his steering paddle to swing the stern around, calling out to the voyageurs the strokes he needed, while the other canoes followed.

They whisked through several rapids without mishap. Usually, in water like this, the canoeists would have pulled over to the riverbank periodically and taken the time to walk along the shore, to get a sense of what lay ahead. But their smooth, early run might have given them a false sense of security, and so as they approached the entrance to a canyon, the lead canoe didn't stop. The second canoe followed, carrying Crooks in the bow and Clappine in the stern with three voyageurs to paddle. Weaving down a swift channel between rocks, scouting ahead from the bow, Crooks spotted a midstream rock in their path. He called out a warning to Clappine, but the steersman didn't hear him, or Clappine didn't have time to pry the steering paddle, or call out to the other voyageurs and swing the heavy cottonwood canoe.

With a hollow thunk the cottonwood canoe slammed head-on into the basalt boulder. Like the cleaving blow of a giant axe, the impact instantly split the fragile hull along its length. Frigid, swirling water engulfed the hull and it rolled easily, spilling out its load of food and gear and voyageurs.

Crooks and one voyageur, both strong swimmers, struck for the safety of the riverbank. Stroking hard across rushing tongues of current, they managed to drag themselves to the rocky shore. The other two voyageurs and the steersman Clappine had far less confidence as swimmers. The threesome clung to the hull of the swamped canoe as it washed downstream like a half-sunken log, with Clappine clinging to its stern.

Clunk!

It slammed its bow end into another boulder. The two voyageurs clinging to the hull released their grip from the canoe and seized the big rock, scrambling onto it.

But Clappine, either from fright or lack of confidence in his ability to swim to the rock, held tight to the canoe's upstream end, its stern, his customary spot as a steersman. The current shoved against the hull and swung the canoe broadside. The canoe spun off the rock, propelling Clappine out into the middle of the powerful current.

His horrified companions watched the turbulent river sweep Clappine and the swamped hull toward the canyon's mouth. The lone head and the swamped canoe bobbed along helplessly. Then they tumbled over the lip of cascading rapids and disappeared from sight.

It was the emotional impact of losing Clappine that struck them first. A friend of all, a steersman with years of experience, he had a fine, powerful singing voice—a prerequisite for taking the stern of a voyageur's canoe. It would have been Clappine who started the rounds of singing, Clappine who prompted the voyageurs' response, Clappine who kept spirits high and kept them paddling and pushing onward.

A la claire fontaine
M'en allant promener,
J'ai trouvé l'eau si belle
Que je m'y suis baigné.

Lui ya longtemps que je t'aime,
Jamais je ne t'oublierai.

At the clear running fountain
sauntering by one day,
I found it so compelling
I bathed without delay

(Chorus from paddlers):
Your love long since overcame me,
Ever in my heart you'll stay

But they would hear his powerful voice no more. The canoes—now only thirteen of them—beached on the rocky shore. The voyageurs and partners and hunters combed the riverbanks up and down. There was no sign of Clappine, or of the split canoe or the trade goods it carried.

It was the Overland Party's first death. It stunned the group— "struck a chill," as Irving later phrased it, "into every bosom."

Then another reality began to sink in. They were at the head of a powerful rapid at the mouth of a canyon. Could they go forward in canoes from here?[*]

---

[*] In 1938, a local rancher panning for gold in the Snake River in a dry year found a corroded deposit of muskets, traps, and other equipment in the riverbed. It was near a rock that matched the description and location of the one that split open Crooks's canoe. These artifacts were later identified as being of the proper vintage to likely be its spilled cargo. From bulletin, "Idaho State Historical Society, Reference Series, Site of Ramsay Crooks 1811 Canoe Disaster, Number 1011, May 1993."

The following day, October 29, their tenth on the unknown river, Hunt trekked ahead with three other men, scouting downstream for a way to bring canoes down the gorge's north bank, while sending another small party to scout the south rim. It was his first time leading a scouting party of his own, and his choice to lead it was a measure of his concern. He didn't plan to stay out overnight. He had brought no food. It was the following day, after an unplanned night out, that he and his little party stumbled back into camp, exhausted and ravenous.

The river, Hunt reported to his fellow partners and the voyageurs, kept its course northwest through a gorge. It was, he said, "no more than sixty to ninety feet wide, it is full of rapids, and its course is broken by falls ten to forty feet high." He and his three men had walked for what they estimated was thirty-five miles along the gorge's north rim in desertlike sagebrush plains. In that entire distance they had discovered only two or three notches where they could even descend the two or three hundred feet down the gorge's cliffy sides to fetch water from the river. They had slept beside their fire on the desert rim, foraging a few rose hips for their supper.

The loss of Clappine now only underscored the deepening predicament of the entire party. At the main encampment, beside a thundering thirty-foot drop, Hunt and the partners conferred. The Scottish partners had dubbed it "Caldron Linn," after a famous waterfall in the Scottish Highlands. Just below it was the narrow gorge that Hunt had scouted, choked with one cascade after another, which they called the "Devil's Scuttle Hole," a term referring to a drainage valve in a ship's hull—presumably Satan's. The party scouting the south rim had walked about six miles downstream and discovered a notch in the gorge's steep side. This had possibilities. The group laid out a plan: Portage canoes and baggage the six miles from the camp at Caldron Linn around what appeared to be the worst of the gorge and descend to the river through this notch. Then they would negotiate whatever rapids lay farther downstream.

"Sixteen men, with four of our best canoes, went to attempt the passage," wrote Hunt.

Six miles was not an unusual distance for the voyageurs to portage. They easily carried canoes and baggage on their powerful shoulders over sagebrush plains and lava rock rather than northern forest and marsh. They negotiated the steep descent to the river without incident. Instead of paddling, they tried to line the canoes through the rapids with ropes. Almost immediately they lost one of the four canoes and all its trade goods. The other three canoes snagged among exposed rocks. Here they wedged fast, pinned by the thousands of pounds of pressure exerted by the current. Even the strong-armed voyageurs, shoving and tugging, were unable to budge them. Abandoning the three canoes, they trekked, disheartened, the six miles upstream to the main camp at Caldron Linn.

"We saw no way to continue our journey by water," reported Hunt.

Like the canoes, the Overland Party was now stuck. They couldn't go forward by canoe. They'd left their horses what they estimated was 340 miles upstream. They had no idea where this river might run, only that it eventually reached the Pacific. But their most immediate problem was this: food. Specifically, food to feed a party of fifty.

"Our situation became critical," reported Hunt. "We had enough food for about five days."

Unless one has experienced it personally, it is difficult to grasp the extraordinary amount of nutrition—raw calories, *food*—the human body demands to sustain itself during heavy exercise in cold weather. Under everyday living conditions, an average-sized adult male requires about 2,200 calories a day; a female 1,800 calories. Winter exertion demands at the very least twice that. The U.S. Army recommends for winter hiking a bare minimum of 4,500 calories. Cross-polar ski expeditions have shown that males making the trek burn 6,000 calories daily, or the equivalent of nine square meals per day, and females 3,000 calories.

Until this point, much of the European exploration of North America had been conducted by sailing ship or canoe, vessels capable of carrying many tons of food. Now the equation had changed dramatically. Hunt's party would have to go on foot. Without the horses they'd abandoned far upstream, and with their canoes stuck in the canyon, they could carry on their own backs relatively little food even if food were available. The Overland Party suddenly found itself trapped in the grim nutritional paradox of the higher latitudes: In winter an active human (unlike, say, a hibernating animal) needs far more food, though food is far harder to find.

With a pound of bison, elk, deer, or comparable lean game animal only offering about 600–800 calories, each person would need to consume three to five pounds of game meat per day (or its caloric equivalent in jerked meat, fat, or other foods) simply to maintain their energy over the many days' travel. To meet this relentless demand, Hunt's fifty-some-member overland expedition would have to kill and eat one large animal such as an elk (200–300 pounds of boneless meat) or bison (400–500 pounds of boneless meat) every three or four days or else the travelers would begin to starve. For these reasons—the tremendous caloric demands of winter travel and relative leanness of wild game—Native Americans and early travelers highly valued "fat meat" with its potent caloric punch, and could eat huge quantities over the course of several sittings.* Native hunters also knew that small parties can usually live off the land far more easily than large ones.

The three tons of bison jerky (or, in modern convenience-store terms, about 25,000 packets) that they had acquired on the other side of the Tetons barely had lasted a month. They had eaten some; they had lost some in the river. Bison and elk were nowhere to be found in the canyon at Caldron Linn, nor, it seemed, on the barren, dry lava plains above its rim. Hunt had wanted to travel in safety in the wilderness with a party large enough to hold off Indian attack—but, as he

---

* Early arctic explorers recorded individual Inuit hunters consuming fifteen pounds and more of meat in a twenty-four-hour period when they returned to their igloos after a successful hunt.

now discovered, with autumn giving way to winter, you also had to be able to feed a party so large.

Hunt now had to make his second big decision. As the situation grew dire, Hunt, consulting with the Scottish partners, mapped a new strategy. As he noted tersely in his journal on November 1, "we changed our plans."

In essence, several small reconnaissance parties led by different partners would split off from the main group and fan out looking for an avenue of escape or a source of food. If a reconnaissance party couldn't find an easy way out and if it couldn't report back to the main group, these small parties would simply keep going until reaching safety or the Columbia's mouth.

It was agreed that John Reed, whose status as clerk almost equaled that of the partners, should lead one small reconnaissance party that would head downriver, trying to locate nearby Shoshone camps and exchange trade goods for horses and food. Three other partners— McClellan, Mackenzie, and Crooks—would head in different directions with three small reconnaissance parties of "chosen" men, meaning those with the best wilderness skills. McClellan would lead a reconnaissance party downstream along the bank of the unknown Mad River to attempt to follow it to the Columbia. Mackenzie would lead a party northward, away from the Mad River, across the barren sagebrush plains toward distant mountains, hoping to hit the main stem of the Columbia more directly somewhere to the north. Another small reconnaissance party, led by Crooks, would strike off to re-cover the estimated 340 miles upstream where they'd left their horses and built canoes. He would bring back those horses to the main party. This main party would stay with Hunt, camped along the Mad River near Caldron Linn waiting for Crooks to arrive with the horses, and then use the horses to carry the expedition farther west to the Columbia or Pacific.

Having made the decision to split up, the Overland Party cached the extra baggage carried in the canoes. They hid tons of traps, trade

goods, and other supplies in six carefully camouflaged holes at Caldron Linn, planning to return for them. Then the reconnaissance parties separated from the big group of fifty and set off on their separate
ways, traveling on foot.

Hunt's main group, numbering thirty-four, paddled back upriver a
short distance from Caldron Linn, scouting for an obvious escape or
some source of food. They set nets but caught only a single fish. The
hunters brought in only a few beaver, whose meat Hunt ordered dried. A
few days after leaving, Crook and his small party returned to the main
group, also empty-handed. It was already early November. They realized they had no chance of traveling far enough upstream to retrieve the
horses before winter descended. Meanwhile, a messenger from John
Reed's downstream reconnaissance party returned, reporting that, as
far as they could see, the river persisted tumultuously through a gorge.

It was growing colder by the day. Their food supply was dwindling.
Delayed by his own logistics and the fruitless sojourn he had made
upstream, Hunt thrashed around for an escape from their predicament. The frustration erupted even in his own minimal journal, when
he reported that, on November 7, his main party returned downstream
to Caldron Linn.

"We had wasted nine days in futile explorations."

Hunt's inexperience with winter in the mountains had finally
caught up to him. His lack of urgency and the delays in months past
now converged with the imminent arrival of winter, the impassable
river, and the lack of food. It is in the nature of exploration that at times
a party hits a dead end, routes that don't "go," in the parlance of the
mountain climber. A guide who knows the terrain can help avoid these
impasses, and it's something of a mystery why Hunt didn't try harder
to find a Shoshone guide before they abandoned their horses and set
out in canoes on the Mad River. If the river were truly navigable by
canoe, the Native Americans in the region probably would have been
paddling it for thousands of years and would know its length and
features well. That he couldn't readily find someone to describe the

river might have been a clue as to what lay ahead. The combination of his lack of urgency, his lack of experience in the wilderness, and the implacable geography of this unknown terrain had now put Hunt in a very difficult spot.

Crooks suggested to Hunt that they further split up the main group, numbering about forty with the reconnaissance parties still absent, so they wouldn't require so much food. Hunt agreed. They decided both parties would head downstream, along the river, but on opposite sides, where at least they knew they'd have water to drink and hoped they'd have fish as well.

Caching more goods at Caldron Linn, they divided the main group into two parties of nineteen each, plus their respective leaders, Crooks and Hunt. Hunt, significantly, kept the Dorion family in addition to the nineteen others—with Marie now eight months pregnant—in his own group. Perhaps it was gentlemanliness; perhaps he intuitively understood the concept of group expeditions, reflected in an adage current among contemporary mountain climbers: A party is only as strong as its weakest member.

They divvied up the entire supply of food. Hunt distributed to each person in his party a ration of five and a quarter pounds of meat, in addition to which the group possessed a small quantity of corn, cooking fat, and bouillon tablets.

"That had to keep more than twenty people alive," he wrote of his portion.

Leaving Caldron Linn, the two parties of twenty, plus the Dorion family, started down opposite riverbanks on the morning of November 9, 1811, Hunt on the north rim of the gorge, Crooks on the south rim. Cliffs, rapids, and massive chunks of shoreline basalt made it virtually impossible to walk along the riverbank itself. Unencumbered by small children, Crooks's party quickly pulled ahead on the south rim and was soon lost from sight. Neither party had any idea where they were headed, or any notion of how many days that meager ration of food would need to last.

G EOGRAPHY IS DESTINY," NAPOLEON BONAPARTE ONCE
pronounced, referring to the fate of empires and armies. Tracing
Hunt's uncertain route through the Rockies in late fall of 1811, however, one could as easily say that "geology is destiny."

The Mad River continued to flow across a vast lava plain. Sagebrush covered the tablelands while in a canyon nearly three hundred
feet below, the river tumbled between walls of black basalt. Crooks
and his group had disappeared ahead on the canyon's south rim. Hunt
and his group walked through late autumn storm and sun over desert
stretches on the canyon's north rim. When the river spread and eased
into calmer stretches, the chunky basalt walls eased back and the travelers could climb down into the shallow canyon. There they followed
Indian trails directly along the riverbank until shelves of basalt narrowed the passage and forced them up to the rim again.

As one Astorian described this thirty-mile section they'd labeled
the "Devil's Scuttle Hole:"[F]or the greater part nothing that walks the
earth could possibly pass between [the precipices], & the water, which
in such places is never more than 40 yds wide, rushing with irresistible
force over a bed of such Rocks as makes the spray fly equal to the surf
of the Ocean, breaking violently on a lee Shore. . . ."

Marie Dorion now showed the large bulge in her belly of a child
soon due. She and the two small boys, Jean Baptiste and Paul, trekked
along uncomplainingly, the two-year-old Paul riding on her back. The

buffalo jerky, five and a quarter pounds per person, was long gone, and at times the party's rations were reduced to nothing but bouillon. They passed an occasional small Shoshone encampment along the river, its dwellings of reeds and grasses piled like haystacks.

"The women fled in such haste," wrote Hunt, "that they did not have time to take their children who could not walk, but simply covered them with straw. The poor little creatures were terrified when I lifted the straw to look at them. Even the men trembled, as though I were some ferocious animal."

Most Shoshone camps had little food to spare from the meager supplies they had gathered for the oncoming winter, but some willingly traded small amounts with Hunt.

"I bought two dogs," he recorded with satisfaction at one stop, "and we ate one for breakfast."

They trekked about twenty to thirty miles per day—an exhausting, weakening pace on so little food. One group of Shoshone communicated that a party of whites recently had come through on the same trail, and still another group of whites had followed the Mad River on the opposite bank. This gave Hunt some reassurance. The first group must have been one of the smaller reconnaissance parties led by Mackenzie or McClellan. The party that the Shoshone reported seeing on the opposite banks must have been Crooks's party of twenty, which still had to be healthy and making progress. The Shoshone reported that the whites had dogs with them. Hunt figured they couldn't be starving entirely or else they would have eaten the dogs by then.

Another band of Shoshone pointed them on a shortcut across the lava plain. This would cut off a big, northward-sweeping bend of the Mad River, so they decided to take it. Cut off from the river, however, they were overcome by thirst, and the voyageurs drank their own urine, until a late-autumn rain puddled in rock hollows and gave relief. Then they reached a tributary of the Mad River—today's Boise River, west of Boise, Idaho. The tributary ran through a shallow, fertile, flat valley where grass and trees grew more lushly and the Indian encampments appeared wealthier. Hunt managed to buy from them a few horses to help carry gear and to provide a supply of meat, then led his party downstream to where the tributary joined the Mad River.

They had resumed their trek along the river, which now had swung around a huge rightward bend to flow toward the north, when another problem arose. Pierre Dorion, the Indian interpreter, had traveled beyond the Sioux languages he knew of the plains. Here, in what today is southwestern Idaho, the few inhabitants spoke Shoshone—the farthest north of the Aztec languages, which reach all the way down into Central America. It became increasingly difficult for Dorion and Hunt to get from the Shoshone clear answers to their questions about the geography that lay ahead, or even to determine whether the Shoshone knew the answer at all.

"On [November] 22nd we met some Indians," recorded Hunt. "As I gathered from the few words that I could understand, the distance from this spot to the Columbia was very considerable; but the Indians told me nothing about the route that I should take."

There was no one to ask. There were thousands of square miles of unknown terrain, and only the river to follow.

The Mad River now flowed due north. Hunt knew that somewhere to the north lay the Columbia. It made sense to follow the Mad River in that direction on the assumption it emptied into the Columbia. The Pacific Coast, he believed, still lay within reach before full-on winter set in.

As they trekked along its banks during these last days of November 1811, however, the Mad River exited the broad lava plain and entered barren foothills where it began to constrict and rush. Beyond the foothills loomed mountains. The Tetons, which they'd left hundreds of miles to their backs, were not, it now appeared, the range "that would be our last." Worse, the mountains ahead, Hunt ruefully observed, were "all covered with snow."

It was here that geology and destiny converged to determine the fate of the Overland Party. John Jacob Astor's West Coast empire may have unfolded quite differently were it not for a giant bubble of lava that percolates from the earth's molten interior and pushes close to its cool surface in today's northwestern Wyoming and eastern Idaho.

This bubble of lava bulges the landscape for many miles around, causing the headwater rivers of the Missouri and Columbia to spill in opposite directions from its highlands—the great creased boulder is actually a massive dome of lava. It spawns Yellowstone's famous geysers, hot springs, and earthquakes. But this lava bulge, known as the Yellowstone hot spot, has not remained in the same location relative to North America over the aeons. Rather, it has literally melted a giant channel across the tall ridges of the Rocky Mountains, as if the mountains were lumps of butter melting in a hot pan; or, as some geologists describe it, as if a blowtorch flame passed underneath a sheet of crumpled paper.

The geologic principle called plate tectonics shows that the earth is an enormous ball of molten lava. On it float giant rafts of cooled rock crust, or "plates." The North American plate drifts slowly westward at a speed of about one inch per year. The Pacific plate creeps eastward. Where the two plates collide along the West Coast, the Pacific plate dives under the North American plate, wrinkling up the earth's crust into mountain ridges and shoving it into deep trenches, as it did with the Rocky Mountains. As the North American plate inched westward during millions of years over the Yellowstone hot spot, which has remained stationary beneath the earth's crust, the hot spot, like the flame beneath the butter, melted a broad path through the Rocky Mountains. Today that melted path is known as the Snake River Plain. By following the Mad River, or the Snake, downstream from its headwaters on the hot spot's bulge, Hunt and his Overland Party were led into this great melted channel through the Rocky Mountains.

But then the Mad River suddenly left the lava plain. The terrain around it buckled. The river twisted its way into barren foothills, then steep mountains that squeezed the river, forcing Hunt's party to clamber up the slopes above its cliffy banks.

"We climbed mountains so high that I could hardly believe our horses would get over them," wrote Hunt. "The heights were covered with pines and snow. We could advance only with the greatest difficulty because of the sharp rocks, and the precipices plunge to the very banks of the river. . . ."

Due to his lack of hurry a few months earlier, at this decisive point in his journey, winter and mountains overtook Hunt at virtually the same moment.

> December 1—"[I]t rained in the valley and snowed in the mountains. As I climbed them to look for a passageway, I found the snow knee deep. . . . Snow fell so heavily on the mountain slopes we had to cross that visibility was no more than a half mile."

> December 2—"We were compelled to rest in camp. . . . The evening before we had caught a beaver, but as we had nothing more to eat I killed another horse."

> December 3—"Rain and snow fell all day. . . . [W]e traveled only nine miles. We unloaded our horses so that we could keep to our trail along the river, and we carried the baggage in our arms, trudging to the northeast."

The next day, December 4, strained them to the utmost. Again they dragged themselves up steep mountainsides above the river's cliffs, laboriously breaking a trail through new-fallen snow up to their knees. Winds blew across the snowy slopes, broken here and there by pine groves. The temperature plummeted. There were twenty of them, almost everyone on foot, with the Dorion toddlers carried on a horse or Marie's back. One can picture Hunt's party trudging along, heads down in a hunched file, breathing hard, occasionally looking up—the cold skies scouring the mountaintops, the steep fields of endless white skirting down, fractured here and there by black cliffs or gray-green swaths of pine. As daylight dims, the cold sharpens. The whiteness deepens to shades of purples and grays. They need to stop for the night. A profound chill takes hold inside one's core the moment one stops climbing and the sweat from panting uphill exertion begins to freeze.

"We were nearly exhausted by the harshness of the weather," recorded Hunt, "when we had the good luck of reaching a patch of pine trees at sunset."

The grove offered shelter from frigid winds and deep snow. They heaped up a bonfire from dead pine boughs and pressed around it, gratefully warming themselves and ripping into the last of their roasted horse meat.

"Although we had struggled ahead all day," wrote Hunt, "we were, because of the twisting course of the river, only four miles from our camp of the day before."

On the fifth the weather turned worse. A heavy snowstorm blew in, swirling on the mountain winds. As the party left their pine grove camp the storm worsened. Snow and wind and cloud churned into a whiteout. Dragging themselves across the snowy mountainside, the party could see only three hundred feet ahead through the blowing snow. From far below, they heard the distant, wavering roar of the Mad River's rapids.

Guided only by the sound of the rapids rushing somewhere in the whiteness far below, they slipped and skittered on their moccasins down the precipitous slopes, the dim shapes of pine trees floating upward past them like gray ghosts as they descended. The horses struggled down, too, under their loads, one of them suddenly slipping. It tumbled down the slope for several hundred feet. Amazingly, it wasn't hurt, its fall perhaps softened by the deep snow. But that night, when the party camped along the Mad River's banks, where the storm was milder and pelted rain on top of slushy, ankle-deep snow, Hunt ordered one of their last two horses slaughtered. Hunt was no longer squeamish about horse meat, as he'd been just ten days earlier when he recoiled at eating a horse he considered a friend.

The next day brought a deeply unpleasant surprise.

"On the 6th," reported Hunt, "to my astonishment and distress I saw Mr. Crooks and his people on the other side of the river."

So hungry and exhausted they could barely stay upright, Crooks and his party of nineteen were struggling along the opposite riverbank the wrong way—*upstream*. As soon as they saw Hunt's party they yelled at the top of their voices for food. Hunt quickly ordered his men to construct a bullboat, using the hide of a slaughtered horse wrapped around a bowl-shaped wooden frame. He sent across one of the voyageurs, Sardepie, to deliver fresh horse meat to the starving men and brought back the group's leader, Ramsay Crooks, and another voyageur, Le Clerc. As the bullboat neared the bank with the passengers, Hunt and company were startled to see how wasted and dejected his counterpart leader and partner had become since they parted a month earlier.

Crooks ate ravenously. Then he talked. He and his group had traveled down the left-hand or south bank of the river (which, as the river swung to the north, became the west bank). The land was especially arid and barren. They encountered few Shoshone. The Indians whom they did meet possessed barely enough food for themselves. His party fell woefully short of rations. For the first eighteen days, Crooks reported, they ate only half a meal each day; then for three days after that they ate a beaver they'd killed, wild cherries, and old moccasin soles. For the last six days all twenty of them had been living off the flesh and entrails of a single dog that had accompanied them. They had seen Mackenzie's and Reed's parties moving along the right bank, but had no way of crossing over to them.

From where he met Hunt, Crooks and his party had already traveled three days farther down the Mad River, with the hope that it would soon join the Columbia. But progress had proved excruciatingly difficult. Cliffs dropped straight into the water, he reported. The river roared through a narrow gorge in an almost continuous stretch of rapids. They had tried to skirt above the cliffs that dropped to the water. The only way past was to climb a mountain that rose steeply from the river. For half a day Crooks and his men trudged upward through snow. They reached a knob that offered a view. They saw they had not yet climbed even halfway from the riverbank over the steep mountain that flanked it. From the heights, they had hoped to see the broad Columbia River plain lying ahead, leading gently to the Pacific. Instead they spotted snowy mountain after snowy mountain stretching as far as they could see. Far, far below them, the river ran. It had entered a monstrous gorge, and after that tremendous effort of climbing, they were still not even halfway up its flank.

Weak, starving, exhausted, they simply didn't possess the strength to go forward into the gorge, to pull themselves over the cliffs and mountains that lined the river's edges. They realized their only hope was to turn around and head back upstream.

"It was impossible for men in their condition to get through," Hunt recorded.

This huge mountain gorge that engulfed the Overland Party is known today as Hells Canyon, of the Snake River. Measuring a mile and a half deep, it is the deepest gorge in all of North America—nearly half again as deep as the Grand Canyon. It is here that the Mad River— the Snake—exits that broad lava plain melted through the Rockies by the Yellowstone hot spot. Veering northward, the river tumbles into an ancient trench creased into the earth's crust by the collision of the Pacific and North American plates. It was almost a topographic inevitability that set Hunt on this doomed route. The geology and hydrology of the huge unmapped region they attempted to traverse had captured the wandering Hunt and his Overland Party, as if they were droplets of rainfall or snowmelt headed toward the Pacific, and funneled them directly into this awesome crack in the earth.

Hunt now faced another dilemma about how to proceed. In this case it was made far more desperate by the alarming weakness of both parties, the near-total lack of food, the rapid onset of winter, and the profound depth of the canyon. Should they struggle ahead down the unknown course of the Mad River toward the Columbia? Set off overland across the snowy mountains? Head upstream the way they'd come in hopes of finding Shoshone Indian settlements and food?

Hunt could see that, in essence, they were trapped in the huge gorge with no good options, no food, and failing men.

"I spent the night reflecting on our situation," recorded Hunt. "I had to answer for the needs of more than twenty famished people and, moreover, to do all that I could for Mr. Crooks and his men."

Hunt carried in his bags a letter of credit from Astor that could buy virtually any of the world's goods—shiploads of silk, herds of horses, or warehouses of food. But Mr. Astor's money was worthless here. Hunt had traveled far beyond the known map of the world, beyond its linked networks of civilized amenities, beyond Astor's ability to work the levers of control he operated from his headquarters in lower Manhattan, and had stumbled into this giant, unknown crack in the earth.

The physical sight of Crooks that day had come as a shock. Hunt had never seen anything like this skeletal creature stumbling along the fractured, rocky shore, someone who just a month earlier had strode the solid earth a healthy man. In Crooks, Hunt witnessed firsthand the onset of the process known as catabolism—when the body eats its own fat and muscle tissue in order to keep its vital organs functioning. John Jacob Astor's blanket letter of credit could do nothing to stop that.

As Hunt tossed that night, he must have realized what a serious mistake it had been to give up the 120 horses in favor of the faster, but far less certain, canoes. Once they had abandoned the canoes at Caldron Linn and taken to foot travel, they had broken into smaller groups, like native bands of hunters, with the hope of living off the land more easily. But to look at Ramsay Crooks made it difficult to see this strategy as successful. Typically, the human body can endure about a month without food, depending in part on its quantity of stored fat. After that, the catabolic process first consumes extraneous muscle, breaking the protein of the muscle fibers down into energy. This way the body saves the vital organs like the heart and nervous system for last to keep itself alive. There comes, however, a point of no return, when the process of catabolism has so damaged the mechanism that converts muscle protein to energy that it no longer functions.

Hunt doesn't mention it in his journal, but Crooks's voice may well have taken on the deep, mournful tone—"sepulchral," is how Arctic explorer journals in the decades ahead would describe it—of the explorer whose body has begun to digest itself during a hard, cold overland journey in order to stay alive.

Hunt was keenly aware that all forty of them could end up like Crooks. He was trapped in North America's deepest gorge with a choice between bad and worse. If they stayed here, they would starve. But to move in any direction at all, they'd have to leave behind several members of Crooks's group who were too debilitated from their exertions to travel any farther.

Did Hunt, the seeker of consensus, known almost universally as a nice fellow, have it in him simply to cast off the failing men? It was no longer a matter of wealth, and empire, and growing rich. They were fighting to stay alive, and Hunt was fighting to save them.

A s THAT HOLIDAY SEASON OF 1811 STARTED IN NEW YORK City, and snow drifted down and mufflers appeared on the coach-men in the streets, John Jacob Astor felt very good about his plans. As far as he knew, the advance party aboard the *Tonquin* had begun con-struction of the great emporium, had sailed up the Northwest Coast and loaded a cargo of precious sea otter furs, and was now sailing in the *Tonquin* across the Pacific to Canton to trade the furs for porce-lains and silks to bring back to New York. Just two months earlier, in October 1811 Astor, had dispatched a follow-up supply ship, the *Beaver,* to the West Coast emporium. It, too, would then sail to China laden with furs and return to New York with Chinese luxuries. And Astor had still a third ship at sea, which preceded the whole endeavor. This was the *Enterprise,* sent to the Northwest Coast for furs and to China two years earlier. She was due to return to New York soon with her rich load of teas, silks, and porcelains, completing the loop of ships cir-cling the globe and returning their enormous profits to Astor's office in New York.

With his global triangle trade in motion, Astor could enjoy a pleas-ant holiday season with Sarah and the children in their double brick house at 223 Broadway, savoring the warmth of its glowing fireplaces and surrounded by family. Sarah no doubt insisted that the family, bundled in the best fur, attend Christmas services at the Reformed Church, where she was a devout member, and encouraged John

Jacob to attend. There would be holiday dinners with close friends and relatives—her relatives, the Brevoorts and the Todds, or John Jacob's prosperous meat-merchant brother Henry and his beautiful wife, Dorothea. Dining by candlelight, they'd eat browned roasts, served on Sarah and John Jacob's best silver (they treasured their fine set of "plate"), and drink good Madeira wine. John Jacob liked to send a couple of large casks of Madeira to sea in the holds of his ships to give the sweet wine an extra-mellow aging, enjoying it with friends when it had reached a perfect ocean-rolled maturity.

Glittering in one of the two drawing rooms of the Astor house may have stood a Christmas tree, an old German custom, although not yet adopted generally by Americans.* There was far less emphasis on Christmas gift-giving in America at the time, although friends exchanged visits between their homes over Christmas and New Year's, and plenty of revelry and pot-banging raucousness went on in taverns and streets among the city's coarser inhabitants. Besides, the Astor household, once full of small children, slowly had started to empty. Only three of the five children remained at home for the festivities of 1811.

Four years earlier, Magdalen Astor, then nineteen, had married a Danish, multilingual former diplomat, Adrian Bentzon. Astor lent the newlyweds one of his properties on Manhattan Island—the graceful country estate known as Richmond Hill, occupying a landscaped knoll overlooking the Hudson just south of Greenwich Village (near today's Holland Tunnel entrance). Richmond Hill had formerly belonged to the high-living Aaron Burr, who, after his duel with Alexander Hamilton, had left politics, survived a trial for treason, and, deeply in debt, finally

---

* It is a historical coincidence that here, in New York City, during the Christmas of only two years earlier, the jolly, portly, gift-giving character we now know as "Santa Claus" was fleshed out, if not quite fully invented, as a Christmas character by none other than Washington Irving, then a young New York lawyer starting a writing career with publication of his comic, mock-history *Knickerbocker's History of New York* (1809).

took off for Europe in 1808. Recognizing a good distressed property when he saw one, Astor purchased Burr's Richmond Hill estate for cheap and let the young couple live in its airy, pillared main house. Astor soon recruited his urbane Danish son-in-law, with his diplomat's experience, to travel to Russia to help advance his great plan for the West Coast empire.

Giving Bentzon detailed instructions, Astor used his government contacts to secure his daughter and her husband berths aboard a U.S. Navy frigate bound for Europe. They arrived in Russia in the summer of 1811. Bentzon was to negotiate with Russian authorities the final details of a contract that would give Astor's ships exclusive right to supply Russian fur posts in Alaska and transport Russian sea otter, seal, and other furs from Alaska to China. For these transport services to China, Astor would receive a healthy commission, in addition to proceeds from his sales of supplies to the Russian posts. The two parties, Russia and Astor, would also agree to stay out of each other's fur territories on the West Coast. For Adrian and Magdalen Bentzon, the Christmas of 1811 was spent in frozen St. Petersburg, working out these contract details. If their efforts were successful, it would be a generous Christmas present for Magdalen's father—another large step toward his global fur monopoly.

John Jacob and Sarah's second son, nineteen-year-old William Backhouse Astor, would likewise miss the family holidays in Manhattan. He was studying abroad for four years at the famed University of Heidelberg, Germany's oldest, located near Astor's hometown of Walldorf. Soon he would return and join his father in the fur business. The absence of Magdalen and William left in the household the three other surviving children—the oldest son, John Jacob II, a strange, inward child who rarely left his upstairs room at the back of the house; and his two younger sisters, Dorothea, now sixteen, and Eliza, now ten. The elder of the two, Dorothea—or Dolly—was outgoing and energetic. Embracing the growing spirit of Romanticism among the day's well-educated youth, she would soon rebel against her staid parents by eloping with an unsanctioned suitor and estranging herself from her father for years.

But, for now, as the holidays arrived, Dolly was behaving properly and Astor's great West Coast empire was, as far as he knew, progressing splendidly. He would soon sit down to write a long, enthusiastic letter to Thomas Jefferson, recently retired to Monticello after two terms as president. Astor would give his mentor-in-empire a progress report detailing the ships and expeditions sent to the Northwest Coast, the negotiations with rival fur companies, and his diplomatic contacts with the Russians to embrace their Alaskan fur trade. He hoped also to ask the ex-president for political advice. He was, in effect, reporting in to his superior: "Sir . . . Since I had the pleasure of speaking with you first at Washington concerning it, my constant study has been to attain the object. . . ."

Astor had invested a tremendous amount of energy, thought, and money in this risky, infinitely complicated, and far-flung endeavor, but even in the absence of news he managed to maintain a remarkable coolness and rationality. Astor had traveled in the wilderness enough himself, paddling canoes and trekking muddy trails with a pack of trinkets in upstate New York, to know that his Overland and Seagoing parties would have faced plenty of hardships en route. In the absence of any other information, however, as well as being aware of the long lag time before news could reach him, and given his meticulous planning and careful instructions to his leaders, he assumed that both Thorn's and Hunt's parties had by now safely arrived on the Northwest Coast and laid the foundations of the emporium, and reached it before the North West Company.

"[A]t all events, I think we must be ahead of them," he wrote to Jefferson. "By what I can learn there is a great deal of fur on the west side of the mountains, and a considerable business is to be done on the coast with the Russians."

He continued enthusiastically to Thomas Jefferson, pleased that his Overland Party had apparently found a better route than Meriwether Lewis:

"The party which ascended the Missouri is under the direction of a very respectable gentleman from Trenton, New Jersey, by the name of Hunt. . . . The last account which I had of the party [was] where they left the Missouri, and took . . . a southern course, this being recommended as nearer and easier to the south branch of the Columbia than the route taken by Mr Lewis. . . . The accounts as to their ultimate success were fair and encouraging, and they had no doubt of meeting their friends who went by sea; which I think they must have done in October last."

Astor couldn't possibly imagine, as he enjoyed the family warmth of the holiday season, his men staggering through barren plains, gnawing on moccasins and drinking their own urine, or a woman eight months pregnant with her two small children in tow, tumbling down mountainsides in a snowstorm toward the unseen roar of an unknown river in a canyon far below.

C ONSENSUS WOULD NO LONGER BE POSSIBLE FOR HUNT. Mackenzie's and McClellan's reconnaissance parties had gone ahead a month earlier to find their way to the Columbia, leaving behind the slower-moving main party. The main party had split into two groups traveling on opposite sides of the unknown river, Hunt's nineteen people on one bank, plus the Dorion family, and Crooks's nineteen on the other. All were severely weakened; some in Crooks's party had become so feeble after their foray three days farther down-river into the giant canyon that they could barely walk.

Hunt, after tossing restlessly through the night of December 6, now had to choose among several bleak options: go farther downstream into the mile-and-a-half-deep mountain gorge; abandon the river and climb westward over steep, snowy mountains toward the Pacific; or retreat upriver to the broad lava plain where they'd encountered the more pros-perous Shoshone camps in fertile valleys, and hope the Shoshone hadn't moved in the meantime. But staying here in the deep gorge as winter arrived simply wasn't an option. It was only a matter of days before they'd grow too weak to travel at all. Then the first would die, and the survivors would have to decide whether to cannibalize their dead.

Despite the fact that Crooks's party had reached the brink of star-vation going forward, Hunt's initial thought was to follow that path forward into the gorge, so fixed was he on reaching the Pacific accord-ing to Mr. Astor's plan and schedule. Hunt, no doubt urged by Crooks himself, then reconsidered. He'd already had a brief taste of fighting the deep snows that blanketed the mountain slopes above the gorge's cliffs. The higher they climbed those mountain slopes, the deeper the snow lay. Crooks surely made it clear to his less experienced colleague and partner that far worse lay ahead.

"To my great regret," Hunt recorded of that morning of December 7 after his restless night, "it was thus necessary to backtrack with the hope of finding some Indians. . . . I counted on buying from them a large enough number of horses to feed us until we reached the Columbia, a move I flattered myself in thinking we could effect this winter."

Even this deep into trouble, Hunt didn't fully grasp the exigencies of winter travel in the mountains. He very nearly succumbed to the temptation to thrash blindly forward into increasingly desperate circumstances, an often fatal mistake made by lost and hypothermic hikers. But going back had its dangers, too. Since leaving the last Shoshone camp upriver more than a week earlier, on November 29, Hunt's group had encountered no game whatsoever and found nothing to eat but a few wild cherries. This meant that to reach the lava plain and Shoshone camps on the tributaries they would have to retreat at least a week upriver without any food at all, except the leftovers from the malnourished horse they had killed, which were now feeding forty people and vanishing quickly. Ramsay Crooks—one of the party's best men, an Astor partner, and an American besides—and the voyageur Le Clerc were so badly weakened by lack of food and their exhausting scouting foray farther downriver that Hunt thought they and several others might simply "break down," in the parlance of the day, before reaching the Shoshone camps.

"What a prospect!" Hunt wrote.

To make matters worse, the river still separated Hunt's and Crooks's groups. The bullboat had somehow got loose from its moorings and drifted away, so Crooks's group remained on the left bank (looking downstream) while Crooks himself was stuck on right bank with Hunt.

That morning, having made the decision to retreat upriver, Hunt's group attempted to improvise a Shoshone-style canoe of bound bundles of reeds, so they could deliver both Crooks and Le Clerc and more horse meat to Crooks's men on the far bank. When it turned out that the frail craft couldn't buck the powerful current, they abandoned it. Grasping the precariousness of their situation, and unwilling to waste any more time, both parties started upriver toward the Shoshone camps that day, traveling on opposite banks.

But soon the parties began to fragment. Ramsay Crooks and Le Clerc soon staggered far behind the rest of Hunt's group, stumbling among boulders that littered the few flat sections of the river's shore or dragging themselves up cliffy hillsides where the banks fell sheer to the water. Hunt slowed his party, believing they should stay with the collapsing men. Not wanting to wait, small groups and lone travelers pushed ahead, hoping to reach food and safety before they, too, gave out. Among these were the Dorion family, who possessed the party's single remaining half-starved horse. Except for a few beaver skins, it was the group's last remaining source of food.

The next day, December 8, members of Hunt's party who still remained with him tried to float another reed raft so Crooks and Le Clerc could ferry themselves to their own party across the river. The pair tried repeatedly to force the craft into the river channel, but the swift current and their own weakness defeated them again, shoving them back to the riverbank. Hunt waited patiently as they fumbled on the cold eddies and frigid currents. The voyageurs at his side now realized their own hopes were slipping away—burdened by Crooks and Le Clerc, weakening each passing moment themselves, and anchored in place by Hunt's obstinate insistence that he stay with the failing men.

The voyageurs bitterly harangued Hunt.

"They said that we would all die from starvation," he recorded, "and urged me by all means to go on."

Hunt's carefully cultivated unity now unraveled under the pressure of profound hunger. Finally, only Hunt and five men remained with the failing Crooks and Le Clerc, the rest having pushed ahead in ones and twos and threes. Hunt and the stragglers camped together that night of December 8. During the night, Crooks fell very ill. Only three beaver skins remained for food. The sheer instinctive necessity of survival was stripping away whatever authority Hunt possessed. Yet he felt weighted by a deep sense of personal responsibility. What had started out as a series of business decisions for this "very respectable gentleman from Trenton, New Jersey," had now evolved into naked choices over life and death. Reading between the spare lines of his journal, one can hear his tortured thoughts.

Where was he needed more? By the side of a good but failing man along the trail? Or with his party leading them and negotiating for food when—and if—they reached the Shoshone camp? Loyalty to a partner? Or loyalty to the success of the mission? How could he abandon one of Mr. Astor's primary partners to die of starvation in a river gorge a thousand miles or more from the nearest white settlement?

Hunt finally chose again: He would go ahead. But he didn't abandon his weaker men entirely—not yet. He left two of the three beaver skins for them to eat, and two men to help Crooks and Le Clerc along the trail.

For ten days they retraced their steps upriver, hoping to find the prosperous tipi village of the Shoshone Indians in the fertile tributary valley. After pausing with Crooks and Le Clerc, Hunt hurried to catch up with his group. He found that some of them hadn't eaten a single thing in four days of hard, cold trekking over boulders and skirting cliffs. Hunt proposed they kill and share Dorion's family horse. Dorion refused to give it over. Surprisingly, the voyageurs backed Dorion, wanting to save the scrawny animal in the event they didn't find Shoshone tipis ahead. Hunt agreed.

Later that day they had a stroke of luck, spotting a new collection of Shoshone tipis along the riverbank, surrounded by a herd of twenty horses. The band apparently had emerged from a tributary mountain valley since Hunt and company had passed the spot downriver. Fearing the Shoshone would flee or hide their horses at the bizarre sight of white men, Hunt approached gingerly and managed to buy (Hunt's account) or grab (Irving's account), or some combination thereof, five of the horses before the Shoshone and horses could scatter. He ordered one horse slaughtered on the spot, and meat delivered on the back of another horse downriver to the ailing Crooks and Le Clerc. The starving group devoured the remainder.

Slightly fortified, Crooks and Le Clerc managed to catch up briefly with the Hunt group. Crooks's men, however, were still on the opposite riverbank. "[H]overing like spectres of famine," as Irving, who interviewed eyewitnesses to the incident, put it, the sight of them repelled Hunt's own struggling group. Crooks ordered a bullboat constructed immediately and sent a supply of horse meat across the river to his men. Everyone in the starving party received the meat eagerly, but one of the voyageurs in the Crooks group, Jean Baptiste Prevost, had become frantic with hunger. He demanded to be ferried across the river immediately to the Hunt group, saying death was certain on his side. Prevost forced his way aboard the returning bullboat. As it approached the shore where Hunt's party roasted hunks of horse meat over fires, Prevost leapt up in the bullboat, clapped his hands in delight, and according to Irving's account, which possibly came from Crooks himself, capsized the fragile craft. The boat's steersman, Pierre Delaunay, barely saved himself. Prevost did not.

"The poor wretch," wrote Irving, "was swept away by the current and drowned. . . ."

It was the Overland Party's second death.

The two groups pushed on upriver toward the tributary stream on the lava plain where they had taken a shortcut three weeks earlier. Again, in the interest of speed, they left behind the desperately weak Crooks and Le Clerc. Hunt gave the pair two horses and part of the meat of a third horse, so they could follow once they had regained some strength.

For the next four days, the two parties continued to struggle upriver on opposite banks. It snowed. The temperature plummeted. Hissing rafts of ice congealed on the surface of the Mad River. Exhausted, hungry, chilled, they finally stumbled out of the mountain gorge and onto the broad lava plain on December 16. They camped that night at a tributary stream they had forded on November 26.

"Thus for twenty days," lamented Hunt in his journal, "we had worn ourselves out futilely trying to find a passage along the lower part of this river."

The following day, December 17, Hunt's group, leaving behind the wretched party on the opposite bank, ascended the tributary through more fertile country and arrived at an entire tipi village of the Shoshone. They found relief—temporarily. Hunt exchanged trade items— an old pewter pot, knives, blue glass beads—for a few horses, a dog, some dried fish and roots, and pounded, dried wild cherries. These last, along with rose hips, a Shoshone staple that Hunt also foraged, were essential to their survival.

Many species of cherries are extraordinarily high in vitamin C. The Hunt and Crooks parties' suffering and weakness was no doubt due partly to the onset of scurvy, a debilitating illness that frequently killed early European seafarers subsisting on a diet of salt meat and grains. Scurvy, both at sea and on land during the winter, posed one of the single greatest obstacles to early exploration. Typically setting in after about ten to twelve weeks without fresh food, its early symptoms included fatigue, weakness, and malaise, followed by a swelling of the gums, loosening of the teeth, and opening of old scars as the body's tough, connective collagen tissues started to unravel. Then the blood vessels and organs began to leak and hemorrhage, followed shortly by death.

Ascorbic acid—vitamin C—functions as a kind of molecular knitting device that tightly binds together the amino acids responsible for producing collagen. Doses of vitamin C can reverse scurvy's deteriorating effects in a few days or even hours. Widely dispersed Native American tribes had, through millennia of trial and error, discovered different strategies to prevent the onset of scurvy during winter

"Mrs. Astor (from a Miniature)." Sarah Todd Astor as a young woman, married to John Jacob in 1785 (*left*); *John Jacob Astor, after a Portrait by Gilbert Stuart.* John Jacob Astor in 1794 as an aspiring fur trader and New York businessman in his early thirties (*right*).

Waldorf.   (*From a water-colour sketch.*)

Astor's childhood home in the German town of Walldorf.

John Jacob Astor by John Wesley Jarvis, ca. 1825.
John Jacob Astor as a prosperous American businessman.

Lieutenant Jonathan Thorn (*left*), young naval hero who became captain of Astor's ship the *Tonquin*, which carried the Seagoing Party to the Pacific Coast; Wilson Hunt Price (*right*), leader of Astor's Overland Party to the Pacific Coast.

Tontine Coffee House, N.Y.C. by Francis Guy, ca. 1797. Tontine Coffee House (*left*) and Merchant's Coffee House (*center*) at the corner of Wall and Water Streets, New York City, where merchants such as Astor gathered to conduct business. Astor's office and home were a few blocks away.

Portrait of Alexander Ross *(left);* portrait of Donald Mackenzie *(right).*

Portrait of Ramsey Crooks *(left);* portrait of Robert Stuart *(right).*

Portrait of Gabriel Franchère.

Portrait of a voyageur.

Canoes in a Fog, Lake Superior by Frances Anne Hopkins, 1869. Voyageur canoes paddling the inland water route to the North American interior, as Hunt's Overland Party did.

View from Floyd's Grave, 1300 Miles Above St. Louis by George Catlin, 1832. A Missouri River scene. The Overland Party worked its way in riverboats up this same stretch of river.

Stu-mick-o-súcks, Buffalo Bull's Back Fat, Head Chief, Blood Tribe
by George Catlin, 1832. Portrait of a chief of the Blackfeet Confederacy,
the Native Americans whom Hunt's party feared and veered south to avoid.

Sha-kó-ka, Mint, a Pretty Girl
by George Catlin, 1832.

Mih-Tutta-Hangkusch, a Mandan Village by Karl Bodmer, 1841. Hunt's party witnessed
a scene similar to this, with women in bullboats on the Missouri River hauling
firewood for their village. These are women of the Mandan peoples, several hundred
miles upriver from the Arikara villages where Hunt's party left the Missouri.

Buffalo Chase over Prairie Bluffs by George Catlin, early 1830s. Hunt's Overland Party witnessed and participated in buffalo hunts on the prairies.

The Interior of the Hut of a Mandan Chief by Karl Bodmer, ca. 1832. A contingent from Hunt's party traveled to the Mandan villages to acquire horses for their long overland trek into unknown terrain.

"The American Falls of Lewis Fork," from a report by later explorer John Charles Fremont. Hunt's canoes ran into trouble here, along the "Mad River," known today as the Snake River.

Hell's Canyon of the Snake River, where Wilson Price Hunt and his party struggled on foot as winter arrived.

Entrevue de l'expedition de M. Kotzebue avec le roi Tammeamea dans l'île d'Ovayhi, Iles Sandwich by Louis Choris, 1827. The royal court of Hawaii, as it greets a party of Europeans. A party from the *Tonquin* was also greeted at the royal court here.

Sea Otter, engraving by S. Smith, after John Webber, the illustrator who traveled with Captain Cook on his voyage to the Northwest Coast. This is the mammal whose fur provided the "soft gold" that brought so much attention to the Northwest Coast.

"Tenaktak canoes," early photograph by Edward S. Curtis. These are typical of the large cedar canoes of the Northwest Coast.

Interior of Whale House of Chief Klart-Reech, Klukwan, Alaska. c. 1895. Many of the peoples of the Northwest Coast had longhouses decorated with elaborate carvings and paintings.

A *TLŪ'WŪLÁHŪ* MASK - TSAWATENOK*

"Tluwulahu mask—Tswatenok," photograph by Edward S. Curtis.
The peoples of the Northwest Coast had an elaborate ceremonial culture.

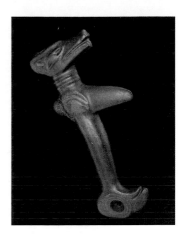

Ka'heit'am (Stone Club), pre-1778, from Yuquot village, Nuu-chah-nulth (Vancouver Island area). Meticulously shaped from stone, with what appears to be a wolf's head and thunderbird design, this was one of many types of clubs used on the Northwest Coast both for killing animals and for dispatching human enemies.

Northwest Coast Art—*Yéil X'eenh* (Raven Screen), ca. 1810, from Klukwan village, Tlingit people. Screens like this stood in traditional longhouses separating family living quarters. From the house of a clan associated with the Raven, this screen shows the Raven's head looking straight ahead at the very top, center. Its tail feathers appear below the round opening at the bottom, which served as the ceremonial entrance to the "house master's" treasure room. The Raven's wings drape down the sides of the screen.

E, E. HENRY, Photographer.

ROBERT McGEE,

Scalped by Sioux Chief Little Turtle in 1864.

It was images like this one that gave Wilson Price Hunt pause when choosing a route across the continent for Astor's Overland Party. Robert McGee (*pictured here),* like Edward Robinson—the trapper and survivor who advised Hunt to avoid hostile Blackfeet territory—was a survivor of scalping.

when fresh food was scarce and they might subsist on starchy roots and dried meat as the Shoshone did. Inuit in the Arctic ate raw and lightly cooked seal meat and other organs, high in vitamin C. Ojibwa Indians in what is now eastern Canada relied on an ascorbic-acid-rich tea made from the ground-up bark and foliage of what has been identified as the white cedar, or arborvitae ("tree of life"). The Shoshone had cherries and rose hips. These, like little pills of vitamin C, certainly helped to revive and prepare the Overland Party for the next brutal leg of their journey.

Hunt asked the Shoshone many times, communicating with difficulty through Dorion and the Aztecan language barrier, how to get to the Columbia, or "Big River," as it was known to Native Americans. He finally understood that the Shoshone knew of a large encampment of Sciatoga Indians located near the Big River. The Sciatoga had many horses, he understood. The Shoshone knew a trail that could take Hunt to the Sciatoga camp. But the trail wasn't easy, and the village wasn't near. Hunt would spend between seventeen and twenty-one nights on the trail, he would have to cross a large mountain range, and "we would be in snow up to our waists."

By now Hunt had learned that without a Shoshone guide he probably would never reach the Sciatoga village. White explorers in North America both before and after him would learn the same basic lesson.

"I offered a gun, some pistols, a horse, etc., to whoever would serve me as a guide."

No one accepted the post.

"They all replied that we would freeze to death and pleaded with me to remain with them during the winter."

Hunt grew desperate. He combed the Shoshone camp searching for a willing guide.

"I went to every tepee along the river banks, but without success. I could not get along without one, for that meant running the risk that we would all die. But to remain in this place would be still worse, after having come so far and at such great cost."

But why would it be so awful to wait out the winter? Wilson Price Hunt was a businessman and brought with him a schedule to lay the foundation of John Jacob Astor's West Coast empire. He was already running two months late, and he refused to compound the delay by overwintering in a Shoshone camp for another three months until the spring snowmelt. The wilderness did not keep to a businesslike schedule of hours or days, minutes or months, or deadlines for human convenience. The native peoples recognized this, tending to stay put when the weather was bad, to move when it was good, and they wondered why someone would choose otherwise. Even after all his trials, Hunt was still learning to adapt his behavior to an ever-changing environment. He would not yield to the winter.

Yet for all his strengths and failings, Hunt remained an astute reader of human character. Though he'd always been well mannered and unfailingly polite—"a gentleman of the mildest disposition" was how Bradbury, the botanist, had described him—Hunt now deliberately and forcefully changed his diplomatic tone. In order to hire a guide, rather than appealing to their desire for possessions, he played to their sense of pride.

"I ended by telling the Indians that they spoke with forked tongues, that they were lying to me. I accused them of being women; in short, I challenged them with whatever expressions would goad them most."

And it worked.

"At last," he wrote, "one of them found courage enough to volunteer to be our guide as far as the village of the Sciatogas."

I N FACT HUNT WAS ABLE TO SHAME THREE SHOSHONE INTO guiding his party. Those three now led them from the safety of the large Shoshone village down the small tributary river westward, back to the banks of the Mad River. As there were no native reed canoes to ferry across the river's swirling current, Hunt killed two of the horses he'd bought from the village and crafted a horsehide canoe, delicately ferrying the party a few at a time across the channel, four hundred yards wide and running with spinning chunks of ice. They felt cheered finally to put to their backs the river they had followed for two months and whose unexplored, mile-and-a-half-deep crack in the earth—Hells Canyon—had for weeks blocked their westward progress to the Pacific.

"*La maudite rivière enragée,*" the voyageurs called it, bidding farewell. "The accursed mad river."

On the far bank, Hunt and company met the remaining thirteen men of Crooks's ragtag party, still waiting, after their struggles in the great gorge, for food and leadership.

"[They] told me that since we had left they had not seen either Mr. Crooks or the two men who were with him," wrote Hunt. "All of Mr. Crooks's men were extremely weak and exhausted, four of them even more than the others."

Three of these weakened voyageurs told Hunt they didn't have the strength to go onward. It's a measure of their deprivation and extreme exertion along *La maudite rivière enragée* that these workhorse-like men, routinely happy to paddle canoes eighteen hours per day and haul two-hundred-pound loads over portages, singing all the way, had simply stopped. Frail, spectral versions of their former selves, they had decided to stay in the wilds rather than with their companions, taking their chances of survival at the Shoshone villages. The fourth frail and exhausted man, Michael Carriere, opted to proceed west-ward into the mountains with Hunt as best he could.

It may have been easier for Hunt to go on while Crooks was still out of sight in the canyon than to have to say goodbye to his friend and weakened business partner before heading west toward the Pacific. Hunt was torn by the tension between the unity of the group and the success of the mission. He had hesitated in the gorge: Should he stay with his good but failing man beside the trail? Was his devotion to his men or to the success of the mission? But in many ways the success of the mission depended on the loyalty of the men, and the loyalty of the men depended on Hunt taking care of them. It was a dilemma that offered only difficult answers.

Hunt had, however, now irrevocably made the decision: The suc-cess of Mr. Astor's enterprise trumped the welfare of the straggling men. He had provided as best he could for Crooks, leaving two men by his side in the gorge, including John Day, the lanky, friendly, forty-year-old Virginian hunter. Hunt had also sent horse meat back to his failing friend. Should he make it out of the gorge alive, Crooks could take shelter in the same Shoshone village and recover his strength. But it was also true that Hunt could have chosen to stay all winter in the Shoshone village and let Crooks and the others catch up and recover. Instead, he chose to go on.

Mr. Astor's Overland Party, once sixty strong, had splintered again. On Christmas Eve, 1811, Hunt left his weakest men and the Mad River and headed west over big, rolling country toward distant mountains.

"My group," Hunt recorded, "was now made up of thirty-two white men, a woman eight months pregnant, her two children, and three

Indians. We had only five puny horses to feed us during our trip over the mountains."

For three days they trudged westward, led by the Shoshone guides. The trail proved a good one that was well traveled by Indians in the warmer months. They could make about fifteen miles per day walking through intermittent showers of rain and snow, as they crossed up and down over dry, open hills and rounded grassy ridges not quite sharp enough to be called mountains. But the trudging climbs and descents still took their toll. On the third day the exhausted voyageur, Carriere, simply lay down, unable to walk anymore. Hunt gave Carriere one of the five scrawny horses to ride.

They worked their way westward from valley to valley. Skiffs of snow clung to the steep, shady north faces. They followed winding stream bottoms bordered by fringes of dwarfed cottonwoods and waded through the frigid water. Strained beyond endurance by yet another set of hills, the voyageur La Bonté, once capable of hauling inhuman weights but now too emaciated to hold his own body upright, also "broke down." Hunt propped him up on another of the horses. When he realized the horse didn't have the strength to carry both La Bonté and La Bonté's twenty-five-pound pack, Hunt added La Bonté's pack to his own.

The rolling terrain gradually rose. They crossed a taller ridge that topped out in pine groves and snow. As they descended the far side, a broad, snowless valley opened up where six Shoshone tipis clustered. Trading two old guns, a tomahawk, and a cooking pot for four horses, three dogs, and edible roots, Hunt's party feasted with immediate relish, preferring dog meat to all else. The Shoshone people in the camp pointed toward a snowy ridge of mountains rising to the west. This was the barrier. They indicated a gap where Hunt would find a pass. They told Hunt he had three more nights to cross those mountains before reaching the camp of the Sciatogas. On the pass, they told him, he would not find much snow.

Hunt remained skeptical.

"They . . . had so often given me erroneous reports that I did not take this news seriously," wrote Hunt. "On every side of us snow blanketed the mountains."

While still in camp early the next morning, December 30, Marie Dorion, at eight months pregnant, went into labor. She was an Iowan woman with a part-Sioux husband and about to give birth in a Shoshone camp; whatever the exact tribal tradition she followed, pregnancy in traditional Native American culture was considered a sacred state for a woman and giving birth a sacred act.

"Silence and isolation are the rule of life for the expectant mother," wrote Charles Alexander Eastman, or Ohíye S'a, a Santee Sioux born in the mid-1800s on the plains who eventually studied Western medicine at Dartmouth College and Boston University. "She wanders prayerful in the stillness of great woods, or on the bosom of the untrodden prairie, and to her poetic mind the immanent [*sic*] birth of her child prefigures the advent of a master-man—a hero, or the mother of heroes. . . . And when the day of days in her life dawns—the day in which there is to be a new life, the miracle of whose making has been intrusted to her, she seeks no human aid. She has been trained and prepared in body and mind for this her holiest duty, ever since she can remember. The ordeal is best met alone. . . ."

Marie Dorion, however, was on something of a forced march in Hunt's party during her pregnancy. How had she been thinking about the life gestating inside her? Were the endless walks and climbs, the hardships and privations, all contributing to her unborn child's spiritual power? Had she even assumed extra hardships to give her child power? The men on the expedition were constantly amazed at how much, and how easily and uncomplainingly, pregnant Marie Dorion walked instead of rode a horse.

The six-tipi Shoshone camp in the broad valley offered a convenient place to give birth before the Hunt party embarked over the snowy mountains. Perhaps it was induced. Meriwether Lewis reported in his journal how Sacagawea underwent a difficult and painful labor at the Mandan villages with her first child. A Mandan medicine man was enlisted, who, saying the method had worked many times before, took two rings from the rattle of a rattlesnake that Lewis possessed, crumpled them into water, and gave it to Sacagawea to drink. She gave birth within ten minutes. (Lewis admitted to some skepticism that the rattle made the difference.)

As Marie went into labor early that morning at the six Shoshone tipis, Pierre Dorion told Hunt to go on ahead.* The Hunt party set out again across the broad and open valley. The following day the Dorion family overtook the main group. Hunt was stunned to see them so soon and so relaxed, Pierre walking in front.

"His wife rode horseback with her newly born child in her arms," wrote Hunt. "Another child, two years old and wrapped in a blanket, was fastened by her side. One would have thought, from her behavior, that nothing had happened to her."

It was New Year's Eve, 1811. Voyageurs typically rang in New Year's Day with singing, dancing, drinking, and feasting.

"My people asked me not to travel on the 1st of January without first celebrating the new year," wrote Hunt. "I agreed to the idea willingly because most of them were very tired from having daily no more than a meager meal of horse meat and from carrying packs on their shoulders while crossing the mountains."

On January 2 they resumed their march, climbing steadily into the mountain range that rose like a long blue wall to the west, first ascending a small river valley, then the fork of a creek. Leaving the creek's head, their Shoshone guides led them clambering up snowy ridges, forested with pine trees, that rose to mountain peaks—today's Blue Mountains in northeastern Oregon. On the heights, the trees thinned and the snow lay deeper. They plowed through it, halfway up their legs, to break a trail. In places they plunged through wind drifts or dropped into hollows, sinking up to their waists.

---

* This Shoshone encampment where Marie Dorion went into labor was located near today's North Powder, Oregon, in the Baker Valley.

With two days of climbing in the deep snow, on January 4, 1812, Hunt's party dragged themselves to the frigid crest of the range, capped with icy gray cloud.

"[W]e were at a point as high as the mountains that surrounded us, some wooded, but all covered with snow," Hunt wrote.

For two more days they worked along the crest, heading generally west, traversing high, rolling ridges, struggling through deep snow and pine forests. On January 6 a crack of sunlight broke through the frigid cloud cap. Looking westward from the heights, just beneath the gray cloud ceiling, they spotted what looked like a wide, sunny, shimmering valley. Could this be the broad Columbia River plain? Was this shaft of sunlight the first waft of the milder Pacific climate that lay beyond the last mountains? They had been wrong so many times before in thinking they were almost there.

The next day, January 7, their Shoshone guides led them to a narrow stream defile that notched the mountain crest. Starting as a small valley on the mountain ridge, it twisted lower all day, dropping, deepening, snaking between immense hillsides that now rose high on each side as the stream fell in elevation. Many of the men, stumbling, dropped behind the main group. Another tragedy befell them.

"The Dorion baby died," Hunt recorded tersely.

There was no mention of a ceremony for the week-old infant. On the same cold night, a number of the stragglers failed to appear in camp. Hunt didn't wait. It was now a staggering dash for a rescue, a race to stay ahead of the starvation and exhaustion that had begun felling the rearmost members of the group, one by one.

The snow thinned as they descended the twisting, deepening defile and disappeared. They noticed deer tracks and horse trails along the streambank and the hillsides. Then the narrow defile suddenly opened up. As if exiting a doorway from the mountains, they emerged into a broad valley etched gently with meandering streams. Its floor shone bright green with grass even in the winter, while the bottomlands along the streams were like oases—microclimates—sheltered from

winter's north winds and exposed to warm southern sun. Their three
Shoshone guides led them onto the valley floor. They spotted a sprawling Indian encampment. With rising joy, they counted thirty-four tipis.
An astounding number of horses grazed contentedly in the meadows
around the camp—at least two thousand of them—an indication of the
richness and abundance of the place. Hunt spotted copper kettles sim-
mering over cook fires. Here was another encouraging sign—an indication of nearby trade with the Pacific Coast. The Columbia River, the
Indians told him, lay an easy two days' travel away.

After two months of wandering lost in search of the Columbia,
they'd arrived. They had just crossed the final range of the mountains
and descended the far side to the Pacific.

"I cannot thank Providence enough for our having reached this
point," wrote Hunt, "for we were excessively tired and weak."

The Indians, once again, had rescued Hunt. He and his party
stayed in the Sciatoga camp for six days to recuperate, some men
gorging on meat and roots until they sickened themselves. It "pleased
me greatly," Hunt recorded, to hear reports from the Sciatogas that
another party of white men—Mackenzie's or McClellan's group, no
doubt—had recently passed down the Columbia. All of Hunt's stragglers of the last few days eventually showed up in the Sciatoga camp,
except one, Carriere, who'd been weakest and riding on horseback.
Also missing were Ramsay Crooks and the four others left far back
at the Mad River. The journal accounts say that Carriere apparently
turned onto the wrong hunting trail. Hunt's men searched briefly for
him from the Sciatoga camp before giving up the debilitated voyageur for lost. In the aftermath, however, suspicions of cannibalism
hung around his disappearance.

PART THREE

PACIFIC EMPIRE AND WAR

ASTORIA, AS IT WAS IN 1813.

WHEN THE *Tonquin* FINALLY CROSSED THE COLUMBIA Bar and anchored in the river's mouth in late March of 1811, the ship had logged 21,852 miles since leaving John Jacob Astor and New York Harbor. Eight men had perished in the attempts to guide her across the Columbia Bar. Wilson Price Hunt and his Overland Party were nowhere in evidence and not expected on the Pacific Coast until sometime in autumn (they were currently pushing their way up the Missouri). Hunt's absence left a power vacuum wherein other men contended.

Captain Thorn and partner McDougall, whom Astor had appointed second in command in Hunt's absence, quarreled about the exact choice of sites for the "emporium"—the large trading post and living quarters, wharves and warehouses, that would serve as the heart of the West Coast empire. Once across the bar, those aboard the *Tonquin* found themselves in a river estuary some five miles wide that gradually narrowed as it reached deeper into the continent's interior. Heavy coastal rain forest—towering cedar and fir trees draped with lichens— descended in a thick green curtain to the river's edge. They needed to find a site within this wall of forest and broad reach of estuary that offered a cove for landing boats and cargo, enough flat ground to build the establishment, and a hill to give views down to the mouth, as well as up the river, to detect the arrival of friends or enemies. Accessibility by ship and defensibility against attack both stood as key considerations for this nodal point of the Pacific trading empire, in the same way that safe anchorages at Jamestown and Plymouth and Boston Harbor had determined the locations of the first English colonies on the Atlantic Coast of North America.

The Astor partners sent scouting parties from the *Tonquin* upriver, looking for potential sites. In scattered villages on both banks lived several different Coastal Indian tribes. Eager to trade for manufactured goods like knives, beads, and pots, the Indians for the most part greeted the new arrivals with friendliness—white trading ships had been stopping occasionally at the mouth of the Columbia for nearly two decades, since the 1792 arrival of the ships of Captain Robert Gray and Captain George Vancouver.

On April 5, ten days after the *Tonquin* had crossed the bar and anchored at Baker's Bay, a sheltered spot at the river's mouth, McDougall and David Stuart, in the longboat, discovered a possible location for the emporium on the south bank, about eleven miles up the estuary from the bar. On their way back to the *Tonquin,* they crossed the estuary and visited a Chinook village of longhouses on the north bank. The Chinooks, led by their elderly, one-eyed chief, Comcomly, known for his canniness, had greeted the Seagoing Party especially warmly.

The wind kicked up, churning large waves on the river. The chief warned them not to row back to their ship over the five-mile-wide river estuary until the wind had died. The partners and their eight men in the longboat attempted it anyway. A large wave broke over the boat, capsizing it. McDougall didn't know how to swim. He would have drowned had Comcomly not taken the precaution to send two of the village's large canoes and expert paddlers to follow the longboat and rescue the floundering occupants. The Chinook built a large fire on the shore, dried the clothes of the partners and men, and took them back to the village. There he sheltered them in the cedar-planked longhouses until the rain and gale subsided, three days later.

"[Comcomly] received them with all imaginable hospitality,"

recorded Franchère, "regaling them with every delicacy his wigwam afforded."

Thorn, under orders from Mr. Astor for the *Tonquin* to get under way while spring and summer weather prevailed to trade for sea otter furs along the Northwest Coast, had impatiently chosen his own spot in the partners' absence. He'd built a shed near the *Tonquin*'s anchorage at Baker's Bay and begun unloading cargo. But Stuart and McDougall had found a better site, forcing the group to abandon Captain Thorn's newly built shed. The *Tonquin* sailed a few miles upstream to a cove in the estuary shore where a small ship could anchor fifty yards from land. Above it rose a bluff, affording a sweeping view downriver of the eleven miles to the breaking seas of the Columbia Bar and a gray-blue slice of the Pacific beyond. Upstream, they could see along the dark, forested banks of the estuary as far as a promontory projecting off the south bank, called Tongue Point. Almost directly across the river from their chosen site lay Comcomly's Chinook village. Here, at the entry point to the western American continent by river, at the shores of the Pacific reaching to Asia, the partners had chosen to stake out the hub of Mr. Astor's empire.

On April 12 the first party landed in the longboat with tools to clear the land and establish a camp. After so many months at sea, the prospect of setting foot on land made the men giddy at first, as it had the Jamestown settlers two centuries earlier.

"The spring, usually so tardy in this latitude, was already far advanced," reported Franchère. "[T]he foliage was budding, and the earth was clothing itself with verdure; the weather was superb, and all nature smiled. We imagined ourselves in the garden of Eden; the wild forests seemed to us delightful groves, and the leaves transformed to brilliant flowers."

They went to work with energy, Franchère reported, clearing underbrush, burning deadfall, rolling away rotted logs wedged beneath the giant pillars of the still-standing fir and cedar trees, amid glades of mosses and ferns. While they labored, they pondered a name. *Virginia, India, Australia*—these had become the world's great colonies. This rude clearing in the forest symbolized the nexus of a great empire on the Pacific Ocean. And so, as they laid the foundation for the colony's first structure—fittingly, the initial warehouse to secure trade goods and the furs destined for China—they named the empire-to-be: *Astoria*.

As quickly as possible, McDougall left the ship and moved ashore to a tent, where he could fully assert his authority. He and Captain Thorn, still aboard the *Tonquin* anchored a few hundred yards away, exchanged officious letters. McDougall requested goods currently buried in the ship's hold, which Captain Thorn found troublesome to fulfill. The captain complained of waiting around while his passengers ashore partook of further "smoking and sporting parties" and planted turnip patches when he needed them to complete the warehouse so he could unload his cargo and get on his way. The Indian canoes crowding around his ship also annoyed him, with their curiosity and light-fingeredness but, so far, only holding up meager offerings of furs to trade. He finally banned Indians from stepping aboard the *Tonquin*.

Clerk Alexander Ross, ashore, marveled ruefully at how unsuited this group of Scottish fur traders, French-Canadian paddlers, blacksmiths, coopers, clerks, and Hawaiians was to fell the enormous trees that stood on the site of the emporium-to-be. Some of these coastal firs and cedars measured fifty feet around, he wrote, and many of the men had never before held an axe.

Assigned four men per tree, they erected scaffoldings eight or ten feet off the ground as platforms on which to stand, then chopped away at the massive trunks, wood chip by wood chip, with their guns propped nearby in case of a surprise Indian attack. It often required two days to fell a single tree, work stopping frequently so the men could investigate suspicious rustlings in the bushes. The tree finally hewn almost through, work stopped "fifty different times" while the axemen studied the tree from various angles and debated which way the giant would fall. At this delicate juncture, the "most impatient or fool-hardy" of these amateur woodcutters would jump back onto the scaffolding and give the tree another whack or two with his axe.

"Much time was often spent in this desultory manner," reported Ross, "before the mighty tree gave way. . . ."

The men then had to dig out the "monster stumps," and blast them with powder to shatter them into pieces small enough to remove. One man blew off his hand with gunpowder during this sort of excavation.

"Nearly two months of this laborious and incessant toil had passed, and we had scarcely an acre of ground cleared," reported Ross.

McDougall, he wrote contemptuously, was next to worthless as director of the enterprise and lived in relative luxury, supplied with the best food and drink from the ship.

"[T]he great pasha," Ross called him, adding that McDougall was not only vain and self-important, letting the Indian chiefs who visited his "tent of state" be sure to know that he was the great chief of what would be a great enterprise—a king of the Northwest. He was also incompetent. He possessed an "irritable, peevish temper" besides.

Still, work progressed, McDougall handing out liquor rations three times a day to bolster the men's enthusiasm. With timber framing that had been carried aboard the *Tonquin,* they built a small schooner, the *Dolly,* to work the fur trade on the river. After laying the foundations for the warehouse, sixty feet long by twenty-six feet wide, they raised up its walls of logs, sheathing it with waterproof cedar shakes. They began work on quarters for the men, as well as a powder magazine.

By the end of May, construction had progressed far enough that Captain Thorn could unload supplies and trade goods from the *Tonquin* into the warehouse. He prepared to sail up the Northwest Coast to Vancouver Island, where the Coastal Indian villages were known to have rich supplies of sea otter furs.

On June 1, Captain Thorn weighed anchor from the cove at Astoria, with the *Tonquin* manned by his Yankee crew, minus those lost on arrival, and sailed the eleven miles down to the river's mouth. There he waited in Baker's Bay, just inside the mouth, for a favorable wind to propel him across the Columbia Bar to the open Pacific. Captain Thorn lacked officers. In addition to having lost its first mate and one of the expedition's ablest sailors, the missing and presumed drowned Mr. Fox and Job Aiken, the *Tonquin* now also lacked its second mate, Mr. Mumford. Often at odds with Thorn, Mumford was left behind at Astoria to command the *Dolly*. Captain Thorn carried three passengers aboard the *Tonquin* for the trading journey up the coast: Astor partner Alexander McKay, the trader who had crossed the continent with explorer Alexander Mackenzie of the North West Company and was expert at dealing with Indian tribes; a clerk from New York by the name of James Lewis; and, as attendant to partner McKay, a young Canadian, Louis Bruslé.

Before boarding the *Tonquin* for the coastal voyage, McKay took Alexander Ross by the hand in the forest clearing at Astoria. According to Ross's account, McKay asked Ross to look after his teenage son, Thomas, whom McKay was leaving behind at Astoria. Wrote Ross of the conversation: "'You see,' said [McKay], 'how unfortunate we are: the captain, in one of his frantic fits, has now discharged the only officer on board,' alluding to Mr. Mumford. 'If you ever see us safe back, it will be a miracle.'"

On June 5, 1811, a favorable wind arose. The *Tonquin* uneventfully crossed the bar and sailed free out into the open ocean, headed northward along the Northwest Coast. She was expected to return to Astoria within several weeks, laden with the first cargo of sea otter pelts to be shipped to China to inaugurate John Jacob Astor's emporium on the Pacific.

With the emporium's first foundations dug, its first vegetable plots tilled, its first pigsties fenced, and its first coastal trading expedition under way, Astor's instructions called for smaller advance parties to establish the sprawling inland network of fur-posts. These were to extend up the Columbia River, branching out along its tributaries like a great web, reaching deep into the western continent's largely unexplored interior. On July 15, a party of nine under David Stuart loaded canoes alongside Astoria's new little wharf for a journey up the Columbia and along unknown tributaries. The group was actually stepping into their two big Chinook cedar canoes when someone spotted another large canoe paddling hard around Tongue Point. They made out eight voyageurs pulling at the paddles, and, to their great surprise, an ensign flying from the stern—the British flag!

At full speed the big cedar canoe sliced toward the beach, and landed.

"A well-dressed man, who appeared to be the commander, was the first to leap ashore," reported Franchère. "[A]ddressing us without ceremony, [he] said that his name was David Thompson, and that he was one of the partners of the Northwest Company."

Even among rivals of opposing nationalities, a formal cordiality often prevailed in distant wilderness outposts. Thompson was invited to lodge in their living quarters, which were temporarily housed in one end of the long log-and-cedar-shake warehouses while a building for regular sleeping quarters remained under construction. After being served food and drink and given the customary hospitality, Thompson remarked that he had been sent here, to the mouth of the Columbia, by the wintering partners of the North West Company.

He stayed for a week while the Astorians puzzled over his visit. This was not just any trader who had wandered in. Thompson was a tremendously accomplished explorer, mapmaker, and partner in a sprawling company that could be either Astor's potential partner or potential rival on the Pacific Coast. A subtle dance unreeled between Thompson and the Astor partners, perhaps over glasses of port, under candlelight, inside the newly hewn log walls that were fragrant of sweet-sharp cedar and mellow wood smoke. Thompson likely wore his best, while the Astor partners in residence, McDougall and the two Stuarts, surely did likewise. The kilts may have come out. A great deal lay at stake in this pageant of Scottish formality under the towering trees of the coastal wilderness. Among the prizes was the possession of the Northwest Coast, the Columbia Basin, the trade with China, an empire on the Pacific.

The North West Company already had a well-defined and very rapid canoe route, lying well to the north of the Missouri River route, from Lake Superior nearly to the Rockies. They had established trading houses near the foot of the Rockies. A few years earlier, David Thompson had crossed the Rockies and started to explore the fur terrain on the far northern tributaries of the Columbia, and the North West Company had established a few posts on the uppermost reaches. But neither Thompson nor any of the other Nor'westers, as the company men were sometimes called, had descended the river very far.

In the summer of 1810, as the Astorians had made their way westward by ship and overland, Thompson had been heading in the opposite direction—back to Montreal on that chain of rivers and lakes, to take a break from the life of a trader and wilderness explorer. Partway back, he'd received a message from the wintering partners sent from their contentious meeting at Fort William on Lake Superior, where they had debated whether to join forces with Astor. The message from the wintering partners told Thompson to turn around and head to the mouth of the Columbia.

Wrote Thompson to a friend back east: "I intended to have paid you a visit at Montreal . . . but the critical situation of our affairs in the Columbia obliged me to return."

Approaching the Rockies in late fall, he pushed over the deep snows of a pass across the Continental Divide and wintered on a far northern branch of the Columbia. Even professional explorer Thompson was daunted by the power of the forest beyond the divide on the moist Pacific slope of the Rockies. He called humans "pigmies" by comparison to the trees towering more than two hundred feet above.

"[I]n such forests what could we do with Axes of two pounds weight?"

Some of his men deserted. Nevertheless, Thompson and his remaining men managed to craft a canoe of split cedar planks sewn to a frame with spruce roots. By early spring, via canoe and horse, they headed downstream toward the Columbia's mouth, with Thompson stopping to smoke pipes at Indian villages to establish good relations. This was new terrain for explorer Thompson, too. At one major river confluence along the Columbia, Thompson planted a British flag on a tall pole, tacked with a message for all to see, claiming both the confluence as a trading post and all territory to the north as British. When he arrived at Astoria, he pointed out to the Astor partners that he would have arrived a good deal earlier at the Columbia's mouth—in other words, before *they* had—if several of his party hadn't deserted while crossing the Rockies during the winter.

What did he want? The Astorians still weren't sure, even after Thompson had stayed a week, supping at their table. Was he a spy? Had he hoped to raise the British flag and start a North West Company post at the Columbia's mouth but failed to arrive before the Americans? It was a subtle dance, with tremendous stakes.

"Mr. Thompson kept a regular journal," reported Franchère, "and traveled, I thought, more like a geographer than a fur-trader."

A wooden case in his canoe cradled a sextant, chronometer, and barometer. During his week at Astoria, Thompson made astronomical observations and fixed its latitude and longitude. Was this somehow to guide the North West Company or British Royal Navy to the exact spot? Clerk Alexander Ross was convinced that Thompson was a spy of some sort, and that McDougall—a former North Westerner himself but now an Astor partner—was, whether knowingly or not, abetting him.

"M'Dougall received him like a brother," wrote Ross with disdain; "nothing was too good for Mr. Thompson; he had access everywhere; saw and examined everything; and whatever he asked for he got, as if he had been one of ourselves."

One explanation for his visit is that Thompson arrived under the North West Company's carefully thought-out strategy equipped with both a Plan A and a Plan B. Plan A might have been to claim the mouth of the Columbia first and establish a fur post there. But if the Astor advance party was already there, Thompson should go to Plan B: offer to divide the vast territory of western North America between the two companies. Thompson showed the Astoria partners a letter from the North West wintering partners that offered the equivalent of Plan B. Wrote Franchère: "[T]he wintering partners had resolved to abandon all their trading posts west of the [Rocky] mountains, not to enter competition with us, provided our company would engage not to encroach upon their commerce on the east side. . . ."

This, if true, was a mammoth proposal, involving thousands of square miles of North America. But matters were left unresolved. With the wealth of much of the western half of the continent hanging in the balance, Astor partner David Stuart and his party embarked upon the Columbia River on July 23 to establish their fur trading posts. Amicably, although perhaps guardedly, David Thompson and his big canoe of voyageurs paddled beside Stuart's canoes, supposedly for mutual security. McDougall had given Thompson food and other supplies to travel back across the Rockies. Ross speculated that McDougall may have extended such hospitality and generosity to potential rival Thompson in order to lure him into revealing what, in fact, he was up to for the North West Company.

"This is more than probable," writes Ross, "for in point of acuteness, duplicity, and diplomatic craft, they were perhaps well matched."

Now, in this last week of July 1811, the ranks at Astoria had thinned dramatically. The *Tonquin* had sailed up the Northwest Coast and David Stuart's and Thompson's expeditions were paddling up the Columbia, while Hunt's party, unbeknownst to those at Astoria, had just left the Missouri to trek overland. It wasn't expected in any case to arrive at the mouth of the Columbia until late summer or fall. The Indians that had crowded around the Astoria settlement also mysteriously vanished. What had teemed with busy workers, curious Indians, and parcels of goods unloading from the ship now fell strangely silent. The weight of the dark forest pushed in on the little clearing. They numbered approximately two dozen men, along with a few uncompleted and unfortified buildings. It struck them profoundly just how isolated they were—and how vulnerable.

It was the lack of activity that was most disconcerting. Nothing stirred in the forest. Nothing moved on the river except the great sliding sheet of downstream current and the ebb and flow of the estuary's tide pushing in from the ocean. The swells from the Pacific pounded endlessly against the bar in the distance. Astoria constituted a tiny dot of "civilization" on this farthest, wild rim of the continent. The ports of China lay 12,000 miles across the Pacific. The ports of the United States lay 21,000 miles around Cape Horn—five times farther than Jamestown or Plymouth had lain from their supply ports in England. The Astorians' presence was not a quick visit to load furs aboard a well-armed ship, or an expedition holed up for a few months in winter's rain like those of the whites who had come before to this coast. These people had landed here to establish a permanent settlement—the first American colony on the West Coast.

Their sense of exposure deepened. Like a two-pound axe up against a two-hundred-foot tree, their camp was nothing but a tiny clearing between the vast wilderness of western North America's mountains, forests, and rivers and the vastness of the Pacific, with its crushing swells and storms. It felt like the ends of the earth. Also woven between sea and forest was an elaborate and unseen network of Indian tribes, each with its own loyalties and pacts, friendships and animosities, linked by a hidden communication network. It was another great unknown. The Astorians could only guess: What were these native peoples thinking?

Should the Astorians need to flee, they had no one to run to, and nowhere to hide. The remoteness and exposure were profound. The nearest reliable help lay at least a year's journey away.

Paranoia set in—for McDougall in particular.

It was as if, in his need for self-importance, he had drawn a giant target on his back. McDougall had set himself up as the king of the Northwest, telling every Indian chief who would listen while visiting his "tent of state" of his importance and the glory and power of his empire-to-be. Now, however, with the *Tonquin* and its protective cannon and complement of men gone, as well as Stuart's party traveling upriver, and with the Indians vanished and forest and river strangely quiet, McDougall realized he was a king who possessed neither castle nor army. Perhaps he also assessed the surrounding Indian tribes through the prism of his own thinking. He hoped to grow wealthy and powerful from this West Coast enterprise, surely knowing that it would come at least in part at the expense of the native inhabitants. Why, given the chance, wouldn't they wish to grow wealthy and powerful at *his* expense? He sat atop a trove of trade goods—axes, knives, pots, as well as guns and gunpowder—that the tribes coveted. After the *Tonquin* had left, and Stuart's party departed upriver, the Indians could plainly see that the treasure lay unguarded.

The paranoia intensified. The younger Stuart, Robert, still at Astoria while his uncle David led the upriver expedition, heard a rumor from an Indian friend: Since the post was undermanned, the tribes were mulling an attack to kill its occupants and steal its goods.

"We hastened, therefore," wrote Franchère, "to put ourselves in the best possible state of defense."

In a frenzied six days of work, lasting deep into the nights, they finished raising the log walls of the living quarters and workshops, which sat across an open space from the warehouse. Others hustled into the forest to chop small trees for pickets to erect a wooden palisade, with the warehouse serving as one wall and living quarters and shops the other, and the palisade joining them into a enclosed square about 90 feet by 120 feet. At the corners of the palisade they raised platforms on which they mounted four small four-pounder cannon, then set a guard watch night and day.

"The whole . . . had a sufficiently formidable aspect to prevent the Indians from attacking us," wrote Franchère.

July turned to August. They started to feel more secure in their palisade. They practiced drills with their weapons. The *Tonquin* had now been away two months. They looked downriver, toward the Columbia Bar and the open Pacific, expecting her arrival soon.

Meanwhile, a large group of Indians from different tribes who lived northward up the coast had gathered at the Columbia's mouth, just inside the bar in Baker's Bay, to fish for sturgeon. The men at Astoria began to hear strange rumors emanating from this fishing encampment.

"It was bruited among these Indians that the *Tonquin* had been destroyed," reported Franchère. "We did not give credence to this rumor."

More native contingents showed up from the north, including the Tschikeylis (known today as Chehalis) and some from nearly as far away as Vancouver Island, almost two hundred miles north up the coast. They, too, were supposedly fishing for sturgeon. Or were they setting up for an attack? Some of these northern tribes were more warlike in appearance than the neighboring Chinook, reported Franchère, which put the men on their guard.

They, too, repeated the strange rumor about the *Tonquin*.

"[W]ithout wholly convincing us," wrote Franchère, "it did not fail to make a painful impression on our minds. . . ."

A STOR'S LEADERS WERE, IN MANY WAYS, HIS SURROGATES. Astor had chosen Captain Thorn to sail the *Tonquin* because he was decisive, because he would fight, because he was sure to defend with steely courage Astor's fledgling empire. Jonathan Thorn would make the perfect commander in a blazing cannon-to-cannon naval battle against a British or Spanish warship that might threaten to attack the West Coast emporium. But it was a very different adversary, as it turned out, that Captain Thorn would face on his first trading voyage up the West Coast.

Impatient as ever to be on his way, Captain Thorn, after unloading his ship at Astoria and crossing the Columbia Bar out to the open ocean on June 5, had sailed north up the Pacific Coast to trade for sea otter furs in the Coastal Indian villages along today's Vancouver Island. He then was to return to Astoria and load more furs for the cross-Pacific voyage to China, furs that had been collected from the beginnings of a vast web of Astor posts reaching into the interior. Instead of officers, Captain Thorn carried on his ship the most experienced Scottish trader, Alexander McKay, and clerk James Lewis. While en route up the coast, the *Tonquin* put in at an Indian village near today's Gray's Harbor, Washington, and took aboard one more passenger when Thorn and MacKay hired an Indian interpreter, Joseachal, who spoke the Coastal dialects of Vancouver Island.

The *Tonquin* sailed for a village known as Newetee on Vancouver

Island, about two hundred miles north of Astoria. As they made their way north, Joseachal warned Captain Thorn that the Indians of New-etee could be treacherous and held a grudge against an earlier American trading vessel whose crew had mistreated them. Ignoring the native's warnings, Thorn dropped anchor in Newetee's cove around that second week of June 1811. (The cove has since been identified as Templar Channel of Clayoquot Sound, British Columbia.) Trader McKay and interpreter Joseachal went ashore to open trade negotiations. The village chiefs received them with warm hospitality, and the two spent the night in a chief's Clayoquot longhouse on the traditional cedar benches draped with thick sea otter furs.

Out in the cove on board the *Tonquin,* negotiations unfolded less smoothly. The Indians' big cedar canoes, with their long snoutlike prows, pulled alongside the ship's hull. Their paddlers, the Clayoquot, wore woven cedar-bark clothing and weatherproof conical hats. The paddlers held up rolls of sea otter furs to trade. Captain Thorn, the naval hero with no experience in the Indian trade, and his chief trader onshore at the villages, ordered a tempting array spread out on his deck of blankets, knives, blue beads, pots, and other trade goods. An elderly Indian chief named Nookamis climbed aboard to establish the prices in trade goods for furs. Captain Thorn made an offer— two blankets and a few smaller items such as fishhooks and beads in exchange for one sea otter fur.

Known to be a shrewd bargainer among the Coastal Indians, Noo-kamis contemptuously rejected Captain Thorn's offer as far too low. It was a clash of two cultures on the purest of economic terms. Accounts vary as to exact details of this interaction between Thorn and Nooka-mis but follow the same general pattern, as do accounts of the *Tonquin* incident as a whole:

Nookamis wanted five blankets instead of the two Thorn had offered for a sea otter fur. Thorn didn't budge.

"He had a vast deal of stern, but honest pride in his nature," wrote

Irving, who knew Thorn personally, "and, moreover, held the whole savage race in sovereign contempt."

The two were at a stalemate. Jonathan Thorn was not a bargainer. He was a Yankee and a navy man with little experience outside those cultures. He believed he had given a fair price. But he had entered a Northwest Coastal Indian trading culture where bargaining was a centuries-old way of life. These people were not the "ignorant savages" Thorn believed they were.

Nookamis dismissed Thorn's low price. Thorn stalked off angrily along the deck. Nookamis followed him, holding up a bundle of sea otter furs. He began to ridicule Thorn's offer, harassing and "pestering" him to trade. Captain Thorn suddenly spun about, his temper exploding. He grabbed a sea otter fur and rubbed it in Nookamis's face.

"Damn your eyes!" he shouted at the chief, angrily kicking away the bundles of furs and trade goods laid out on the deck.

Then he threw Nookamis off the *Tonquin*.

The other Indians immediately left in their canoes. McKay and Joseachal returned to the ship later that day and, when they heard what had happened, urged Captain Thorn to weigh anchor immediately. The Indians would look for revenge for such a deep insult, they warned. Thorn contemptuously laughed them off.

"You pretend to know a great deal about the Indian character," he said to McKay, according to Alexander Ross's account, which captured the spirit of this tense encounter, whether or not its exact wording, too. "You know nothing at all. . . . They'll not be so saucy now."

IT IS ANOTHER of Astoria's historical ironies that John Jacob Astor, for all his own wealth, came up against two of the wealthiest Indian groups in North America. These were the Blackfeet with their buffalo herds, a tribe that Hunt carefully avoided, and the Coastal Indians with their annual salmon runs. Captain Thorn was willing to confront the latter tribes head-on. The salmon runs reached staggering proportions during those pre-European times—somewhere around 300 million fish *each year,* or about 1.8 billion pounds of protein. And they ran in predictable routes up coastal inlets and river mouths—a veritable pipeline of fish—and leaping up waterfalls where they could easily be netted or speared.

This abundance of salmon on the Northwest Coast—plus clams, mussels, oysters, geoducks, seals, whales, halibut, and much more—thrived where cold, nutrient-rich North Pacific seawaters met countless freshwater rivers and estuaries pouring off the rain-drenched continent, then stirred by powerful tides into a giant, blooming, marine-life stew. Here lay the West Coast equivalent of the cod-rich Grand Banks off Newfoundland. They would prove as significant a draw in bringing the first Europeans around Cape Horn to the Northwest Coast as the Grand Banks had first been in bringing the first Europeans across the Atlantic to the East Coast.

The incredible wealth of marine life supported a Northwest Coastal Indian standard of living that was in many ways superior to late-eighteenth-century living conditions for much of the population of London, Boston, or New York. The Coastal Indians lived several families together in huge longhouses, up to one hundred feet long, or more, housing up to eighty people, tightly built of post-and-beam construction and cedar planking split from giant coastal rain forest trees. Fire pits ran down the center of these longhouses, one fire per family. Drying racks for damp clothing or fish hung from the ceiling, and cedar sleeping benches rimmed the walls, plushly upholstered with sea otter furs. Carved and painted totemic objects guarded the entrances, and one entered some longhouses through the giant mouths of these mythical creatures.* Unlike the more nomadic and egalitarian socie-

---

* The longhouse of Chief Wickaninnish of the Clayoquot could seat eight hundred people and was decorated with "festoons of human skulls, arranged with some attention to uniformity," as reported by one of the first fur-trading captains on the Northwest Coast, John Meares, in 1789.

ties of the interior, Northwest Coastal Indians were divided into social classes. A chiefly rank topped the social hierarchy, followed by commoners, and at the bottom labored a slave class—many of them war captives—who performed the menial tasks.

So great was the wealth of the Northwest Coast that the ceremonial life of these societies centered on the potlatch. These were elaborate ceremonies in which a family gained social status by giving away—and even destroying—its own wealth. What all this wealth of the Coastal Indians meant for John Jacob Astor and his proposed West Coast empire was that, should these tribes find it in their interests, they possessed a great deal of motivation to resist outsiders. Fortunately for Astor, the Coastal tribe in the immediate vicinity of Astoria's headquarters at the Columbia's mouth, the Chinook, and their Chief Comcomly welcomed the fur traders and valued their trade goods. Farther up the coast, however, the relationship between white traders and the tribes—along today's Vancouver Island and beyond toward Alaska—was more complex and strained.

Powerful, tightly knit, and more warlike societies, these were cultures of the "voyaging" or "war" canoe, massive craft up to sixty-five feet long and eight feet wide that could carry up to sixty paddlers, their bows fiercely carved with a bald eagle or a human face or other figures, painted in the characteristic red, black, or white. Some, like the Clayoquot, were whaling societies, which demanded feats of tremendous seamanship and bravery as the canoes put out into the open sea with a harpooner in the bow who had undergone weeks or months of ritualized purification. A great deal of intertribal trade occurred up and down this rich, two-thousand-mile coast. Tribes that crafted especially finely woven rain hats of the inner bark of a cedar tree might trade them to tribes rich in salmon or whale, or villages that hewed the best voyaging canoes might trade the vessels for strings of detalium—mollusk shells that looked like miniature tusks and served as Northwest Coastal currency.

In short, the Northwest Coastal Indians were extremely sophisticated traders and bargainers, to the surprise and sometimes the distress of the first Europeans to arrive, including Captain Thorn. The first few European trading ships to Vancouver Island found they could purchase the sea otter furs cheaply. The Northwest Coast Indians used the plush furs to cover their sleeping benches and for other purposes, but didn't hunt it with any more verve than they did other sea mammals. The Russian fur traders who had begun to work the Alaskan coast had come to call the sea otter furs "soft gold" for the incredible prices they brought on the Chinese market, a discovery also made by Captain Cook's men. An enormous demand grew from China's wealthy and educated mandarin class, who used furs to line their vests and trim their robes.

Sea otter pelts mesmerized the luxury-loving beholder. With nearly one million fine hairs per square inch, the sea otter possesses the densest fur of any mammal known. The fineness and denseness of the hairs give it a soft, luxurious touch. It's this coat that allowed the sea otter to thrive in frigid coastal waters all along the northern Pacific Rim—from California, to Alaska and the Aleutians, to Kamchatka, to the northern islands of Japan. Unlike other cold-water marine mammals such as the seal, it has no insulating blubber layer and relies on this double coat of fur for warmth. Outer guard hairs protect the soft, dense inner hairs, which trap air bubbles and serve as an insulating layer that keeps the otter's actual skin dry.

Even then, since the sea otter needs to maintain a very high metabolism to keep its inner furnaces hot, it eats up to 25 percent of its body weight daily—diving for bottom-dwelling mollusks such as clams, mussels, abalone, and creatures like sea urchins and octopus. It pries these off the rocks, stuffs them into an armpit pouch of skin along where it also carries a rock, swims to the surface, and lies floating on its back, where it can eat in repose, pounding open the hard shells with its rock, using its belly as a kind of table. Sea otters gather in large groups of one hundred or more called "rafts," where they float together amid kelp beds and ocean swells and groom and fluff their fur meticulously to maintain its insulating properties. A mother sea otter nurses her baby pups while they rest on her belly, and when she dives for food, she wraps them in strands of kelp so they don't drift away in her absence.

The native hunters of the Northwest Coast learned how to exploit the sea otter's habits, and did so especially efficiently after fur traders arrived from Russia and then other nations coveting the furs. The Aleuts, in Alaska's Aleutian Islands, paddled *baidarkas*—seagoing kayaks—in the predawn darkness in large groups and stealthily surrounded the floating otters. Shooting in unison, they released arrows or spears at the animals. Each hunter's arrow carried a distinctive marker so he would get credit for the kill with the Russian traders who accompanied them. Farther south, Coastal Indians used special canoes for sea otter hunting, paddling out in wide rows to scout a broad expanse of calm seas and kelp beds, and releasing on discovery special arrows tipped with bone points.

The first American and British ships traded for sea otter furs on the Northwest Coast in the late 1780s. The next wave discovered that the Indian bargainers—knowing demand when they saw it—had raised the price heftily. Angered at the price rise, some American and British trading ships took furs by force or threat of violence. This quickly escalated with retaliations and counter-retaliations. Thus, as mentioned earlier, John Boit's complaint in his journal in 1792 that his commander ordered him to destroy the village called Opitsatah: "[I] am grieved to think Capt. Gray shou'd let his passions go so far. . . ."

As it happened, that very village, Opitsatah, and the nearby village of Clayoquot were Captain Thorn's first trading stop in the *Tonquin*. Boit's incident at Opitsatah had occurred almost two decades before, but only the previous year another unfortunate incident took place when an American fur-trading ship took aboard about a dozen Clayoquot Indians as hunters on a fur-trading voyage far down the West Coast, promising to return them home afterward. Their usefulness at an end, however, their Captain Ayres of Boston casually abandoned the Clayoquot hunters on some uninhabited islands off the California coast. Only a few had survived the long overland trek back home through hostile tribal territories.

That memory was still fresh for the Clayoquot, and so interpreter Joseachal had warned Captain Thorn against entering this particular inlet along Vancouver Island. Astor, likewise, had explicitly warned Captain Thorn in his instructions. Having spent his early business career trading directly with the Iroquois and related tribes of upstate New York, Astor had some grasp of Native American culture, the system of economics, the respect they demanded, and also, surely, the vengeance that could result when such respect was not given. Captain Thorn did not.

"If you find them kind, as I hope you will," wrote Astor in his instructions, "be so to them. If otherwise, act with caution and forbearance, and convince them that you come as friends . . . be particularly careful on the coast, and not rely too much on the friendly disposition of the natives. All accidents which have as yet happened there arose from too much confidence in the Indians."

Astor, in other words, had warned Captain Thorn: *Be kind . . . and beware.*

The Clayoquot, however, in the interest of conducting a beneficial trade with the *Tonquin,* seemed willing to overlook Captain Thorn's insult to their chief Nookamis. Just after daybreak the morning after the contretemps on deck, another big cedar canoe paddled its carved prow alongside the ship. Captain Thorn and McKay still slept belowdecks. The Indians held up packets of furs to trade, apparently signaling a willingness to accept Thorn's prices. The watch on deck let the first canoe of paddlers on board.

Captain Thorn and McKay were summoned from below, along with Joseachal. As the threesome emerged on deck, Clayoquot Indians stood at the ready to trade with sea otter fur packets in hand. James Lewis, the clerk from New York, monitored the display of bales of blankets, metal pots, blue glass beads, knives, and other trade goods. More canoes pulled alongside the *Tonquin.* More Clayoquot climbed over the rail with their bundles of furs, eager to trade. McKay and Joseachal grew anxious. They had warned Captain Thorn not to let more than a few Indians aboard at one time.

The captain again dismissed McKay and his warnings. He pointed to his ten bristling cannon, and his many loaded firearms belowdecks, not to mention the nine thousand pounds of gunpowder in the hold.

"I won't believe that a parcel of lazy, thieving Indians has the courage to attack a ship like this," he told McKay, according to the account by Astorian Ross Cox, which again captured the spirit of this encounter on the deck of the *Tonquin,* even if not its exact wording.

Captain Thorn let the trade open, sticking, apparently with satisfaction, to his low terms, trading the Clayoquot one blanket and one knife for each of the lustrous sea otter furs that he would sell in Canton for many times that value. As far as Captain Thorn was concerned, John Jacob Astor's West Coast empire had finally opened for business. It went well. The Clayoquot traded one fur after the other, tossing the blankets they acquired into the waiting canoes below, paddled by Clayoquot women.

Joseachal, suspicious, watched closely. He noticed that some Indians on deck wore fur mantles over their shoulders, and he wondered if they might hide something underneath. He pointed it out to McKay, who brought it to the attention of Captain Thorn. With a smile of contempt, according to the accounts, the captain dismissed Joseachal's and Mackay's concern, noting that with all the firearms on board, the *Tonquin* "would be more than a match for three times the number" of Clayoquot.

As more climbed aboard, however, Thorn himself grew concerned at the throng of Indians roaming the *Tonquin's* deck. Others in their big cedar canoes nosed up to its copper-clad hull. They could see still more canoes setting out from the village along the cove. Following McKay's urgings, Captain Thorn issued the order to clear the decks, unfurl the topsails, and weigh anchor. The *Tonquin* would sail out of the cove and away from Clayoquot village, removing the ship from the fray.

Seven sailors scrambled aloft to let loose the sails. As they climbed the ratlines a Clayoquot chief on deck gave a signal. In unison, the Clayoquot warriors on deck emitted a ferocious war cry. They jerked war clubs and knives from their bundles of fur and from beneath their mantles. And then they attacked.

Known as *pogamoggan*s or *Ka'heit'am* ("killing object"), the war clubs were highly decorated and coveted objects, crafted of polished materials such as whalebone and stone, finely shaped with balls or knobs or spikes at the end of a slender bone or wooden handle—sometimes flexible and whiplike—the graceful whole designed to inflict maximum blunt-force trauma to the skull. The *pogamoggan* offered a weapon par excellence in close, hand-to-hand combat—for instance, in tight spaces like the deck of the *Tonquin*.

None of the Americans or Europeans on deck was armed—neither Captain Thorn, nor McKay, nor the sailors themselves. As was routine, they had left firearms, although loaded, belowdecks. Nor did Captain Thorn's ten cannon, aimed seaward, away from the ship, or his nine thousand pounds of gunpowder in the hold prove remotely useful on the Clayoquot Indians' chosen, and very cramped, field of battle.

Who first fell to the deck differs with various accounts, but the melee aboard the *Tonquin* appears to have occurred like this:

The clerk Lewis, whose job was to keep track of transactions with trade goods, was bending over a bale of blankets when the war cry erupted. A Clayoquot chief instantly stabbed him in the back as the cry reverberated, and Lewis stumbled over the blankets and tumbled down a companionway.

McKay, arms crossed, observing, was leaning against the taffrail (stern rail) on the larboard (left) side of the ship as the attack began. According to one account, he alone had taken the precaution to arm himself with a pair of pistols stuck in his pockets and briefly defended himself, killing a warrior. But his was a one-shot defense. Other Clayoquot clubbed him over the head with their *pogamoggan*s, then shoved him over the taffrail into the sea, where he was seized by women who waited in the canoes below.

Captain Thorn was third. Standing in his customary spot on the quarterdeck as the war cry sounded, he reached into his pocket and jerked out the only weapon he carried on his person when striding the decks of his ten-cannon vessel—a pocketknife. As the warriors rushed at him with clubs and knives, he thrust and slashed at their bellies with his knife, eviscerating four of them, but suffering bad wounds himself. Staggering with blood loss, he fought toward the cabin entryway where the firearms were stored.

"Covered with wounds, and exhausted from the loss of blood," as one testimonial described the moment, "he rested himself for a moment by leaning on the tiller wheel, when he received a dreadful blow from a . . . *pautumaugan,* on the back part of the head, which felled him to the deck."

The Clayoquot finished him off with knives and clubs, tossing his body over the rail into the sea.

The other Clayoquot aboard had spread out on the ship's deck while the trading was under way, both fore and aft, two or three of them surreptitiously following each sailor. As the war cry sounded, they attacked their chosen victims, who, unarmed, didn't stand a chance. The sailors crumpled to the deck under crushing head blows from *pogamoggan*s and thrusting stab wounds from the just-traded steel knives that the Clayoquot had hidden beneath their fur mantles.

Rather than confronting head-on and against impossible odds the massive power of Western warfare technology in the form of the *Tonquin*'s ten cannon and countless firearms, the Clayoquot had executed a well-planned, disciplined attack on their own terms. Had he survived, Captain Thorn, master and commander of that tremendous firepower, surely would have called the Clayoquot ambush "cowardly." On the deck of the *Tonquin,* as in so much warfare, each side played by whatever "rules of warfare" and definition of "bravery" and "cowardice" gave it maximum advantage.

The Clayoquot chief and his warriors, however, failed to account for one factor in their surprise attack: the seven sailors who had climbed aloft on Captain Thorn's order to unfurl the sails.

Though unarmed, the sailors could easily enough repel or avoid any Indian attackers who tried to clamber up the ratlines after them. From yardarms and rigging, they watched the chaotic massacre on the *Tonquin* below, the blood and the sprawled bodies of their shipmates spilling across the decks, the last death groans falling silent in just a few minutes. The sailors aloft could either jump from the rigging down into the sea, where the war canoes surely would pursue them, or attempt to reach the cabin, where the firearms were stored.

They chose the latter. With the alacrity of sailors who have spent a lifetime aloft, they seized with calloused hands the running lines, such as halyards and sheet ropes, "slipped" down them, and leapt into a hatchway open to belowdecks. One of them fell from the rigging and perished either from the fall or blows from the Clayoquot. Another was killed outright. A third, believed to be the armorer, Stephen Weeks, who had barely survived the awful night with the Hawaiians in the small boat off the Columbia Bar, suffered a critical wound making his escape down the hatchway.

There were five or six survivors taking refuge belowdecks in the cabin at this point, although accounts vary as to the exact number: four still-healthy sailors who had jumped down from the rigging, another man from aloft (probably Weeks) who had sustained a bad wound, and, it seems, the New York clerk, James Lewis, who, on being stabbed, had tumbled over a bale of blankets and down the hatchway.

The survivors barricaded themselves in the cabin belowdecks, broke out pistols, rifles, and muskets stored there, and fought back, shooting through the cabin skylights and out the companionway. Their fusillade sent the Clayoquot warriors jumping over the rails and down to their canoes. The survivors then opened fire on the fleeing canoes with the *Tonquin*'s roaring deck cannon. Captain Thorn's long-distance and industrial instruments of war flung balls and shards of metal whistling across the cove at some 1,700 feet per second and ripped through the paddlers' mostly naked bodies. Many nevertheless made it safely to the shore.

Silence fell over the cove. Bodies and blood lay spilled over the *Tonquin's* deck. Other corpses drifted beside the hull or slowly sank beneath the sea, among them Captain Thorn's. McKay, who at the start of the battle had been bludgeoned over the head and shoved over the taffrail to the waiting women in the canoes below, originally might have been singled out for lighter treatment. Astorian participant and chronicler Ross Cox believed the Clayoquot wished to take McKay hostage and ransom him to Astoria, and had tried to detain him on shore before the planned attack to keep him safe.

"Mr. M'Kay," observed another chronicler and Astorian, Alexander Ross, "was a great favourite among the Indians."

For all his adaptability to Native American culture, however, McKay also stood out as something of an oddball within his own society— "very active, but whimsical and eccentric," was how Ross described him. Ross told the story of McKay, for amusement, setting fire to a tall fir tree when a man was climbing in its upper limbs, forcing him to leap to the limbs of another tree for safety, like a squirrel. Captain Thorn, on the other hand, while fierce and rigid aboard ship, was known to be a well-mannered gentleman within polite society.

"[W]e remember him well in early life," wrote Irving, who had known Thorn as a young man, "as a companion in pleasant scenes and joyous hours."

One could argue that Alexander McKay and Captain Thorn represented two competing approaches to the world's remote coasts on the part of the first European visitors. Thorn performed well within a tightly structured and disciplined system, but was absolutely at a loss when outside clear-cut rules and boundaries, while McKay was a free-form improviser who seemed vastly adaptable to other societies. Neither approach, however, worked out well for them when the *Tonquin* met the Clayoquot, although it seems McKay almost escaped.

After he was bludgeoned over the head and shoved over the taffrail, McKay was said to remain alive for a time either in the sea along-side the women's canoes, or in one of the canoes itself. Then, however, the Clayoquot women observed Thorn, with his slashing pocketknife, killing their chief Shee-wish, son of the great chief Wickaninnish and supposed instigator of the attack. The women took revenge on their hostage McKay, either by ramming him with the pointed blades of their paddles or employing the traditional war clubs, or, perhaps, both.

"The last time the ill-fated gentleman was seen," wrote Cox, "his head was hanging over the side of a canoe, and three savages, armed with *pautumaugan*s, were battering out his brains."

Night fell. No more Clayoquot canoes embarked from shore. The interpreter Joseachal remained in the village. When the attack erupted, he had jumped over the rail into the sea and offered himself up as a slave to the women in the canoes, who hid him under woven mats.

What exactly occurred overnight aboard the *Tonquin* among the five or six survivors is partly testimony, partly conjecture. They most certainly deliberated sailing the ship out of the cove under the cover of night. This would offer their safest route of escape, equipped with all that firepower to defend themselves against the Clayoquot war canoes. But the task of setting sail on a square-rigged ship with only four able-bodied men proved utterly daunting, this on a ship that normally car-ried a crew of more than twenty, where sailors climbed aloft to unfurl sails, teams of others stayed on deck to haul in unison on halyards, oth-ers sheeted-in the sails, worked the windlass to raise the anchor, took the wheel to steer. The strenuous job demanded many hands working precisely in tandem. Besides, according to Irving's account, a head-wind blew into the cove. The ship would struggle even with a full crew to sail clear of the cove's entrance and gain the open water beyond.

The second option was to take to the longboat and make a run for it. Under the cover of darkness, they could slip out of the cove and head down the coast, where, if their luck held with the weather and they stayed well offshore, they could row and sail undetected the two hundred miles down to Astoria and safety.

Four of the five survivors chose this option. However, one of the five, believed to be either James Lewis, the clerk, or Stephen Weeks, the armorer, apparently elected not to make the escape by longboat, and insisted he would remain aboard the *Tonquin*. Either he suffered wounds too severe to allow him to travel, or he believed he had a better chance of survival on board the ship, or he had some other plan in mind. Perhaps, mortally wounded and utterly exhausted, the single individual Lewis or Weeks (and the other may have been his dead or dying comrade) simply no longer cared and wished only that his comrades save themselves. According to Irving's account, Lewis had claimed on the voyage around Cape Horn to the West Coast that he would prefer suicide to being taken and tortured by Indians.

Four men slipped into the longboat during the night and stealthily rowed out of the cove. As day broke, they weren't to be seen. Clayoquot canoes from the village set off from shore to make their way to the *Tonquin,* approaching slowly, cautiously. They wished to seize the ship and its precious cargo of trade goods, and tow it to shore.

Nothing stirred at first aboard the *Tonquin*. Then a single figure, either Lewis or Weeks, slowly appeared on deck.

"The wounded man showed himself over the railing, made signs that he was alone, and wanted their assistance," stated one account.

He then disappeared below. Slowly, cautiously, the Clayoquot canoes nestled around the *Tonquin's* hull. The first Clayoquot climbed over the rail and onto the deck. They realized that no one manned the ship but the wounded man who had disappeared below. Seeing the ship was now theirs, the Clayoquot excitedly pried opened hatches and doorways, scrambled over the decks and through passageways below, to loot its vast treasure of trade goods.

Dozens and dozens of Clayoquot Indians now scrambled aboard the *Tonquin* as she rode in the cove, with many more clustered alongside her copper-sheathed hull in their big cedar canoes. Joseachal, the interpreter, watching from the shore, estimated there were four or five hundred Indians in total.

Suddenly, reported Joseachal, who watched from the shore, the ship disappeared in a blinding flash and a billowing explosion of smoke. A thunderous roar rolled across the water, echoing for miles along the wooded coast. Torsos, limbs, heads, and pieces of flesh arced over the cove. Shattered bits of wood from the *Tonquin*'s thick hull and the cedar canoes rained down on the sea.

Lewis—or Weeks—had taken revenge for Captain Thorn and all aboard the *Tonquin*. He'd apparently waited for the Indians to gather aboard to loot the ship. Then he lit off the ship's powder magazine, all nine thousand pounds of it packed in the hold like a bomb, blowing himself and everyone nearby into the sky.

Somewhere around two hundred Clayoquot perished. Joseachal reported that body parts washed up on the beach for days afterward. He also reported the fate of the four crew members who escaped in the longboat. They eventually were blown by a gale to shore. Discovered by Indians, they were brought back to the Clayoquot village. Joseachal apparently heard from them the story of their attempted escape. Then the Clayoquot slowly tortured the four survivors to death.

I N ASTORIA, THE PLEASANT WEATHER OF LATE SUMMER and early autumn in 1811 abruptly ended when the late October rains swept in. The mood darkened further. The *Tonquin's* voyage should have lasted just a few weeks. It had now been more than four months since she'd left. The only news came from the continued rumors of her destruction delivered from the tribes to the north. Likewise, they expected Hunt's Overland Party to arrive any day. But they sighted no voyageurs canoes emerging from behind Tongue Point and stroking hard down the broad Columbia, paddle blades flashing and songs rolling across the water.

With the chill autumn storms blowing in from the Pacific, their little clearing in the forest turned to mud. The fortifications they had erected so hastily at Astoria did little to repel the choking sense of vulnerability or leaven the dark anxiety of the unknown on this sodden, storm-battered coast, three thousand miles from home. Possessing neither numbers, nor ships, nor large cannon, McDougall thought hard about how to regain advantage over the unseen Indians who he feared lurked in the forests around him, ready to overrun the palisaded settlement under his command. Clever with ruses and behind-the-scene strategies to safeguard his interests, McDougall finally hit on an inspiration.

Of the new diseases that the first Europeans brought to the Americas, one of the leading killers was smallpox. The virus, transmitted through close contact and expelled mucus or bedding, could race quickly through whole villages, covering its inhabitants with lesions, followed by death. About twenty years earlier, the Northwest Coastal Indians had suffered a severe smallpox epidemic brought by the first coastal trading ships. They lived in mortal fear of the disease.

Knowing this history, McDougall invited the local chiefs to Mr. Astor's new emporium on the Columbia. Once they'd gathered, according to an account Irving heard from one of the participants, McDougall held up a small glass vial. In this bottle, McDougall told them, hid the deadly smallpox. If the Indians didn't treat the traders well, there would be consequences.

"I have but to draw the cork, and let loose the pestilence, to sweep man, woman, and child from the face of the earth."

They backed away. The ruse gave him some leverage—for a while.

Work continued, even with no sign of the *Tonquin* or the Overland Party. The *Tonquin* had gone missing, a major loss, but they knew that other Astor ships were due to supply the emporium in the coming spring, and that Hunt's Overland Party should eventually arrive with more men to reinforce their thinned ranks.

Still, they had yet to spend a winter at the new colony on the West Coast. They began to prepare. Hunters, both Indian and Astoria's own, brought back deer and elk to supply the men with nutritious fresh meat. Other natives paddled up to the settlement in canoes laden with dozens of fresh and dried salmon to exchange for goods. The Astorians worried they wouldn't have enough food for winter. There were many reasons to be anxious. Two centuries earlier, the first winter and starvation had decimated the Jamestown colony on the East Coast. Winter's cold and scurvy had nearly wiped out some of the first French settlements in New France, and likewise killed 52 of the 102 original Plymouth colonists during their first winter of 1620–21.

They finished the dwelling house on September 26, and the small schooner, named *Dolly,* after Astor's effervescent teenage daughter, on October 2. David Stuart, one of the Scottish partners and a kind of unofficial elder, had left in early summer by canoe to explore and establish an interior fur post high on a Columbia tributary known to the Indians as the Okanagan, taking with him clerk Alexander Ross and a few voyageurs. Now his nephew Robert Stuart took the *Dolly* to explore the Columbia's lower reaches and establish a fur trade with the natives there. The unpopular McDougall remained in charge at Astoria.

On November 10, the Astorians discovered that three men had deserted. Leaving under the pretense of a hunting expedition, the trio "absconded," as Franchère put it, with a canoe and fowling guns and other men's clothing. The threesome evidently believed they could reach the Spanish settlements that lay nearly a thousand miles south down the Pacific Coast. They meant to escape the dark, sodden Northwest and the heavy labor of clearing the forest. McDougall dispatched a search party led by Franchère, which got lost in a maze of islands a short way up the Columbia and spent several very unpleasant nights beating through thick forest in blustery rain. With the help of Indians who identified the fugitives' footsteps on a sandy river beach, the searchers eventually located the three escapees, held captive by an Indian chief on a nearby southern tributary of the Columbia. The river was called the "Willamet" or "Wolamat," as some wrote it. Known to the natives as the *Cathlanaminim,* the Willamette Valley was then unknown and unexplored by whites. It would figure prominently in the future of both the Astorians and the entire West. Grudgingly, the chief ransomed the trio of escapees back to Franchère for eight blankets, a brass kettle, a tomahawk, and a broken pistol.

Hauled back to Astoria, the three were put in irons and on half rations for eleven days, then freed to return to the work of sawing logs into planks and other tasks for the budding settlement. That they had been willing to walk to the Spanish settlements so far through unknown terrain gives one a sense of the level of discontent at Astoria that fall. But then things got worse. The days grew short and dark. Winter rains charged in from the open sea, blasting into the river's mouth, moaning through the swaying forest of giant trees, occasionally toppling one with an earthshaking crash into rain-soaked underbrush. The Astorians felt exposed.

"It rained in torrents and was dark as pitch," Franchère wrote of nights in the forest during the search for the fugitives, when rain doused their campfire and a gale blew away the woven mats they used for tents.

By early December, they'd given up on the *Tonquin* for the season. Had she sailed directly for China? Or were the Indian rumors true? With the winter storms' huge North Pacific swells crashing onto the Columbia Bar, she clearly wasn't returning anytime soon. They were so sure of this that McDougall auctioned off the personal articles that clerk James Lewis had left behind when he sailed off aboard the *Tonquin* for Vancouver Island. The downpour leaked into the fort's cellars and powder magazine. Work parties bailed out the cellar, elevated the floors, and tightened the cedar shingle roofs. With the late autumn gales, the local Indians migrated from their exposed villages along the wide Columbia's banks to smaller, sheltered tributaries inland, no longer providing the Astorians with a regular supply of fresh game meat.

Yet not all events were discouraging that fall. A small expedition arrived at Astoria that October by canoe from upriver, sent from David Stuart's new post high on the Okanagan. It carried promising reports—friendly Indians and bountiful furs. The Astorians also heard reports from the natives that the valley of the river Willamette, where the deserters had been held, was particularly rich in beaver. Young Robert Stuart set out on December 5 to explore the Willamette as a possible fur post. It was encouraging to learn that, as at the Okanagan, and surely on many other unknown rivers, lay rich new territory for Mr. Astor's fur empire on the Pacific. Here in abundance lay the resources to feed his transglobal trade.

The Astorians dug up the last of the root crops that they had planted upon their arrival in May, spading on November 26 sixty potatoes, sixty turnips, and a few carrots. Another twenty-five bushels of turnips were unearthed on December 20, one of them, noted McDougall, measuring thirty-three inches around. It was a victory of sorts. They had physically shoved back the overpowering wildness on this ragged, stormy juncture between continent's edge and ocean's breadth to create a haven where they nurtured domestic crops. Their pigs were another, messy triumph. Tended by the Hawaiians, they also had survived well, rooting content-edly in the mud and rain and the food slops tossed out to them.

The Astorians celebrated a rainy Christmas Day in 1811 happily enough. They remained unaware, of course, of Hunt's struggles over the snowy mountains at the same time, but perhaps imagined Astor with his browned roasts and warm fires in New York. They drank an extra dose of grog. New Year's Day—the traditional voyageur day of celebration—presented an even bigger occasion. Franchère noted that it had rained almost without interruption since early October. The new year of 1812 dawned beautifully at Astoria, with clear blue skies, sun-shine, and a white frost on the ground that sparkled against the dark green forest.

"At sunrise," wrote McDougall, who kept Astoria's official log, "the Drum beat to arms and the colours were hoisted. Three rounds of small arms & three discharges from the great Guns were fired, after which all hands were treated with grog, bread, cheese & Butter."

The dinner provided a wonderful break from what Franchère described as a meager diet for the last several months, consisting mainly of "sun-dried fish." Then more grog was served out, and the French-Canadian voyageurs, the Hawaiians, and the Scottish traders danced together in front of the fire at Mr. Astor's new settlement on the Pacific until 3:00 A.M.

IN MID-JANUARY the men at Astoria were going about their usual daily work building the emporium to handle the expected influx of furs in the thousands—the cooper splitting staves for barrels, the blacksmith assembling dozens of axes for upriver trade goods, the carpenters framing a shed, voyageurs hauling timbers from the forest for boatbuilders to build barges for the river trade, Hawaiians clearing brush. The sick list showed six men. Scurvy had begun to set in after many weeks without fresh food. McDougall himself was ill. He often was, keeping to his quarters, not recording his illness in the official log. At 5:00 P.M. on Saturday, January 18, 1812, the Astorians looked up from their appointed tasks to see two canoes paddling around Tongue Point, headed toward their settlement. The canoes appeared to contain white men.

They neared the beach. Wrote Franchère: Mr. M'Dougal . . . being confined to his room by sickness, the duty of receiving the strangers devolved on me. My astonishment was not slight, when one of the party called me by name, as he extended his hand, and I recognized Mr. Donald M'Kenzie, the same who had quitted Montreal, with Mr. W. P. Hunt, in the month of July, 1810."

It had been a year and a half since they'd seen each other. Since then, Astor partner Mackenzie had been traveling nearly nonstop across North America's wilderness. Franchère was taken aback at his appearance.

"[They] arrived at the establishment, safe and sound, it is true," he wrote, "but in a pitiable condition to see; their clothes being nothing but fluttering rags."

Accompanying Mackenzie were partner McClellan, clerk John Reed, American hunter William Cannon, and seven voyageurs. Two small reconnaissance parties had gone ahead when the Overland Party had first split up at Caldron Linn in early November, one under Mackenzie and one under McClellan. Farther along the Mad River the two small parties had run into each other and rejoined in their trek toward the Columbia and the Pacific. They'd suffered extremely. Unable to descend to the Mad River to fetch water, they had been plagued by thirst so intense that it killed their dogs and forced the travelers to drink their own urine. Crossing mountains northward and struggling through the deep gorge for three weeks, they had gone without food for days on end, surviving on bits of roasted beaver skin and old moccasins. Finally they had reached a canoeable tributary of the Columbia, traded for two canoes from the Nez Percé Indians, and paddled downstream to the Columbia's mouth.

For the first time, they saw the new settlement. It existed. But they also learned the disturbing news about the loss of the *Tonquin*.

Now the fear at Astoria was this: If Mackenzie's group had suffered so deeply on the trek along the Mad River, what about Hunt and his much bigger party? With far less wilderness experience than Mackenzie, and moving more slowly, Hunt and his party surely would suffer worse. Rumors floated about that they had died of starvation, or been killed by Indians.

A month later, on February 15, a pod of six canoes emerged in the distance from behind Tongue Point and soon paddled up to the beach at Astoria. It was Wilson Price Hunt and his party of thirty-three, which included the Dorion family. These men, too, looked awful. Wrote Alexander Ross: "The emaciated, downcast looks and tattered garments of our friends, all bespoke their extreme sufferings during a long and severe winter."

Yet there was joy also in reunion. The parties celebrated warmly at Astoria—voyageurs embracing voyageurs; clannish Scottish fur traders joined again, clasping hands, smoking their pipes and speaking their Gaelic. Inexplicable gaps, however, remained in the Overland Party's unity, as well as strange additions. Still missing were partner Ramsay Crooks, Virginia hunter John Day, and the several struggling voyageurs who had stayed behind at the Shoshone villages. The weakened Carriere, riding a horse, had simply vanished. Two men had drowned in the Mad River—Clappine, swept away in the rapids after Crooks's canoe smashed into a rock, and the starving Prevost, who tumbled out of a bullboat. Besides these losses, Mackenzie's party had added to its numbers a white stranger picked up en route.

He was a young New England teenager by the name of Archibald Pelton. They'd found him wandering aimlessly deep in the wilder-

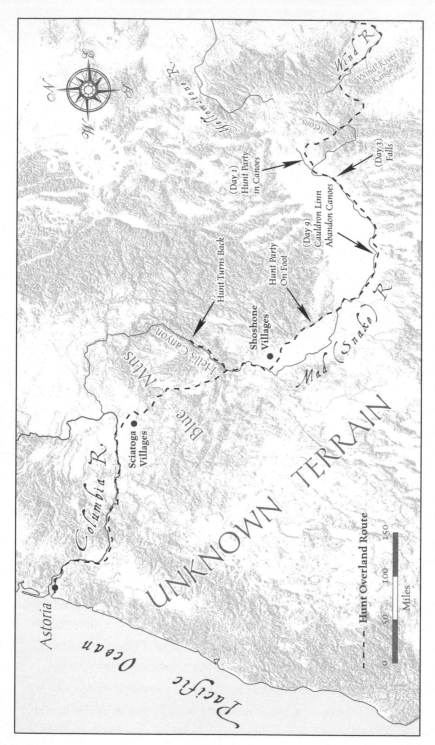

Hunt Overland Party, November 1811–February 1812

ness. Pelton had run away from his family's farm a few years earlier in Northampton, Massachusetts, and ended up in St. Louis. Here he had joined Andrew Henry's ill-fated attempt in 1809 to establish a fur post on the Upper Missouri at Three Forks. Pelton had witnessed the massacre of his close companions by the Blackfeet but had managed to flee. He wandered in the unmapped wilds for nearly two years, eventually taken in by a friendly tribe (probably a group of Nez Percé), where Mackenzie and McClellan had found him as they struggled toward the Pacific.

The trauma of the massacres and wanderings, however, had told deeply on young Archibald Pelton. He'd gone mad. He spoke incoherently and acted strangely, but was otherwise harmless. His name would eventually enter the Chinook trade jargon as a term for losing one's sanity. Technically speaking, this half-mad nineteen-year-old runaway was the first American across the continent after Lewis and Clark. He was also a walking testament to the powerful distorting effect that extreme and prolonged exposure to danger in these distant wilds could have on the psyche. He would not be the only Astorian to suffer this fate.

When the combined Overland Party, with Archibald Pelton among them, arrived at Astoria in the winter of 1812, it marked only the second time in recorded history that a party of Americans had crossed the North American continent. Hunt's consensus style of leadership—his relatively gentle touch compared to that of authoritarian Captain Thorn and the subsurface machinations of fur trader and partner McDougall—had maintained morale and led his party out of the western wilderness. But Hunt's leadership had come at a heavy cost—including getting them lost in the first place, the endless delays that allowed winter to catch them in the mountains, nearly starving them all to death, and the several failing men they'd left far behind.

Even as his party finally arrived at Mr. Astor's new emporium on the shores of the Pacific, two thousand miles after leaving the known Lewis and Clark route up the Missouri for fear of the Blackfeet, Hunt's toughest leadership challenges still lay ahead. To make the West Coast empire successful, he would need to know exactly where to put his energy. And, in the face of yet more daunting challenges, he would need to grasp just how deeply Astor backed the grand venture.

It wasn't clear that Hunt was capable of either.

A NEW SENSE OF OPTIMISM ARRIVED AT ASTORIA WITH the coming of spring in 1812. The half-starved members of the Overland Party recovered their vitality and muscle mass, feasting on the spring runs of fat-rich candlefish that now swarmed up the Columbia and were harvested by the Chinook and brought to the traders. The reports from the inland tributaries such as the Okanagan and the Willamette indicated rich harvests of furs, the Okanagan post alone trading less than $200 worth of merchandise to the Indians for $10,000 worth of furs. Astoria's thin ranks, defended by McDougall's smallpox-in-a-bottle, was now, after the arrival of the Overland Party, suddenly bustling with nearly one hundred men. Here was Astor's vision taking shape in reality—the beginnings of his great emporium on the Pacific Rim.

Hunt brought a renewed energy to the leadership of Astoria. Taking command from McDougall—much to the relief of voyageurs, Hawaiians, and clerks who toiled under the Scotsman—Hunt immediately put to good use his business management skills. He intended to make a success of the grand enterprise, as instructed, despite the shocking setbacks they had all suffered so far. The men knew that Astor's great resources backed their venture, and that he would keep a stream of supply ships arriving at the emporium on the Pacific.

Hunt now laid out his priorities. First, get messages back to Mr. Astor as quickly as possible via the overland route, as this would be faster than waiting for an Astor supply ship that would then sail for Canton. Second, via canoe, deliver supplies upriver to the new fur posts in the interior, and establish more posts, over a still broader swath of terrain. If necessary, the Astor posts would compete directly with the North West Company, whose traders had crossed the Rocky Mountains and established a few small posts high on the northern tributaries of the Columbia. Finally, a party should recover the tons of cached trade goods and traps left at Caldron Linn.

Hunt wasted no time. In March, as spring snowmelts began to swell the river, and barely a month after his arrival, he dispatched canoes up the Columbia to carry out these three tasks. Robert Stuart would lead the party resupplying his uncle David Stuart at the Okanagan River post and bring back that post's winter harvest of furs. To carry out the second task—returning to the caches at Caldron Linn— Hunt sent two clerks, Farnham and McGillis, a guide, and a party of eight voyageurs to travel by canoe and on horses to be purchased from upriver Indians.

The third mission—the long trek back across the North American continent with messages for Mr. Astor—would be led by clerk John Reed, an Irishman, along with hunter Ben Jones. Despite its sufferings, Hunt's Overland Party had discovered a plausible route across the continent south of the Lewis and Clark route and Blackfeet territory—a viable "line of communication" across the continent. The Astorians would now employ this line of communication by sending a message back to Astor in New York. The true significance of this major geographical accomplishment wouldn't become clear until decades later.

Believing he was taking an extra precaution, Reed ordered a waterproof tin box soldered together by the metal workers at Astoria. In this he would carry the precious letters to Astor strapped to his back. Removing it only to sleep, willing to part with the tin case only upon death, Reed, as Irving described him, possessed the "zeal of a true Irishman" as well as an Irishman's "want of forethought." As it turned out, the shiny metal box would be a terrible liability.

The three parties set out together from Astoria by canoe on March 22. The first obstacle lay about 150 miles upriver where the Columbia squeezes past Mount Hood and channels through the Cascade Mountains. Here they approached the section of the Columbia called the Narrows (today known as The Dalles) and the Indian village of Wishram. This was a prime fishing spot where the Wishram and Wasco tribes erected platforms that projected from the riverbanks over the narrow, foaming chutes of rushing water. Standing on scaffolding and using hooplike nets on long poles like butterfly nets, the tribal members swept the frothing waters to catch the salmon fighting upstream toward their spawning beds. On a good day, noted Robert Stuart in his journal, an experienced net handler could scoop up one or two fish with every downstream sweep and by day's end bring in more than five hundred fish—a stunning amount of food. It was then dried, pounded into a fine powder, and packed into reed bags lined with dried salmon skins that made weighty packages about one foot wide by two feet long. The people of Wishram traded this *ch-lai* to other tribes in return for dried buffalo meat and other goods, making Wishram and the Narrows a regional Native American marketplace.

But as the people of Wishram captured salmon swimming upriver, they also levied whatever tolls they could from canoes wanting to pass through the Narrows, where the parties, whether native or white, had to portage rapids and waterfalls. This trading and toll-taking presumably had gone on from time immemorial—by some archaeological estimates the villages at the Narrows are among the oldest continuously inhabited human settlements in North America, lived in for eleven thousand years or more.* It was no different for them when the first

---

* The native settlements at the Narrows lost this distinction, and in fact their existence, after federal agencies built The Dalles dam for hydroelectric power and irrigation, which in 1957 flooded the ancient salmon-netting site of Celilo Falls and inundated the villages. In Ken Kesey's novel *One Flew Over the Cuckoo's Nest*, the fictional inmate Chief Bromden is the son of the chief who "lost" Celilo Falls to the dam.

canoes of white traders, such as Robert Stuart, wanted to pass through the Long Narrows and Falls of the Columbia. The Indians no doubt viewed the white parties as an incursion on their territory and a threat to their tremendous wealth of salmon. The young Scotsman Robert Stuart saw it differently. "[They] are saucy, impudent Rascals, [who] will steal when they can, & pillage whenever a weak party falls into their clutches. . . ."

The shiny metal box on Irishman John Reed's back became an object of particular attention. During the first leg of the portage at the Narrows, Stuart hired local Indians to help haul canoes and carry the heavy bales of trade goods. Portaging the goods on horses, a few of the Indians vanished up a rocky canyon with two bales of merchandise. Others threw rocks to damage a canoe hull, apparently hoping its leaks would maroon some of the Astorians and their trade merchandise on the riverbank, where it could be plundered. On the portage's second leg, around the Falls of the Columbia (Celilo Falls), the white traders countered with stealth. Robert Stuart directed the 1:00 A.M. portage operation by moonlight while the Indians slept. At dawn, only two loads of goods remained at the portage's lower end. John Reed and McClellan were standing guard over these last two loads when Reed, according to Stuart's account, "very imprudently" refused the help of extra men to guard the merchandise.

The moment the two were alone, canoes of warriors paddled from the opposite side of the river and went for the two loads of goods. McClellan, he of the quick trigger finger who had so wanted to shoot Manuel Lisa on sight back on the Missouri, told the gung ho Irishman Reed to pull back with him away from the goods and, as Stuart quoted McClellan, "they would give it to them while plundering."

Reed, however, had forgotten to remove the leather cover over his rifle's firing mechanism. An Indian tried to wrestle Reed's rifle away. Another threw a robe over McClellan's head and tried to stab him. McClellan untangled himself from the robe, raised his rifle, and shot the warrior dead through the chest. Another Indian struck Reed in the side of the head with a war club. He fell senseless to the riverbank. McClellan drew his pistol and shot that warrior, too. Several warriors still pressed forward. One struck Reed's head with five quick tomahawk blows. McClellan rushed at them with his empty rifle raised as if to fire. He managed to push them back, quickly reloaded, and charged at them with a war cry. They dispersed, and McClellan went off chasing three warriors who made motions to return. Up at the head of the portage, Robert Stuart heard McClellan's shots. He immediately sent men to the lower end. They found Reed wandering among the rocks, totally dazed. Soaked with blood from his five head wounds, he walked, as Stuart put it, "not knowing whither he went."

Missing in the melee was the shiny tin box of messages for Mr. Astor that John Reed had carried on his back.

At the upper end of the portage, they climbed into their canoes, Reed having fainted. McClellan bandaged the five, two-inch tomahawk gashes in Reed's head. A short distance upstream, a force of 120 mounted warriors gathered at a narrow point of the river to stop them. The Stuart party tied their canoes together and moored to a rock just offshore, guns at the ready. The war chief was paddled out to the Stuart armed flotilla. The families of the two fallen warriors demanded revenge, the war chief told them. It could be satisfied simply by handing over the body of Reed (who the Indians assumed was dead), which would be cut into pieces. After that, promised the chief, in Stuart's account of the conversation, "the greatest harmony would prevail for the future."

"Our answer was NO, the man you wounded is our Brother and you must destroy [all of] us before you get him—We are prepared and ready for your Warriors, bring them on and we will teach you a more serious lesson than you learned this morning."

The chief returned to the shore to consult. It was finally negotiated that the blood debt could be settled with three blankets, "to cover the dead," as well as tobacco, "to fill the Calumet of Peace."

Once beyond the Narrows and its gauntlet of warriors, the three combined parties paused. They had to decide: Where to proceed from here? Reed was now in no shape to trek overland back to the United States with messages for Mr. Astor. Nor did he possess any messages to deliver. All parties decided to turn back to Astoria. First, however, the combined group paddled farther up the Columbia to the high tributary where Robert's uncle, David Stuart, had established his post on the Okanagan River.

Heading upriver beyond the Narrows, and past Mount Hood and the Cascade Range, the terrain opened on both riverbanks into dry plains and sagebrush—the Columbia Plain. This huge expanse of desertlike landscape lies like a giant valley between the rainy, snowy peaks of the Cascades, which catch the moisture-heavy storms blowing in off the Pacific, and the distant spine of the Rockies.

The group arrived at the Okanagan post on the Columbia River on April 24, a month after leaving Astoria. With this post, David Stuart had staked a claim for John Jacob Astor to the trading territory on the river's northern reaches. A kind of testing and jostling was under way between Astor's company and the North West Company over the huge and still only partially explored Columbia Basin. When David Thompson of the North West Company had canoed down the Columbia the previous summer to Astoria, he had tried to convince the tribes that controlled the "Forks" of the Columbia that the river's northern branch should be his company's trading territory, while the southern fork (the Snake River) he apparently suggested could be Astor's. He had erected a British flag and posted a message at the Forks—where the Snake joined the Columbia—claiming the region for the North West Company. But immediately after Thompson's posting, David Stuart had come upriver from Astoria and convinced the same Indians at the Forks to let him trade on those same northern branches for Astor.

David Stuart had accrued a rich harvest of beaver furs during the winter by trading with the friendly Sinkaietk Indians on the Okanagan—they had 2,500 furs, according to Alexander Ross, who served as Stuart's clerk. Here was more evidence of the potential of Astor's West Coast empire.

That "good old soul" David Stuart, as Alexander Ross described his boss, joined his nephew Robert Stuart for the return trip to Astoria for a visit, having last seen his colleagues at the Columbia's mouth the previous summer, in 1811, when they had landed together from the *Tonquin*. Leaving the Okanagan post on April 27, the Stuart flotilla, which included Reed, McClellan, and others, had by early May descended the Columbia some two hundred miles and reached the mouth of the Umatilla River—still about three hundred miles upriver from Astoria. Just past sunrise one early May morning they were paddling their four canoes downstream where the river cut a trough across the big, arid Columbia Plain when they passed a camp of Indians on the riverbank.

They heard a shout.

"Come onshore!"

It sounded like English. They drew their canoes alongside each other. They paused. The big craft drifted together on the current. The men listened closely.

"Come onshore!" the shout echoed across the water.

They stroked for the riverbank. To their amazement, they found standing on the shore among the Indians their lost colleagues—Ramsay Crooks and John Day.

"[S]o changed and emaciated were they," writes Ross, "that our people for some time could scarcely recognize them to be white men."

Ramsay Crooks then told the remarkable tale of his and John Day's ordeal, which Ross set down in his narrative.

Some five months earlier, back in mid-December 1811, Hunt and his Overland Party had left Crooks and Day weakened and struggling upstream out of the Mad River gorge. The two had eventually reached the relative safety of a Shoshone camp near the lava plain. The Shoshone had treated them kindly, giving them shelter and sharing food when the Shoshone themselves had food. Eventually, however, the Shoshone packed up their encampment and moved on, leaving Crooks and Day to fend for themselves.

They built a wigwam of grass and branches. They gathered fire-wood. Then John Day faltered. It may have been scurvy. He grew so weak he couldn't stand up on his own. Ramsay Crooks tried to cook camas roots in the Shoshone style for sustenance. He mistakenly dug up what was apparently the "deathcamas" instead of the similar-looking *camassia,* which thrives in broad, moist mountain valleys and when baked resembles a sweet potato. He almost fatally poisoned both of them. Reduced to a "torpid" state by the steroid alkaloid toxins of the deathcamas, Crooks and Day let their fire die. Fireless, foodless, poisoned, and alone in the mountain valleys in the middle of winter, they would have died if two Shoshone Indians hadn't strayed by their shelter, relit their fire, fed them, stayed with them for two days, and left them a two-pound piece of venison.

Their next visitor was a wolf that hovered around outside the wig-wam, perhaps sensing that death was imminent within. Despite his weakness, John Day remained a crack shot and managed to drop it. Pounding the marrow out of its bones, they made a nutritious broth and ate the wolf hide. Restored enough that they could walk, they started westward again, carrying a supply of dried wolf meat and hunt-ing what little game they could find. They located the Hunt Party's trail through the snow. They followed it for some days. Then they lost it in a broad and snowless prairie. They then spent much of the winter wandering, unsure where they were, probably in the valleys east of the Blue Mountains. By the end of March, the snow had melted enough to make the final crossing over the mountain crest. On the far side, they followed the Umatilla River downstream.

In mid-April they reached the Columbia where the Umatilla River joins it near the Forks of the Columbia, or Great Bend. Here they found an Indian encampment and met a friendly and hospitable chief, Yeck-a-tap-am, who fed them and acted toward them "like a father." Revived, they struck off on foot down the bank of the Columbia toward what they hoped was a settlement—Astoria—that their colleagues had established at its mouth, as planned. After nine days of walking, they had approached to within twenty miles of the Narrows and the village of Wishram. Crooks and Day were sitting on the riverbank one morning when a party of Indians came up, greeted them in the friendly manner that Crooks and Day had experienced upriver, sat with them, and, according to some accounts, offered them food.

During this pleasant springtime encounter overlooking the Columbia, one of the Indians indicated he wished to measure the length of Crooks's rifle. He picked it up and held his bow alongside it as a gauge. At the same moment, another picked up John Day's rifle. The two ran off a distance, followed by the rest of the Indian party. They aimed the two rifles and drawn bows at the surprised Crooks and Day. With sign language, they communicated that a recent party of white men heading upriver in canoes (which, unbeknownst to Crooks and Day, was Stuart and Reed and McClellan's group) had killed two of their warriors at the Narrows. Day drew his knife. He proposed to Crooks that he rush the warriors and grab back his gun. Crooks insisted that this would result in instant death.

"The Indians then closed in upon us, with guns pointed and bows drawn, on all sides," according to Ross's recounting of Crooks's story, "and by force stripped us of our clothes, ammunition, knives, and everything else, leaving us as naked as the day we were born. . . ."

The Indians now debated heatedly among themselves—apparently over whether to kill Crooks and Day. In the midst of the argument, two or three elderly men intervened among the younger warriors, apparently warning them of the possible consequences of killing the two. They gestured for Crooks and Day to leave. Crooks and Day slowly turned, starting to walk back upriver, expecting at any moment to be killed. But when they dared look back the Indians instead were preoccupied in divvying up the clothing and other items they had stripped from the pair of white men.

They walked naked, upriver, for four days. They spent four nights without fire trying to sleep naked in the chill of early spring. Finally they reached a small Indian encampment. The inhabitants gave them food and bits of clothing. Several days more on foot brought them upstream to the camp of Yeck-a-tap-am, at the Umatilla mouth, who a few weeks earlier had treated them as a father would his sons. According to Ross's telling of it, the two were preparing to head all the way back to St. Louis via the just-explored overland route when they spotted Stuart's canoes paddling that morning down the Columbia from the Okanagan post.

"Come onshore!"

Five months after their ordeal began, Crooks and Day finally were safe.

CHAPTER NINETEEN

A S THE STUART FLOTILLA OF CANOES CARRYING CROOKS
and Day approached Astoria on May 11, a large sailing ship
rode at anchor at Baker's Bay just inside the Columbia's mouth.
As the Stuart party touched at the new wharf under construction
at Astoria, to the "great surprise and great joy" of all, they learned
that the ship anchored ten miles downstream was the *Beaver*. Astor
had dispatched the vessel the previous autumn to resupply what he
hoped—but hadn't heard—was his new emporium on the Pacific. At
490 tons, nearly twice the size of the *Tonquin,* well armed, and laden
with an enormous load of trade goods, the *Beaver* had arrived at the
Columbia's mouth only four days before. Its Captain Sowles, a careful
man, following Astor's instructions precisely, cautiously sailed back
and forth beyond the Columbia Bar until he could learn whether the
emporium existed and remained in friendly hands. The *Beaver* signaled by firing cannons, until cannons had answered in the distance
and Comcomly's big canoe paddled out to meet it, with an oared boat
following behind bearing McDougall and one of the clerks as the official greeting party.

The *Beaver* brought a huge boost of energy to the outpost on
the Pacific—dozens of men, hundreds of bales of trade goods, arse-
nals of armaments, good food and live animals, barrels of liquor, and
instructions and support directly from the hand of Mr. Astor himself.
At Astor's wish, the *Beaver* carried many Americans, as he wanted to

ensure that his enterprise on the Pacific would be primarily managed and staffed by American rather than British personnel, especially as tensions continued to rise between the two nations in the Atlantic. Aboard were fifteen American laborers, five clerks ("young gentlemen," as Irving put it, "of good connexions in the American cities"), including John Jacob Astor's own nephew, George Ehninger, in addition to six Canadian voyageurs. Aboard the *Beaver* was also another prominent manager in the Astor enterprise, this one of American citizenship like Hunt—John Clarke. Unlike Hunt, Clarke had experience in the American fur trade of the upper Midwest. Astor hoped his American man Clarke, as the Scotsman Ross put it, would stand out as a "brightest star" in the Pacific enterprise.

A kind of convergence of parties arrived at Astoria all at once. This same day, May 11, that the Stuart party canoes paddled into the settlement from upriver and the *Beaver* rode at anchor in Baker's Bay, Donald Mackenzie also returned to Astoria from further explorations up the Willamette River. He brought highly favorable reports of a broad valley between low hills covered with pine and spreading oaks.

"Between these high lands, lie what is called the Valley of the Wallamitte, the frequent haunts of innumerable herds of elk and deer . . . a very rich country," Ross wrote.

Astoria jumped with planning and strategy now that all partners were finally present—among them Hunt, McDougall, the two Stuarts, Mackenzie, and the newly arrived Clarke—as well as scores of men and tons of fresh supplies. Hunt was in charge. As ever, following Mr. Astor's instructions, he aimed for consensus among the partners and was able to effect an agreement on a comprehensive plan. The partners would send out expeditions in virtually all directions to establish a vast network of posts. These tendrils of John Jacob Astor's empire on the Pacific would spread out like a giant web from the epicenter at Astoria to capture the fur trade of this entire sector of the North American continent, funnel it through the emporium, and leverage its wealth into a round-the-world global trading empire:

North—To establish posts beyond David Stuart's on the Okanagan and counter any activity of the rival North West Company in what they called New Caledonia.

East—To the interior mountain valleys of the Kootenai and Salish people and to build posts in the Snake River country.

South—To establish posts in the great rich valley of the Willamette.

Overland—To fetch the supplies cached at Caldron Linn, and to set off overland to St. Louis with the messages for Mr. Astor that had been stolen on the first attempt.

Sea-ward—To collect sea otter furs, exchange trade goods with the Russian posts in Alaska, and load Russian furs. On this mission, Astoria's leader, Wilson Price Hunt, would board the *Beaver* and sail up the Northwest Coast.

THREE THOUSAND MILES AWAY, on May 12, 1812, the day after that happy arrival at Astoria, John Jacob Astor opened his newspaper, the *New York Gazette and General Advertiser.* A prominent item on the second page confirmed vague rumors he'd been hearing recently, emanating from ship captains on the tarry wharves of New York: The *Tonquin,* and its crew, had been lost.

A letter from Mr. Nathaniel Woodbury of Danvers, dated Kegharni (in the South Sea), Sept. 5, 1811, contains the following melancholy report: "That in June last the ship Tonquin, Thorn, master, was lying at anchor, at a village near Nootka Sound . . . for the purpose of trade—that a great number of Indians were on board, when, on some misunderstanding, they suddenly attacked the crew, killed all on board except the captain and one more, who [fled to] the magazine, and seeing no possibility of escape, chose to be their own executioners, and accordingly put fire to powder, which blew the ship to pieces, and destroyed many Indians. . . . The ship brought out a large number of persons, part of a company who have commenced a settlement on the Columbia River—and the place where she was taken is not more than two degrees north of the place where she landed her settlers."

That night, John Jacob and Sarah Astor attended a play, as they often did. Performed on the Manhattan stage that week were two romances, *The Child of Nature: A Dramatic Piece, from the French of Madame the Marchioness of Sillery* and *The Lady of the Lake: A Melo-Dramatic Romance,* based on Walter Scott's poem. Astor ran into a friend in the audience. The friend consoled him about the stunning news in the *Gazette.* According to Irving's account of the incident, the friend remarked that he was surprised to see Astor out at the theater after so severe a blow to his enterprise.

"What would you have me do?" Astor replied. "Would you have me stay at home and weep for what I cannot help?"

It was a shock, to be sure, this sudden and violent end to his ship, captain, and crew the previous summer. But he was not about to give up of his dream of empire over the loss of a single ship. Rather the *Tonquin*'s loss seemed to harden his determination and prepare him to deepen his already staggering investment. His eminent business practicality trumped whatever sentimentality he felt for the loss of life. He had known all along he was in this for the long haul and that there would be difficult obstacles to overcome. He knew it would take several years at best for the West Coast empire to turn a profit.

A few weeks after he read the grim account of the *Tonquin,* Astor received good news. Reports started coming in from other sea captains of his ship *Enterprise* nearing New York Harbor after her two-and-a-half-year voyage to the Northwest Coast and China. The *Enterprise*'s cargo, when finally tabulated, returned John Jacob Astor his initial investment in cheap trade goods many times over. Based on the *Enterprise* returns, he estimated that $20,000 worth of trinkets in New York could be traded for furs on the Northwest Coast that would bring $80,000 to $100,000 from the merchants at Canton—and another huge jump in profit beyond that when he used those returns to purchase Chinese luxury goods and sell them in New York.

It had *worked*. The Pacific Rim and transglobal triangle trade had made the kind of immensely profitable returns for which he'd hoped. The pieces of his West Coast empire were coming together, although he still didn't know exactly what had happened to the Overland Party. He frequently wrote to St. Louis with inquiries as to any news.

What worried him most now was not the explosion of the *Tonquin*. Rather, in this May and June 1812, it was the fast-escalating tension between the United States and Great Britain. Britain was fighting Napoleon and needed a steady supply of fresh recruits to send into battle. The British Royal Navy had taken to stopping American commercial ships on the Atlantic Ocean, boarding them, dragging off crew members who were thought to be British subjects, and conscripting them into the British armed forces.

U.S. president James Madison declared this and other obnoxious British practices and encroachments had to stop. But they didn't stop.

Astor suspected trouble was on the way.

THE FRENZY OF PLANNING AND PREPARATION at Astoria lasted late into June. The emporium buzzed with more than a hundred men, each assigned a task to forward the grand plan—packing goods for the canoes, preparing food, burning charcoal for the ironworks, clearing brush, erecting structures. Chinook and Clatsop Indians rode canoes to Astoria bearing elk and venison, salmon and furs, to trade for beads and axes, blankets and pots, from the emporium's warehouses. Plans were laid for a large shingled building to serve as a hospital and a lodgings for the tradesmen, such as the blacksmiths and carpenters who served this first American colony on the Pacific. Amid all this activity were other good tidings. Astor's potential rival, the North West Company, wasn't much in evidence in the lower and middle reaches of the Columbia—as if they had withdrawn to the north and left this great unclaimed chunk of the continent to the Americans. The Astorians knew that the North West Company had recently set up posts elsewhere, on some of the Columbia's northern branches, such as the Spokane River. The partners at Astoria, now under the American businessman Hunt instead of the former Nor'wester and Scotsman McDougall, pledged to build Astor's posts directly alongside the rival company and compete with the Nor'westers head-to-head on the Columbia's northern tributaries.

That early summer of 1812 unfolded as a relatively peaceful and prosperous time at Astoria. But just beneath the surface of this society lay the small fractures of psychological stress. On May 12, the day after Ramsay Crooks arrived at Astoria after his five-month ordeal, he simply threw in his shares of the Astor enterprise and quit. He'd been dragged in a travois, starved in a canyon, poisoned by deathcamas, lost in mountains, stripped by Indians. It didn't matter to him whether the *Beaver* had arrived bearing fresh supplies. Likewise for his companion in naked exile, the Virginia hunter John Day. And another Scottish fur trader and partner who'd been with Hunt's Overland Party, the hair-trigger McClellan, threw in his shares and quit. Several voyageurs had already deserted the previous fall. Joseph Miller had quit near the Tetons, splitting off with a leash of trappers. The immense potential profits were no longer enough to lure them. They wanted only to return east as quickly as possible.

They were "partners dissatisfied with the enterprise," Franchère wrote, "and who had made up their minds to return to the United States."

The list went on. There was young Mr. Nicoll, one of the educated clerks of good connections from New York, who had arrived aboard the *Beaver*. He'd hardly set foot on this wild coast of the Pacific when he rudely demanded to Hunt to be taken back to New York aboard the *Beaver*—"being discouraged," as one of his shipmates and fellow clerks, Alfred Seton, put it, "by the hardness that the country presented."

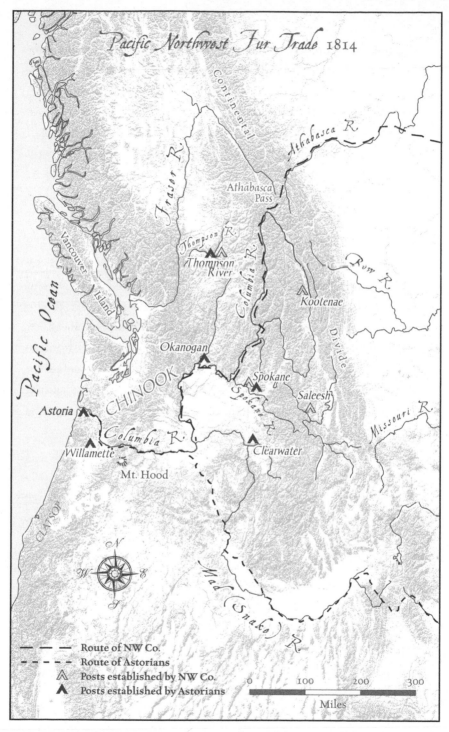

Pacific Northwest Fur Trade 1814

Continental

Athabasca R.

Fraser R.

Athabasca Pass

Thompson R.

Thornton River

Columbia R.

Bow R.

Koolenae

Vancouver Island

Pacific Ocean

Divide

Okanogan

Spokane

Saleesh

Spokane R.

CHINOOK

Astoria

Columbia R.

Clearwater

Missouri R.

Willamette

Mt. Hood

CLATSOP

N
W   E
S

Mad (Snake) R.

— · — Route of NW Co.
– – – Route of Astorians
⋀ Posts established by NW Co.
▲ Posts established by Astorians

0   100   200   300

Miles

COLUMBIA BASIN REGION WITH TRADE POSTS

Hunt said he could go—but due to his rude manners he would have to work as a sailor aboard ship instead of traveling as a gentleman passenger.

And there was Archibald Pelton.

"Our Madman (Pelton) continuing the same," recorded McDougall on June 15, adding a few days later, when Pelton's bizarre behavior still hadn't changed. "[T]hat he is in reality insane there is now little doubt and has become an object of compassion."

McDougall, too, was frequently sick, withdrawing to his quarters.

For all the progress at Astoria, it's not surprising, really, that these profound signs of strain were appearing. The partners who had accompanied the Overland Party, for instance, had survived an incredibly difficult eighteen months overland, with the constant threats of fatal rapids, Indian ambush, starvation, brutal cold, and utter exhaustion, aside from having no idea, for much of the time, where they were. In their sufferings they surely envisioned the rich food, and crackling warmth, the comfort and safety, perhaps even the sense of luxury, that awaited them at their destination—Mr. Astor's emporium on the Pacific.

Then imagine the rude shock of arrival in the coastal winter or early spring: It's cold, it's raining—as it is nearly two hundred days a year at the mouth of the Columbia; the infinite gray coastline stretches away, backed by the thick, dark rain forest—soggy, choked with rotting cedar logs, prehistoric sword ferns, and the dark columns of towering fir and spruce whose outstretched limbs are draped with lichen in giant, ghostly cobwebs. This was a far cry from the euphoric expanses and brilliant starry skies of the high plains, or even the snowy sparkle of the Rockies. The great "emporium" you've fantasized about for so long turns out to be a muddy clearing—rooting pigs, ragged turnip patches, half-blasted stumps, and a ramshackle log palisade—hacked out of the endless wilderness. You learn that your supply ship, the *Tonquin,* has disappeared off the face of the earth. After dreaming for months of luxury and comfort and, above all, safety, you're greeted by this vision of mud and rain, raw logs and squealing pigs, with no other white settlement within a thousand miles, and bands of Indians—who can guess whether for trade or ambush?—always pressing closer.

Virtually every person involved, starting with Astor himself, grossly underestimated the psychological toll both journey and settlement would take on men and leaders alike.

On Tuesday, June 30, 1812, the great flotilla meant to establish Astor's several new posts launched from a staging area at Tongue Point near Astoria and headed up the Columbia. The main body numbered more than sixty men in nine canoes and two bateaux, including thirty-two Canadian voyageurs, twelve Hawaiians, seven clerks, and three partners—Mackenzie, David Stuart, and John Clarke. The Dorion family was among them, Pierre serving as a hunter. This fleet of nine canoes would split into different directions once it reached the Forks of the Columbia. Yet a tenth canoe carried the "Return Overland Party," which would buy horses at the Forks and head all the way to St. Louis bearing fresh messages for Mr. Astor. Led by bold, young Robert Stuart, this canoe carried two of the three partners who had quit—Robert McClellan and Ramsay Crooks—as well as John Day. Crooks and Day had arrived only six weeks earlier.

As soon as the flotilla of canoes embarked from Tongue Point, John Day began to act strangely. Formerly cheerful and popular, he had begun to shown signs of "derangement" when wandering lost in the wintry mountains with Crooks, the latter now reported. As the huge canoe party pitched camp in a beautiful grove of oaks and ash late the second day out from Astoria, Day, who had been "restless" the previous few days, "now uttered the most incoherent absurd and unconnected sentences," reported Robert Stuart.

"Several spoke to him, but little satisfaction was obtained, and he went to bed gloomy and churlish."

The next day, Thursday, July 2, the canoes passed the mouth of the Cowlitz River, which emptied in on the north bank from a source among the high glaciers of Mount Rainier, about one hundred miles away. The parties camped that night on broad, meadowy Deer Island. The weather had cleared since leaving Astoria, and a series of fine days set in—the brief Northwest Coast summer. From certain vantages, they could see the spectacular glacier-capped cones of several volcanoes—Mount Rainier, Mount St. Helens, and especially Mount Hood, towering to the east above the river's surface and forested foothills, its glacier-covered pyramid emerging from winter's cloud veil and gleaming white against the summer's cerulean skies.

"[T]his gigantic mass appears as a Steeple overlooking the lowest Houses of a City," is how Robert Stuart described it.

It should have been a joyous, uplifting sight. For John Day, however, it may well have been what's known as a "trigger." The sight of it viscerally reminded him of what lay twenty miles beyond Mount Hood—the Narrows. And he knew that a short distance beyond the Narrows was the spot where he'd been stripped by the Indians and sent naked into the wilds. And still beyond that terrible place began the vast unmapped region where he and Crooks had wandered the previous winter.

"[D]uring the night," wrote Robert Stuart of their Deer Island camp, "John Day's disorder became very alarming, and several times he attempted getting possession of some of our arms, with the intention of committing suicide, but finding all his attempts fruitless, he at length feigned great remorse. . . ."

Day's remorse lulled his companions into dropping their guard. The camp slept soundly on the grassy island, with the exception of the new clerks from New York just off the *Beaver,* who complained about mosquitos whining in their ears. John Day also didn't sleep. In the hour before dawn, Day quietly managed to get hold of two loaded pistols. He put both of them to his head. He pulled the triggers.

The simultaneous pistol blasts shook the camp. Sleeping partners, voyageurs, hunters, clerks, Hawaiians jumped up in alarm. They instantly grabbed Day. His aim, as Stuart put it, was "fortunately too high to take effect."

Stuart put Day under guard in one of the boats sitting along the riverbank where he couldn't easily reach the many firearms lying around camp. As Day was supposed to accompany Stuart and his Return Overland Party all the way to St. Louis, Stuart now had to figure out what to do with him.

From a modern perspective, we'd say that John Day likely was suffering from post-traumatic stress disorder, or PTSD. The syndrome, formerly known as "shell shock" or "battle fatigue," has been around as long as humans have faced physical danger—whether from saber-toothed tigers or enemy tribes. It's possible that it is some version of an evolutionary adaptation that, in times of mortal danger, puts our senses on high alert and prompts us to avoid the peril. In practice, it is a deterioration of normal responses under prolonged or extreme stress. It can appear in combat veterans, rape victims, survivors of natural disasters and other intense situations. Its victims can be hypervigilant, irrationally angry, restless, depressed, suicidal, and careful to avoid situations that remind them of their trauma. PTSD may have played a significant but largely unrecognized role in the early exploration of North America. This especially may have been the case with expeditions traversing hostile Indian territory, where, for months on end, explorers were in an almost continuous state of profound threat and often witnessed traumatic events—all of which are associated with PTSD.* Among the Astorians, there are documented cases of something very like PTSD in Archibald Pelton and John Day, but there were almost surely others whose behavior was

---

* Meriwether Lewis himself may have been one of PTSD's victims. He had also traversed hostile Indian territory for months on end. He was almost surely a victim of depression. He fatally shot himself in the head and chest in the fall of 1809 at Grinder's Tavern in Tennessee, three years after the triumphant return of his expedition.

not dramatic enough, or deemed unusual enough to be recorded in the Astorian journals. (Even John Day's suicide attempt goes unmentioned in most of them.)

The next day, July 3, provided Stuart with a solution for Day. Under guard, he was now making threats to companions he believed were conspiring against him. From the camp at Deer Island, the flotilla continued to paddle upstream toward Mount Hood. In a few miles they crossed over to the north bank and Cathlapootle Island (today's Bachelor Island, just downstream from Portland, Oregon).

At Cathlapootle Island, it became clear that Day couldn't go on. On the mainland nearby stood a large village of nine hundred inhabitants and fourteen longhouses of the Cathlapootle people. Robert Stuart knew and liked their chief. John Day, however, had started to rave against Indians at every opportunity, apparently even against the friendly Cathlapootle. What might happen when they reached native villages that were less friendly?

"[I]t was . . . the opinion of all the Gentlemen," wrote Stuart, "that it would be highly imprudent to suffer [John Day] to proceed any farther for in a moment when not sufficiently watched he might embroil us with the natives, who on all occasions he reviled by the appellations of Rascal, Robber etc etc."

Day had become "entirely useless" to the expedition, in Robert Stuart's estimation. There was no sense in taking him farther. Stuart struck a deal with the chief of the Cathlapootles. For the price of a few trade items, the chief agreed to escort John Day by canoe back downriver to Astoria.

Concluded Stuart: "[H]is insanity amounted to real madness. . . ."

Relieved of the volatile Day, the flotilla worked its way upstream to the Narrows, which they passed through without major incidents by posting guard parties along the portages. It took them two weeks of hauling to carry their canoes and trade goods around the rapids, as they had to use much of their manpower simply to guard the goods from Indian pilfering rather than hauling it. Finally, they had ascended the rapids and traveled beyond the last of the mountain range that bounded the wet Pacific Coast. The country on both sides of the river now flattened and opened into the broad, arid Columbia Plain.

Above the Narrows, the flotilla passed the spot where Crooks and Day had been robbed and stripped. Crooks, to his "great delight," as Irving recounted, happened to recognize two of the thieves in a group of Indians along the riverbank. These two were quickly captured, bound, placed in a canoe, and held as hostages until the stolen rifles and other equipment were returned. While the two were terrified of being killed, Crooks, not being of a "revengeful disposition," had them released otherwise unharmed.

On July 27, they reached the mouth of the Walla Walla River, where the Columbia made a huge sweeping bend toward the north, and the Snake River also entered from the east, this known as the Forks of the Columbia. The following day, July 28, the big flotilla would split up and head in its many directions, sending messages back to New York, recovering cached goods, establishing the great web of fur posts throughout the Northwest. The long tendrils of John Jacob Astor's West Coast fur empire had now unfolded.

That night, in celebration, the voyageurs and a great group of the Walla Walla people, welcoming the traders, made a big bonfire at one end of camp and danced into the night.

A STOR'S ANXIETY GREW THROUGH May AND INTO June 1812. With every report of the threatening mood in Washington, D.C., war seemed more likely. On June 1, President Madison sent a list of U.S. grievances against Great Britain to Congress. For the next four days the House of Representatives debated in a closed-door session. They voted. The tally was announced: by 79 to 49 the U.S. House passed a declaration of war. Their verdict went to the Senate. If the Senate should pass it, and President Madison signed a proclamation of war, it would be the first war declared by the young United States.

In New York City, Astor hungered for news. For a wealthy man Astor lived relatively modestly, but one luxury for which he would spare no expense was timely information. At crucial moments in his business dealings, he employed private express couriers to carry messages and news up and down the East Coast. He well knew that the rapid delivery of information could translate to tremendous advantage—whether on the battlefield or in politics, or amid the thickets of trade barriers and quirks of international markets, to turn massive profits or avoid massive loses.

An intense debate over war now raged in Washington. On June 12, the Senate voted on the declaration. It deadlocked.

A few days later, Astor mounted his horse and set off for Washington, D.C., as fast as he could.

He knew powerful people in the U.S. government. President Jefferson, who had so championed his great plan, had retired. He was now living at Monticello. But Astor had also met James Madison back in 1808 when he met with Jefferson, and Madison was serving as secretary of state. Now Madison was president but he didn't share Jefferson's passion for the West and for exploration. Perhaps Astor's best connection was his personal acquaintance Albert Gallatin, secretary of the treasury under both Jefferson and Madison. A well-born and highly educated Swiss who was a disciple of Rousseau and follower of the Enlightenment, Gallatin had emigrated to the United States about the same time as Astor and struggled as a young businessman before entering politics. Appointed by President Jefferson to his cabinet, Gallatin had been instrumental in helping Jefferson plan the Lewis and Clark expedition and had a deep interest in the West as well as Native American ethnology. Like Astor, he spoke German, in addition to several other languages. He had followed Astor's enterprise since the beginning and, while no direct evidence exists, he may have helped initiate it. Soon after the return of the Lewis and Clark expedition, Albert Gallatin himself may have tipped off Astor that Thomas Jefferson and Meriwether Lewis were discussing the need for an American fur post at the mouth of the Columbia.

Now, four years later, Astor had put tremendous resources and energy behind his West Coast master plan. But a declaration of war could throw his whole globe-girdling enterprise into jeopardy. War could overwhelm even his enormous resources. The British Royal Navy, one of the world's most powerful armed forces, would surely blockade American ports, which would prevent Astor's next supply ships to his West Coast emporium from leaving New York Harbor. Likewise, it would prevent his cargoes of Chinese luxury goods, and with them his astronomical profits, from returning to the United States.

Perhaps even worse, war could render Astoria itself—as an establishment flying the American flag—a potential target for the Royal Navy. And still worse, Astor's Canadian rival, the North West Company, loyal to Britain, could very well incite the Royal Navy to take the fledgling colony as a prize and try to claim the Columbia Basin (or the whole West Coast) out from under him.

His men at his West Coast emporium could possibly prevent this, but how to get word to them? And did they have the will and the resources to defend against a Royal Navy attack? Could they stave off the North West Company? He couldn't be sure. He knew some would remain absolutely loyal to him—Wilson Price Hunt, for instance. But the others? The Scottish fur traders who were former employees of the North West Company and whom he'd hired for their expertise—could they be trusted? If forced to choose in time of war, would they stay with his American enterprise, or turn against him to join with their native country and former employer?

Astor had thought far ahead about this very possibility. Two years earlier, back in the summer of 1810, he'd brought the first Scottish fur traders down from Montreal to meet in his offices in Manhattan. He'd made them partners—given them shares and a stake in his West Coast enterprise. They personally stood to profit enormously from the venture should it succeed. But Astor took a further measure than money to ensure their loyalty. Before the *Tonquin* embarked from New York for the Northwest Coast, he asked those Canadians who would be traveling on it to get U.S. citizenship.

He was under the impression they had done so. But they hadn't. McKay and David Stuart had instead visited the British consul to the United States, Francis James Jackson, who happened to be visiting New York.

What would happen if war broke out? McKay had asked, according to Franchère, a British citizen and much interested in this same point.

"After some moments of reflection Mr. Jackson told him, 'that we were going on a very hazardous enterprise; that he saw our object was purely commercial, and that all he could promise us, was, that in case of a war we should be respected as British subjects and traders.'"

Astor knew nothing at the time of this meeting. He, too, had thought carefully about exactly whom he could trust. This is why,

not wishing to risk giving too much leadership to a British subject
like Mackenzie, he had sent the letter to Hunt in St. Louis specify-
ing that he was the sole leader of the Overland Party. The loyal Hunt
would also serve as head of the entire West Coast emporium. As for
the others—Mackenzie, McDougall, McKay, the Stuarts? They were
Scotsmen all, British citizens, former Nor'westers—again, would they
remain loyal?

Astor had put all his faith in the loyal, steady, consensus-seeking,
conflict-avoiding Wilson Price Hunt to serve as the anchor of the West
Coast emporium. What he hadn't counted on, as he rode fast toward
Washington amid the growing threat of war in June 1812, was that
Hunt was about to leave Astoria.

In early November 1812, Astor partner Donald Mackenzie left
his new post on a branch of the Snake River to visit his colleague John
Clarke at the latter's new post on the nearby Spokane River. Despite
the early loss of the *Tonquin,* John Jacob Astor's trade empire was
unfolding largely according to plan. The many parties dispatched that
summer in the flotilla from Astoria had established outposts all over
the Northwest's interior, casting Astor's giant net. Besides Clarke's
and Mackenzie's posts were Stuart's on the Okanagan, another in
the Willamette, posts being established to the north of these on the
Thompson River, to the east in the Kootenai region, in the Flathead
region, and on a river called by the voyageurs Coeur d'Alene.

Furs had been found in rich supply in all these areas, seemingly,
except one—the post on the Snake tributary known as the Clearwater. This was the post headed by Donald Mackenzie. For much of
the last two years, the "man of perpetual motion" had been traveling
steadily in the wilds with Hunt's Overland Party. Settled in at last, his
restlessness now manifested itself again. He complained that the local
Indians didn't want to trap, and Astor's trade goods wouldn't compel
them to bring in furs. They preferred to go off and make war and

hunt buffalo. As Alexander Ross, manning a more productive post on the Thompson River, put it, "They spurned the idea of crawling about in search of furs; 'Such a life,' they said, 'was only fit for women and slaves.'"

"Mackenzie," writes Ross, "soon got sick of them, and weary of the place."

The restless Astor partner mounted a horse he'd purchased from the Indians and rode several days north to John Clarke's post on the Spokane to consult with his colleague and to smoke pipes with him. While Clarke and Mackenzie shared the warmth of the fire one November day, a deputation arrived at their door.

It was from the North West Company and at its head stood an official named John George McTavish. He had recently arrived at the Spokane post from other North West Company posts on the other side of the Rockies and carried an important message. He formally handed it to the two Astorians:

> *Whereas the Congress of the United States, by virtue of the constituted authority vested in them, have declared by their act bearing date the 18th day of the present month [June 1812] that war exists between the United Kingdom of Great Britain and Ireland and the dependencies thereof and the United States of America and their Territories:*
>
> *Now, therefore, I, James Madison, President of the United States of America, do hereby proclaim the same to all whom it may concern. . . .*

They were stunned. The North West Company message had raced by express canoe from Montreal to the company's Fort William on Lake Superior. It was then forwarded farther west by light canoe on the inland system of rivers and lakes. McTavish, traveling among the company's remote western posts, happened to be at Lake Winnipeg (north of today's Minnesota), when instructions from North West

Company partners reached him, along with President Madison's proclamation of war.

The basic message delivered from McTavish of the North West
Company to Clarke and Mackenzie of the Astor enterprise, that day in
the smoky warmth of the log post, boiled down to a startlingly simple
fact: Astoria now presented a fair target for British attack.

It was the first news that any of the Astorians had heard of the
war. McTavish carried still more news. According to Irving's account,
McTavish delivered it with officious delight to his former colleague
Mackenzie and the American Clarke. McTavish was resupplying his
scattering of fur posts on these northern branches of the Columbia
to compete head-to-head with Astor's posts. And still more ominous
news: McTavish informed the two Astorian traders that the North West
Company's twenty-gun ship, the *Isaac Todd,* had sailed from Montreal
bound for England. In Britain she would acquire armed escorts from
the Royal Navy. She would then sail for the Columbia's mouth, arriving
probably in March. The armed British ships would proceed to capture
America's colony on the West Coast.

Message delivered, McTavish and company retired for the moment
to the North West Company's post nearby on the Spokane. Mackenzie
hastened by horseback the several days south to his Astor post on the
Clearwater. He and Clarke knew they had to get news of war to Astoria
as quickly as possible. Mackenzie gathered in his men, some of them
trapping several days away. He ordered them to bundle the furs at the
post, pull up the floorboards, and dig caches underneath the structure.
Having cached the furs and other goods, they carefully replaced the
floorboards.

They celebrated New Year's Day 1813 at the Clearwater post,
according to the young New Yorker Alfred Seton, who served as the
post's clerk, "as jollily as was in our power."

"We had a famous horse pye & a couple of quarts of real Boston
particular with which we regaled ourselves *pas mal* [not badly] as the
Frenchmen say," Seton wrote jauntily.

Then Mackenzie, the man of perpetual motion, abandoned the post. Before leaving, he ordered the Clearwater post burned down, its dying embers falling in a heap over the cached furs. He and his men climbed into their canoes. With ice freezing to the paddle blades at every stroke, and the greenhorn New Yorker sitting miserably with numbed hands and cold feet amidships, the voyageurs powered the canoes to the mouth of the Columbia—singing, Seton noted with frigid amazement, the entire way.

ASTOR HAD BEEN ON HORSEBACK en route to Washington when, just past Baltimore, he got the news in late June 1812: *War declared*. Returning to New York, he had laid out a comprehensive strategy and made a flurry of preparations to protect his West Coast trade empire.

His first task was to get word to his people in Astoria as quickly as possible. They had to prepare to defend the emporium from British attack or seizure. Astor already had one ship in the Pacific, the *Beaver*. He knew her itinerary—during the summer months of 1812, as he'd instructed, she should be at the emporium and working the Northwest Coast and Alaska loading furs, then sail to China before autumn storms swept the North Pacific. Astor immediately drafted messages to Captain Sowle of the *Beaver* for dispatch to Canton aboard other commercial ships headed there. Captain Sowle was to turn the *Beaver* around and proceed with fresh supplies directly back to the West Coast emporium. Once there, Sowle was to follow Hunt's orders to protect the emporium however Hunt deemed necessary.

Astor then reconfigured his next regular supply ship to Astoria. He had planned to send a ship that autumn of 1812, as he had sent the *Tonquin* in autumn of 1810 and the *Beaver* in the fall of 1811. Now his next ship would run the risk of being blockaded trying to leave New York or seized outright by the British. No marine insurer would want to touch this vessel or its cargo. The risk would fall entirely on him. He possessed the resources, should he want to use them, to cover the loss himself. He weighed the risks and struck on a solution: Outfit a special ship that could outrun the British gunships. For extra safety, he would work his diplomatic connections to the Russian embassy in Washington in order to secure Russian papers for the ship, exempting her from the British blockade or seizure. For this high-risk ship he selected the *Lark*—"remarkable," as Irving described the well-armed vessel, "for her fast sailing."

Finally, he considered whether he could engage the U.S. Navy to protect his West Coast emporium. President Jefferson had four years earlier apparently promised him some sort of military protection for his West Coast venture, at least according to Astor. James Madison now held the presidency, however, and he wouldn't necessarily make good on Jefferson's verbal promises, assuming Jefferson had made them. And there was another obstacle—one of simple resources. As both Jefferson and Madison ideologically opposed a standing army and navy for the young United States, as the country went to war, the U.S. Navy possessed only a dozen or so ships ready for sea duty. By contrast, the Royal Navy had six hundred.

AS SOON AS THE NEWS OF WAR ARRIVED in Montreal, the North West Company had jumped into action, too. The partners dispatched an express canoe westward carrying a copy of the document. While Astor's message to his men at Astoria slowly made its way by ship to Canton, the North West Company's highly efficient message system delivered the news of war in less than a month's time to the wintering partners at their July meeting at Fort William on Lake Superior. Seeing a great opportunity in the declaration, this time the North West Company partners quickly reached a consensus about John Jacob Astor and his West Coast pretensions.

They voted to send emissaries from Montreal to London aboard their armed company ship, the *Isaac Todd*. Their agents in London would ask high British authorities for Royal Navy escort ships to sail with their company ship to the Columbia's mouth. They also sent a light express canoe westward with the proclamation of war and messages for McTavish. He was to head westward toward the Pacific. He and his overland party would gather North West Company recruits from fur posts along the way, cross the Rockies, and descend the Columbia. There McTavish and his group of Nor'westers were to wait for the *Isaac Todd* to arrive by sea at the Columbia's mouth, accompanied by Royal Navy escort ships.

Together, as Astor's land and sea parties had combined to found Astoria, the North West Company's land and sea parties would combine to crush it.

OTHER PLAYERS HAD NOW ENTERED THE GAME—big players, possessing huge resources. The stakes had climbed still higher for Astor, and so had the risks. He still had no notion what had happened to Hunt and the Overland Party. Manuel Lisa had returned downriver to St. Louis the previous fall of 1811 and predicted that Hunt and his entire party, leaving the Missouri to trek overland, would be slaughtered by Indians. Astor had received confirmation of the loss of the *Tonquin,* through other ship captains in addition to the newspaper accounts. But no direct word of Hunt's fate had yet come to New York. Despite all this loss and uncertainty, Astor's commitment to the West Coast empire had only deepened, and he played his hand surely.

He summoned two of his best sea captains to a secret meeting and wrote them a draft of twelve thousand pounds sterling. Then he sent them undercover to London. Here the two would end up purchasing a heavily armed and very swift *British* vessel that would be secretly in Astor's employ. Under the pretense of sailing to Canton, it should have no problem passing the British blockade and heading to Astoria to defend her against possible attack from the British themselves. Or that was the hope. With this secret ship and his other armed vessels, plus a possible U.S. naval escort, John Jacob Astor would, if all went according to plan, possess virtually his own navy in the Pacific.

It was an audacious and clever plan and a major risk, but the time had come to take it. Astor was now not only deeply invested financially in the West Coast empire—it had become the driving passion of this otherwise, cool, calculating man. After four years of steady and meticulous work on top of a tremendous investment to make it a reality, he felt that this West Coast empire would be his life's legacy. He would be regarded as the founder of what someday would be a great and thriving colony on the Pacific, and his name would be handed down, as Jefferson had put it, "with that of Columbus & Raleigh."

He would soon write his trusted Mr. Hunt—who he assumed had reached Astoria and would be in charge of its defense against British attack—these impassioned instructions, sending his letter aboard the *Lark,* his fast, armed supply ship departing from New York:

> *Were I on the spot, and had management of affairs, I would defy them all; but, as it is, everything depends on you and your friends about you. Our enterprise is grand, and deserves success, and I hope in God it will meet it. If my object were merely gain of money, I should say, I think whether it is best to save what we can, and abandon the place; but the very idea is like a dagger to my heart.*

CHAPTER TWENTY-ONE

W ITH THE FREEZING ALFRED SETON HUDDLED IN THE
canoe, Mackenzie's party left the upriver posts in early January 1813 and paddled fast down the Columbia toward Astoria. Mackenzie carried a copy of the surprise U.S. declaration of war that the rival North West Company's McTavish had delivered to him with such flourish. In the misty dusk of January 16, the canoes pulled alongside the new wharf at Astoria. As they disembarked, Mackenzie and his party received their own bit of shocking news from the settlement. They were told that the *Beaver,* with Mr. Hunt aboard, had disappeared.

In early August, the ship had crossed the bar and left the Columbia's mouth. Its mission was to head up the Northwest Coast to supply the Russian posts in Alaska, as Astor had worked out with the Russians, and load thousands of Russian furs. Then, according to plan, in October the *Beaver* would return to Astoria to drop off Hunt, and he would take charge again. The ship would load still more furs from Astoria's warehouses and sail with its cargo for the rich markets of Canton.

But something had gone badly amiss. Wrote Franchère, clerk at Astoria: "The months of October, November, and December passed away without any news of the 'Beaver,' and we began to fear that there had happened to her, as to the Tonquin, some disastrous accident."

Late fall had been difficult. As during the first autumn at Astoria, it had rained in cold torrents. The Indians had retired to their camps deeper in the forest. The Astorians again ran short of food. No Indian hunters or salmon fishers could supply them in this season of scarce game. Without fresh meat and greens, scurvy set in. Men fell sick. The days shortened with early northern darkness. The emporium's grounds turned to a swamp of cold mud.

McDougall himself, largely confined to the post and not working physically like the others, may have been suffering from scurvy. Early European explorers in North America long before had noted a relationship between scurvy, listlessness, and depression. The listless and negative members of an expedition tended to succumb more readily to scurvy. Likewise, once scurvy set in, it afflicted its victims with a sense of hopelessness.

"He no longer evinced the bustling confidence and buoyancy which once characterized him," wrote Irving of McDougall. "Command seems to have lost its charms for him; or rather, he gave way to the most abject despondency, decrying the whole enterprise, magnifying every untoward circumstance, and foreboding nothing but evil."

The *Beaver* was missing. The *Tonquin* was gone. McDougall thought he heard the whispers of certain Indian attack. It was as if he'd become trapped on the bad-luck coast. The arrival of Mackenzie's canoes in mid-January should have been a happy moment for McDougall. It wasn't. Mackenzie climbed out of his canoe bearing the copy of the U.S. proclamation of war. With it came the threat of British warships. Surely it would mean a blockade of Astor's supply ships to Astoria. And with Mackenzie also came twenty men—twenty more mouths to feed from the dwindling supplies.

Mackenzie, too, was done with his post. He let McDougall know it. He had burned it to the ground. There was no good fur territory there, he had decided. He was ready to move on.

Together, the restless Mackenzie and depressive McDougall produced a kind of synergy of negativity.

"The intelligence [of war] thus brought," wrote Irving, "completed the dismay of MacDougal, and seemed to produce a complete confusion of mind."

This vortex of bleakness intensified through the last half of January 1813. It upwells between the lines of McDougall's log of the daily doings at Astoria:

January 16—"That part of the country in which he [Mackenzie] had begun an establishment did not answer for the ends expected, and for this reason left it. . . ."

January 23—"[O]ur small stock of provisions will not warrant keeping so many people as we have here at present. . . ."

January 24—"Comcomly . . . now tells us that the Indians from the Northward . . . intimated their designs of destroying us. . . ."

January 25—"We are now under the necessity of stopping from most of our men two meals a day. . . . We cannot purchase a sufficiency to support the people."

And again the same day—"Events from every quarter wear unfavorable appearances."

January 28 appears to have brought a breaking point. "An Inventory being consequently taken of the Goods and Stores at this place, it was found far short of what would be necessary in the present crisis; it is therefore judged prudent for the safety of so large a party as we now form in all the Columbia to suspend all trade except what may be necessary for our support. . . ."

So read the official language. McDougall kept the official log. In a way, he whitewashed it. Franchère tells it differently, or certainly more completely.

"We held, therefore, a sort of council of war," wrote Franchère.

Clerks like himself were invited to attend but had no vote. Only the partners could vote—in this case, McDougall and Mackenzie.

"Having maturely weighed our situation," wrote Franchère, "after having seriously considered that being almost to a man British subjects, we were trading, notwithstanding, under the American flag; and foreseeing . . . the impossibility that Mr. Astor could send us further supplies or reinforcements while the war lasted . . . we concluded to abandon the establishment in the ensuing spring, or, at the latest, in the beginning of the summer."

Alexander Ross put it more bluntly: "M'Dougall and M'Kenzie, weighing circumstances, concluded all was hopeless."

ACROSS A VAST WILDERNESS and three thousand miles distant, Astor was meeting at almost the same moment, in late January 1813, with U.S. secretary of state James Monroe in Washington, D.C. Through every channel he could think of, Astor was attempting to get word to President Madison of the towering importance to future U.S. national interests of protecting his West Coast emporium and colony. Astor's intelligence agents in London had told him that the North West Company was sending its armed ship, the *Isaac Todd,* to the West Coast, and trying to enlist armed escorts from the Royal Navy.

During their meeting, Astor explained to Secretary Monroe how deeply the West Coast and its fur trade mattered both economically and strategically. In a polite follow-up letter, Astor asked Monroe, in effect, if the United States planned to claim this rich country, the Northwest, or let the British have it: "[I]t becomes very interesting to know . . . whether it will be deemed expedient for the government to take possession of a country which will afford wealth and comfort to many. . . ."

He suggested sending a naval ship to cruise the waters off the Columbia for British ships, and also land forty or fifty troops at the settlement itself or a barracks nearby to protect it.

Secretary of State Monroe didn't reply.

Astor once again approached his friend Albert Gallatin to get word to the president. Gallatin made a proposal to Madison: a U.S. frigate could be sent to cruise the waters off Canton. En route to doing so, it could drop off a contingent of marines at the mouth of the Columbia, "so as to embrace this opportunity of taking possession."

There was still no response. As historian James P. Ronda points out, President Madison had many other urgent matters before him, with an increasingly unpopular war going poorly. "Madison and others in his administration must have found it difficult to think seriously about the West at a time when the tide seemed to be running against American survival," Ronda writes.

Astor could wait no longer for a reply, and for official naval escort. He ordered the *Lark* to put to sea. He had managed to acquire both Russian and American papers for her, so she would be able to avoid either British or American harassment.

On March 6, 1813, the fast, armed *Lark* sailed from New York for Astoria. A few weeks later Astor received word from his agents in London that the *Isaac Todd,* the North West Company ship, was preparing to sail from Portsmouth, England, for the mouth of the Columbia. Although she was known to be a slow sailer, she was also carrying heavy guns. At the same time, Astor's stealth ship, named the *Forester* and under British flag, was preparing to sail from Portsmouth, too.

AT ASTORIA, once McDougall and Mackenzie made the decision to abandon the whole enterprise, they summoned partners David Stuart and John Clarke from their upriver posts. Traveling separately, the two of them headed downriver in spring 1813 in canoe flotillas low to the water with heavy packs of furs—thousands of furs. It had been an extremely profitable winter at their upriver posts. They saw no need to abandon the West Coast enterprise. They felt it had a great future, and, in Irving's words, "considered it rash and pusillanimous to abandon, on the first difficulty, an enterprize of such great cost and ample promise."

They planned to tell Mackenzie and McDougall so.

Another dark cloud fell over that bright future, however, while they were heading down the Columbia.

Mr. Astor had sent two silver goblets aboard the *Beaver* under the care of John Clarke to be presented to Alexander McKay. Clarke had discovered on his arrival at Astoria that McKay was presumed dead along with everyone else who had sailed north aboard the *Tonquin*. Clarke decided to keep Astor's silver goblets for himself. During his winter at his new Spokane post, the goblets became one of his prized possessions, a bit of elegance in the shaggy wilds.

"He was a tall, good-looking man, and somewhat given to pomp and circumstance," noted Irving. "He was stately, too, in his appointments. . . ."

As he left his Spokane post, on his way to the Columbia and Astoria, Clarke and his party passed through the nation of the Catatouch Indians, a tribe of the Nez Percé, who had kept the traders' big canoes safe over the winter. That day, May 30, Clarke held a ceremonial meeting with the Catatouch chief. He took a silver goblet from his traveling wine case and passed it to the chief with a little wine.

The chief drank it.

"[You're] a greater man now than ever before," Clarke told the chief, according to Ross's account.

The chief passed the goblet, like a pipe, to the other warriors in the circle, who marveled at it. Then it was put aside.

In the morning, the silver goblet was gone from Clarke's tent.

Clarke, said to be normally even-tempered and experienced with Indians, went into a rage. It was as if he'd invested the goblet with the power of Mr. Astor—as Native Americans invested natural objects with spiritual power—and that power now had been stolen from him. He assembled the whole Catatouch camp and demanded the return of the goblet. In his rage, he threatened to kill the thief.

The entire tribe went off, as Ross describes it, returning as a group soon thereafter. The chief was at their head. Spreading his robe on the ground, he placed the stolen silver goblet upon it.

Clarke was still enraged.

"Where is the thief?" he demanded.

The chief pointed to a man sitting in the circle of Catatouch men, according to Ross's account.

"'I swore,' said Mr. Clarke, 'that the thief should die, and white men never break their word.'"

The thief didn't believe him at first, as it was the custom that if property were returned the punishment was excused. But Clarke ordered the thief's lodge dismantled. He ordered the tipi poles made into a tripod scaffold. He ordered a rope produced, and a noose tied. The thief begged for his life. His tribal companions begged for his life. Clarke's fellow Astorians told him it was too severe a punishment, but from his boyhood, writes Irving, Clarke "had lived in the Indian country among Indian traders, and held the life of a savage extremely cheaply."

"Mr. Clarke," wrote Alfred Seton, "was inexorable."

Farnham, a clerk from Vermont, whose pistol had been stolen, served as executioner. The order came. The noose tightened. The Indian was strung up on the tripod, screaming, kicking, and struggling until all movement stopped.

The many Catatouch Indians watching, according to accounts, said not a word. They mounted their horses and took off.

Clarke and his party continued downriver. At the mouth of the Walla Walla—where less than a year before the Astorians had celebrated with the Walla Walla people, a tribe closely related to the Catatouch—he met with Stuart, also headed downriver with his winter furs, and Mackenzie, who had come upriver to recover his cached furs. Thinking they would be pleased, Clarke told them what he had done to the goblet thief.

"What did Stuart and McKenzie say? What could any man say?"

recorded Ross of this pivotal moment near the mouth of the Walla Walla in the first days of June 1813. "The reckless deed had been committed, and Clarke's countenance fell when the general voice of disapprobation was raised against him. The Indians all along kept flying to and fro, whooping and yelling in wild commotion. At this time, Tummeatapam came riding up to our camp at full speed. 'What have you done, my friends?' called out the old and agitated chief. 'You have spilt blood on our lands!'"

Tummeatapam, the chief of the friendly Walla Walla, pointed to an approaching cloud of dust in the distance raised by the Indian horses.

"'There, my friends, do you see them? What can I do?'" said the chief, wheeling his horse around and galloping away.

"Taking the hint, we lost no time," writes Ross. "Tents were struck; some had breakfasted, some not—kettles and dishes were all huddled together and bundled into the canoe, and, embarking pell-mell, we pushed with all haste from the inauspicious shore."

When the combined Stuart, Clarke, and Mackenzie parties reached Astoria on June 12—six canoes and two boats, for a total of fifty-three people and 119 packs of beaver—they held an extremely tense reunion with McDougall.

"Two days were spent in mutual recriminations," wrote Ross.

McDougall was incensed that these upriver parties had not purchased horses from the Indians, as he had instructed, so they could all abandon Astoria in July, a month from now, and head back overland to the East. He would now have to spend an entire *year* more at this godforsaken outpost. Stuart and Clarke were enraged that McDougall had single-handedly, with Mackenzie's urging and consent, decided to shut down the West Coast enterprise.

The bitter argument raged in the partners' quarters over whether or not to abandon Astor's West Coast emporium. Hanging like a vulture over the proceedings was McTavish of the North West Company. He, too, had recently arrived at Astoria from far upriver with his own party. He had set up camp a short ways down the shore, awaiting what he was sure would be the imminent arrival of the armed company ship, *Isaac Todd,* to claim the whole place.

McDougall and David Stuart, the two Scotsmen and Astor partners, went head-to-head. The American partner, Clarke, sided with Stuart to stay the course. Their territories on the northern tributaries were rich with furs. The empire would succeed, they claimed. McDougall demanded immediate abandonment. War had been declared. British warships were on their way. Sell out now to the North West Company while the selling was good.

Where, however, were the threatened warships? McTavish had originally claimed that the *Isaac Todd* and an armed British convoy would arrive at the Columbia's mouth in March. Now it was June. They were still nowhere to be seen. Was this all a bluff on the part of the North West Company? But if the British Royal Navy convoy did appear it could simply take Astoria as a prize of war, along with its valuables and furs.

And Astor's supply ship? Where was that? Had the British blockaded the U.S. ports and prevented it from leaving New York Harbor? And Wilson Price Hunt and the *Beaver*? Had they utterly disappeared?

Mackenzie stood off to the side while the cedar roofing of the partners' quarters reverberated with angry words and accusations. The recriminations reached a standoff. Mackenzie spoke up. He'd prepared his argument as carefully as a barrister, in Alexander Ross's detailed recounting of the moment.

"'Gentlemen,' said he, 'why do you hesitate so long between two opinions? Your eyes ought to have been opened before now to your own interests. In the present critical conjuncture, there is no time to be lost. . . . We have been long enough the dupes of a vacillating policy. . . .'"

Mackenzie then enumerated the ways that the Americans John Jacob Astor and Wilson Price Hunt had wronged the British citizens who were supposedly equal partners in the West Coast enterprise:

First, at Montreal, Hunt had refused to hire enough Canadian men because they were not Americans.

Second, Astor's "private missive" to Hunt at Nodaway winter camp had given the American Hunt exclusive leadership of the Overland Party and had given offense—"umbrage"—to all the other (in other words, British) partners.

Third, Mr. Astor had sent orders to Hunt aboard the *Beaver* regarding Astor's American nephew, clerk George Ehninger, also traveling on the ship, that he be placed in charge of all the other clerks. "Could there be anything more impolitic and more unjust . . . more at variance with the spirit of the articles of agreement?" asked Mackenzie to his fellow Britons.

Fourth, Mr. Astor's orders to his American ship captains, such as Thorn of the *Tonquin* and Sowle of the *Beaver,* served to "annihilate the power and authority of the partners."

And fifth, the two Astor supply ships, *Tonquin* and *Beaver,* had sailed off from Astoria carrying all the most valuable trade goods still aboard, leaving only the poorest articles for the British partners remaining at Astoria to use to buy furs. Additionally, this year, "there is no ship at all!"

"Has it not been obvious from the beginning that under Astor's policy we can never prosper?"

Mackenzie admitted that certain circumstances lay beyond Astor's control, such as the U.S. declaration of war. Likewise, it was not a question of prosperity of the country, he argued. The country was rich with furs. "[B]ut Astor's policy, and a chain of misfortunes, have ruined all."

Mackenzie pointed out that the original agreement between the partners and Astor allowed the partners, within five years of signing, to abandon the West Coast enterprise if it wasn't profitable or practicable. Now he was arguing that it was neither, and that Astor, "with all his sagacity, either does not or will not understand the business."

"We owe it to Astor—we owe it to ourselves . . . to deliver the whole back into the hands from which we received it—and the sooner the better."

Mackenzie said, in short, that Astor favored the Americans over the British partners, that Astor's policies were doomed from the start, and that the outbreak of war would end it all anyway. Stuart and Clarke thought it over and eventually agreed with Mackenzie and McDougall. They would pull up stakes and abandon Astor's West Coast enterprise.

Another tough question arose: How?

It was now June. There was no way to pack up their goods and cross the Rockies before winter. They would have to spend another winter at Astoria. Furthermore, McTavish and the North West Company were encamped nearby, waiting for their armed ships to seize everything. But McTavish was anxious, too—growing desperately low of supplies and trade goods while waiting for the promised ships. Everything hung in stasis. What had been a jostling rivalry between the two companies, amid a certain professional collegiality, had become a high-stakes stand-off that awaited the arrival of mutually hostile and heavily armed ships and the possibility of a bloodbath for control of the West Coast, Columbia Basin, and Pacific Rim trade. There was also, thanks to Clarke's decision to execute the thief upriver, the possibility of Indian attack.

McDougall made a proposal for the upcoming year. It's impossible to know if behind this proposal simmered some backroom deal struck between McTavish of the North West Company and McDougall of Astor's company. Likewise, when McTavish had first showed up at Astor's Spokane post with the proclamation of war, it's impossible to know if McTavish had pulled Astor partner Mackenzie aside to deliver some tempting and whispered offer to sell out Astor and to join his firm, the North West Company, bringing Astor's assets with him.

Whatever the case, McDougall and McTavish now came to an official agreement to cover the upcoming year until the Astorians abandoned the settlement. McDougall would sell some of Astoria's trade goods to McTavish to resupply the North West Company. The two companies would further agree to split up the fur posts already established in the Columbia Basin—striking, as historian Robert F. Jones has put it, a "market-sharing agreement."

It was a temporary reprieve both for the stretched McTavish and, although McDougall didn't necessarily intend it that way, the grand plan of John Jacob Astor. With this agreement in place until the next spring, when the Astorians would abandon the settlement, the various parties dispersed back up the Columbia to their respective winter posts.

Astoria emptied out again. McDougall led the small contingent that remained. A palpable sense of uncertainty and anxiety hung over Astoria during that summer of 1813. British attack? Indian attack? The Indians at the Walla Walla continued to promise revenge and those at Astoria heard stories from posts upriver of the way Indians tortured their enemies.

Ross Cox, working as a clerk on the upper tributaries, described in his memoir how a captured Blackfeet Indian was tortured by the Flatheads, the two tribes mortal enemies. While Cox's story may have been exaggerated or even apocryphal, it illustrates whites' fear of Indian torture. The Blackfeet warrior, tied to a tree, unceasingly taunted his torturers as they pressed a red-hot rifle barrel to his body, cut out his fingernails, and severed his fingers joint by joint. Cox asked a translator what the Blackfeet was saying.

"You can't hurt me. . . . You are fools. . . . You do not know how to torture. . . . We torture your relations a great deal better, because we make them cry out loud, like little children. . . ."

Then turning to a one-eyed Flathead warrior.

"It was by my arrow *you* lost *your* eye."

Whereupon the Flathead warrior "darted" at the bound Blackfeet and scooped out an eye with his knife. And so it continued—"I killed *your* brother, and scalped your old fool of a father"—the taunting and retribution, the stoic display under excruciating pain, until the Blackfeet warrior was scalped, and finally shot through the heart by the enraged Flathead captors. Meanwhile, writes Cox, the Flathead women directed the torture of the female Blackfeet captives in a manner too gruesome to describe.

McDougall's paranoia seemed to rise in inverse proportion to the number of men with him at Astoria. With only a small contingent remaining at Astoria, McDougall, himself a schemer who constantly saw schemes forming against him, cast about for self-protection. Previously, he had concocted the smallpox-in-the-bottle threat. He now conjured up another insurance policy against Indian attack. He paid a visit to Chief Comcomly of the Chinook in the villages across the river. As was customary in these situations, McDougall laid down offerings of presents to the chief. Then emissaries who accompanied McDougall asked in his name for the hand of Comcomly's daughter in marriage. Comcomly consulted his daughter and opened negotiations with McDougall over the gifts that would be exchanged.

Early in the afternoon on July 20, according to Irving's account, a canoe procession of Chinook paddled across the Columbia and landed at Astoria, bearing the anointed bride to McDougall, who received her at the fort. From then on, according to Irving, Comcomly paid a daily visit to his son-in-law's fort. He kept Astoria's blacksmith shop busy making various iron implements for him.

Another alliance had been sealed. Duncan McDougall rested more easily at night knowing his father-in-law would protect him and his fort. The fate of John Jacob's Astor's western empire, however, still hung in the balance.

A MONTH AFTER MCDOUGALL'S MARRIAGE, on the fresh, sunny morning of August 20, a canoe raced across the Columbia from the Chinook villages on the opposite bank. Comcomly's son, Gassacop, announced excitedly that his people had spotted a sailing vessel cruising back and forth in the sea off the Columbia's mouth. The Chinook had sent two canoes out through the crashing surf to discover its identity.

McDougall now jumped into his own dory. He ordered his men to row hard downstream toward the mouth. As they pulled at the oars, a big ship hove into sight at the river's mouth. It sailed cleanly across the Columbia Bar on an incoming tide and westerly breeze, and flew upriver with full sails along the opposite bank. On the riverbank at Astoria, the tension built. Was she a British ship come to capture Astoria? Was she an American ship come to help? Was she Spanish? Was she Russian?

As McDougall's dory rowed across the broad river, the ship dropped anchor on the far shore of the Columbia directly opposite John Jacob Astor's emporium and lowered sails. Only the five miles of the river's breadth now separated the unidentified ship and Astor's fort. Glassing her, Franchère and others at the fort spotted an American flag flying. Franchère ordered her saluted with three guns booming from the fort. The ship saluted back with three guns. She was American. But they still didn't know who she was or why she had come.

The long summer dusk settled over the Columbia's broad estuary. McDougall's dory reached the ship. It then turned back across the river toward Astoria bearing extra passengers. Darkness fell. Franchère and company waited nervously. In the darkness, they finally heard the splash of oars as the dory approached the wharf.

She came alongside. Out of the darkness stepped the passenger. To their amazement, it was the long-given-up-for-dead Wilson Price Hunt.

A YEAR EARLIER, Hunt had climbed aboard the *Beaver* with Captain Sowle for a coastal trading mission to the Russian fur posts in Alaska. Hunt soon had found himself in the heart of a fortress perched atop a rocky promontory on the Alaskan coast, sitting across the table from Russia's Count Baranoff, futilely trying to match the Count cup of rum for cup of rum. The Count's stronghold, called New Archangel, possessed one hundred cannon and guns, sixty Russians, and an untold number of Indian hunters paddling canoes and the seagoing kayaks called *baidarkas,* and commanded a vast network of trade in sea otter and other furs along the Alaskan and Aleutian Island coasts.

Pleased to have company in his lonely outpost, the Count offered full Russian hospitality to whoever happened by. He expected in return, however, that his guest eat, drink, and make merry as hard as he.

"He is continually giving entertainments by way of parade," Hunt reported in his journal, "and if you do not drink raw rum, and boiling punch strong as sulfer, he will insult you as soon as he gets drunk, which is very shortly after sitting down to table."

The Count was a cagey businessman as well as a heavy drinker. According to the careful plan worked out by Astor with the Russians, the *Beaver* was to deliver trade goods from New York to the Count and his fortress. Astor's representatives aboard the *Beaver* would be paid for these trade goods in the Russian's furs. Then the *Beaver* was also to load the Count's additional thousands of stockpiled furs and deliver them across the Pacific to the wealthy markets of Canton. Astor's enterprise would take a commission on the sale of the additional Russian furs in the Chinese market.

Whether by design or happenstance, the Count managed to delay the amiable Wilson Price Hunt for *six weeks* at New Archangel with his drinking bouts and endless show of parading men. Autumn storms began to roil the North Pacific. Hunt knew he had to leave to return to Astoria, and quickly. Hunt's haste to depart no doubt gave the Count, as the Count may have calculated, the best possible deal in terms of what he had to pay in furs for Hunt's trade goods.

The bargain finally sealed, Captain Sowle, Hunt, and the *Beaver* sailed still another three weeks out into the Bering Sea to St. Paul Island to load Baranoff's huge stockpile of eighty thousand seal furs stored there. It took days simply to bale the furs into bundles. A storm blew the *Beaver* out to sea. She was recovered with a damaged rudder. Captain Sowle, cautious as the late Captain Thorn was arrogantly confident, told Hunt that, with winter storms coming in and their huge Pacific swells, he wouldn't risk sailing his damaged ship in the rough waters off Astoria. Instead he would sail the *Beaver* straight for those flower-scented islands of Hawaii to repair the storm-damaged ship.

Hunt protested, though one wonders how hard. Hunt's journal for this portion of the Astoria undertaking is missing, and one can only guess his thinking. The cautious Captain Sowle was pushing for Hawaii for the safety of his ship. Hunt still knew nothing about the outbreak of war, but he knew Mr. Astor wanted him at Astoria to take command and to ensure the West Coast emporium's smooth and loyal business operations. To follow Astor's wishes meant he would return to that difficult and highly insecure post at the Columbia's mouth just as the long, cold winter rains set in and its occupants, as clerk Franchère phrased it, were subject to "insufferable ennui . . . in the midst of deep mud."

The *Beaver,* according to Captain Sowle, was in danger of being permanently damaged or lost if they returned to Astoria in winter. That would represent a significant loss to Astor, if Captain Sowle was being truthful about the risks. Here was another crucial decision point for Wilson Price Hunt. What was more important? Avoiding risk to the *Beaver* and its valuable cargo of furs, or ensuring that a loyal American was in command of Astor's West Coast emporium? Or, given Hunt's nice-guy, consensus-seeking personality, was Captain Sowle simply able to overwhelm him?

However Hunt might have rationalized it, or whatever the personality dynamics, a winter in Hawaii surely looked more attractive than winter in a ragged forest clearing of cold mud. Hunt acquiesced to Captain Sowle and together they sailed off to Hawaii on the *Beaver.*

Hunt planned to catch a ride back to Astoria on Astor's next supply ship, due to come through Hawaii in the next few months and presumably able to get him back to the West Coast by spring. No supply ship arrived in Hawaii, however, because of the war. Hunt was stranded, unaware of the war and luxuriating on those palmy islands for six months. In June 1813, the American ship *Albatross* stopped at Hawaii after sailing from Canton. She brought the year-old news of war. Hunt instantly saw the threat that war posed to Astoria. He now showed the sense of urgency that had been absent in so many of his earlier doings. With two thousand dollars in Astor funds, he chartered the *Albatross* to carry him directly to Astoria. When he rowed up to the fort's wharf that night of August 20, 1813, he had been gone from his leadership position for thirteen and a half months and had toured much of the North Pacific.

The normally mild, polite Wilson Price Hunt now grew livid in the soft August night as McDougall told him that the partners had signed an agreement to abandon Astoria and return to the East.

"[H]e blamed us severely for having acted with so much precipitation," reported the clerk Franchère, "pointing out the success of the late coasting voyage. . . . [I]t was a thousand pities to sacrifice, and lose the fruits of the hardships he had endured and the dangers he had braved, at one fell swoop, by this rash measure."

His rage changed nothing. The partners wouldn't budge in their decision. A week after he arrived, Hunt sailed off again on the *Albatross,* as he had chartered the ship only to take him to the West Coast and it had other cargo duties to fulfill in the South Pacific. He said he would return soon with another ship to get Mr. Astor's furs. It was now the end of August. The threatened British warships still hadn't arrived. There was still time, should someone be so determined, to save John Jacob Astor's West Coast empire.

Certainly Astor had no intention of giving it up.

As Hunt was making his brief stop at Astoria in mid-August 1813, Astor's ship, the fast-sailing *Lark,* was bearing down hard toward the West Coast emporium in order to protect it from the British. Somewhere behind the Lark was Astor's stealth ship, the *Forester,* secretly purchased in England. And as far as Astor knew, his large ship, the *Beaver,* armed with its own considerable complement of cannon, was headed toward Astoria, too. In effect, Astor had dispatched his own private navy to the Pacific to defend his West Coast colony against possible Royal Navy attack.

It was on August 13, when the *Lark,* bearing Astor's impassioned letter to Hunt, was a few hundred miles off the coast of Maui headed hard toward Astoria that a tremendous gale blew up. As huge seas overtook the *Lark,* Astor's trusted Captain Northrup had to rely on inexperienced sailors due to the needs of the U.S. Navy to fight the British on the East Coast and Great Lakes and other factors that had made recruiting difficult for the captain. As the captain fought to keep her steady, she swung sideways to the massive waves, and then was suddenly knocked down by a huge sea, throwing the ship into a "great Confusion and disorder," as Captain Northrup recorded.

When another swell hit, it knocked her almost entirely over, so that her keel rose out of the water, yardarms, masts, and rigging dragging underwater like fishing nets, pulling the ship over. The *Lark* threatened to overturn completely. The crew clung for their lives. Captain Northrup had to decide whether to try to ride it out and hope she'd right herself, making it possible to save Astor's dreams for a West Coast empire and Jefferson's hopes for a Pacific democracy.

But the danger of losing the ship entirely appeared too great. He issued the order: *Dismast her!*

With the ship laid on her side, her sails and rigging dragging in the sea, slammed by wind and waves, the crew, seizing whatever they could grab hold of on the now-vertical deck, worked furiously to cut the shrouds that affixed the masts to the hull. They sliced away this rigging on the windward side of the ship—that side which remained just barely above water. The severed masts swung away into the sea. But they had not cut the rigging on the submerged leeward side of the hull. The ship now dragged alongside her a great tangle of rigging and spars and yardarms. Worse, the inexperienced crew had inadvertently sliced the lines holding the dories and other auxiliary craft. These small boats—their only escape—skittered away on the gale.

She was now mastless, heaving on her side in the storm's powerful waves, her hatches smashed in, her holds taking on water. The overturned *Lark* nonetheless carried enough weight in her holds that she finally turned herself upright. Still a partly submerged hulk, shoved along by the crashing seas and shrieking gale, she wallowed through the storm as the nest of rigging and yardarms smashed and clunked beside her, and the sailors, washed over and over again by the waves breaking across her deck, hung on for their lives.

For four days, from August 13 to August 17, the *Lark* blew along like this. One sailor drowned belowdecks in the cabin at the outset. Another died of exposure and exhaustion on the second day. Seas swept him overboard. Three days later the high seas swept off two more exhausted sailors, drowning them, then flung the bodies back on deck, where they washed about until the survivors tied them down as an emergency food supply. Slowly they pulled themselves together. They built a platform out of broken spars above the submerged deck so they could sleep above the waves. They jury-rigged a sail. A Hawaiian swimmer aboard managed to dive below and bring up salt pork and porter. The black cook died. Thrown overboard, he was instantly devoured by the sharks that swarmed around the ship.

Two weeks of drifting brought them within sight of the coast of Maui. Hawaiian canoes paddled out. Too exhausted and starved to land the wreck of the *Lark* themselves, Captain Northrup and crew abandoned her and climbed into the canoes. From the beach they watched their hulk crash aground in the surf, spilling out tons of Mr. Astor's trade goods in barrels, casks, chests, and bales. King Kamekameha claimed the goods under his salvage rights to any abandoned ship that washed ashore on his islands.

Somewhere in all this wreckage lay the letter from John Jacob Astor to Wilson Price Hunt, Astor's chosen leader of his West Coast empire, telling him to stand tall against the British. Hunt wouldn't have been able to receive the letter until months later in any case. He had just left Astoria a few days earlier aboard the *Albatross,* bound for the ship's destination, the South Pacific's beautiful Marquesas Islands.

J. JACOB ASTOR'S FORMER RESIDENCE 88TH ST. NEAR EAST RIVER.
House in which Washington Irving wrote his Astoria.

John Jacob Astor's country house at Hell Gate, overlooking the East River
at what is today 88th Street. It was here that Washington Irving and Astor
collaborated on Irving's account of the Astor's West Coast endeavor.

A STOR'S LIFE CONTINUED TO REVOLVE AROUND ITS CALM domestic center in Lower Manhattan. The wreckage of his empire, however, lay scattered over much of the Pacific Ocean.

A few weeks after the *Lark* had wrecked off Maui, and Hunt had sailed off aboard the *Albatross,* McTavish, of the rival North West Company, returned downriver to Astoria from his posts on the far upper tributaries of the Columbia. He brought a large flotilla of ten canoes carrying a force of seventy-five men of the company as well as a letter to McDougall and the Astorians. It had been written by McDougall's own uncle, Angus Shaw, a principal partner with the North West Company. The letter warned that the British Royal Navy ship *Phoebe* was en route around Cape Horn along with the company's own *Isaac Todd,* "to take and destroy every thing American on the north-west coast."

Or, as the "Top Secret" orders from the British Admiralty to the *Phoebe*'s Captain James Hillyar put it, "totally annihilate" any American settlements it found.

As the great flotilla of canoes landed at Astoria, McTavish of the North West Company now made an offer to Astor's de facto leader, McDougall. In effect: *Sell out Astoria now while you still have a chance. Otherwise, we will simply take it.*

McDougall accepted, though the Americans at Astoria were outraged. They believed they could easily enough defend the fort against a heavy British frigate that couldn't come close to the settlement because it would hit bottom in the river shallows. Or, if the frigate did threaten, they could simply remove all the Astor company furs and other valuables a short distance into the interior, where the British Royal Navy couldn't touch them.

Nonetheless, on October 23, 1813, Duncan McDougall sold out John Jacob Astor's West Coast enterprise and first American colony on the Pacific and all its goods—including some thousands of furs—for about thirty cents on the dollar.

"It was thus," lamented Franchère, "that after having passed the seas, and suffered all sort of fatigues and privations, I lost in a moment all my hopes of fortune."

He was not the only one.

Five weeks later, on November 30, a sail appeared in the distance off Cape Disappointment, crossed the bar, and anchored in Baker's Bay just inside the river's mouth. It was the British sloop-of-war *Racoon.* Wrote Franchère: "The officers [of the *Racoon*] . . . seemed to me in general very much dissatisfied with their fool's errand, as they called it: they had expected to find a number of American vessels loaded with rich furs, and had calculated in advance their share of the booty of Astoria."

Or as the folksier Irving put it: "They felt as if they had been duped and made tools of by a set of shrewd men of traffic, who had employed them to crack the nut, while they carried off the kernel."

With a British warship anchored at the Columbia's mouth, and the furs sold off to the North West Company, the end of Mr. Astor's dream of a West Coast empire appeared near. A date was set for a formal transfer to the British. Shortly before the ceremony, however, McDougall's new father-in-law, Comcomly, paddled across the Columbia estuary to Astoria with canoes bearing warriors dressed and painted for battle. In a long formal speech, Comcomly addressed his son-in-law. He told McDougall that the Americans had arrived first. They had been good trading partners. He didn't want King George's men to make those in Astor's American company, including his new son-in-law, their slaves.

Comcomly now made his son-in-law an offer. The forest grew almost to water's edge all along the river. He and his Chinook warriors would hide in the woods near the wharf. As the British stepped from their longboats to claim Astoria, he and his warriors would ambush them. The Americans thus would avoid becoming slaves to the British. It would be an easy matter to rush from the woods and kill them all.

"Mr. McDougall thanked them for their friendly offer," wrote Ross Cox.

The son-in-law explained that the exchange of the fort would be on friendly terms. No American would be made a British slave. Comcomly and his warriors had difficulty believing it.

On the evening of December 12, 1813, Captain William Black of the *Racoon* was rowed to Astoria from his ship anchored at the river's mouth. He was hosted to a proper dinner. He then rose from the table to break a bottle of Madeira on the fort's flag post, hoist the Union Jack, and proclaim Astoria and all surrounding country the territory of the British Crown.

Captain Black and his *Racoon* sailed away. They left the British flag flying and a complement of North West Company men at the fort. About two months later, on February 28, 1814, yet another unidentified ship appeared off the mouth of the Columbia. Chinook canoes paddled out to meet it. They returned bearing a letter from Wilson Price Hunt. He had traveled to the Marquesas, then to Hawaii, purchased the ship *Pedlar* with Mr. Astor's funds, and returned to Astoria to remove Mr. Astor's furs to Count Baranoff's fortress in Alaska, out of British naval reach.

"It may be imagined what was the surprise of Mr. Hunt when he saw Astoria under the British flag," wrote Franchère.

But where had he been? In the two years since his exhausted Overland Party had stumbled into Astoria, Hunt, its appointed leader, had only been in residence at the emporium on the Pacific a total of about five months. McDougall had filled the vacuum. Hunt had, in effect, relinquished power by his absence. It now became clear that, starting just before Christmas, and without announcing it, McDougall had switched over to the North West Company. This news further outraged the Americans at the settlement. McDougall offered to sell Astor's furs from the North West Company back to Hunt and Astor's company. Days of bitter arguments and haggling followed at the fort, as Hunt fought with McDougall and other representatives from the NWC over the price of Mr. Astor's sold-out inventory.

Finally, on March 20, three weeks after the *Pedlar*'s arrival, they reached agreement adjusting the terms of the sale. On April 2, the *Pedlar* and Hunt crossed the Columbia Bar and headed out to sea, carrying off the clerks who wanted to leave Astoria, but not the furs, which remained with the North West Company. On leaving aboard the *Pedlar* after two years along the Columbia, the clerk and young New Yorker, Alfred Seton, missing his family and friends, gave the Northwest Coast an obituary of sorts, a good deal of it surely inspired by McDougall: "I leave the Country & most of those I have met here, without regret, so much meanness, Selfishness, & Hypocricy among an equal number, are seldom met with."

Astoria was breaking up. Two days after the *Pedlar* weighed anchor with Hunt, Seton, and others, another large expedition on April 4 set off in canoes up the Columbia River to return to the East across the inland waterway route of the North West Company. This party included

Astorian voyageurs and clerks who wished to return to their homes in
Montreal and elsewhere in Canada, among them Franchère, as well as
North West Company traders headed to their upriver posts. The British
now ran the establishment at the mouth of the Columbia, renamed Fort
George. The big canoe party had paddled up as far as the Walla Walla
River when they spotted three canoes struggling to catch up with them.

   "Arrêtez donc, arrêtez donc"—Stop! Stop!—they heard a child cry
out in French, reported Franchère.

   The flotilla pulled to the shore. The three canoes approached. The
traders saw that one of the canoes carried Marie Dorion and her two
boys.

   She gave them the bad news: All the other Astorians in the Snake
River country were dead.

   It had happened the past winter. Her husband, Pierre, and Jacob
Reznor and Le Clerc had been out trapping. She had remained at their
cabin with her boys, preparing furs and food. One January day Le
Clerc appeared at the cabin, badly wounded. Shortly before collapsing,
he said that they'd been attacked by Indians while attending the traps.
Pierre Dorion and Reznor had been killed.

   Marie Dorion quickly gathered up her children and the wounded
Le Clerc, and mounted them on two horses. She traveled four or five
days to the cabin of John Reed. En route to Reed's cabin the little group
hid from a band of Indians for a cold night, not wanting to risk a fire.
Le Clerc died during the frigid night. Alone with her children, Marie
Dorion arrived at the cabin Reed shared with other trappers. Deserted,
it was covered with bloodstains.

   She fled. For two days she traveled hard with her children toward
the west, seeking the safety of the Columbia. She came to a mountain range—the same where her baby had died two years earlier, the
Blue Mountains. The snows lay too deep in January to traverse them.
She found a hidden ravine, safe from attack. She killed the two horses.
Over a fire, she smoked the horse meat to preserve it for the weeks
ahead, and using the horsehides built shelter for herself and her chil-

dren. Hidden in this makeshift shelter in a ravine with her two boys, Marie Dorion had spent the winter.

In March, as the snows melted, Marie and her children crossed the mountain range on foot and came down its far slopes to the Columbia, knowing that a springtime flotilla of traders would come upstream from Astoria. She had been given hospitality by the Indians at the Walla Walla mouth. When the flotilla appeared, two weeks later, the Walla Walla had paddled her out from shore to meet it.

"We had no doubt," wrote Franchère, "that this massacre was an act of vengeance, on the part of the natives, in retaliation for the death of one of their people, whom Mr. John Clark had hanged for theft the spring before."

In all the Snake River country, Marie Dorion was the only survivor.[*] She and her two fatherless boys bore one more heavy cost of John Jacob Astor's attempt at West Coast empire.

JOHN JACOB ASTOR OPPOSED GAMBLING. He refused to play cards for money. He abhorred speculation in stocks, which during his youth had become an emerging practice among the coffeehouse-frequenting merchants of Manhattan, leading to the birth of the New York Stock Exchange. But John Jacob Astor in many ways was the consummate gambler, his wagers for huge sums and vast stretches of territory extending over thousands of miles and several decades.

He didn't give up his West Coast empire for lost—not for years, and really not even then. At first, he didn't know what had happened. It took months for news of various disasters to reach him in New York, interspersed with reports of Astoria's achievements. But even after he learned of the repeated setbacks and disasters, he pushed forward, long after his own men had essentially given up.

---

[*]   Franchère lists the dead in this massacre as John Reed, Jacob Reznor, Pierre Dorion, John Hubbough, Gilles Leclerc, François Landry, and André la Chapelle.

"Good god," he had written to the State Department in the spring of 1813, "what an objict is to be secured by Smale means. . . ."

You needed big, bold strokes to accomplish big, bold ends. That summarized his message to the government bureaucrats who moved cautiously on his repeated requests throughout 1813 to send an armed U.S. naval ship and a small complement of marines to the mouth of the Columbia to defend the American settlement there—*his* settlement—against the British Royal Navy. He had bolstered the nation's under-funded war effort, no doubt out of a mixture of patriotism and profit, willing to lend the U.S. Treasury $2.5 million in its attempt to raise $16 million from America's wealthiest individuals.

But the Madison administration vacillated on whether to help Astor defend his West Coast colony.

"And for want of one ship and crew," writes historian James P. Ronda, "an empire appeared lost."

> 8 lost on the Columbia Bar
>
> 5 lost on the Overland Party
>
> 27 perished with the Tonquin
>
> 3 died or were killed at Astoria
>
> 8 lost in the wreck of the Lark
>
> 9 massacred by Indians in the Snake River country
>
> 1 died in the final departure
>
> ———————————————————————
>
> 61 Total
>
> *Astorians who perished as tallied by clerk Alexander Ross; figures do not include untold Native American losses. Historian Hiram Chittenden puts the total at 65 Astorians.*

One of the last to die was young Archibald Pelton. A few weeks after the other Astorians had left by ship and canoe in early April 1814, he one day was tending the charcoal pit alone in the forest, now in the employment of the North West Company. Two Tillamook Indians mistook him for a white man who had wronged them and vowed revenge, ambushing him and splitting open his skull with his own tomahawk.

Astor had sent a total of about 140 men to the mouth of the Columbia, between the *Tonquin,* the *Beaver,* the *Lark,* and Hunt's Overland Party. Of these, at least sixty-one, or over 41 percent, died in a gruesome spectrum of violent deaths. It's fair to ask: Was this a bold display of perseverance on John Jacob Astor's part, to send expedition after expedition to a dangerous and remote coast? Or was it simple callousness to human life?

"[Mr. Astor] assumed the financial risks," wrote one commentator; "the traders mortgaged their lives."

"My plan was right," Astor allegedly said, according to another, "but my men were weak. Time will vindicate my reasoning."

One could argue that other Americans who built great business empires since John Jacob Astor's day likewise showed the same deep focus on the vision and were willing to sacrifice almost everything else to see it succeed, often ignoring human costs. Astor does not come across this distance of two centuries as capricious or cruel. Rather, he's gentlemanly. But he's also unsentimental—except for his own family—and relentlessly focused.

Astor explicitly parceled out blame, and blame fell directly on his chosen leaders. Irving was undoubtedly speaking for Astor himself in the conclusion to his 1836 account commissioned by Astor, some twenty-five years after the incidents, when he singled out Captain Thorn. The captain had ignored Astor's orders and "earnest injunctions" about how to approach the native peoples of the Northwest Coast. His poor judgment resulted in "dismal catastrophe" that "prepared the way for subsequent despondency."

In other words, the explosion of the *Tonquin* in those very first months set the mood of life on the Northwest Coast—the anxious, paranoid, exposed life in the dripping rain forest, along the swashing tidal rivers and surf-pounded headlands. This was not a warm, friendly place. In this dank, dark setting, fringed by violent death, personalities like McDougall spied malevolence lurking behind every tree.

Through Irving, Astor also criticized Wilson Price Hunt for wandering off on the *Beaver,* around the Pacific, to Hawaii, then to the Marquesas, again in direct contradiction to instructions and Astor's overall plan. These wanderings produced "a series of cross purposes disastrous to the establishment" and kept Hunt away from Astoria "when his presence was of vital importance to the enterprize."

The eruption of war complicated everything, making it extremely difficult and risky for Astor to supply his emporium on the Pacific. The United States could have helped greatly but the government dallied in its response and finally wouldn't provide armed escorts. The *Lark* might have saved Astoria single-handedly, but she shipwrecked off Maui. Astor's stealth ship, the *Forester,* made it as far as Hawaii, and there the crew, perhaps hearing of the various disasters that had preceded them aboard the *Tonquin* and *Lark,* apparently mutinied. If Astor had had either the commitment of his leaders or the protection of the U.S. government, his vision might have succeeded. So spoke Astor through Irving.

Some of his leaders didn't understand Astor's vision and commitment, Irving wrote. Others were loyal not to Mr. Astor but to the rival North West Company and switched allegiances once war was declared. If Mr. Hunt hadn't been off wandering about the Pacific, he would have prevented Astoria from being sold out by McDougall, Mackenzie, and the others.

"It was [Astor's] great misfortune that his agents were not imbued with his own spirit," wrote Irving.

Yet neither Irving nor Astor acknowledges a central fact: John Jacob Astor wasn't there. While Astor was vastly exposed, his exposure was purely financial. His men, in contrast, were exposed to the constant proximity of a violent death. How would John Jacob Astor himself have fared in the remote rain forest on the Pacific Coast rather than a solid-brick, double row house on Lower Broadway?

So much of Astoria's fate, and the future of the Pacific Coast, ultimately hinged on a few individual personalities, its leaders, coming under the severest kind of strain—their fight for physical survival.

Captain Thorn, both the simplest example and the shortest-lived of Astoria's leadership, brought a rigid system of values and narrowly defined worldview when he arrived among the native peoples of the Northwest Coast, along with a macho arrogance and a volatile temper. It was a combination almost fated to go wrong. Astor recognized this possibility in advance and gave Captain Thorn fair warning and detailed instructions, but even these couldn't prevent the inevitable clash. Why did Astor hire him? Astor wanted a "gunpowder man" capable of destroying enemy European ships. Surely Astor thought of the trade-offs. He didn't believe Captain Thorn was so rash as to trigger a violent confrontation with the native peoples at his very first unsupervised meeting with them. While Astor wanted the bravest man he could find, Thorn illustrated that there lies a point when bravery shades into arrogance, and arrogance shades into idiocy.

Yet one can also maintain some sympathy for Thorn, the object of endless ridicule, tricks, and insubordination by the clannish Scottish traders and their frisky clerks aboard the *Tonquin*. They played mind games with Captain Thorn, working him into a frenzy of paranoia and anger. By the end of the voyage Thorn seethed with frustration. When confronted with what he considered more insouciance from the natives of the West Coast, he erupted. He carried a fixed hierarchy and rules of engagement derived from Atlantic naval battles, which he tried to impose through sheer fierceness on others—first with the Scottish fur traders during the voyage and then with the Coastal Indians while trading. The more fiercely he forced his own rigid sense of order upon the intricacies of other, more fluid, cultures, however, the more likely it was to be subverted.

McDougall, in contrast, possessed the flexibility to adjust to these fluid cultural situations, which he did, relentlessly, to his personal advantage. That he had a talent for strategizing—or scheming, depending on how one might look at it—is obvious from his plans for the smallpox-in-a-bottle, from his marriage to Comcomly's daughter, from his taking control so thoroughly of Astoria at the colony's outset and ultimately selling the place out. Even Franchère, one of the most generous of the Astoria chroniclers and a fellow Canadian besides, finally takes to calling the Scotsman "the crafty M'Dougall" and declares that the "charge of treason will always be attached" to Astoria's leadership.

While some secret backroom deal transacting between McDougall and the North West Company—*if you sell us Astoria we'll in turn make you a partner*—certainly seems plausible, it has never been proven. McDougall might have resisted selling to the NWC if he had felt more secure at Astor's emporium on the Pacific. Barricaded in Astoria's fort, building up its palisades, often ill, McDougall succumbed to the worst imaginings, some real, some exaggerated—everything from Indian attack to starvation. His sense of vulnerability deepened during the rainy coastal winters, when upriver trading expeditions thinned the numbers at the fort. His strategies served as his defense against surroundings he saw conspiring against him. But McDougall's own nature provided a dark lens on the world that he glassed beyond the fort's palisades. He could see conspiracies everywhere in part because he was constantly concocting his own.

Among Astoria's leaders, Wilson Price Hunt remains the most complex character who has come down to us through the various journals and accounts and the one who responded in the most nuanced way to extreme exposure and risk. He neither lashed out aggressively like Thorn nor conspired darkly like McDougall. Accounts agree almost universally that he was a man of upstanding character and loyalty. He clearly remained faithful to Astor, and, by his own nature and by Astor's instructions, attempted to lead in the most inclusive way possible. But he lacked a sense of urgency at key periods, and lacked a firm hand when one was sometimes called for. His greatest strength may have proved his greatest flaw—one that finally sunk John Jacob Astor's West Coast empire. Wilson Price Hunt vastly preferred cooperation to confrontation.

Almost immediately Hunt left Astoria aboard the *Beaver*. Arriving at the Russian fortress on the Alaskan coast, he let himself be manipulated by Count Baranoff. He wouldn't stand up to Captain Sowle. When the captain swung the *Beaver* from Alaska toward the Sandwich Islands—Hawaii—for repairs, Hunt either would not or could not demand firmly enough that the ship first return to Astoria to drop him off. His penchant for avoiding confrontation in favor of compromise played a pivotal role, right then, in Astoria's fate. Ship repairs offered a plausible reason to defer to the authority of Captain Sowle and depart from Astor's instructions. Or was this less a plausible reason than a reasonable excuse? Instead of returning to Astoria for a dark, rainy, uncertain winter, he would spend it on Hawaii. Hunt had traveled hard and nearly steadily for the last two and a half years, crossing the continental wilderness of North America, leading a party that had nearly starved to death. Young and vigorous though he may have been at the start, by this point Hunt may have simply been exhausted. Maybe he needed a break.

And maybe it wasn't just Hunt. Maybe all the Astorians had finally exhausted themselves. In an age-old tradition, young men had flung themselves at the wilderness, measuring themselves against it. Yet on the Pacific Coast lay a wilderness of unimaginable size and power and remoteness. Finally there comes a point—after one year? two years? three years of naked exposure?—when you have had enough.

Whichever it was, Hunt's decision left him absent from the mouth of the Columbia at a crucial time and left the door open for McDougall to sell out. If McDougall acted with stealth and subterfuge, and Thorn by direct confrontation, it seems that Hunt often made choices by default. The result was that Astoria lacked a strong leadership loyal to John Jacob Astor. Instead it had a "crafty" leadership loyal to its own interests. Foreshadowing certain American business practices two centuries in the future, McDougall, in the absence of anyone present to tell him no, fashioned himself and Mackenzie a "golden parachute."

Then he bailed out.

Twenty-two years later, in the fall of 1835, Washington Irving moved in with John Jacob Astor and grandson at Astor's country estate overlooking the spinning currents of the East River. Known as Hell Gate after the river strait on which it sat, and located at what is now East Eighty-Eighth Street but was then Manhattan Island countryside, the graceful, pillared, two-story mansion was designed in the neoclassical style. Also in residence were Astor's personal secretary and de facto advisor on all things literary and artistic, the witty and charming poet Fitz-Greene Halleck, and at times Irving's nephew Pierre. His every need provided by a staff of servants, free to do as he pleased, Irving called the Hell Gate mansion "a kind of bachelor hall."

"I have not had so quiet and delightful a nest since I have been in America," Irving wrote in a letter to his brother.

Astor had commissioned Irving, then a famous American author who had lived in Europe for seventeen years, to write the story of his great enterprise, as Irving would come to call it. Irving had enlisted Pierre to research and compile the story from many sources—journals, letters, and interviews with surviving participants, for whom Astor happily sent whenever they needed to fill in a missing part of the story.

Irving was taken by Astor's energy, even at age seventy-two, and desire to commit the story to writing. Astor had recently retired, and his wife, Sarah, had recently died. Irving thought Astor was looking for "occupation and amusement" and so launched the project.

The world had moved on in some ways since the fall of Astoria, and in other ways it had not. The city of New York had climbed up Manhattan Island from the lower tip as far as about Twentieth Street. Astor personally happened to own a great deal of it. He had also been busy over the last two decades building an enormous fur empire *east* of the Rockies. He had hired both Robert Stuart and Ramsay Crooks as two of his principal fur traders and managers, even though Crooks, battered from his overland ordeal, had initially quit Astoria upon arrival on the West Coast. With their able help and his drive and resources, Astor and his son William Backhouse Astor rolled over the competition (some said ruthlessly) and dominated the fur regions from the Great Lakes to the Rocky Mountains. During the 1820s and 1830s era of the "mountain men" and the great trappers' rendezvous in places like Jackson Hole, many of the furs ended up in Astor warehouses.

Astor sold his sprawling fur business to Ramsay Crooks in the mid-1830s and retired. But even then, in the fall of 1835, as Irving worked over his manuscript at Astor's Hell Gate country house, with the "old gentleman's" encouragement and enthusiasm, the fate of the Northwest Coast still hung in limbo, as it had for the last twenty-two years. After McDougall sold out Astor in the fall of 1813, Captain Black of the *Racoon* had declared the whole country a British possession. Therein, however, lay a problem.

"What the vague term of the 'whole country' in the present case meant, I know not," wrote Alexander Ross. "Does it mean the Columbia? Does it mean all the country lying west of the Rocky Mountains? Or does it merely mean the coast of the Pacific?"

It remained unclear for decades which nation had strongest claim to the "whole country." After the War of 1812 came to an amicable settlement in late 1814, in a kind of stalemate, with no territory or borders changed, it was eventually decided between the United States and Britain that the disputed Northwest would remain under "joint occupation" for a period of ten years. But the British had already firmly established themselves in Astor's former fur posts and started more of their own. Astor still couldn't quite let it go, although his initial anger had turned to a kind of resignation.

"[W]hile I breath & so long as I have a dollar to spend I'll pursue a course to have our injuries repair'd & when I am no more I hope you'll act in my place; we have been sold, but I do not dispond," he had written in 1814 to Mackenzie upon receiving the news of Astoria's sale. Soon Mackenzie came under Astor's suspicions, too.

McDougall, meanwhile, remained on the West Coast safely out of reach of Astor's wrath. The low price he received for his goods particularly incensed Astor.

"Had our place and our property been fairly captured," wrote Astor to Hunt afterward, "I should have preferred it. I should not feel as if I were disgraced."

Astor later estimated that, through McDougall's "fraudulent" sellout to the North West Company, Astor's company had received from the company about $40,000 for what Astor estimated was $200,000 worth of goods.

Four years later, as the joint occupation agreement started in the Northwest, Astor's tone had mellowed. "If I was a young man, I would again resume the [Pacific] trade," he wrote to his friend Albert Gallatin.

What could have been on the Pacific Coast? Surely Astor thought about it. In those quiet moments on his horseback rides or walks he must have mused on what he could have possessed if not for the odd quirks of his chosen men, the gaps in leadership, the fateful arrival of Pacific storms or Atlantic politics. Would he have possessed the whole West Coast? The region all the way to the crest of the Rockies? From Alaska to Mexico? Would it be a wealthy trans-Pacific trade empire? Or a political entity as well? Would it become, in short, the country of *Astoria*?

"I remember well having invited your proposition on that subject," a retired Thomas Jefferson had written Astor in early spring of 1812, about Astor's then-thriving colony on the West Coast. "[I] looked forward with gratification to the time when it's descendants should have spread themselves thro' the whole length of that coast, covering it with free and independent Americans, unconnected with us but by the ties of blood & interest, and enjoying like us the rights of self-government."

Again, a year later, Jefferson wrote to Astor, replying to Astor's letter confirming the settlement had been established as planned. Wrote Jefferson:

*. . . I learn with great pleasure the progress you have made
towards an establishment on the Columbia river. I view it as the
germ of a great, free & independent empire on that side of our
continent, and that liberty & self government spreading from that
as well as this side will ensure their compleat establishment over the
whole. [I]t must be still more gratifying . . . to foresee that your
name will be handed down with that of Columbus & Raleigh, as
the father of the establishment and founder of such an empire. . . .
[W]ith fervent wishes for a happy issue to this great undertaking
which promises to form a remarkable epoch in the history of
mankind, I tender you the assurance of my great esteem & respect.*

Th: Jefferson

To have these words of encouragement from a former president
of the United States, and this possible legacy, was no small thing to
relinquish, especially one possessed of a continental vision like Jefferson's. We'll never know exactly what vision Jefferson and Astor
shared—or what they didn't share. In their enthusiastic discussions in
the president's house in 1808 they may have left the exact details of a
West Coast colony a blank. How large an empire? What kind? Would it
become, as Jefferson hoped, "a great, free and independent empire." In
other words, a democracy? Or a sprawling and powerful trade empire
controlled by a dictatorial fur and real estate baron based in Manhattan? Or, somehow, would it be a melding of both?

This schism still lives with Americans today. It is especially pronounced in the nation's role in lands that lay, as Astoria did, beyond
the borders of the United States. In these places is America a beacon
of democracy that will unflaggingly support individual rights? Or is
it a trade empire looking out for its best economic interests? Which
comes first? Where is the priority? If Astoria had become a reality,
this was an issue that almost certainly would have arisen—and perhaps been bitterly fought, or even resolved—in the empire on the
Pacific.

Astor never quite got over his sense of loss about Astoria, embarking two decades later on the literary project to record for posterity what he had created on the West Coast— and what it *could* have been. But neither Astor nor Irving understood the larger significance of Astoria when writing in 1835. Its most important contributions to shaping the continent's destiny were still to come.

The Overland Party's excruciating journey from the Missouri River to the Columbia in 1811 would prove far more important than what seemed at the time sheer folly and catastrophe. In their wandering, hunger-ridden route, in all their wrong turns and suffering and dead ends, Hunt's Overland Party happened to discover the best way to cross the last third of the continent. The route finding occurred in the most haphazard, unsystematic fashion—motivated by a drive to profit rather than by exploration or science—but they had done it.

A year later, in 1812, the Return Overland Party discovered another key piece of geography—the South Pass through the Rocky Mountains. Carrying messages to the East for Mr. Astor and led by Robert Stuart, the Return Party took nearly a year and suffered a journey nearly as harrowing as Hunt's, robbed by Indians, almost starved, and hiding for the winter from possible ambush. But on October 22, 1812, Robert Stuart and Ramsay Crooks and their companions walked through rolling high country in today's southwestern Wyoming from one watershed to the next. They realized that they had strolled across the Continental Divide. For the Native Americans, this gentle route over a divide of hills represented simply another of innumerable ways across the Rocky Mountains. But the Indians didn't use wheeled vehicles. Stuart and Crooks had discovered a place where a loaded wagon could cross the Rocky Mountains and Continental Divide. That crucial discovery, along with the channel Hunt had found cut through the mountain ranges by the Yellowstone hot spot, would become the Oregon Trail.

For the next thirty years after the Astorians discovered it, however, this route remained obscure, even forgotten. There was little American activity in the Northwest. But the idea of American claims to it persisted. In 1815 and again in 1816, the determined Astor pressed the U.S. government through Albert Gallatin once more for a small, shipborne U.S. military force to be sent to the mouth of the Columbia to reestablish the American presence on the West Coast. Gallatin, who was traveling back and forth between Europe and the United States in this period, and who had helped negotiate the Treaty of Ghent, which ended the War of 1812, brought up the matter to President Madison, yet again. And yet again, nothing happened.

The first "joint occupation agreement" between Britain and the United States to share the Oregon Country was signed in 1818. But into the 1820s, an outspoken contingent of American politicians strived to bring the region solely to U.S. control, leaning heavily on Astoria as the foundation of American claims to the West Coast.

"The settlement on the Oregon, connecting the trade of that river [the Columbia] and the coast with the Missouri and Mississippi, is to open a mine of wealth to the shipping interests and the western country, surpassing the hopes of even avarice itself," argued John Floyd, representative from Virginia, who was distantly related to Sergeant Floyd of the Lewis and Clark expedition (and its only member to die en route), in a speech to the U.S. House in 1822. "The lands of the Oregon are well adapted to the culture of rye, corn, barley, and every other species of grain."

Thomas Hart Benton, senator from the newly admitted state of Missouri, was another passionate supporter of taking the Northwest for the United States. Later known to history as a great advocate of what became called Manifest Destiny—that Americans were destined, for any number of reasons, to sweep westward across the continent to the Pacific—Benton asserted in a speech to the Senate in February 1823 that Astoria had "consummated" the U.S. title to the region. He also invoked fears of a British empire on the Pacific.

"Not an American ship will be able to show itself beyond Cape Horn, but with the permission of England."

Congress nevertheless voted down Floyd's and Benton's proposals.

The British fur companies—the North West Company and the Hudson's Bay Company—took over the former Astor posts. They built more of their own throughout the Columbia Basin. American trappers stayed farther east in the Rocky Mountains. As a result of Astoria's collapse, and the lack of prompt U.S. action to try to recover it, this huge region remained in question, what came to be known as the "Oregon Country." It stretched from the northern border of today's California all the way to Alaska and extended inland hundreds of miles to the Rockies' crest. For comparison, if a region this size were projected onto the East Coast, it would extend roughly from Jacksonville, Florida, to Boston, and stretch inland nearly as far as the Mississippi River. That entire region—what would have been Astoria, if all had gone according to John Jacob Astor's plan—continued to hang in limbo for three decades.

A few wagons in the 1830s followed this route over the Rockies discovered by the Astorians and carried fur traders or missionaries as far as the Snake River. Then in 1840 a few bold American settlers in wagons kept on going, dragging their heavy loads over the Blue Mountains to the Columbia. Under the "joint occupation" agreement they were free to do so even though the British held the fur posts on the river.

The reports came back to the United States. Near the Pacific Coast lay a virtual Eden—a great valley of rich, moist, impossibly green land, perfect for farming. This was the Willamette. In 1843 the first large group of wagons, known as the "Great Migration," made for the Willamette from Independence, Missouri, along the route pioneered by the Astorians. When they arrived after their journey of five months they found a few settlers already living in the Willamette. Among them was an elderly Marie Dorion and her third husband.

"She, from various traditions," wrote one early Oregon historian, "was looked up to and revered as an extraordinary woman, the oldest in that neighborhood, kindly, patient and devout."

Before Marie Dorion died in 1850, the Willamette had become a magnet for the western movement. Thousands of heavily loaded wagons carrying European agriculturalists and their plows and pianos and bedsteads, trailing their cattle behind, rolled through Native American hunting grounds and the easiest passes to the Pacific—up the Platte River, through South Pass, along the Snake River plain, over the Blue Mountains, and down the Columbia. This was the route that had been discovered with great difficulty by the explorations of the Astorians—the Oregon Trail.

The United States and Britain resolved the "Oregon Question" in 1846, finally drawing the border after a great deal of contention. Britain wanted it drawn at the Columbia River (the border between today's Washington and Oregon), while the more adamant U.S. advocates demanded that the United States take all the Pacific Coast as far north as the Russian posts in Alaska at about 54 degrees, 40 minutes north—thus the rallying cry of the American advocates of Manifest Destiny, "Fifty-four forty or fight!"

Britain and the United States compromised at 49 degrees north—the current U.S.-Canadian border today across the Northwest. The long period of limbo and joint occupation ended. A great chunk of the West Coast was suddenly stamped "American." It officially opened to U.S. settlement. Immediately, a relentless wave of settlers crowded out of the East and pushed westward to claim their plots of farmland in the rich Willamette Valley. The Native American Coastal tribes, powerful as they were, were driven out or confined to reservations.

Britain held on to a five-hundred-mile stretch of Pacific Coast and lands reaching far inland to the Rockies' crest (roughly today's British Columbia). But it might have turned out very differently.

"It is no flight of fancy, but rather a sober and legitimate conclusion, to say that if the Astorian enterprise had succeeded," wrote historian Hiram Chittenden 1902, "the course of the empire on the American continent would have been altogether different than it has been . . . no part of the Pacific Coast line would now belong to Great Britain."

Wrote Charles M. Harvey in a 1911 *North American Review* essay titled "Our Lost Opportunity on the Pacific": "[W]hen California came into our hands, in 1848 and when Russia handed Alaska over to us in 1867, we should have had an unbroken coast-line from San Diego up to Point Barrow, far above the Arctic Circle."

Whether this great stretch of the western continent would have been called "Astoria," a separate and a free country, is another question altogether.

John Jacob Astor lived just long enough to see part of the Oregon Country become U.S. territory. He died at age eighty-four in 1848, two years after Britain and the United States settled the issue. He was by then the richest man in the United States, worth $20 million, or $110 billion in today's dollars by one calculation, which ranks him fourth on the list of the all-time wealthiest Americans. Astor personally controlled wealth equivalent to about 1 percent of the nation's gross national product at that time. Much of the fortune derived from furs and real estate, especially property in Manhattan. He left most of his fortune to his second son and business partner, William Backhouse Astor, a powerful and successful businessman in his own right. (John Jacob and Sarah's eldest son remained mentally incapacitated his entire life.) At his death, John Jacob Astor came under criticism from some quarters, like educator Horace Mann, for not showing more generosity to charity than the half million dollars he gave. His largest bequest amounted to $400,000, which went to found the Astor Library—forerunner of the New York Public Library.

While John Jacob and Sarah left many descendants from their five surviving children, the bulk of actual fortune followed primogeniture of a sort in the male line. One branch of the family moved to Britain, taking the control of a great deal of the fortune with it and became titled there. In the United States, the last of the direct male Astor line (which included John Jacob Astor IV, who went down on the *Titanic* but left children behind) ended with Vincent Astor. He and his third wife, Roberta Brooke Russell Astor, had no children, nor had he any offspring with his previous wives. Upon his death in 1959, his fortune went to his charity, the Vincent Astor Foundation. The money that this foundation gave away to schools, hospitals, the arts, and countless other causes could be said to date back to the original John Jacob Astor, the young German immigrant selling cakes on the streets of late-eighteenth-century Manhattan. All its funds finally spent, as intended, it closed in 1997. Brooke Astor died in 2007 at age 105.

Not long before her death, a crab fisherman in Clayoquot Sound, on Vancouver Island, British Columbia, snagged his traps on something protruding from the sandy bottom of Templar Channel. Divers sent down discovered that the traps had become enmeshed on the shaft of an old anchor. The ten-foot-long, thousand-pound anchor was hauled to the surface, and, upon analysis, found to date to a late-eighteenth- or early-nineteenth-century sailing ship. It is believed to be the anchor of the *Tonquin,* further confirmed by Clayoquot oral history identifying the spot of the *Tonquin*'s destruction. Remarkably, the anchor was encrusted with blue glass beads of the kind the *Tonquin* used for trading for furs with Coastal Indians. The anchor represented the first archaeological evidence confirming the destruction of the *Tonquin*. Further searches of Templar Channel's bottom have not yet turned up other remains of the ship.

Today the name Astor mostly conjures images of New York society, luxury hotels, the later John Jacob who went down on the *Titanic*. The momentous drama of John Jacob Astor's great Pacific enterprise has largely been forgotten by the general public, although it is still studied by western historians. A century and a half ago, when the nation was still coalescing geographically, it was a well-known and oft-cited chapter of American history. Irving's book was a bestseller in 1836 and, it is said, required reading in New York schools.

The prominence of the Astorians and their story has been in some ways overshadowed for decades by the much-vaunted successes of Lewis and Clark. Americans love heroes and winners. In Astoria, there are few clear-cut winners and no unblemished heroes. Although the story has been largely supplanted in American folklore by sturdier icons, a powerful legacy nevertheless remains from John Jacob Astor's attempt at a West Coast empire.

Whatever else one can say about him, it's hard to deny that John Jacob Astor, as well as Thomas Jefferson, had a far-reaching vision of the Pacific Rim. By many measures, they were two hundred years ahead of their time. Only in recent decades, and increasingly in recent years, has the Pacific entered fully on the world stage as both an economic and political nexus in the way that the Atlantic was for several centuries previously. Astor and Jefferson envisioned what we now call a global trade that crisscrossed the Pacific and linked the countries bordering its shores.

The Astorians served as that first push of American settlers across the continent, finding the route, placing an American presence on the Pacific Coast, and bringing the idea of settlement into consciousness. Without them, the shape of the nation might look very different. If Astoria hadn't put down roots in the Northwest, would a foreign power more easily have controlled the entire West Coast? In a way, John Jacob Astor did finally achieve his dream of a West Coast empire. But it wasn't his. It was everyone's.

A less tangible but equally powerful American legacy derives from the nature of John Jacob Astor himself. His personal drive and vision served as a template for later American entrepreneurs. Astor possessed the resilience and confidence to fail, along with the focus and drive to keep going despite failure.

In this, Astor's attempt at a West Coast empire echoes the story of the early European settlement of the East Coast. It required a visionary and risk-taking leader to take the first leap. In many, if not most, cases, that first visionary leader failed. Raleigh's Roanoke Colony failed, as did the first French colonies in Acadia and elsewhere in eastern Canada. These founders were willing to expose themselves and their people to huge risk. They left wreckage in their wake. They had to fail first—leaving colonists exhausted, broke, dead, or all three—in order for those coming later to succeed.

It makes sense, then, to give a follower of one of these visionaries the last word. This comes from Robert Stuart, the bold young Scotsman who led the Return Overland Party, bearing messages for Mr. Astor in Manhattan. On Tuesday, October 13, 1812, Stuart and his party, which included the long-suffering Ramsay Crooks, were failing from starvation in the high country of what's now southwestern Wyoming, just short of the crucial pass they were about to discover. They figured they had not many days to live. One of the voyageurs traveling with them proposed drawing lots, shooting the loser, and eating him. Stuart, horrified, put an end to the proposal at gunpoint. But for the first time in his life, he couldn't sleep at night, amid all his tossing and troubled thoughts.

Some of these thoughts Stuart recorded. He may have directed them at humankind in general. Or he might have addressed them obliquely to the visionaries who sent forth this expedition that was causing such suffering, John Jacob Astor and Thomas Jefferson, living in comfort on the eastern seaboard. Wandering starving in these uncharted lands, Stuart came to understand that enormous wealth, such as Astor's, meant nothing here. Lofty political ideals about liberty and equality, such as Jefferson's, took on an entirely different meaning in a barren wilderness. Here one is humbled by freedom—either find sustenance, or die.

> Let him but visit these regions of want and misery; his riches will prove an eye sore, and he will be taught the pleasure and advantage of prayer—If the advocates for the rights of man come here, they can enjoy them, for this is the land of *liberty and equality,* where a man sees and feels that he is a man merely, and that he can no longer exist, than while he can himself procure the means of support.

WILSON PRICE HUNT—Served for many years as postmaster of St. Louis, where he upheld an impeccable reputation both for honesty and for the conscientious delivery of the mail.

DUNCAN MCDOUGALL—Stayed at the Fort George (formerly Astoria) post, appointed a North West Company partner in 1816. The following year he traveled East and took charge of the NWC's Winnipeg district, where, from unspecified causes (one suspects retribution by a wronged party), he soon "died a miserable death." Seeking the last word, he claimed in a codicil to his will that the "malicious and ungenerous" conduct of his former associates at Astoria had unjustly damaged his reputation.

RAMSAY CROOKS—After Crooks had quit Astoria and returned overland to the East, the tireless Astor recruited him to build his next large fur enterprise. Crooks would eventually run operations for Astor's American Fur Company, which covered a great deal of the Great Lakes and West during its height. Though a fierce competitor, Crooks was regarded as a principled and tactful individual and a devoted family man. He died peacefully in New York City in 1859.

CHINOOK NATION—Chinook reservation lands were designated in 1851 by the Superintendent of Indian Affairs for the Oregon Territory in their traditional homelands along the lower Columbia and on the Pacific Coast. These reservation lands were not ratified at the time by the U.S. Senate. The Chinook refused to move to reservations elsewhere. The federal government thereafter ceased relations with most of the Chinook bands in 1954. The Chinook tribe, of which there are 2,700 members, are currently seeking federal recognition as a tribe. They appeared to have won recognition in 2001 but the decision was reversed in 2002. Christopher Stevens, the ambassador to Libya slain in 2012 during an attack on U.S. consular offices in Benghazi, was a member of the Chinook tribe through his mother, and closely related to Chinook tribal elders.

CLAYOQUOT NATION—Known today as the Tla-o-qui-aht First Nation, it is part of a confederation of fourteen First Nations along the west coast of Vancouver Island, British Columbia, numbering a total of about 8,000 people, about 900 of them Tla-o-qui-aht, and maintaining cultural ties to their past. The village of Opitsaht, where Captain Gray destroyed two hundred houses and countless carvings by cannon fire (one of the cannonballs recently unearthed), still exists and as of 2006 had a population of 174. Oral tradition among the Tla-o-qui-aht places the explosion of the *Tonquin* off the former village of Echachis. The trade blankets scattered by the force of the explosion were much valued and known as *claokwahitshe*.

"The Martin family of the Tla-o-qui-aht First Nation," according to the 2005 archaeological report about the finding of the *Tonquin*'s anchor, "state that it was their ancestor, Chief Nuukmiis that led the attack on the *Tonquin*, prompted not only by an insult perpetrated on Nuukmiis by Captain Thorn, but also by previous acts of treachery on the part of American traders, as well as Chief Wickaninnish's desire to obtain an armed vessel."

As part of the research for the 2005 report, a Tla-o-qui-aht tribal historian was asked why previous researchers had not cited the abundance of traditional Tla-o-qui-aht knowledge regarding the *Tonquin* incident.

"No one ever bothered to ask us," he replied.

ROBERT STUART—Only a month after returning from his brutal overland journey across the continent and his three years in the wilds, Stuart married the former Elizabeth Emma Sullivan in New York, with whom he would have nine children. With friend Ramsay Crooks, he soon joined John Jacob Astor's next fur enterprise, the American Fur Company, and served for many years as Astor's resident agent at Michilmackinac Island, where, at the operation's height, he oversaw four hundred clerks and traders, in addition to two thousand voyageurs. Known as a fair but exacting man, he was said to have brought his quick temper to bay after a spiritual awakening during a revivalist movement in the late 1820s. He died peacefully in his sleep after reading a book in front of the fireplace of his Chicago hotel room in 1848, his wife beside him.

DONALD MACKENZIE—Pursued a long and varied career as a fur trader with the Northwest Company and Hudson Bay Company, in the Northwest and in the Red River region, fathering many children first with his "country wife" and then with his children's young Swiss nanny, whom he married. He retired to an estate overlooking Lake Chautauqua, New York, and died in 1851 after being thrown by his horse.

ALFRED SETON—After leaving Astoria in April of 1814 with Wilson Price Hunt aboard the *Pedlar,* the young clerk Seton underwent another long and inadvertent series of adventures—drinking bouts with Count Baranoff in Alaska, romances with Spanish girls in California, serious bouts of malaria in Panama. Still trying to make his way back to New York, he was stranded in Cartagena, Colombia, when, as a "gentleman," he managed to talk his way into a passage with a British Royal Navy vessel to Jamaica, whence he returned to New York, "as poor as a Starved Rat"—this despite having dropped out of Columbia University to make his fortune and reverse his family's tough financial times by joining Astor's great venture. After some years as a fur merchant, he and several other partners founded the Sun Mutual Insurance Company, offering ship's insurance, and became very wealthy, moving to a country home in Westchester County, New York, where he died in 1859. Seton's lost journal was discovered in 1947 in a cupboard in Washington Irving's home, "Sunnyside," in Tarrytown, New York, when the home was undergoing historic restoration.

JOSEPH MILLER—The former army officer and Astor partner from a "respectable family" in Baltimore, suffering a bodily malady that pained him to ride on horseback, gave up his shares and quit Hunt's Overland Party just past the Tetons in October 1811. He and a string of trappers that included the three Kentuckians—Robinson, Hoback, and Reznor—were trapped for the winter toward the south, probably in what is today northern Colorado. Twice robbed of goods and horses by Indians, they made their way back north, and were found in August 1812 fishing beside a stream, horseless and nearly starved, by the Return Overland Party. While the three Kentuckians remained to trap in the Snake River country (and later were massacred with John Reed), Miller accompanied the Return Overland Party to St. Louis. He there disappears from the historical record.

ROBERT MCCLELLAN—After struggling overland from Hell's Canyon to Astoria, McClellan of the hair-trigger temper "threw in his shares" and quit. He then turned around and struggled back to the United States with the Stuart and Crooks Return Overland Party. Within a month of their arrival in St. Louis, McClellan was thrown into prison for unpaid debts. He declared bankruptcy and was freed, then briefly ran a store in Cape Girardeau, Missouri. He gave it up due to poor health, but seems to have purchased two racehorses nevertheless. He died at St. Louis only two and a half years after his arrival from Astoria, nearly impoverished.

ALEXANDER ROSS—Leaving Astor's concern, he worked for the North West Company and then for the Hudson Bay Company in the Northwest after the two outfits merged. He became an administrator in the Red River colony in today's Manitoba, fathered thirteen children with his native wife, and later in life wrote three books on his experiences in the Northwest and West.

ROSS COX—Worked briefly for the North West Company in the Northwest, returned to the East, and tried unsuccessfully to get a posting with the Hudson Bay Company. Returning to his native Ireland, he worked as a clerk in the Dublin police headquarters and as a correspondent for the London *Morning Herald,* publishing his book, *Adventures on the Columbia River,* in 1831.

GABRIEL FRANCHÈRE—Returned to Montreal when Astoria was sold and married his sweetheart, whom he had left behind. He remained employed in the fur trade, eventually becoming John Jacob Astor's chief agent in Montreal for Astor's American Fur Company, then moved to New York City. After Astor sold his American Fur Company and it eventually went bankrupt, Franchère, said a friend, acted "in an extremely honorable manner, [and] sacrificed his own personal fortune to assist in meeting its liabilities."

BAPTISTE DORION, *son of Marie and Pierre Dorion*—Baptiste Dorion served as guide and interpreter to early settlers in the West and for the naturalist John Kirk Townsend.

JOHN DAY—Irving says Day's health was broken after his ordeals with the Overland Party and he died within a year, but that appears to be mistaken. Apparently Day went to work as a hunter for the North West Company, and in 1819 or 1820, being "infirm of body," died in the Snake River country in a place traders called "Day's Defile" (today's Little Lost River, Idaho). He is memorialized in both the town of John Day, Oregon, and the John Day River.

ACKNOWLEDGMENTS

This book started with a happenstance encounter. One day in May 2008, during research for my previous book, *The Last Empty Places,* I was driving through the largely uninhabited regions of eastern Oregon. As dusk fell, I found myself cruising down a long, empty highway that tumbled through high prairies, over forested ranges, along twisting river-valleys. It seemed I hadn't seen another car for hours. I began to wonder where I would spend the night. Past dark, by now around 10:00 P.M., I came to a small town—more a village, really—tucked among forested hills. I found a motel. I slept.

The next morning, I discovered where I was: John Day, Oregon. What a curious name for a town, I thought. Who was John Day? A person?

A quick bit of online research in my motel room revealed that he was a member of the Wilson Price Hunt expedition sent by John Jacob Astor across the continent in 1810–1811. I'd never heard of it. Or so I thought. I read that John Day had been left behind. He'd been captured by Indians, stripped naked, and sent into the wild. Rescued but faced with having to retrace the same route, he had tried to kill himself. This story piqued my curiosity even more.

The deeper I delved into the story of John Day and the other Astorians, the wilder it became: canoes trapped in canyons, overbearing sea captains, longboats caught in surf, an exploding ship. And behind it all stood a poor immigrant who had become a wealthy New York fur baron and alongside him, cheerleading this first effort to plant an American settlement on the largely unclaimed West Coast, a U.S. president—Thomas Jefferson.

Why hadn't I heard of it? I'd lived for three decades in the heart of Lewis and Clark country, steeped in the stories of their heroics, but I hadn't heard a word about the Astorians, a much larger expedition that had followed right afterward. I wanted to know more. I learned that Washington Irving had written a story about it. The story had become a bestseller in 1836 but was now largely forgotten. I started to dig into the story of the Astorians more deeply, and the more I dug, the more compelling the story became.

As I researched, I realized I had caught glimpses of this story years before.

On a long-ago family ski trip to Jackson Hole, Wyoming, my father, William F. Stark, veered the rental van onto a side road in a mountain valley.

"The Astorians came through here," he had said, or something to that effect. "These were men sent by John Jacob Astor from New York."

I hadn't paid much attention at the time, not understanding the significance of the story. My father was a Wisconsin businessman, with a passion for history and for writing, and the author of several regional and local histories. For many years, he was also on the board of directors of the Wisconsin State Historical Society, a longtime leading resource in the history of the fur trade. He knew a great deal about the fur trade, especially in the upper Midwest. When I was a grade-schooler, we took canoe trips as father, son, and grandfather down the Wisconsin River, and my father told stories about the voyageurs who had paddled this same key route (which included Wilson Hunt Price and his Overland Party) for two centuries. For a time, hanging above our mantelpiece in my childhood home in Wisconsin, was a reproduction of a Frances Anne Hopkins painting of the voyageurs.

So it's to my father that I owe my first debt of gratitude for this book. In what has otherwise been a pleasure to research and write, it has been a deep regret that my father, who died in 2003, has not been alive as I've worked on *Astoria*. He would have so loved to be involved in the research. I'm sure I would be receiving daily phone calls from Wisconsin and almost daily packages in the mail with new information about Astor, Ramsay Crooks, fur posts, Michilimackinac Island, and countless other historical matters relating to this story that he would have devoted himself to uncovering. I think he would have been very proud, on my behalf, of the result.

As I dug into the story of the Astorians, I realized I'd been hearing about it for years, obliquely, from another family source. The family of my wife, Amy Ragsdale, has for decades had a summer cabin on Hartstene Island in Puget Sound next door to the summer cabin of the Murray and Rosa Morgan family of Tacoma, Washington. The families have remained the closest of friends. Until his death in 2000, at age 84, Murray was one of the Northwest's best known popular historians, and the author, among many other books, of *Skid Road,* one of the most widely read and beloved histories of Seattle.

From the time I first met him, in the 1980s, Murray was working on and off on what he called "the work by which I want to be remembered." This was a history of the first European explorers who came to the Northwest Coast, and in particular the first ships that arrived to exploit the precious sea otter furs. It was through Murray, a wonderful storyteller—and no doubt over a long lunch or dinner sipping wine on the Morgans' or Ragsdales' rickety porch and looking out across Puget Sound at the shimmering glaciers of Mount

Rainier—that I first learned of the significance of the sea otter that led to the trans-Pacific trade and European settlement of the Northwest Coast. Murray's story was a huge one, covering many decades and expeditions, his research assisted, as usual, by Rosa. It was still in progress when he died. Murray and Rosa's daughter, Lane Morgan, also a writer and editor, has since taken up the manuscript and is currently preparing it for publication.

So my second debt is to Murray Morgan, who opened my eyes to the significance of the sea otter trade on the Northwest Coast. Its historical significance resonated with me when I stumbled across the story of the Astorians. Thus I've dedicated *Astoria* to Murray and Rosa, and to Rags, the name by which my father-in-law, Wilmott Ragsdale, was universally known. A foreign correspondent and then–professor of journalism at the University of Wisconsin, Rags (who was also my journalism professor in graduate school), taught me much about writing and gave me unflagging encouragement even in the darkest of times that almost inevitably intrude at points in a freelance writer's career.

Countless other individuals and institutions have helped me in the course of researching and writing *Astoria*, and I'd like to acknowledge them here, aware that I may nevertheless inadvertently overlook someone.

Historical researcher John Robinson of Spokane, Washington, and Missoula, Montana, has done a superb and amazingly efficient job of helping me find obscure articles and dig out deeply buried facts, as well as collaborating in compiling and writing the endnotes, and many other research tasks. He is truly a "J-STOR Ninja"—a master of the massive online database of academic articles. He also happens to have been born in Astoria, Oregon; knows the terrain; and, for his doctoral thesis in history, is writing on the federal status (or lack thereof) of the Chinook tribe at the mouth of the Columbia who helped the Astorians. I'd also like to thank John's thesis advisor, Dan Flores, A. B. Hammond Chair in Western History at the University of Montana and author of numerous books on the American West, for putting me in touch with John Robinson.

Several individuals read the book's proposal in the early stages and gave me valuable responses: Bryan Di Salvatore, David Cates, Fred Haefele, Connie Poten, Kate Stark Damsgaard, Ted Stark, and Bob Hayssen. I am also grateful to several editors who read the completed proposal and gave their editorial insight: Leslie Meredith, Marc Resnick, Roger Scholl, Gillian Blake, Nancy Miller, Anton Mueller, Susan Canavan, and Tom Mayer. Jack Macrae early in the process recognized Astoria as a largely unknown story of exploration that deserved a greater audience. Alex Philp, historical geographer, has been a great sounding board for my ideas over the years, as has Scott Elrod.

As I began to research and write the book, I visited as many of the locales portrayed in the Astoria story as time and circumstance (and wilderness accessibility) allowed, in order to capture with vividness and immediacy what the Overland and Seagoing Parties experienced in these rugged landscapes and seascapes themselves. It is amazing to me how much of the Hunt route remains wilderness, or near-wilderness, or much as he saw it two centuries ago. With the exception of a few small pockets, this is not a part of North America that has been subdivided into housing developments or paved over into mall parking lots. Much remains sparsely populated rangeland, farmland, rugged near-wilderness, or—in the case of Hell's Canyon, the Wind River Mountains, the Bighorn Mountains, and parts of the Blue Mountains—actual designated wilderness under the federal Wilderness Act of 1964.

In September 2012, we took a four-day canoe trip down the South Fork of the Snake River, very near to the section of the Snake where Wilson Price Hunt and his Overland Party ran into such difficulty with rapids and canyons on their "Mad River." I'd like to thank my paddling companions on that trip: Jim Ritter and his daughter, Kate, and my daughter, Molly Stark-Ragsdale, who also captured portions of the trip and the rugged terrain and canyon walls on videotape. Jim, both a journalist and a widely read history buff, is not only one of my oldest friends and paddling companions, but has been a tremendous resource throughout my research and writing of *Astoria*, both as a reader from the proposal stage onward and a sounding board for ideas.

On the Snake River trip, Jeff Hawkes of Rexburg, Idaho, helped us with canoe rentals, happens to live very near where the Overland Party built their canoes on the Henry's Fork, and has a deep interest in local history. For my hike into the Seven Devils area near Hell's Canyon, where Hunt's Overland Party encountered impassable mountains, I'd like to thank the Hell's Canyon National Recreation Area office in Riggins, Idaho, for advice.

My understanding of the Seagoing Party's dilemmas at the mouth of the Columbia, as well as en route on the open ocean, was informed in part through my visit to Astoria itself and Cape Disappointment at the Columbia's mouth, as well as a four-day sailing experience with a group from Sussex School in Missoula, Montana, aboard the *Adventuress*, a one-hundred-foot, traditional wooden schooner that sails on Puget Sound. There, we not only learned—and performed—traditional sail-hauling and other techniques but also had the experience and knowledge of our captain, Daniel Evans, to draw on as well as the help of his crew.

My understanding of square-rigged sailing ships such as the *Tonquin* was greatly enhanced by countless hours of conversation with my father, William Stark, who as a young man in 1949 served as an ordinary seaman aboard the last commercial windjammer to round Cape Horn, the Pamir. I helped my father write a memoir of this experience, *The Last Time Around Cape Horn,* and in the course of it heard in detail how square-rigged sailing ships perform in squalls and storms at sea, including a hurricane that the *Pamir* endured in the Atlantic while my father was aboard and, for part of the storm, aloft in the rigging.

To learn more about Northwest Coast Native Americans and their large sea-going canoes, I was pleased to be able to attend two annual gatherings of nations from up and down the Northwest Coast. Every August, representatives from each nation paddle—in some cases for weeks—on open ocean or inland waterways to reach a designated gathering spot for a week of celebration, dancing, feasting, and honoring of ancient traditions. In August 2012, I attended the Paddle to Squaxin, hosted by the Squaxin Island tribe on Puget Sound near Olympia, Washington, a gathering of 102 large canoes, and in August 2013, I attended the Paddle to Quinault, hosted by the Quinault Indian Nation on the open Pacific Coast near Taholah, Washington. I am very grateful to these tribes and this event for opening themselves so willingly to the general public, and to the event's founders and participants for keeping these ancient traditions and the Northwest Coast canoeing arts alive.

I further learned about the original peoples of the Northwest Coast (as well as the violent end of the *Tonquin*) during a visit to Clayoquot Sound, on the West Coast of Vancouver Island, and to the town of Tofino, British Columbia. It was there that I took a room for several days at the House of Himwitsa Lodge and Gallery in Tofino, overlooking Clayoquot Sound, and owned by the George family. I am very grateful to their hospitality and helpfulness. The title of Maquinna, hereditary chief of Ahousaht, has been handed down in their family for seventeen generations.

During my stay at Clayoquot Sound, Brandon Hilbert, of Tofino Water Taxis, took me on a boat tour of the possible site of the *Tonquin*'s destruction and other points of interest in the sound.

My research was made a great deal easier by the helpful staffs at Baker Library at Harvard Business School, and by Tim Mahoney, Special Collections Librarian; the New York Historical Society; the Manuscripts and Archives Division at the New York Public Library; Beinecke Rare Book and Manuscript Library at Yale University, and Ingrid Lennon-Pressey; Clatsop County Historical Society and its Heritage Museum in Astoria, Oregon; Tacoma Public Library; Mansfield Library at the University of Montana; Grand Portage National Monument in Grand Portage, Minnesota, and Karl Koster; Fort William Historical Park in Thunder Bay, Ontario; Fort Michilimackinac State Park, Michigan; the Stuart House Museum, Mackinac Island, Michigan; Headwaters Heritage Museum at Three Forks, Montana; Nez Perce County

Historical Society and Museum in Lewiston, Idaho; Spokane House Interpretive Center at Riverside State Park in Spokane, Washington; Museum of the Mountain Man in Pinedale, Wyoming; and Museum of the Fur Trade in Chadron, Nebraska.

I am also extremely grateful to historians who came before and have researched the efforts of John Jacob Astor to establish his West Coast trade empire. These include Washington Irving himself, who with his nephew and researcher, Pierre, assembled a great deal of the Astoria story from documents, journals, and interviews. While some critics and historians of the 1800s disparaged Irving's efforts as romantic, exaggerated, or embellished, I have found—as have others before me—that on close examination, much of what he wrote is based directly on the documented material. He also had the advantage of interviews with living participants and access to letters and other documents that have since been lost or destroyed. Other historians who laid the groundwork for the Astoria story are Hiram Chittenden and Kenneth Wiggins Porter, both writing in the early 1900s. For the modern reader who wishes to learn about the Astoria story in greater detail from a more academic perspective, I recommend the impeccably researched *Astoria & Empire* by Western historian James P. Ronda.

As the manuscript neared completion, it was read by several individuals who made valuable suggestions and offered insights. These were Mike Kadas, Noel Ragsdale, John Brown, and Jane Ragsdale, who also has contributed her enthusiasm and helped with research. Sally Thompson, archaeologist with a great deal of knowledge of the Lewis and Clark expedition and Native American history along its route, initially suggested to me that Sacagawea and Marie Dorion probably met along the Missouri River in 1811, and also provided insightful feedback on the manuscript itself. Jack Nisbet, writer of Northwest history, read the manuscript and gave helpful suggestions relating to the Northwest fur trade and geography. Jack's book on David Thompson, *Sources of the River,* provided a key guide in helping me track that extraordinary explorer's movements. Jim and Linda Hunt enthusiastically embraced the book and helped introduce it to other Northwest historians, while Ashby Kinch brought it to his group of readers. Nancy Cook and Tom Berninghausen provided helpful information on Washington Irving and other early American literature. Bailey Stark helped with additional research.

I feel fortunate beyond measure to work with the people at Ecco and HarperCollins who made this book possible, got behind it from the start, edited it so skillfully and intelligently, designed it so beautifully, and marketed and publicized it so enthusiastically. To Daniel Halpern, Martin Wilson, Suet Chong, Michael McKenzie, Doug Jones, Bob Alunni, Gabriel Barillas,

Jim Hankey, and Emma Janaskie, you have my deep gratitude. To Ross Harris and Shana Cohen, many thanks. To Hilary Redmon, editor extraordinaire, and Stuart Krichevsky, agent extraordinaire, it's been a pure pleasure to work together on this book. I've felt from the start it's been a team effort and that it's been a great team.

To research and write a book like this—or more generally to pursue a career as a freelance writer, and as a writer of adventure and exploration—demands a certain willingness to venture into unknown realms, sometimes geographically, but more often to stray into uncertain terrain psychologically and emotionally, not to mention financially and professionally. I would never be able to do this without the support and understanding and participation of my family—both my extended family and my immediate family. So to all of them, and especially to Amy, Molly, and Skyler, my deepest offering of love and gratitude.

NOTES

PROLOGUE

1   *she swung sideways to the onrush of wind and water*: Washington Irving, *Astoria, or, Anecdotes of an Enterprise Beyond the Rocky Mountains,* author's revised edition (New York, 1849), pp. 476–77.

    "[W]e were in great Confusion and disorder": Samuel H. Northrop to John Jacob Astor, March 1814, in Kenneth Wiggins Porter, *John Jacob Astor, Business Man,* vol. 1 (1931; reprint, New York: Russel & Russel, 1966), pp. 552–54.

2   *Another wave hit*: Alexander Ross, *Adventures of the First Settlers on the Columbia River, Being a Narrative of the Expedition Fitted Out by John Jacob Astor* (London: Smith, Elder, 1849), pp. 261–62, and Irving, *Astoria* (1849), p. 477.

3   *contemplated adding a post down near San Francisco Bay*: A Russian fur post, eventually known as Fort Ross, on the Pacific Coast in today's Sonoma County, was established in 1812, two years after Astor had launched his enterprise on the Columbia.

CHAPTER ONE

7   *"[Y]our name will be handed down with that of Columbus & Raleigh"*: Thomas Jefferson to John Jacob Astor, November 9, 1813, in *The Papers of Thomas Jefferson, Retirement Series,* vol. 6 (Princeton: Princeton University Press, 2010), p. 603.

    He smoked his pipe, sipped from a glass of beer: James Parton, *Life of John Jacob Astor* (New York: American News Company, 1865), p. 50.

8   *Walldorf, one of seven "forest villages"*: Elizabeth L. Gebhard, *The Life and Adventures of the Original John Jacob Astor* (Hudson, NY: Bryan, 1915), p. 7. Gebhard, writing in 1915, corresponded with individuals in Walldorf familiar with the Astor family history in Germany and the early history of the town. She apparently was a descendant of John Gabriel Gebhard, who had also left Walldorf as a young man, when Astor was a boy of five, and who had known Astor when the two were in America. See Gebhard's foreword for her many sources.

8   *The eldest Astor brother, George*: Parton, *Life of John Jacob Astor*, p. 18.
     Parton, writing in 1865, also cites a small biography about Astor, written
     by a Lutheran clergyman from Baden who interviewed living individu-
     als in Walldorf who knew Astor as a youth. The pamphlet was published
     in Germany about ten years earlier (c. 1855) and served as the source
     for some of Parton's material about Astor's early life. Parton, *Life of John
     Jacob Astor*, p. 26.
     His father was a Huguenot: Gebhard, *The Life and Adventures of the Origi-
     nal John Jacob Astor*, p. 13, and John Upton Terrell, *Furs by Astor* (New
     York: William Morrow, 1963), pp. 23–25.
     "loved not . . . John Jacob": Gebhard, *The Life and Adventures of the Origi-
     nal John Jacob Astor*, p. 20, and Parton, *Life of John Jacob Astor*, p. 19.
     apprentice John Jacob to a clockmaker or master carpenter: Gebhard, *The
     Life and Adventures of the Original John Jacob Astor*, p. 3.
     youngest son: Ibid.
     "I'm not afraid of John Jacob; he'll get through the world": Parton, *Life of
     John Jacob Astor*, p. 24.
     "with a bundle over his shoulder": Porter, *John Jacob Astor, Business Man*,
     vol. 1, p. 7, citing Oertel.
9   *seven finely crafted flutes*: Ibid., vol. 1, p. 10; Parton, *Life of John Jacob Astor*,
     p. 29.
     the New Land: Gebhard, *The Life and Adventures of the Original John Jacob
     Astor*, pp. 23–24.
     Making his way to New York City: John Jacob Astor to Washington Irving,
     November 25, 1836, in Porter, *John Jacob Astor, Business Man*, vol. 1,
     p. 353. In this letter to Irving, Astor described his arrival in America and
     his first weeks there, receiving the hospitality of a Swiss man and wife
     living in Baltimore; the husband, Nicholas Tuschdy, had a shop where he
     let Astor display some of his musical instruments.
     met aboard the ship a friendly fellow German: Parton, *Life of John Jacob
     Astor*, pp. 31–32.
     then with a population of twenty-three thousand: Gebhard, *The Life and
     Adventures of the Original John Jacob Astor*, p. 68.
     and reaching no farther north than Cortlandt Street: Ibid., p. 60.
10   *"I'll build . . . a grander house"*: Ibid., p. 73.
11   *voyage back to London*: Porter, *John Jacob Astor, Business Man*, vol. 1, p. 23.
     "Jacob Astor [has] just imported: Ibid., pp. 30–31.
     "Jacob was nothing but a baker's boy": Ibid., p. 20 [remark edited to remove
     "German" pronunciation].
     controlled retail selling prices in the Manhattan meat stalls: Parton, *Life of
     John Jacob Astor*, p. 37, and Gebhard, *The Life and Adventures of the Origi-
     nal John Jacob Astor*, p. 84.

12   *John Jacob married his landlady's daughter, Sarah Todd*: Porter, *John Jacob Astor, Business Man,* vol. 1, p. 24.

     81 Queen Street: Gebhard, *The Life and Adventures of the Original John Jacob Astor,* p. 72. Queen Street is now Pearl Street.

     best judge of furs: Ibid., p. 80.

     Greenwich Village, and another property called Eden Farm: Porter, *John Jacob Astor, Business Man,* vol. 2, pp. 920–21.

13   *British merchants had organized the Hudson's Bay Company*: Harold A. Innis, *The Fur Trade in Canada* (New Haven: Yale University Press, 1962), p. 119. The Hudson's Bay Company was chartered May 2, 1670.

     highly astute bargainers: Gebhard, *The Life and Adventures of the Original John Jacob Astor,* p. 61.

     Seneca, Mohawk, or Oneida: Ibid.

     "I have seen John Jacob Astor with his coat off": Porter, *John Jacob Astor, Business Man,* vol. 1, p. 38.

14   coureurs de bois—*the French-Canadian "runners of the forest"*: Innis, *The Fur Trade in Canada,* pp. 59–62.

15   *starting in 1788*: Robin Inglis, *Historical Dictionary of the Discovery and Exploration of the Northwest Coast of America* (Lanham, MD: Scarecrow Press, 2008), p. 141.

     That nation, Mackenzie wrote: Alexander Mackenzie, *Voyages from Montreal Through the Continent of North America to the Frozen and Pacific Oceans in 1789 and 1793,* vol. 2 (New York: Allerton, 1922), p. 358.

     double row house at 223 Broadway: Parton, *Life of John Jacob Astor,* pp. 49–50; Gebhard, *The Life and Adventures of the Original John Jacob Astor,* pp. 124, 143–44.

16   *"would not lose the sale of a bale of fur"*: Jefferson to Astor, November 9, 1813, *The Papers of Thomas Jefferson, Retirement Series,* vol. 6, p. 603.

     to create a seaport on the Pacific Rim: Stephen E. Ambrose, *Undaunted Courage: Meriwether Lewis, Thomas Jefferson, and the Opening of the American West* (1996; reprint, New York: Simon & Schuster, 2002).

17   *"It was my intention to have presented myself"*: Astor to Jefferson, February 27, 1808, Thomas Jefferson Papers, Library of Congress, American Memory Project.

     "a man of large property": Porter, *John Jacob Astor, Business Man,* vol. 1, p. 167. Porter quotes a letter from to Jefferson from General Henry Dearborn, who apparently, at Jefferson's request, had inquired about Astor's reputation from New York City mayor DeWitt Clinton.

     "The field is immense, & would occupy a vast amount of capital": Jefferson to Astor, April 13, 1808, Thomas Jefferson Papers, Library of Congress, American Memory Project.

     on a warm summer Sunday in 1810: Franchère, *Narrative,* p. 25.

18 *Feathers and ribbons fixed to their hats*: Ibid., p. 25, and Irving, *Astoria,*
    p. 49.
    "Dans mon chemin": Hiram Martin Chittenden, *The American Fur Trade
    of the Far West,* vol. 1 (New York: Rufus Rockwell Wilson, 1936), p. 64.
    the lower Manhattan docks, now so packed with spectators: Ross, *Adven-
    tures,* p. 11.
19 *"[D]elighted with the vivacity and dexterity of the two men"*: Ibid., p. 12.
20 *framed his global commercial vision*: Irving, *Astoria,* pp. 37–40.
22 *didn't extend much farther west than the Ohio Valley*: For a popula-
    tion map of the United States in 1800, see http://etc.usf.edu/maps/
    pages/2300/2397/2397.htm, retrieved September 24, 2013.
23 *Though Hunt had no experience in the wilderness*: Irving, *Astoria,* p. 124.
24 *his new entity the Pacific Fur Company*: Ibid., p. 43, Porter, *John Jacob Astor,
    Business Man,* vol. 1, p. 182, and James P. Ronda, *Astoria & Empire* (Lin-
    coln: University of Nebraska Press, 1990), p. 59.
    "gunpowder fellow": Irving, *Astoria,* p. 54.
25 *"blow all out of the water"*: Ibid.
26 *"the germ of a great, free and independent empire"*: Jefferson to Astor, Novem-
    ber 9, 1813, *The Papers of Thomas Jefferson, Retirement Series,* vol. 6, p. 603.

CHAPTER TWO

27 *How could Captain Thorn tell them*: Irving, *Astoria,* pp. 53–55.
    blacksmith, carpenter, and cooper: Franchère, *Narrative,* p. 30.
28 *Known for his expertise in scouting:* Ross describes him as whimsical and
    eccentric, p. 78. Franchère calls him "bold and enterprising," p. 20.
    "To prevent any misunderstandings": Irving, *Astoria,* pp 52.
29 *"We will defend ourselves"*: Ross, *Adventures,* pp. 14–15.
    "to go to inhabit with strangers": Franchère, *Narrative,* p. 33.
30 *She carried ten guns*: Ibid., p. 38.
31 *with many of his passengers then hauled off to fight*: Ibid., pp. 35–36.
    Captain Thorn grew fed up: Irving, *Astoria,* p. 55.
34 *"The Order of the Good Times"*: Francis Parkman, *France and England in
    North America,* Volume 1, pp. 201–3. For the French in America generally,
    see also Marc Lescarbot, *The History of New France.*
    From then on, Scottish Highlanders, immigrating: For the shifting power
    balance in the fur trade, see Harold A. Innis, *The Fur Trade in Canada,*
    chap. III, esp. pp. 166–88.
35 *On the night of November 11*: See Franchère, *Narrative,* p. 40, and Ross,
    Adventures, p. 19. Ross and Franchère disagree as to the date by one day,
    though it is certainly the same storm.
36 *"but the frail machine"*: Franchère, *Narrative,* p. 33.
    "[The] terrible tempest": Ibid., p. 40.

37 *making a distance downwind*: See Ross, *Adventures,* p. 20. For further description gale forces, see Franchère, *Narrative,* pp. 40–41.
breaking two of his ribs: Franchère, *Narrative,* pp. 40–41.
they were running dangerously low: Ross, *Adventures of the First Settlers on the Columbia River,* p. 20.
38 *"This pious attention to two dead men"*: Ibid., pp. 46–47.
39 *"to our infinite surprise and dismay"*: Ross, *Adventures,* pp. 23–24.

CHAPTER THREE

41 *Astor's "gilded prospectus"*: Ross, *Adventures,* p. 9.
42 *Mackenzie objected*: Ronda, *Astoria & Empire,* p. 89, and Ross, *Adventures,* pp. 10, 171.
hated to sit still: Cecil W. Mackenzie, *Donald Mackenzie: "King of the Northwest"* (Los Angeles: Ivan Beach Jr., 1937), p. 26.
"To travel a day's journey on snowshoes was his delight": Ibid., p. 26. Mackenzie the author was quoting Ross's description from other writings of Ross.
43 canot du maître: Grace Lee Nute, *The Voyageur* (New York: D. Appleton, 1931), p. 24. See also Irving, *Astoria,* pp. 125–26, for canoe and paddler description.
forty to sixty strokes per minute: Nute, *The Voyageur,* p. 27.
44 degradé: Ibid., p. 28.
"I can liken them to nothing but their own ponies": Ibid., p. 14, quoting Thomas L. McKenney.
"[T]hey haven't lost an iota of French gaiety": Alexis de Tocqueville, *Letters from America,* ed. Frederick Brown (New Haven: Yale University Press, 2010), p. 154.
mangeurs de lard, *or "pork-eaters"*: Nute, *The Voyageur,* p. 5.
45 *"I could carry, paddle, walk and sing with any man"*: Ibid., p. vi.
On July 22, 1810: Chittenden, *The American Fur Trade of the Far West,* vol. 1, p. 182. The exact dates of the Hunt Party departure from Montreal and arrival at Michilmackinac vary slightly in different accounts, but agree on an early July departure and late July arrival.
paddling at top speed, voyageurs singing: Nute, *The Voyageur,* p. 60. Nute gives a vivid description of the arrival of a typical voyageur canoe.
46 *"resembled a great bedlam"*: Ross, *Adventures,* p. 176.
47 canot du nord: Nute, *The Voyageur,* p. 24.
"Perhaps Satan never reigned": Bryan Leigh Dunnigan, *A Picturesque Situation: Mackinac Before Photography, 1615–1860* (Detroit: Wayne State University Press, 2008), p. 91. The quotation is in a letter from Alice Parks Bacon, wife of a Protestant missionary, in winter 1803.

47   *A whispering campaign*: Irving, *Astoria,* p. 129, and Ronda, *Astoria &*
      Empire, p. 119.
      the first Mackinac recruit signed: Ronda, *Astoria & Empire,* pp. 119–20.
      Ronda cites the company ledger, and says that Landry is the first name
      that appears among the recruits at Mackinac.
48   *"stool-pigeon"*: Irving, *Astoria,* p. 129.
      $11.25 fine levied against him: Ronda, *Astoria & Empire,* p. 120.
49   *"inevitable pipe"*: Nute, *The Voyageur,* p. 13, citing various travelers'
      accounts for voyageur clothing. See also Orville D. Menard, "Voyageurs
      with the Lewis and Clark Expedition," in *We Proceeded On* 38, no. 1 (Feb-
      ruary 2012): 21–29. This article gives illustrations of the dress of voya-
      geurs.
      "Je suis un homme du nord": Irving, *Astoria,* p. 128. Irving had traveled
      in voyageur canoes and knew voyageurs personally, as well as their pad
      dling techniques and construction of their canoes.
      brightly colored feather: Nute, *The Voyageur,* p. 60.
50   *Leaving Mackinac Island in mid-August*: Irving, *Astoria,* p. 132.
51   *under the leadership of Andrew Henry*: Chittenden, *The American Fur*
      Trade of the Far West, vol. 1, pp. 138–44.
      Reports had come downriver: Ibid., vol. 1, p. 142, and Irving, *Astoria,* p. 140.
      knew they had to get a start: Irving, *Astoria,* p. 136.
      Two days later: Ibid., p. 137.

CHAPTER FOUR

53   *making good speed*: Franchère, *Narrative,* pp. 46–47, and Ross, *Adven-*
      tures, pp. 23–25.
54   *"The weather now grew more violent"*: Ross, *Adventures,* p. 25.
      "upon those barren rocks": Franchère, *Narrative,* p. 48.
55   *"you are a dead man"*: Ross, *Adventures,* p. 25.
      "The coast of the island": Franchère, *Narrative,* p. 54.
      watching the island's approach: Ibid., pp. 53–54. Ross gives the name of
      the young man overboard as Joseph LaPierre. Ross, *Adventures,* p. 28.
56   *The* Tonquin *had rounded the Horn*: Franchère, *Narrative,* p. 51.
      "Sullen and silent, both parties passed and repassed": Ross, *Adventures,* p. 26.
57   *"Had the wind not hauled ahead"*: Irving, *Astoria,* p. 62.
      When the Tonquin *had rounded Cape Horn*: Franchère, *Narrative,* p. 50.
      "Crews with clique structures": Sheryl L. Bishop, "From Earth Analogs to
      Space: Getting There From Here," in *The Psychology of Space Exploration,*
      ed. Douglas A. Vakoch (Washington, DC: National Aeronautics and Space
      Administration, 2011), p. 72.
58   *Arguments and power struggles*: Irving, *Astoria,* p. 63.

58   *"[A]nd within fifteen minutes"*: Ibid., p. 63.
     never learned to swim: "Sailors Who Cannot Swim," *New York Times,* May
     3, 1883.
59   *sliced the lines that secured it*: Franchère, *Narrative,* p. 53.
     by rolling him in blankets and rubbing him with salt: Ross, *Adventures,*
     pp. 28–29.
     Dozens of native canoes paddled out: Franchère, *Narrative,* p. 55.
60   *"For other traits, they are very lascivious"*: Ibid., p. 74.
     "not accustomed to have his intentions frustrated": George Gilbert, *The
     Death of Captain James Cook (From Gilbert's Narrative of Cook's Last Voy-
     age, 1776–1780)*, Hawaiian Historical Society Reprints, No. 5 (Honolulu:
     Paradise of the Pacific Press, 1926), p. 11.
61   *they now wanted souvenirs*: Irving, *Astoria,* p. 68.
62   *"Storming and stamping on deck"*: Ross, *Adventures,* p. 32.
63   *served as boatswain aboard a New England ship*: "Boatswain John Young,
     His Adventures in Hawaii Recalled," *New York Times,* February 14, 1886.
     rowed ashore at Tohehigh Bay: Franchère, *Narrative,* pp. 59–60.
     "He received us kindly": Ross, *Adventures,* pp. 32–33.
     generating profits for the royal treasury: Franchère, *Narrative,* pp. 60–61.
     anchored in Waikiki Bay: Ross, *Adventures,* p. 34.
64   *"It would be difficult to imagine"*: Irving, *Astoria,* pp. 75–76.
     wanted to hire thirty or forty Hawaiians: Ibid., p. 75.
65   *"[F]rom the good conduct of the sailors"*: Ross, *Adventures,* p. 41.

CHAPTER FIVE

67   *Here wind squalls from the northwest*: Franchère, *Narrative,* pp. 85–86.
     They can literally stand: Interview with Daniel Evans, professional sea
     captain, *Adventuress,* May 2012.
68   *Captain Thorn gave orders to prepare*: Franchère, *Narrative,* p. 86; Ross,
     Adventures, pp. 54–56; Irving, *Astoria,* pp. 78–80. Ross gives the most
     complete and detailed account of the interaction between Thorn and Fox
     over the launching of the small boat. He was on the *Tonquin* at the time
     and added details that did not appear in Irving's account, which was pub-
     lished earlier than Ross's account.
69   *"Mr. Fox, if you are afraid of water"*: Ross, *Adventures,* p. 55.
     A mere twenty ships had: William Henry Gray, *A History of Oregon, 1792–
     1849, Drawn from Personal Observations and Authentic Information* (Port-
     land, OR: Harris & Holman, 1870), pp. 13–15.
     Spaniards first had sailed northward: *Oxford Atlas of Exploration,* p. 140.
     as far as today's Oregon: Sir Francis Drake, sailing for Queen Elizabeth,
     coasted Oregon in 1579 during his circumnavigation, though whether he
     landed there remains under debate. See John Barrow, *The Life, Voyages,*

and Exploits of Sir Francis Drake, with Numerous Original Letters from Him and the Lord High Admiral to the Queen and Great Officers of State, 2nd ed., abridged (London: John Murray, 1844), pp. 59–66.

70   *With Russia poking around Alaska's Pacific Coast:* Ruby and Brown note the Russians discovered the value of sea otter in Kamchatka at the end of the seventeenth century. Ruby and Brown, *The Chinook Indians,* p. 36. A group of merchants formed an association to hunt otters in Alaska in 1785 (p. 78). Later, in 1799, that association became the "Russian American Fur Company," officially sanctioned by the czar (p. 78). Ruby and Brown note that Russians had been operating from Kodiak Island as early as 1783. The *Juno,* formerly an American ship, now owned by the RAFC, sailed past the Columbia Bar in 1806, while Lewis and Clark were encamped near the river's mouth. They were looking for another place to begin trade as they'd run into trouble in Sitka. They did not cross into the river (p. 109). Ruby and Brown provide more detail of Russian presence along the Northwest Coast on pp. 117–118, 126, 138.

Franchère tells of meeting an old blind man: Franchère, *Narrative of a Voyage to the Northwest Coast of America,* pp. 112–13. Ruby and Brown also relate stories told by Lower Columbia tribes of Spanish sailors surviving wrecks and ending up among them. Ruby and Brown, *The Chinook Indians,* pp. 26–29.

Starting in 1769, Franciscan Father Junípero Serra: For Serra, see Stephen W. Hackel, *Junípero Serra: California's Founding Father,* esp. chaps. 8–10.

assigned Cook a secret mission: James Zug, *American Traveler: The Life and Adventures of John Ledyard, the Man Who Dreamed of Walking the World* (New York: Basic Books, 2005), p. 64.

the last major section of the earth's continental coastline: Oxford Atlas of Exploration, p. 161.

71   *they discovered that the spectacularly lustrous sea otter furs:* Ruby and Brown, *The Chinook Indians,* p. 37.

"*The rage with which our seamen*": Zug, *American Traveler,* p. 114, quoting Officer King's official account of the voyage.

he had become the first native-born American citizen: Zug, p. 78.

72   *Promoting with his memoir:* Ibid., pp. 132–138.

his innovative theory: Zug, pp. 186–87.

"*My friend, my brother, my Father*": John Ledyard, *John Ledyard's Journey Through Russia and Siberia, 1787–1788,* ed. Stephen D. Watrous (Madison: University of Wisconsin Press, 1966), p. 114.

73   *Ledyard's stories opened Jefferson's eyes:* Donald Jackson, *Thomas Jefferson and the Rocky Mountains* (Norman: University of Oklahoma Press, 1981), p. 56. "Ledyard . . . affected Jefferson's thinking profoundly. . . . [H]e

could also see in Ledyard a man whose dreams made sense and were not unlike Jefferson's own dreams for American growth."

73   *"[M]y tour round the world by Land"*: Ledyard to Jefferson, St. Petersburg, March 19, 1787, *The Papers of Thomas Jefferson,* vol. 11 (Princeton: Princeton University Press, 1955), pp. 216–18.

      As the lone romantic adventurer struck off: Ledyard later was arrested by Russia authorities and deported. He died several years later in Cairo while making arrangements to attempt to cross the Sahara Desert.

74   *sail for the Northwest Coast*: Barry M. Gough, *Dictionary of Canadian Biography,* vol. 5, s.v. "John Meares."

      Russian traders built a permanent fur post in Alaska: Ruby and Brown, *The Chinook Indians,* p. 78.

      finally returning home to Boston Harbor: Dorothy O. Johansen, *Empire of the Columbia,* 2nd ed. (New York: Harper & Row, 1967), pp. 52–54.

      "I was sent": John Boit, "Log of the Columbia," ed. F. W. Howay, T. C. Elliott, and F. G. Young, *Quarterly of the Oregon Historical Society* 22, no. 4 (Portland: Oregon Historical Society, 1921), p. 303.

75   *became the official Euro-American discoverer:* Inglis, *Historical Dicitonary of the Discovery and Exploration of the Northwest Coast of America,* p. 81. Bruno de Hezeta, a Spanish explorer, noted the existence of a large river in August 1775 but did not enter its mouth, although its mouth was subsequently marked on Spanish charts.

      Five months later a rival explorer: Bern Anderson, *Surveyor of the Sea: The Life and Voyages of Captain George Vancouver* (Seattle: University of Washington Press, 1960), pp. 114–17.

77   *He prepared himself should the partners*: For Thorn's suspicions of the partners, see Irving, *Astoria,* pp. 93–94. Conversely, Franchère writes that the "idea of a conspiracy against him on board [was] absurd." Franchère, *Narrative,* pp. 373–74.

      "My uncle was drowned here": Ross, *Adventures,* p. 55.

CHAPTER SIX

79   *on March 22, 1811*: Franchère, *Narrative,* p. 86.

80   *"At last she hoisted the flag"*: Ross, *Adventures,* p. 56.

      Franchère reported that when those aboard: Franchère, *Narrative,* p. 87.

      "an anxious night": Ross, *Adventures,* p. 57.

83   *But no one aboard ship made a move to help*: Ibid., pp. 59–60.

85   *spilling the crew*: Franchère, *Narrative,* p. 91, and Ross, *Adventures,* p. 65.

      averages about 45 degrees: Paul S. Auerbach, M.D., ed., *Wilderness Medicine: Management of Wilderness and Environmental Emergencies,* 3rd ed. (St. Louis: Mosby, 1995), p. 105.

      body's core temperature begins: Ibid., Fig. 4-4, p. 109.

86   *has lost a good part of his or her ability*: Ibid., pp. 115–16.
     After four hours in water: Ibid., Fig. 4-10, p. 116.
     Modern research shows: Jack Wang et al., "Asians Have Lower Body Mass
     Index (BMI) but Higher Percent Body Fat than do Whites: Comparisons
     of Anthropometric Measurements," *American Journal of Clinical Nutrition*
     (July 1994): 23–28.
87   *seized Weeks's clothing in their teeth*: Ross, *Adventures*, p. 64.
     keep working his muscles to generate body heat: Franchère, *Narrative*, p. 92,
     and Irving, *Astoria*, p. 83.
     Around midnight, with a rising wind: Franchère, *Narrative*, pp. 89–90.
88   *The following morning, March 26*: Franchère and Ross disagree on the date
     of the *Tonquin*'s bar crossing. Ross places it one day later. Ross, *Adventures*,
     p. 58; Franchère, *Narrative*, p. 87.
     "You did it purposely": Ross, *Adventures*, p. 63.
     the other Hawaiian lay down atop him: Franchère, *Narrative*, p. 92.
89   *"I paused for a moment"*: Ross, *Adventures*, p. 65.
     feet bleeding, legs swollen: Franchère, *Narrative*, p. 96.
90   *brothers Lapensèe and Joseph Nadeau*: Ibid., p. 86.

CHAPTER SEVEN

93   *dancing had lasted until midnight*: Porter, *John Jacob Astor, Business Man*,
     vol. 1, pp. 66–67. Also see journal entry of Samuel Bridge, from Montreal,
     ibid., pp. 412–13.
94   *In essence, Astor would buy into the existing*: Ronda, *Astoria & Empire*, p. 55.
     with china and white linen tablecloths: From personal visit to Fort William
     Historical Park, Ontario, Canada, July 2012. The North West Company's
     Fort William has been meticulously re-created as it was circa 1815 at this
     site near the original Fort William on Lake Superior's western shore.
95   *wilderness delicacies such as fatty beaver tail*: Irving, *Astoria*, p. 24, and
     from inventories in the Great Hall at Fort William Historical Park.
     wintering partners voted in favor: David Lavender, *The Fist in the Wilder-
     ness* (1964; reprint, Lincoln: University of Nebraska Press, 1998), pp. 125,
     443 fn. 7, and Ronda, *Astoria & Empire*, p. 63.
96   *guard their own interests on the Pacific side*: Ronda, *Astoria & Empire*, p. 64.
97   *Astor wrote to Hunt*: Ibid., p. 139.
     "No establishment of the [United] States on that river or on the coast": Ibid.,
     p. 56.
98   *Koo-koo-Sint*: Jack Nisbet, *Sources of the River: Tracking David Thompson
     Across Western North America* (Seattle: Sasquatch Books, 1994), p. 151.
     The message from the North West Company wintering partners: Ronda,
     Astoria & Empire, pp. 62–64. The instructions themselves from the win-
     tering partners to Thompson do not survive.

CHAPTER EIGHT

99 *On the morning of May 26*: John Bradbury, *Travels in the Interior of America, in the Years 1809, 1810, and 1811, Including a Description of Upper Louisiana* (London: Sherwood, Neely & Jones, 1817), pp. 77–78.
He had been scalped: Ibid.

101 *his own hair-raising encounter the previous year*: Irving, *Astoria*, pp. 130–31; Chittenden, *The American Fur Trade of the Far West*, p. 161; Bradbury, *Travels in the Interior of America*, p. 90.
thirty-some members to a full sixty: Irving, *Astoria*, p. 131.
"Mr. Hunt, in his eagerness to press forward": Ross, *Adventures*, p. 182.
ten-oared riverboat: Bradbury, *Travels in the Interior of America*, p. 11.

102 *Astor had promised Jefferson to share*: Ronda, *Astoria & Empire*, p. 124.
Daniel Boone: Bradbury, *Travels in the Interior of America*, p. 16.

103 *which he wrote down*: Ibid., pp. 17–21. Bradbury reported that he had heard about Colter's sighting of the forty-foot-long fish from William Clark, of Lewis and Clark fame, then in charge of U.S. Indian affairs for Louisiana Territory, based in St. Louis.

104 *The whoops grew fainter:* For a physiological description of this phenomenon, known as EIPH, see A. J. Ghio, C. Ghio, M. Bassett, "Exercise-Induced Pulmonary Hemorrhage After Running a Marathon," *Lung* 184, no. 6 (Nov.–Dec. 2006), pp. 331–33. Abstract retrieved December 14, 2013, from http://www.ncbi.nlm.nih.gov/pubmed/17086462.
isolated fur post on the Yellowstone River: Ibid., p. 21n; Chittenden, *The American Fur Trade of the Far West*, vol. 1, p. 119.

105 *commissioned by the Linnaean Society*: Irving, *Astoria*, p. 143.
Psoralea esculenta: Bradbury, *Travels in the Interior of America*, p. 21.
Meriwether Lewis as being at least partly responsible: Ibid., p. 18n, and Irving, *Astoria*, pp. 146, 179.
Several young Blackfeet tried to steal: Ambrose, *Undaunted Courage*, pp. 360–63.
take all possible precautions: Irving, *Astoria*, p. 146.

106 *twenty-four-year-old Ramsay Crooks*: Crooks was born in January 1787, in Scotland, to a shoemaker. *Dictionary of Canadian Biography*, vol. 8, s.v. "Crooks, Ramsay," http://www.biographi.ca.
steady, even-tempered, and considered: Irving, *Astoria*, p. 130, and *Dictionary of Canadian Biography*, vol. 8, s.v. "Crooks, Ramsay."
piercing, deep-set, dark eyes: Irving, *Astoria*, p. 138.
Born in Baltimore to a respectable family: Ibid., p. 135.

107 *he would shoot him on sight*: H. M. Brackenridge, *Journal of a Voyage up the Missouri River, Performed in 1811*, in *Early Western Travels*, vol. 6, ed. Reuben Gold Thwaites (Cleveland: Arthur H. Clark, 1904), p. 111.
served as a Sioux interpreter: Ronda, *Astoria & Empire*, p. 138.

107 *she escaped into the woods along the river*: Bradbury, *Travels in the Interior of America*, pp. 12–14, and Irving, *Astoria*, p. 144.
     Five-year-old Jean Baptiste: "Marie Dorion," entry in National Women's History Museum, http://www.nwhm.org, retrieved October 1, 2013.
108 *Sacagawea had adopted European dress and manners*: Brackenridge, *Journal*, pp. 32–33.
     on April 21, 1811: Bradbury, *Travels in the Interior of America*, p. 46.
109 *voyageurs as* embarrass: Ibid., p. 32, April 2, 1811.
110 *"Behind our house there is a pond"*: Ibid., p. 13. Bradbury recorded that the Canadians were "measuring strokes of their oars by songs" and that there were singing calls and responses from oarsmen in bow and stern, or the steersman sang while the rest of the oarsmen provided the chorus.
     Two years earlier, in the spring of 1809: Chittenden, *The American Fur Trade of the Far West*, vol. 1, p. 141–44. Chittenden gives an account of Andrew Henry and Manuel Lisa's Missouri Fur Company's early venture at Three Forks.
     "The [Blackfeet] Indians were so intensely hostile": Ibid., vol. 1, p. 142.
111 *let their empty canoes drift away downstream*: Bradbury, *Travels in the Interior of America*, p. 77, entry for May 26, 1811.
112 *leave the Missouri River*: Ibid., pp. 78–79, and Irving, *Astoria*, pp. 179–80.
     infused more with the spirit of brotherly love than mortal combat: Chittenden, *The American Fur Trade of the Far West*, vol. 1, p. 57 and p. 64 n2.
     Old photographs of scalping victims: See photograph of scalping survivor Robert McGee, in Library of Congress collections at http://www.loc.gov/pictures/resource/cph.3c05942. Other accounts of scalping survivors can be found at http://www.futilitycloset.com/2008/02/20/how-the-west-was-won.
113 *constrict the blood vessels quickly and slow the loss*: Conversation with emergency physicians Dr. Doug Webber and Dr. Gary Muskett, December 2, 2011.
114 *that Hunt had received a letter from Astor*: Ross, *Adventures*, p. 244.
     "O mon Dieu! Abattez le voile!": Bradbury, *Travels in the Interior of America*, p. 78.
115 "Ou est le fou?": Brackenridge, *Journal*, p. 102.
     1,075 miles up the Missouri: Bradbury, *Travels in the Interior of America*, p. 78.
     "anxious enquiry": Ibid., p. 79.
     Hunt polled them: Irving, *Astoria*, p. 180.

CHAPTER NINE

118 *The chief's powerful Indian oratorical voice*: Bradbury, *Travels in the Interior of America*, pp. 110–11, journal entry for June 12, 1811.
     "M'Clellan, in particular, carefully watched": Ibid., p. 111.

118 *Arikara women bobbing down*: Brackenridge, *Journal,* p. 112, entry for June 12, 1811.

119 "O meu Dieu! Ou est mon couteau!": Bradbury, *Travels in the Interior of America,* p. 103.
"I had several times to stand between": Brackenridge, *Journal,* p. 107, entry for June 5, 1811.

120 *an elderly chief, or priest, climbed to the lodge's rooftop*: Bradbury, *Travels in the Interior of America,* p. 112. The account of the meeting with the Arikara chiefs is contained in both Bradbury and, in more condensed form, Brackenridge.

121 *"[They] were going on a long journey to the great Salt lake"*: Brackenridge, *Journal,* p. 113.
"This candid and frank declaration": Brackenridge, *Journal,* p. 113.

122 *the Sioux had blockaded Hunt's riverboats*: Bradbury, *Travels in the Interior of America,* pp. 82–89, journal entry for May 31, 1811.

123 *"Smoking"*: Ibid., p. 113n. The custom was explained to Bradbury by Ramsay Crooks.

124 *"No people on earth discharge the duties of hospitality"*: Ibid., p. 169.
worked out in advance: Ibid., p. 125.
"I was wondering": Brackenridge, *Journal,* p. 130, entry for June 18, 1811. Both Brackenridge, an American and a journalist, and Bradbury, who was British and a scientist, give a great deal of enthnographic information about the Arikara, although in Brackenridge's case, it is frequently of a disapproving nature.
a total of eighty-two horses: Wilson Price Hunt, "Voyage of Mr. Hunt and His Companions," journal entry for July 18, 1811, in *New Annals of Voyages, Geography and History,* vol. 10. (Paris: J. B. Eyies and Malte-Brun, 1821), translation available at http://user.xmission.com/~drudy/mtman/html/wphunt/wphunt.html, retrieved October 2, 2013.

125 *Sacagawea was ill and wanted to return*: Brackenridge, *Journal,* pp. 32–33. Brackenridge was also on Lisa's riverboat, with Sacajawea and Charbonneau.
They had left their son: Editor's footnote in ibid., pp. 32–33, about Jean-Baptiste.
filled their heads with horror stories: Irving, *Astoria,* p. 219.

126 *"[T]he grass was knee-high*: Hunt, "Voyage of Mr. Hunt and His Companions," journal entry for July 24, 1811.

127 *"honest and clean"*: Ibid., journal entry for August 5, 1811.
Hunt's riverboats, having been sold to Lisa: Brackenridge, *Journal,* p. 146.
"experience many difficulties": Ronda, *Astoria & Empire,* p. 168. Gratiot is a business correspondent of Astor, from ibid., p. 50.

129 *gracious hospitality*: Irving, *Astoria,* p. 224.

130 *piney forests*: Hunt, "Voyage of Mr. Hunt and His Companions," journal entry for September 6, 1811.

"*There, among others*": Ibid., journal entry for September 4, 1811.

131 *for trout or grayling*: Ronda, *Astoria & Empire*, p. 175.

132 "*Spanish River*": Hunt, "Voyage of Mr. Hunt and His Companions," journal entry for September 16, 1811.

133 *He posed the question*: Irving, *Astoria*, p. 268. "The vote, as might have been expected, was almost unanimous for embarkation," writes Irving, who had direct access to several participants.

134 *The voyageurs instead planned to hew canoes:* For a hands-out study of the relative merits of dugout canoes hewn from cottonwood trunks, see William W. Bevis, "The Dugout Canoes of Lewis and Clark" at "Discovering Lewis & Clark," lewis-clark.org, 2014.

135 *clear view of the Tetons' snowy and rocky peaks*: From visit to put in point as marked by historical marker, near St. Anthony, Idaho, by author, April 2012.

136 *fifteen large and heavily loaded canoes*: Irving, *Astoria*, p. 275.

"*Three bonnie ducks go swimming 'round*": Nute, *The Voyageur*, p. 131, translation of voyageur song "En Roulant Ma Boule."

CHAPTER TEN

138 *They were happy*: Irving, *Astoria*, p. 276.

139 "*I sent my canoe and one other to the rescue*": Hunt, "Voyage of Mr. Hunt and His Companions," journal entry for October 20, 1811.

Hunt had split off the first "string" or "leash" of trappers: Irving, *Astoria*, p. 170. The first leash, splitting off east of the Tetons on the Mad River, was Alexander Carson, Louis St. Michel, Pierre Detayé, and Pierre Delauney. The second leash, splitting off at the canoe-building and put-in spot where Andrew Henry had wintered, was Robinson, Hoback, Reznor, Cass, plus Miller. See Irving, *Astoria*, p. 171. Thus nine trappers split off altogether.

An estimated 60–400 million beaver: Steve Boyle and Stephanie Owens, *North American Beaver (Castor canadensis): A Technical Conservation Assessment,* prepared for USDA Forest Service, Rocky Mountain Region, Species Conservation Project, February 6, 2007, http://www.fs.fed.us/r2/projects/scp/assessments/northamericanbeaver.pdf, retrieved October 3, 2013, p. 10. For more details on the beaver's role in the fur trade and its habits and habitat see also Eric Jay Dolin, *Fur, Fortune, and Empire: The Epic History of the Fur Trade in America* (New York: Norton, 2010), pp. 13–23, and Innis, *The Fur Trade in Canada,* pp. 3–6.

140 *Fur trappers exploited this habit*: Kent Klein, "Trapping Techniques of the Mountain Man," HistoricalTrekking.com, p. 6, retrieved October 3, 2013.

Klein assembles excerpts from early explorers' and trappers' journals on methods of trapping beaver.

141 *that he would not be going to the Pacific Coast*: Irving, *Astoria*, pp. 273–74.

"[He] had been in a gloomy and irritable state of mind": Ibid., p. 171.

143 *"[H]is fear of us was so great"*: Hunt, "Voyage of Mr. Hunt and His Companions," journal entry for October 26, 1811.

144 *they approached the entrance to a canyon*: Ibid., journal entry for October 28, 1811.

but the steersman didn't hear him: Irving, *Astoria*, p. 281.

145 *the basalt boulder*: Boulder location described in Idaho State Historical Society Reference Series: "Site of Ramsay Crooks 1811 Canoe Disaster."

146 At the clear running fountain: Nute, *The Voyageur*, p. 106, translation of "A La Claire Fountaine" (The Clear Running Fountain), one of the most popular voyageur boatsongs.

147 *The following day, October 29, their tenth*: Hunt, "Voyage of Mr. Hunt and His Companions," journal entry for October 29, 1811.

148 *The other three canoes snagged among exposed rocks*: Ibid., entries for October 31 and November 1, 1811; Irving, *Astoria*, p. 283.

340 miles upstream: Ibid., p. 179.

burn 6,000 calories daily: Auerbach, *Wilderness Medicine*, p. 158.

149 *With a pound of bison, elk, deer, or comparable lean game animal*: A 3-ounce piece of roasted elk is 124 calories, 1 ounce of roasted venison 46 calories, and 3 ounces of lean bison is 122 calories, according to http://caloriecount. about.com. A pound of elk would thus provide 657 calories and a pound of deer would provide 736 calories. Even without exertion or cold weather, an adult male needs around 2,000 calories per day, which would require an adult male to consume around 3 pounds minimum per person of deer or elk or bison. The Overland Party included 50 people, each of them requiring 3 pounds of wild game meat per day, or 150 pounds per day for the whole party. A large elk provides around 200–300 pounds of boneless meat, and a bison about 500 pounds, so the Overland Party would need to kill a large game animal every three to four days or possibly every day or two, if the animal were smaller.

elk (200–300 pounds of boneless meat): "The Elk Carcass," University of Wyoming. See table at http://i32.photobucket.com/albums/d45/2rocky/Hunting/elkmeatyield.jpg.

bison (400–500 pounds of boneless meat): Ag Canada La Combe Research Centre, http://www.canadianbison.ca/producer/Resources/documents/ExpectedMeatYieldfromaBisonBullCarcass.pdf.

150 *would head in different directions*: Hunt, "Voyage of Mr. Hunt and His Companions," journal entry for November 1, 1811; Irving, *Astoria*, p. 284.

CHAPTER ELEVEN

153 *"[F]or the greater part nothing that walks the earth"*: Robert Stuart, *Robert Stuart's Narratives,* in *The Discovery of the Oregon Trail,* ed. Philip Ashton Rollins (New York: Scribner's, 1935), p. 112. Stuart is describing on the return journey the stretch of river from thirty miles below Caldron Linn to Caldron Linn, or the stretch known as the "Devil's Scuttle Hole." (Today this is known as Murtaugh Canyon.)

154 *"The women fled in such haste"*: Hunt, "Voyage of Mr. Hunt and His Companions," journal entry for November 11, 1811.

156 *Yellowstone hot spot*: Joel Achenbach, "When Yellowstone Explodes," *National Geographic,* August 2009.
   Today that melted path is known as the Snake River Plain: Mark Anders, "Yellowstone Hotspot Track" (map).

158 *a horse he considered a friend*: Hunt, "Voyage of Mr. Hunt and His Companions," journal entry for November 27, 1811. "I could eat it only with regret because I had become attached to the poor animal."

159 *one of the voyageurs, Sardepie*: Irving, *Astoria,* p. 299. In this account of the meeting between Hunt and Crooks parties in the canyon, I've relied on both Hunt's journals as well as Irving's account, which fills in many details not found in Hunt. Irving, when writing his account, had access to several of the surviving participants, including Crooks. The details he includes of this incident clearly came from some of these interviews with particpants.
   For the first eighteen days: Irving, *Astoria* (1849), p. 300.

160 *"It was impossible for men in their condition to get through"*: Hunt, "Voyage of Mr. Hunt and His Companions," journal entry for December 6, 1811.

161 *"I spent the night reflecting on our situation"*: Ibid., journal entry for December 6, 1811.
   The physical sight of Crooks that day had come as a shock: Irving, *Astoria* (1849), pp. 299–300.

162 *"sepulchral"*: John Franklin, "Franklin's First Retreat," in *Ring of Ice: True Tales of Adventure, Exploration, and Arctic Life,* ed. Peter Stark (New York: Lyons Press, 2000).

CHAPTER TWELVE

164 *treasured their fine set of "plate"*: "The Will of John Jacob Astor," in Porter, *John Jacob Astor, Business Man,* vol. 2, pp. 1260–96. Astor made several stipulations about how his "plate" was to be distributed after his death. Other references to his and Sarah's practices to entertain guests give special importance to their "silver plate."
   revelry and pot-banging raucousness: Stephen Nissenbaum, *The Battle for Christmas,* Kindle ed. (New York: Vintage Books, 1997), loc. 1108. Nis-

senbaum also cites a reference for Washington Irving's role in shaping our modern Christmas and developing the tradition of Santa Claus, quoting an article by Charles Jones. "Without Washington Irving there would be no Santa Claus. . . . Santa Claus was *made* by Washington Irving." See ibid., loc. 1409, and chapter 2 fn. 20. Nissenbaum quotes from Charles Jones, "Knickerbocker Santa Claus," *New-York Historical Society Quarterly* 38 (1954): 356–83 (see 367–71).

165 *details of a contract*: Ronda, *Astoria & Empire*, p. 86.

166 *"Since I had the pleasure of speaking with you"*: Astor to Jefferson, March 14, 1812, in Porter, *John Jacob Astor, Business Man,* vol. 1, p. 508.
     "[A]t all events, I think we must be ahead of them": Astor to Jefferson, March 12, 1812, in ibid.

CHAPTER THIRTEEN

170 *"What a prospect!"*: Hunt, "Voyage of Mr. Hunt and His Companions," journal entry for December 6, 1811.

171 *Ramsay Crooks and Le Clerc soon staggered far behind*: Irving, *Astoria* (1849), p. 302, and Hunt, "Voyage of Mr. Hunt and His Companions," journal entry for December 7, 1811.
     small groups and lone travelers pushed ahead: Irving, *Astoria* (1849), p. 302.
     Crooks and Le Clerc could ferry themselves: Ibid., p. 303.
     "They said that we would all die from starvation": Hunt, "Voyage of Mr. Hunt and His Companions," journal entry for December 8, 1811.
     five men remained: Irving, *Astoria* (1849), p. 303.

173 *managed to buy (Hunt's account) or grab (Irving's account)*: Hunt, "Voyage of Mr. Hunt and His Companions," journal entry for December 10, 1811; Irving, *Astoria,* p. 305.
     "[H]overing like spectres of famine": Irving, *Astoria* (1849), p. 305.
     clapped his hands in delight: Ibid., p. 306.

174 *"Thus for twenty days*: Hunt, "Voyage of Mr. Hunt and His Companions," journal entry for December 16, 1811.
     after about ten to twelve weeks: Peter Stark, *Last Breath: Cautionary Tales from the Limits of Human Endurance* (New York: Ballantine Books, 2001), p. 112.

175 *"But to remain in this place would be still worse"*: Hunt, "Voyage of Mr. Hunt and His Companions," journal entry for December 19, 1811.

176 *"a gentleman of the mildest disposition"*: Bradbury, *Travels in the Interior of America,* p. 52.
     "I ended by telling the Indians": Hunt, "Voyage of Mr. Hunt and His Companions," journal entry for December 19, 1811.

CHAPTER FOURTEEN

177 "La maudite rivière enragée": Irving, *Astoria* (1849), p. 310.

"[They] told me that since we had left": Hunt, "Voyage of Mr. Hunt and His Companions," journal entry for December 21–23, 1811.

Three of these weakened voyageurs: Irving, *Astoria*, p. 310, and Rollins, *The Discovery of the Oregon Trail*, p. 325, notes 235 and 236, and account on p. lxxxvii. These three voyageurs who opted to stay behind were Jean Baptiste Turcotte, André LaChapelle, and François Landry. In addition Hunt had left behind the weakened Crooks and Day, plus the voyageur Dubreuil.

179 *make about fifteen miles per day*: Irving, *Astoria* (1849), p. 199, says fourteen miles a day. Hunt's journal indicates 106 miles in about six days, which would be about seventeen miles per day.

Carriere, simply lay down: Ibid., p. 311.

carry both La Bonté and La Bonté's twenty-five-pound pack: Ibid., p. 312.

"They . . . had so often given me erroneous reports": Hunt, "Voyage of Mr. Hunt and His Companions," journal entry for December 30, 1811.

180 *"Silence and isolation"*: Charles Alexander Eastman (Ohiyesa), *The Soul of the Indian: An Interpretation* (Boston: Houghton Mifflin, 1911), pp. 28–30.

181 *"His wife rode horseback with her newly born child in her arms"*: Hunt, "Voyage of Mr. Hunt and His Companions," journal entry for December 31, 1811. The location of the Dorion baby birth site was near today's North Powder, Baker Valley, Oregon, according to Rollins, *The Discovery of the Oregon Trail*, p. 325 fn. 247.

then the fork of a creek: Rollins, *The Discovery of the Oregon Trail*, p. 325 fn. 248, for the probable exact route in various stream drainages of the Blue Mountains.

182 *"[W]e were at a point as high as the mountains"*: Hunt, "Voyage of Mr. Hunt and His Companions," journal entry for January 4, 1812.

183 *They spotted a sprawling Indian encampment*: Ibid., journal entry for January 8, 1812.

"I cannot thank Providence enough": Ibid.

CHAPTER FIFTEEN

187 *the ship had logged 21,852 miles*: Ross, *Adventures*, p. 68.

188 *McDougall and David Stuart, in the longboat*: Franchère, *Narrative*, pp. 99–101; see also Irving, *Astoria*, p. 88, and Ross, *Adventures*, p. 68.

"[Comcomly] received them with all imaginable hospitality": Franchère, *Narrative*, p. 101.

189 *Upstream, they could see*: Ross, *Adventures*, pp. 70–71.

"The spring, usually so tardy in this latitude": Franchère, *Narrative*, p. 102.

191 *"Much time was often spent in this desultory manner"*: Ross, *Adventures*, p. 73.

191 *"[T]he great pasha"*: Ibid., p. 75.

    liquor rations three times a day: See McDougall journal, July 26, 1811, in Robert F. Jones, ed., *Annals of Astoria: The Headquarters Log of the Pacific Fur Company on the Columbia River, 1811–1813* (New York: Fordham University Press, 1999), p. 36.

    sixty feet long by twenty-six feet wide: Ross, *Adventures,* p. 81.

192 *"'You see,' said [McKay], 'how unfortunate we are"*: Ibid.

193 *"A well-dressed man"*: Franchère, *Narrative*, p. 120.

194 *"I intended to have paid you a visit at Montreal"*: Nisbet, *Sources of the River,* pp. 173–74.

    "[I]n such forests what could we do": Ibid., p. 178, quoting Thompson journal.

195 *Thompson planted a British flag*: Ross, *Adventures,* p. 128.

    Had he hoped to raise the British flag: See Franchère, *Narrative,* p. 122 fn. According to Franchère, everyone at Astoria was of the opinion that Thompson intended to arrive first and plant the British flag at the mouth of the Columbia, claiming it for the North West Company, but he was too late. Instead he found the Astorians' fur post flying the American flag.

196 *"[T]he wintering partners had resolved"*: Ibid., p. 121.

    "This is more than probable": Ross, *Adventures,* p. 86.

198 *In a frenzied six days of work*: Franchère, *Narrative,* pp. 123–24.

199 *"[W]ithout wholly convincing us"*: Ibid., pp. 124–25.

CHAPTER SIXTEEN

201 *Captain Thorn carried on his ship*: Franchère, *Narrative,* p. 117.

    Joseachal, who spoke the Coastal dialects: Jones, *Annals of Astoria,* p. 59. The interpreter's identity remains a topic of some question. He is variously described as Lamazee (and other spellings of the same), Jack Ramsay, and Joseachal. See Robert F. Jones, "The Identity of the *Tonquin's* Interpreter," *Oregon Historical Quarterly* 98, no. 3 (Fall 1997): 311–12.

202 *Indians of Newetee*: Irving, *Astoria,* p. 107.

    Captain Thorn made an offer: McDougall journal, August 11, 1811, and June 18, 1813, in Jones, *Annals of Astoria,* pp. 41, 194.

    Nookamis wanted five blankets: McDougall journal, June 18, 1813, in ibid., p. 194.

203 *"pestering" him to trade*: Ibid.

    McKay and Joseachal returned: Irving, *Astoria,* p. 109.

    "You pretend to know a great deal": Ross, *Adventures,* p. 162.

204 *through the giant mouths*: Description from John Meares in Valerie Sherer Mathes, "Wickaninnish, a Clayoquot Chief, as Recorded by Early Travelers," *Pacific Northwest Quarterly* 70, no. 3 (July 1979): 111.

205 *bald eagle or a human face*: Ross, *Adventures,* p. 98.

    ritualized purification: For a general description, see ibid., pp. 311–12.

206 *on the Chinese market*: Dolin, *Fur, Fortune, and Empire*, pp. 138–43.

207 *The Aleuts*: Letter to the editor, "Russian and American Settlements on the North West Coast of America," *North American Review*, c. 1, vol. 2 (1815): 301–3.

by force or threat of violence: James R. Gibson, *Otter Skins, Boston Ships, and China Goods: The Maritime Fur Trade of the Northwest Coast, 1785–1841* (Seattle: University of Washington Press, 1992), pp. 163–64.

another unfortunate incident: Franchère, *Narrative*, pp. 126–27.

208 *"If you find them kind"*: Irving, *Astoria*, p. 52.

209 *"a parcel of lazy, thieving Indians"*: Ross Cox, *Adventures on the Columbia River, Including the Narrative of a Residence of Six Years on the Western Side of the Rocky Mountains, Among Various Tribes of Indians Hitherto Unknown: Together with a Journey Across the American Continent* (New York: J & J Harper, 1832), p. 63.

one blanket and one knife: Alfred Seton, *Astorian Adventure: The Journal of Alfred Seton, 1811–1815*, ed. Robert F. Jones (New York: Fordham University Press, 1993), p. 92.

With a smile of contempt: Ross, *Adventures*, p. 163.

"would be more than a match": Cox, *Adventures on the Columbia River*, p. 64.

210 *a Clayoquot chief on deck*: Ibid.

Who first fell to the deck differs with various accounts: The account that follows is based partly on testimony and, to a lesser degree, partly on conjecture and reconstruction. Accounts of the battle aboard the *Tonquin* appear in the following sources: Seton, McDougall, Irving, Franchère, Cox, Ross, and a *Missouri Gazette* article of May 15, 1813. This last account is not based on the testimony of the interpreter, Joseachal, but on some earlier unknown source. Howay gives a discussion of the different sources. Howay, "The Loss of the *Tonquin*," *Washington Historical Quarterly* 13, no. 2 (April 1922): 83–92. There were also clearly a number of accounts of the incident, which is still remembered today in Clayoquot Sound, from the Indians themselves who made their way to the Astorians. The account I use here generally follows Irving's version, supplemented with these other accounts, as Irving had most complete access to both interviews with Astorians and the records of McDougall, Seton, and others.

bending over a bale of blankets: Franchère, *Narrative*, p. 183.

a pair of pistols: Ross, *Adventures*, p. 162.

211 *the only weapon he carried*: Ibid., p. 164.

"Covered with wounds, and exhausted from the loss of blood": Cox, *Adventures on the Columbia River*, p. 65.

212 *they seized with calloused hands*: Franchère, *Narrative*, p. 184.

There were five or six survivors: Irving, *Astoria*, pp. 111–12; Franchère, *Narrative*, p. 184.

212 *The survivors then opened fire*: Irving, *Astoria*, p. 112.
213 *take McKay hostage*: Cox, *Adventures on the Columbia River*, p. 65.
     "favourite among the Indians": Ross, *Adventures*, p. 161.
214 *"The last time the ill-fated gentleman was seen"*: Cox, *Adventures on the Columbia River*, p. 65.
     a headwind blew into the cove: Irving, *Astoria*, p. 113.
215 *he would prefer suicide*: Ibid., p. 114.
     "The wounded man showed himself over the railing": Howay, "The Loss of the *Tonquin*."
216 *Shattered bits of wood*: This eyewitness account below of the explosion of the *Tonquin* is from Kevin Robinson and David W. Griffiths, "Investigations of a Potential Shipwreck Site, Templar Channel, Clayoquot Sound, B.C.," Tonquin Foundation, May 2005, p. 60: "In the 1860's Ten-ta-coose, a former slave of the Tla-o-qui-aht, told Jason Allard of Fort Langley that he had been at Clayoquot when he had seen a large ship attacked and blown up. *'Ten-ta-coose, the slave . . . saw the tall masts break and crumble . . . bodies thrown into the air to fall broken into the water, and wood, and iron and tattered fragments of sailcloth and humanity he saw blasted high into the sky. . . .'"*
     Joseachal apparently heard: Irving, *Astoria*, pp. 113–114.

CHAPTER SEVENTEEN

218 *Knowing this history, McDougall invited*: McDougall journal entry, July 1, 1811, in Jones, *Annals of Astoria*, p. 30.
     "I have but to draw the cork": Irving, *Astoria*, p. 117.
     52 of the 102 original Plymouth colonists: Nathaniel Philbrick, *Mayflower: A Story of Courage, Community, and War* (New York: Viking, 2006), p. 90.
     named Dolly, *after Astor's effervescent teenage daughter*: Jones, *Annals of Astoria*, p. 52.
219 *reach the Spanish settlements*: McDougall journal entry, November 14, 1811, in ibid., p. 58.
     Known to the natives: The origins of the name of the Willamette River are controversial. Writing in 1947, Howard Corning claimed the river had no name among the Indians. Rather, the tribes named each stretch after its inhabitants. The modern spelling came to prominence when Charles Wilkes brought his exploring expedition to Oregon in 1841. Howard McKinley Corning, *Willamette Landings: Ghost Towns of the River* (Portland, OR: Binfords & Mort, 1947), pp. 8–10.
     as the Cathlanaminim: Franchère, *Narrative*, p. 135.
220 *"It rained in torrents and was dark as pitch"*: Ibid., pp. 134–36.
     The downpour leaked into the fort's cellars: McDougall journal entry, October 11, 1811, in Jones, *Annals of Astoria*, p. 52.

220 *particularly rich in beaver*: Jones, *Annals of Astoria*, p. 90. See footnote regarding Mackenzie's report that led to a fur post on the river near Salem.

222 *The sick list showed six men*: McDougall journal, in ibid., p. 68. Franchère indicates that McDougall was also suffering illness around this time, badly enough to confine him to his quarters. Franchère, *Narrative*, p. 144.
"but in a pitiable condition": Franchère, *Narrative*, p. 150.
Crossing mountains northward and struggling: Rollins, *The Discovery of the Oregon Trail*, pp. 80–82.

223 *Wilson Price Hunt and his party*: McDougall journal entry, February 15, 1812, in Jones, *Annals of Astoria*, p. 72; and Stuart journal.
"The emaciated, downcast looks": Ross, *Adventures*, pp. 182–83.
voyageurs embracing voyageurs: Irving, *Astoria*, pp. 325–26.
the several struggling voyageurs: McDougall writes that the Overland Party left behind Crooks and five other men. Journal entry, February 15, 1812, in Jones, *Annals of Astoria*, p. 72.
teenager by the name of Archibald Pelton: J. Neilson Barry, "Archibald Pelton, the First Follower of Lewis and Clark," *Washington Historical Quarterly* 19, no. 3 (July 1928): 199–201.

225 *His name would eventually enter the Chinook trade jargon*: Jones, *Annals of Astoria*, p. 86, and Ruby and Brown, *The Chinook Indians*, p. 150. Two dictionaries of the Chinook jargon by George C. Shaw and Edwin Harper Thomas indicate *pelton* means "crazy." George C. Shaw, *The Chinook Jargon and How to Use It: A Complete and Exhaustive Lexicon of the Oldest Trade Language of the American Continent* (Seattle: Rainier, 1909), p. 45; Edwin Harper Thomas, *Chinook: A History and Dictionary*, 2nd ed. (Portland, OR: Binfords & Mort, 1970), p. 113.

CHAPTER EIGHTEEN

227 *trading less than $200 worth*: Jay H. Buckley, "Life at Fort Astoria: John Jacob Astor's Pacific Fur Company post on the Columbia River," *Proceedings of the 2012 Fur Trade Symposium,* ed. Jim Hardee (Pinedale, WY: Sublette County Historical Society/Museum of the Mountain Man, 2013). Ross relates that the Indians at Okanagan were so eager to trade that he need only give five tobacco leaves per pelt, and one of the chiefs gave twenty beaver skins for one yard of white cotton. Ross, *Adventures,* p. 200. According to Franchère, the Okanagan trade produced 140 packets of furs that Stuart and McKenzie transported back to Astoria. Franchère, *Narrative*, p. 170. McDougall wrote in his journal that Stuart "gave a very satisfactory account of the country, as abounding in Beaver, etc." McDougall journal entry, January 27, 1812, in Jones, *Annals of Astoria*, p. 69.

228 *Hunt sent two clerks*: Rollins, *The Discovery of the Oregon Trail*, p. 67 fn. 29.
"zeal of a true Irishman": Irving, *Astoria*, pp. 344, 348.

229 *The three parties set out*: Ross, *Adventures,* p. 184.
     On a good day: Stuart, *Robert Stuart's Narratives,* p. 52.

230 *"saucy, impudent Rascals"*: Stuart journal entry, July 14, 1812, in ibid., pp. 51–52.
     The shiny metal box: Irving, *Astoria,* p. 348.
     according to Stuart's account: Stuart journal entry, July 20, 1812, in *Robert Stuart's Narratives,* p. 56.
     "they would give it to them while plundering": Stuart journal entry, July 20, 1812, in ibid., p. 56.
     Reed, however, had forgotten to remove: Irving, *Astoria,* p. 348. The accounts of Stuart and Irving regarding the fight at Celilo Falls vary in minor ways, but they are in agreement regarding the overall results.

231 *"Our answer was* NO": Stuart journal entry, July 20, 1812, in *Robert Stuart's Narratives,* p. 59.

232 *The group arrived at the Okanagan post*: Ross, *Adventures,* pp. 186–87.
     he had tried to convince the tribes: Ibid., pp. 128–29.
     claiming the region for the North West Company: According to Ronda, Thompson's proclamation read: "Know hereby that this country is claimed by Great Britain as part of its territories, and that the North West Company of Merchants from Canada, finding the factory for this people inconvenient for them, do hereby intend to erect a factory in this place for the commerce of the country around." Ronda, *Astoria & Empire,* p. 64.
     they had 2,500 furs: Ross, *Adventures,* p. 187. Accounts vary as to the number of furs. McDougall claims one thousand, in the journal entry for May 11, 1812, in Jones, *Annals of Astoria,* p. 89.

233 *"Come onshore"*: Ross, *Adventures,* p. 187.

234 *They followed it for some days*: Irving, *Astoria,* p. 352. Other accounts of the journey of Crooks and Day include Ross, *Adventures,* pp. 187–92; Rollins, *The Discovery of the Oregon Trail,* pp. lxxxvii–lxxxix; and Seton, *Astorian Adventure,* pp. 97–98.

235 *according to some accounts, offered them food*: Irving, *Astoria,* p. 353; Seton, *Astorian Adventure,* p. 97. Ross's account does not indicate the Indians fed them, nor does Rollins's.
     "The Indians then closed in upon us": Ross, *Adventures,* p. 190.

236 *the two were preparing to head all the way back*: Ibid., p. 192.

CHAPTER NINETEEN

237 *"great surprise and great joy"*: Franchère, *Narrative,* p. 154.
     with an oared boat following behind: Cox, *Adventures on the Columbia River,* p. 53.
     The Beaver *brought a huge boost of energy*: Irving, *Astoria,* p. 359.

238 *Astor's own nephew, George Ehninger*: p. 280.

238 *"brightest star"*: Ross, *Adventures,* p. 195.

explorations up the Willamette River: McDougall journal entry, May 11, 1812, in Jones, *Annals of Astoria,* p. 89.

"Between these high lands": Ross, *Adventures,* p. 236.

Astoria jumped with planning and strategy: Ronda, *Astoria & Empire,* p. 240.

239 *"A letter from Mr. Nathaniel Woodbury"*: "Account of the Tonquin," *New York Gazette and General Advertiser,* May 12, 1812.

240 The Child of Nature: Theater listings, *New York Gazette and General Advertiser,* May 11 and 12, 1812.

"What would you have me do?": Irving, *Astoria,* p. 116.

241 *estimated that $20,000 worth of trinkets*: Porter, *John Jacob Astor, Business Man,* pp. 173–81.

242 *the hair-trigger McClellan*: Ronda, *Astoria & Empire,* pp. 238–39.

"partners dissatisfied with the enterprise": Franchère, *Narrative,* p. 160.

There was young Mr. Nicoll: Seton, *Astorian Adventure,* pp. 98–99.

244 *"Our Madman (Pelton) continuing the same"*: McDougall journal entry, June 15, 1812, in Jones, *Annals of Astoria,* p. 97.

McDougall, too, was frequently sick: Irving, *Astoria,* p. 444.

It's cold, it's raining: According to climate-zone.com, Astoria experiences 193 days with more than .01 inches of rainfall in the average year. Days where the skies are "clear" number only 38.

245 *in nine canoes and two bateaux*: Seton, *Astorian Adventure,* p. 100. See also Jones, *Annals of Astoria,* pp. 100–101 fn. 38.

Formerly cheerful and popular: Irving, *Astoria,* p. 360.

"now uttered the most incoherent": Stuart journal entry, July 1, 1812, in Rollins, *The Discovery of the Oregon Trail,* p. 29.

246 *meadowy Deer Island*: Today, Deer Island is a tiny town along U.S. Highway 30 about thirty-three miles from downtown Portland, between Rainier to the north, and St. Helens to the south.

"[T]his gigantic mass appears as a Steeple": Stuart journal entry, June 29, 1812, in Rollins, *The Discovery of the Oregon Trail,* p. 60.

247 *Day likely was suffering from post-traumatic stress disorder:* According to the *Diagnostic and Statistical Manual of Mental Disorders,* 4th ed., Text Revision (Washington, DC: American Psychiatric Association, 2000), a diagnosis of PTSD requires that "the person has been exposed to a traumatic event in which both of the following were present: 1. the person experienced, witnessed, or was confronted with an event or events that involved actual or threatened death or serious injury, or a threat to the physical integrity of self or others. 2. the person's response involved intense fear, helplessness, or horror." It is fair to say that Day's experiences lost in the wilderness and his encounters with hostile Indians fit at least this part of the diagnostic criteria.

248 *Cathlapootle Island*: Stuart journal entry, July 3, 1812, in Rollins, *The Discovery of the Oregon Trail*, p. 31. Rollins indicates it is Bachelor Island on p. 43 fn. 53.

"[H]is insanity amounted to real madness": Stuart, journal entry July 3, 1812, in ibid., p. 31.

249 *The country on both sides of the river*: Stuart journal entry, July 20, 1812, in ibid., pp. 59–60.

to his "great delight": Irving, *Astoria*, p. 363. Stuart recounts it in his journal entry of July 21, 1812, in Rollins, *The Discovery of the Oregon Trail*, p. 60.

That night, in celebration: Stuart journal entry, July 28, 1812, in ibid., p. 62.

CHAPTER TWENTY

252 *But Astor had also met James Madison*: Ronda, *Astoria & Empire*, pp. 45–46.

Perhaps Astor's best connection: Porter, *John Jacob Astor, Business Man*, p. 146, and Ronda, *Astoria & Empire*, pp. 258–59.

253 *he asked those Canadians*: Ronda, *Astoria & Empire*, p. 99.

What would happen if war broke out: Franchère, *Narrative*, pp. 28–29.

Astor knew nothing at the time: Ronda, *Astoria & Empire*, p. 99.

254 *posts being established to the north of these*: Ibid., p. 241.

This was the post headed by Donald Mackenzie: Ibid., pp. 240, 264.

255 *"'Such a life,' they said"*: Ross, *Adventures*, p. 219.

256 *McTavish delivered it with officious delight*: Irving, *Astoria*, p. 445.

the Isaac Todd, had sailed: Ronda, *Astoria & Empire*, p. 264.

"We had a famous horse pye": Seton, *Astorian Adventure*, p. 109.

257 *Returning to New York*: Ronda, *Astoria & Empire*, p. 251.

Captain Sowle was to turn: Irving, *Astoria*, p. 430; Ronda, *Astoria & Empire*, p. 251.

No marine insurer would want to touch this vessel: Irving, *Astoria*, p. 431.

258 *"remarkable," as Irving described*: Ibid.

promised him some sort of military protection: Ronda, *Astoria & Empire*, p. 45.

the wintering partners at their July meeting: Ibid., p. 252.

They voted to send emissaries from Montreal: Ibid.

259 *There McTavish and his group*: Irving, *Astoria*, p. 449. See also *The Dictionary of Canadian Biography*, s.v. "McTavish, George."

The stakes had climbed still higher: See Irving, *Astoria*, p. 431, for an accounting of Astor's uncertainty during this time.

But no direct word of Hunt's fate: Ronda, *Astoria & Empire*, p. 258.

He summoned two of his best sea captains: Ibid., pp. 252–54.

260 *"the very idea is like a dagger to my heart"*: Irving, *Astoria*, p. 432. Ronda speculates that Irving may have engaged in poetic license here, but that certainly he captured Astor's true sentiment. Ronda, *Astoria & Empire*, p. 262.

CHAPTER TWENTY-ONE

261 *In the misty dusk of January 16*: McDougall journal entry, January 16, 1813, in Jones, *Annals of Astoria,* pp. 145–46.

"The months of October, November, and December": Franchère, *Narrative,* p. 165.

262 *"he gave way to the most abject despondency"*: Irving, *Astoria,* p. 444.

264 *"[I]t becomes very interesting to know"*: Ronda, *Astoria & Empire,* p. 260.

265 *a U.S. frigate could be sent to cruise the waters off Canton*: Ibid., p. 261.

"Madison and others in his administration": Ibid.

they summoned partners David Stuart and John Clarke: Irving, *Astoria,* p. 446.

with heavy packs of furs: Franchère indicates the parties arrived with 140 packs of furs. Franchère, *Narrative,* p. 170. Ross states Clarke left the Spokane post with "thirty-two horses loaded with furs." Ross, *Adventures,* p. 214.

266 *He took a silver goblet from his traveling wine case*: Ross, *Adventures,* pp. 214–15, and Cox, *Adventures on the Columbia River,* p. 107.

"[You're] a greater man now than ever before": Ross, *Adventures,* p. 215.

Different accounts of the execution vary in detail, but generally agree.

267 *"Mr. Clarke," wrote Alfred Seton*: Seton, *Astorian Adventure,* p. 115.

Thinking they would be pleased: Irving, *Astoria,* p. 452.

268 *"Taking the hint, we lost no time"*: Ross, *Adventures,* p. 226.

269 *"'Gentlemen,' said he, 'why do you hesitate so long'"*: Ibid., p. 244.

271 *McTavish and the North West Company*: For the deal struck between McTavish and the Astorians, see Ronda, *Astoria & Empire,* pp. 281–82.

a "market-sharing agreement": Jones, *Annals of Astoria,* p. 198 fn. 89.

273 *He now conjured up another insurance policy*: McDougall journal entry, July 20, 1813, in Jones, *Annals of Astoria,* p. 203; see also fn. 98.

knowing his father-in-law would protect him: Seton, *Astorian Adventure,* p. 116.

on the fresh, sunny morning of August 20: McDougall journal entry, August 20, 1813, in Jones, *Annals of Astoria,* pp. 210–11. For the arrival of the ship, see also Franchère, *Narrative,* p. 173; Ross, *Adventures,* p. 251; and Irving, *Astoria,* pp. 463–64.

274 *A year earlier, Hunt had climbed aboard the Beaver*: Irving, *Astoria,* pp. 465–68.

275 *"He is continually giving"*: Ibid., pp. 466–67. Ronda indicates Irving had access to Hunt's journal, though it is now lost. Ronda, *Astoria & Empire,* p. 283.

276 *"insufferable ennui . . . in the midst of deep mud"*: Franchère, *Narrative,* p. 164.

277 *The partners wouldn't budge*: Ibid., p. 179. Ronda analyzes this meeting in *Astoria & Empire,* pp. 285–286.

277 *he would return soon with another ship*: Franchère, *Narrative,* p. 179, and Irving, *Astoria,* pp. 474–75.

  Astor's ship, the fast-sailing Lark: Porter, *John Jacob Astor, Business Man,* pp. 552–54.

278 *a tremendous gale blew*: Ibid., pp. 552–54; Irving, *Astoria,* p. 477; Ross, *Adventures,* p. 261; Seton, *Astorian Adventure,* p. 202; and Cox, *Adventures on the Columbia River,* pp. 135–36.

279 *the South Pacific's beautiful Marquesas Islands*: Ronda, *Astoria & Empire,* p. 297.

EPILOGUE

281 *McTavish, of the rival North West Company*: Irving, *Astoria,* p. 482.

  McDougall's own uncle, Angus Shaw: Ibid.; Franchère, *Narrative,* p. 191.

282 *"to take and destroy"*: Irving, *Astoria,* p. 482.

  "totally annihilate": Ronda, *Astoria & Empire,* pp. 256–57.

  for about thirty cents on the dollar: Irving, *Astoria,* p. 484.

  "I lost in a moment all my hopes of fortune": Franchère, *Narrative,* p. 193.

283 *He and his Chinook warriors would hide*: Cox, *Adventures on the Columbia River,* pp. 132–33.

284 *"I leave the Country"*: Seton, *Astorian Adventure,* p. 151.

285 *It had happened the past winter*: Franchère, *Narrative,* pp. 273–76; Irving, *Astoria,* pp. 492–95; and Ross, *Adventures,* pp. 277–81.

287 *"Good god," he had written*: Porter, *John Jacob Astor, Business Man,* p. 524.

  $2.5 million: Ronda, *Astoria & Empire,* p. 266.

  "And for want of one ship and crew": Ibid., p. 269.

  Astorians who perished as tallied by clerk Alexander Ross: Ross, *Adventures,* p. 283.

288 *splitting open his skull with his own tomahawk*: Barry, "Archibald Pelton," pp. 200–201.

  Astor had sent a total of about 140 men: Chittenden, *The American Fur Trade of the Far West,* pp. 887–88.

  "[Mr. Astor] assumed the financial risks": John Denis Haeger, *John Jacob Astor: Business and Finance in the Early Republic* (Detroit: Wayne State University Press, 1991), p. 117.

  "My plan was right": Elbert Hubbard, *Little Journeys to the Homes of Great Businessmen* (1916, reprint [New York]:Cosimo Classics, 2005), pp. 224–25.

  Irving was undoubtedly speaking for Astor himself: Irving, *Astoria,* pp. 497–501.

289 *"It was [Astor's] great misfortune"*: Ibid., p. 498.

291 *"the crafty M'Dougall"*: Franchère, *Narrative*, p. 227.

"charge of treason will always be attached": Ibid., p. 204.

293 *"I have not had so quiet and delightful a nest"*: Gebhard, *The Life and Adventures of the Original John Jacob Astor,* p. 288. Gebhard includes an illustration of Hell Gate.

for whom Astor happily sent: Stanley T. Williams, *The Life of Washington Irving* (New York: Oxford University Press, 1935), p. 83.

"occupation and amusement": Irving, *Astoria,* pp. xix–xx.

294 *"old gentleman's"*: Irving, *Astoria,* pp. xix–xx.

"What the vague term of the 'whole country'": Ross, *Adventures,* p. 259.

"[W]hile I breath & so long as I have a dollar to spend": Porter, *John Jacob Astor, Business Man,* p. 239.

Soon Mackenzie came under Astor's suspicions: Ronda indicates Astor and Mackenzie had a falling-out in the fall of 1814. Ronda, *Astoria & Empire,* p. 304.

295 *"Had our place and our property been fairly captured"*: Irving, *Astoria,* p. 485.

Astor later estimated: Letter from Astor to James Monroe, August 17, 1815, in Porter, *John Jacob Astor, Business Man,* p. 585.

"If I was a young man": Letter from Astor to Gallatin dated December 30, 1818, quoted in Ronda, *Astoria & Empire,* p. 315.

"I remember well having invited": Letter from Thomas Jefferson to Astor, May 24, 1812, in *The Papers of Thomas Jefferson, Retirement Series,* vol. 5 (Princeton: Princeton University Press, 2008), p. 74.

296 *"I learn with great pleasure the progress you have made"*: Letter from Jefferson to Astor, November 9, 1813, in *The Papers of Thomas Jefferson, Retirement Series,* vol. 6, p. 603.

297 *But on October 22, 1812*: Rollins, *The Discovery of the Oregon Trail,* pp. 163–66.

298 *Astor pressed the U.S. government through Albert Gallatin*: Letter from Gallatin to Astor, August 5, 1835, reprinted in Irving, *Astoria,* pp. 507–509.

American politicians strived to bring the region solely to U.S. control: For a detailed account of this, see Ronda, *Astoria & Empire,* pp. 330–36.

"The settlement of the Oregon": Floyd quoted in ibid., p. 333.

"Not an American ship will be able to show itself beyond Cape Horn": Benton, quoted in ibid., p. 334.

299 *Among them was an elderly Marie Dorion*: J. Neilson Barry, "Madame Dorion of the Astorians," *Oregon Historical Quarterly* 30, no. 3 (September 1929): 275.

"She, from various traditions": T. C. Elliott, "The Grave of Madame Dorion," *Oregon Historical Quarterly* 36, no. 1 (March 1935): 104.

300 *"It is no flight of fancy"*: Chittenden, *The American Fur Trade of the Far West,* vol. 1, p. 227.

301 *"[W]hen California came into our hands"*: Charles M. Harvey, "Our Lost Opportunity on the Pacific," *North American Review* 193, no. 664 (March 1911): 402.

   which ranks him fourth: See http://www.forbes.com/2007/09/14/richest-americans-alltime-biz_cx_pw_as_0914ialltime_slide_5.html.

   At his death, John Jacob Astor came under criticism: Porter, *John Jacob Astor, Business Man,* pp. 1096–97.

   which went to found the Astor Library: Ibid., pp. 1094–97.

   ended with Vincent Astor: Axel Madsen, *John Jacob Astor: America's First Multimillionaire* (New York: John Wiley & Sons, 2001), p. 292.

302 *The ten-foot-long, thousand-pound anchor*: See Robinson and Griffiths, "Investigations of a Potential Shipwreck Site, Templar Channel, Clayoquot Sound, B.C."

304 *"Let him but visit these regions of want and misery"*: Stuart journal entry, in Rollins, *The Discovery of the Oregon Trail,* pp. 157–58.

FATE OF THE ASTORIANS

305 *Wilson Price Hunt*: T. C. Elliott, "Wilson Price Hunt, 1783–1842," *Oregon Historical Quarterly* 32, no. 2 (June 1931): 132.

   Duncan McDougall: *Dictionary of Canadian Biography,* s.v. "McDougall, Duncan," http://www.biographi.ca/009004-119.01-e.php?id_nbr=2538.

   Ramsay Crooks: *Dictionary of Canadian Biography,* s.v. "Crooks, Ramsay," http://www.biographi.ca/en/bio/crooks_ramsay_8E.html.

   Chinook Nation: John Robinson, "From Boston Men to the BIA: The Unacknowledged Chinook Nation," in *Recognition, Sovereignty Struggles, and Indigenous Rights in the United States,* ed. Amy E. Den Ouden and Jean M. O'Brien (Chapel Hill: University of North Carolina Press, 2013), pp. 263–86. For Christopher Stevens, see "Slain Ambassador Was Member of Local Chinook Tribe," *Chinook Observer,* September 13, 2013.

306 *Clayoquot Nation*: See http://www.tla-o-qui-aht.org/.

   Robert Stuart: Rollins, *The Discovery of the Oregon Trail,* p. xl.

   Donald Mackenzie: *Dictionary of Canadian Biography,* s.v. "Mackenzie, Donald," http://www.biographi.ca/009004-119.01-e.php?&id_nbr=4075.

   Alfred Seton: Seton, *Astorian Adventure,* introduction and pp. 176–77.

307 *Joseph Miller*: Rollins, *The Discovery of the Oregon Trail,* pp. c–ci, 86.

   Robert McClellan: Ibid., pp. xci–xcv.

   Alexander Ross: *Dictionary of Canadian Biography,* s.v. "Ross, Alexander," http://www.biographi.ca/en/bio/ross_alexander_8E.html.

308 *Ross Cox*: *Dictionary of Canadian Biography,* s.v. "Cox, Ross," http://www.biographi.ca/en/bio/cox_ross_8E.html.

308 *Gabriel Franchère*: *Dictionary of Canadian Biography*, s.v. "Franchère, Gabriel," http://www.biographi.ca/en/bio/franchere_gabriel_9E.html.
Baptiste Dorion: See http://www.oregonpioneers.com/JeanBaptisteDorion .htm.
John Day: Chittenden, *The American Fur Trade of the Far West*, vol. 2, p. 889; Rollins, *The Discovery of the Oregon Trail*, p. xcvii.

SELECTED SOURCES

ORIGINAL JOURNALS AND ACCOUNTS BY PARTICIPANTS

Brackenridge, H. M. *Journal of a Voyage up the Missouri River, performed in 1811.* In *Early Western Travels,* vol. 6, ed. Reuben Gold Thwaites. Cleveland: Arthur H. Clark, 1904.

———. *Views of Louisiana: Containing Statistical, Geographical, and Historical Notices of that Vast and Important Part of America.* Baltimore: Schaeffer & Maund, 1817.

Bradbury, John. *Travels in the Interior of America, in the Years 1809, 1810, and 1811, Including a Description of Upper Louisiana.* London: Sherwood, Neely & Jones, 1817.

Cox, Ross. *Adventures on the Columbia River.* New York: J. & J. Harper, 1832.

Franchère, Gabriel. *Narrative of a Voyage to the Northwest Coast of America in the Years 1811, 1812, 1813, and 1814, or, The First American Settlement on the Pacific.* Ed. and trans. J. V. Huntington. New York: Redfield, 1854.

Gilbert, George. *The Death of Captain James Cook (From Gilbert's Narrative of Cook's Last Voyage, 1776–1780).* Hawaiian Historical Society Reprints, No. 5. Honolulu: Paradise of the Pacific Press, 1926.

Henry, Alexander, and David Thompson. *New Light on the Early History of the Greater Northwest: The Manuscript Journals of Alexander Henry, Fur Trader of the Northwest Company and of David Thompson, Official Geographer and Explorer of the same Company, 1799–1814.* Ed. Elliot Coues. New York: Francis P. Harper, 1897.

Hunt, Wilson Price. "Voyage of Mr. Hunt and His Companions." In *New Annals of Voyages, Geography and History,* vol. 10. Paris: J. B. Eyies and Malte-Brun, 1821. Translation available at http://user.xmission.com/~drudy/mtman/html/wphunt/wphunt.html, retrieved October 2, 2013.

Jones, Robert F., ed. *Annals of Astoria: The Headquarters Log of the Pacific Fur Company on the Columbia River, 1811–1813.* New York: Fordham University Press, 1999.

Ross, Alexander. *Adventures of the First Settlers on the Columbia River, Being* a Narrative of the Expedition Fitted Out by John Jacob Astor. London: Smith, Elder, 1849.

Seton, Alfred. *Astorian Adventure: The Journal of Alfred Seton, 1811–1815.* Ed. Robert F. Jones. New York: Fordham University Press, 1993.

Stuart, Robert. *Robert Stuart's Narratives.* In *The Discovery of the Oregon Trail,* ed. Philip Ashton Rollins. New York: Scribner's, 1935.

OTHER SOURCES

Achenbach, Joel. "When Yellowstone Explodes." *National Geographic,* August 2009.

Ambrose, Stephen E. *Undaunted Courage: Meriwether Lewis, Thomas Jefferson, and the Opening of the American West.* 1996: rept., New York: Simon & Schuster, 2002.

Anders, Mark. "Yellowstone hotspot track" (map). Lamont-Doherty Earth Observatory, Columbia University Earth Institute. http://www.ldeo.colum bia.edu/~manders/SRP_erupt.html, retrieved October 6, 2013.

Anderson, Bern. *Surveyor of the Sea: The Life and Voyages of Captain George Vancouver.* Seattle: University of Washington Press, 1960.

Auerbach, Paul S., M.D., ed. *Wilderness Medicine: Management of Wilderness and Environmental Emergencies.* 3rd ed. St. Louis: Mosby, 1995.

Barrett, Walter (pseudonym for Joseph A. Scoville). *The Old Merchants of New York City.* New York: Carleton, 1863.

Barrow, John. *The Life, Voyages, and Exploits of Sir Francis Drake, with Numerous Original Letters from Him and the Lord High Admiral to the Queen and Great Officers of State.* 2nd ed., abridged. London: John Murray, 1844.

Barry, J. Neilson. "Archibald Pelton, the First Follower of Lewis and Clark." *Washington Historical Quarterly* 19, no. 3 (July 1928): 199–201.

———. "The Indians of Oregon—Geographic Distribution of Linguistic Families." *Oregon Historical Quarterly* 28, no. 1 (March 1927): 49–61.

Beach, Moses Yale. *Wealth and Biography of the Wealthy Citizens of New York City, Comprising an Alphabetical Arrangement of Persons Estimated to be Worth $100,000 and Upwards. With the Sums Appended to Each Name, Being Useful to Banks, Merchants, and Others.* New York: Sun Office, 1845.

Bevis, William W. "The Dugout Canoes of Lewis and Clark." At *Discovering Lewis & Clark,* lewis-clark.org, 2014.

Bishop, Sheryl L. "From Earth Analogs to Space: Getting There from Here." In *The Psychology of Space Explorations.* Edited by Douglas A. Vakoch. Washington, D.C.: National Aeronautics and Space Administration, 2011.

"Boatswain John Young, His Adventures in Hawaii Recalled." *New York Times,* February 14, 1886.

Boit, John. "Log of the Columbia." Ed. F. W. Howay, T. C. Elliott, and F. G.

Young. *Quarterly of the Oregon Historical Society* 22, no. 4. Portland: Oregon Historical Society, 1921.

Boyle, Steve, and Stephanie Owens. *North American Beaver (Castor canadensis): A Technical Conservation Assessment.* Prepared for USDA Forest Service, Rocky Mountain Region, Species Conservation Project, February 6, 2007, http://www.fs.fed.us/r2/projects/scp/assessments/northamerican beaver.pdf, retrieved October 3, 2013.

Buckley, Jay H. "Life at Fort Astoria: John Jacob Astor's Pacific Fur Company Post on the Columbia River." *Proceedings of the 2012 Fur Trade Symposium.* Edited by Jim Hardee. Pinedale, WY: Sublette County Historical Society/ Museum of the Mountain Man, 2013.

Bullfinch, Thomas. *Oregon and Eldorado; or, Romance of the Rivers.* Boston: J. E. Tilton, 1866.

Carpenter, Kenneth J. *The History of Scurvy and Vitamin C.* Cambridge: Cambridge University Press, 1988.

Cerami, Charles A. *Jefferson's Great Gamble: The Remarkable Story of Jefferson, Napoleon, and the Men Behind the Louisiana Purchase.* Naperville, IL: Sourcebooks, 2003.

Chittenden, Hiram Martin. *The American Fur Trade of the Far West.* Vols. 1–2. New York: Rufus Rockwell Wilson, 1936.

Corning, Howard McKinley. *Willamette Landings: Ghost Towns of the River.* Portland, OR: Binfords & Mort, 1947.

Dictionary of Canadian Biography. http://www.biographi.ca.

Dolin, Eric Jay. *Fur, Fortune, and Empire: The Epic History of the Fur Trade in America.* New York: Norton, 2010.

Dunnigan, Bryan Leigh. *A Picturesque Situation: Mackinac Before Photography, 1615–1860.* Detroit: Wayne State University Press, 2008.

Durand, Elliot. *Memoir of the Late Thomas Nuttall.* From *Proceedings of the American Philosophical Society* 7, p. 297. Philadelphia: C. Sherman & Sons, 1860.

Eastman, Charles Alexander (Ohiyesa). *The Soul of the Indian, an Interpretation.* Boston: Houghton Mifflin, 1911.

Elliot, T. C. "Wilson Price Hunt, 1783–1842." *Oregon Historical Quarterly* 32, no. 2 (June, 1931).

Franklin, John. "Franklin's First Retreat." In *Ring of Ice: True Tales of Adventure, Exploration, and Arctic Life,* ed. Peter Stark. New York: Lyons Press, 2000.

Gebhard, Elizabeth L. *The Life and Adventures of the Original John Jacob Astor.* Hudson, NY: Bryan, 1915.

Ghio A. J., C. Ghio, and M. Bassett. "Exercise-Induced Pulmonary Hemorrhage After Running a Marathon." *Lung* 184, no. 6 (Nov.–Dec. 2006): 331–33.

Gough, Barry. *Fortune's a River: The Collision of Empires in Northwest America.* Madeira Park, B.C.: Harbour Publishing, 2007.

Gray, William Henry. *A History of Oregon, 1792–1849, Drawn from Personal Observations and Authentic Information.* Portland, OR: Harris & Holman, 1870.

Haeger, John Denis. *John Jacob Astor: Business and Finance in the Early Republic.* Detroit: Wayne State University Press, 1991.

"Here Astor Once Lived: The Up-Town Home of the Old Merchant Prince." *New York Times,* February 16, 1896.

Himes, George H., ed. "Wallamet or Willamette." Portland, OR: Privately printed by Geo. H. Himes, 1875.

Holloway, Marguerite. *The Measure of Manhattan: The Tumultuous Career and Surprising Legacy of John Randel Jr., Cartographer, Surveyor, Inventor.* New York: Norton, 2013.

Howay, F. W. "The Loss of the *Tonquin.*" *Washington Historical Quarterly* 13, no. 2 (April 1922): 83–92.

Hubbard, Elbert. *Little Journeys to the Homes of Great Businessmen.* 1916, reprint [New York]:Cosimo Classics, 2005.

Idaho State Historical Society Reference Series. "Site of Ramsay Crooks 1811 Canoe Disaster." No. 1011, May 1993, http://www.history.idaho.gov/sites/default/files/uploads/reference-series/1011.pdf, retrieved October 3, 2013.

Inglis, Robin. *Historical Dictionary of the Discovery and Exploration of the Northwest Coast of America.* Lanham, MD: Scarecrow Press, Inc., 2008.

Innis, Harold A. *The Fur Trade in Canada.* New Haven: Yale University Press, 1962.

"Investigations of a Potential Shipwreck Site, Templar Channel, Clayoquot Sound, B.C." Kevin Robinson, MA, NS, David W. Griffiths, with contributions by Roderic S. Palm, Melissa Darby, MA, RPA, and Richard Linden. Tonquin Foundation, May 2005 (with amendments, December 2005).

Irving, Washington. *Astoria, or, Anecdotes of an Enterprise Beyond the Rocky Mountains.* Vol 8 of *The Works of Washington Irving,* new rev. ed. New York: George P. Putnam, 1849.

Jackson, Donald. *Thomas Jefferson and the Rocky Mountains.* Norman: University of Oklahoma Press, 1981.

Jefferson, Thomas. *The Papers of Thomas Jefferson.* 39 vols. Princeton: Princeton University Press, 1950–.

———. *The Papers of Thomas Jefferson. Retirement Series.* 10 vols. Princeton: Princeton University Press, 2005–.

———. Thomas Jefferson Papers. Library of Congress: American Memory Project. Series 1: General Correspondence 1651–1827. http://memory.loc.gov.

Johansen, Dorothy O. *Empire of the Columbia.* 2nd ed. New York: Harper & Row, 1967.

Johansen, Dorothy O., and Charles M. Gates. *Empire of the Columbia: A History of the Pacific Northwest.* New York: Harper & Brothers, 1957.

Klein, Kent. "Trapping Techniques of the Mountain Man." HistoricalTrek-
king.com, p. 6, retrieved October 3, 2013.

Lang, H. O., ed. *History of the Willamette Valley, Being a Description of the
Valley and Its Resources, with an Account of Its Discovery and Settlement
by White Men, and Its Subsequent History; Together with Personal Reminis-
cences of Its Early Pioneers.* Portland, OR: Geo. H. Himes, 1885.

Lavender, David. *The Fist in the Wilderness.* 1964; reprint, Lincoln: University
of Nebraska Press, 1998.

Ledyard, John. *John Ledyard's Journey Through Russia and Siberia, 1787–1788.*
Ed. Stephen D. Watrous. Madison: University of Wisconsin Press, 1966.

Mackenzie, Alexander. *Voyages from Montreal Through the Continent of North
America to the Frozen and Pacific Oceans in 1789 and 1793.* Vols. 1–2. New
York: Allerton, 1922.

Mackenzie, Cecil W. *Donald Mackenzie: "King of the Northwest."* Los Angeles:
Ivan Beach, Jr., 1937.

Madsen, Axel. *John Jacob Astor: America's First Multimillionaire.* New York:
John Wiley & Sons, 2001.

Manning, William Ray, "The Nootka Sound Controversy." In the Annual
Report of the American Historical Association for the Year 1904. Washington, DC: U.S. Government Printing Office, 1905.

Meinig, D. W. *The Great Columbia Plain: A Historical Geography, 1805–1910.*
Seattle: University of Washington Press, 1968.

Menard, Orville D. "Voyageurs with the Lewis and Clark Expedition." *We Proceeded On* 38, no. 1 (February 2012): 21–29.

Nisbet, Jack. *Sources of the River: Tracking David Thompson Across Western
North America.* Seattle: Sasquatch Books, 1994.

Nissenbaum, Stephen. *The Battle for Christmas.* New York: Vintage Books,
1997. Kindle ed.

North American Review, c. 1, vol. 2, 1815. Boston: Wells & Lilly, 1816.

Nute, Grace Lee. *The Voyageur.* New York: D. Appleton, 1931.

Oertel, W. *Johann Jacob Astor: A Sketch of the Life of a Man of the People.*
Arranged by W. O. von Horn (W. Oertel.). 2nd ed. Wiesbaden: Julius Nied-
ner, 1877. Trans. into English in ms. version in Astor Family Papers, Manuscript and Archives Division, New York Public Library.

Oxford Atlas of Exploration. New York: Oxford University Press, 1997.

Parton, James. *Life of John Jacob Astor.* New York: American News Company,
1865.

Philbrick, Nathaniel. *Mayflower: A Story of Courage, Community, and War.* New
York: Viking, 2006.

Porter, Kenneth Wiggins. *John Jacob Astor, Business Man.* Vols. 1–2. 1931;
reprint, New York: Russel & Russel, 1966.

Robinson, John R. "From Boston Men to the BIA." In *Recognition, Sovereignty Struggles, and Indigenous Rights in the United States: A Sourcebook*. Ed. Amy E. Den Ouden and Jean M. O'Brien. Chapel Hill: University of North Carolina Press, 2013.

Ronda, James P. *Astoria & Empire*. Lincoln: University of Nebraska Press, 1990.

Ruby, Robert H., and John A. Brown. *The Chinook Indians: Traders of the Lower Columbia*. Norman: University of Oklahoma Press, 1976.

"Russian and American Settlements on the North West Coast of America." *North American Review,* c. 1, vol. 2 (1815): 301–303.

"Sailors Who Cannot Swim." *New York Times,* May 3, 1883.

Shaw, George C. *The Chinook Jargon and How to Use It: A Complete and Exhaustive Lexicon of the Oldest Trade Language of the American Continent*. Seattle: Rainier, 1909.

Sparks, Jared. *Life of John Ledyard, American Traveller*. Boston: Charles C. Little & James Brown, 1847.

Stark, Peter. *Last Breath: Cautionary Tales from the Limits of Human Endurance*. New York: Ballantine Books, 2001.

Terrell, John Upton. *Furs by Astor*. New York: William Morrow, 1963.

Thomas, Edwin Harper. *Chinook: A History and Dictionary*. 2nd ed. Portland OR: Binfords & Mort, 1970.

Thwaites, Reuben Gold, ed. *Original Journals of the Lewis and Clark Expedition, 1804–1806: With Facsimiles, Maps, Plans, Views, Portraits, and a Bibliography*. New York: Dodd, Mead, 1905.

Tocqueville, Alexis de. *Letters from America*. Ed. Frederick Brown. New Haven: Yale University Press, 2010.

United States Geological Survey. Yellowstone Volcano Observatory. http://volcanoes.usgs.gov/observatories/yvo/, retrieved October 6, 2013.

Vakoch, Douglas A., ed. *Psychology of Space Exploration*. Washington, DC: National Aeronautics and Space Administration, Office of Communications, 2011.

Wang, Jack, John C. Thornton, Mary Russell, Santiago Burastero, Steven Heymsfield, and Richard N. Pierson Jr. "Asians Have Lower Body Mass Index (BMI) but Higher Percent Body Fat than do Whites: Comparisons of Anthropometric Measurements." *American Journal of Clinical Nutrition* 60, no. 1 (July 1994): 23–28.

Williams, Stanley T. *The Life of Washington Irving*. Vols. 1–2. New York: Oxford University Press, 1935.

Zug, James. *American Traveler: The Life and Adventures of John Ledyard, the Man Who Dreamed of Walking the World*. New York: Basic Books, 2005.

"The American Falls of Lewis Fork," Rare Books Division, Special Collections, J. Willard Marriott Library, University of Utah

Snake River Canyon, Idaho Historical Society, 62-1.0

Entrevue de l'expedition de M. Kotzebue avec le roi Tammeamea dans l'ile d'Ovayhi, Iles Sandwich by Louis Choris, 1827, National Library of Australia, 2872081

Sea Otter, by S. Smith, after John Webber, in James Cook, *A Voyage to the Pacific Ocean . . . Performed under the Direction of Captains Cook, Clerke, and Gore . . . 1776, 1777, 1778, 1779, and 1780* (London: W. Strahan, 1780), engraving, Rare Book & Special Collections Division (16.5)

"Tenaktak canoes," Northwestern University Library, in Edward S. Curtis, *The North American Indian* (Cologne: Taschen, 2003)

Interior of Whale House of Chief Klart-Reech, Klukwan, Alaska. c. 1895, P87-0013, Alaska State Library, Winter & Pond Photograph Collection

"Tluwulahu mask—Tswatenok," Northwestern University Library, in Edward S. Curtis, *The North American Indian* (Cologne: Taschen, 2003)

Yéil X'eenh (Raven Screen), ca. 1810, attributed to Kadyisdu.axch', Tlingit, Kiks.adi Clan, active late eighteenth to early nineteenth century, Gaanax-teidi', Klukwan village, Frog House, spruce and paint, Seattle Art Museum, gift of John H. Hauberg, 79.98, photograph by Paul Macapia

Ka'heit'am (Stone Club), pre-1778, Northwest Coast, Nuu'chah'nulth, ground and pecked basalt, human hair, and spruce pitch, Seattle Art Museum, gift of John H. Hauberg, 91.1.21

"View of the Falkland Islands," in Parsons Avery and Gabriel Franchère, *Narrative of a Voyage to the Northwest Coast of America*

"Entrance of the Columbia River," in Parsons Avery and Gabriel Franchère, *Narrative of a Voyage to the Northwest Coast of America*

Illustration of an engraving of voyageurs portaging a canoe by Carl W. Bertsch, in Grace Lee Nute, *The Voyageur*

"Astoria, as It Was in 1813," in Parsons Avery and Gabriel Franchère, *Narrative of a Voyage to the Northwest Coast of America*

"J. Jacob Astor's Former Residence, 88th St. near East River," print collection, Miriam and Ira D. Wallach Division of Art, Prints, and Photographs, New York Public Library, Astor, Lenox, and Tilden Foundations

Portrait of Robert Stuart, Missouri History Museum, St. Louis, MO

Portrait of Donald Mackenzie, Chautauqua County Historical Society, Westfield, NY

Portrait of Gabriel Franchère, Minnesota Historical Society, por 27358 p1

Portrait of Alexander Ross, Archives of Manitoba, Ross, Alexander 4 (N21467)